I0210000

LEAVING FOOTPRINTS IN THE TAIGA

Studies in the Circumpolar North

Editors:
Olga Ulturgasheva, *University of Manchester*
Alexander D. King, *Franklin & Marshall College, PA*

The Circumpolar North encapsulates all the major issues confronting the world today: enduring colonial legacies for indigenous people and the landscape, climate change and resource extraction industries, international diplomatic tensions, and lived realities of small communities in the interconnected modern world system. This book series provides a showcase for cutting-edge academic research on the lives of Arctic and Sub-arctic communities past and present. Understanding the contemporary Circumpolar North requires a multiplicity of perspectives and we welcome works from the social sciences, humanities and the arts.

Volume 1
Leaving Footprints in the Taiga
Luck, Spirits and Ambivalence among the Siberian Orochen Reindeer Herders and Hunters
Donatas Brandišauskas

Volume 2
Sustaining Russia's Arctic Cities
Resource Politics, Migration and Climate Change
Edited by Robert Orttung

Leaving Footprints in the Taiga

Luck, Spirits and Ambivalence among the Siberian Orochen Reindeer Herders and Hunters

Donatas Brandišauskas

berghahn

NEW YORK · OXFORD

www.berghahnbooks.com

Published by
Berghahn Books
www.berghahnbooks.com

© 2017, 2019 Donatas Brandišauskas
First paperback edition published in 2019

All rights reserved. Except for the quotation of short passages
for the purposes of criticism and review, no part of this book
may be reproduced in any form or by any means, electronic or
mechanical, including photocopying, recording, or any information
storage and retrieval system now known or to be invented,
without written permission of the publisher.

Library of Congress Cataloging-in-Publication Data

Names: Brandisauskas, Donatas, author.
Title: Leaving footprints in the taiga : luck, spirits and ambivalence among the
    Siberian Orochen reindeer herders and hunters / Donatas Brandisauskas.
Description: New York : Berghahn Books, 2017. | Series: Studies of the
    circumpolar north series | Includes bibliographical references and index.
Identifiers: LCCN 2016021757| ISBN 9781785332388 (hardback : alk. paper) |
    ISBN 9781785332395 (ebook)
Subjects: LCSH: Oroch (Asian people)—Russia (Federation)—Transbaikalia. |
    Oroch (Asian people—Social life and customs. | Oroch (Asian people)—
    Religion. | Reindeer herders—Russia (Federation)—Transbaikalia. |
    Ethnology—Russia (Federation)—Transbaikalia.
Classification: LCC DK759.O7 B73 2016 | DDC 305.894/1—dc23
LC record available at https://lccn.loc.gov/2016021757

British Library Cataloguing in Publication Data

A catalogue record for this book is available from the British Library

ISBN 978-1-78533-238-8 hardback
ISBN 978-1-78920-532-9 paperback
ISBN 978-1-78533-239-5 ebook

Contents

Tables, Maps and Figures

Tables

Maps

Figures

Preface

This book has grown out of seventeen months of ethnographic field-work in 2004–2005, 2010 and 2011 among a small community of Orochen hunters and reindeer herders living east of Lake Baikal, mainly in the Tungokochen District of Zabaikal Province. In July and August of 2004, I visited the Orochen of Tungokochen for the first time as a member of an ethno-archaeological expedition and a postgraduate student at the Department of Anthropology of the North at Aberdeen University, Scotland. The expedition, led by my supervisor, Prof. David Anderson, and the Irkutsk-based archaeologist Dr Victor Vetrov, aimed to reach the remote camps of the only group of reindeer herders in the region, headed by the prominent herder and hunter Nikolai Aruneev, along the Bazarnaia and Poperechnaia Rivers. We planned to map the summer habitation sites of Orochen reindeer herders as part of our involvement with the ethnological module of the Baikal Archaeology Project (SSHRCC MCRI 2000–1000). During our trip we had to rely on the various unpredictable means of transportation that were available after the collapse of the Soviet state, including military all-terrain vehicles, which were used locally as the main means of transportation, travelling at irregular intervals between villages and to remote places in the taiga.

Our journey in search of the reindeer herders' camps could not have been accomplished without our Orochen guides Oleg Taskerov and Gosha Chernykh from the small village of Ust' Karenga, located at the confluence of the Karenga and Vitim Rivers. As the only herders remaining in the village, they took care of several reindeer that were used by a group of indigenous people for hunting. The group of Zhumaneev-Aruneev reindeer herders from Tungokochen village participated in the commodity economy only to a very small degree and had no radio connection. No one in the villages had a clue where the reindeer herders' camps could be found in the taiga. For this reason, Oleg and Gosha were irreplaceable taiga guides, skilfully reading tracks and identifying the Zhumaneev-Aruneev group's movements in the sub-boreal forest. They finally discovered the group's current campsite while transporting our camping gear on their pack reindeer.

During the expedition, we had to walk more than 150 km through difficult, hilly terrain without any roads, covered with larch trees and bushes as well as swamps filled with clouds of mosquitoes in extremely hot weather, with temperatures topping 45 degrees Celsius. The return journey involved paddling kayaks on the Nercha River. This six-week trip gave me a taste of first-hand knowledge of how local people searching for human and animal tracks find their way in the taiga, build shelters and harvest game animals on their seasonal migration routes. Hiking with a backpack in the northern part of Russia and Siberia was not a new experience for me, as I had travelled and camped in the wilderness of Karelia in the Russian part of Lapland, and later in the Altai Republic, during many summers between 1992 and 2003. However, this expedition was the first step towards my professional career as a social anthropologist. It taught me about various taiga skills and philosophies, as well as ways of being among people in the taiga, where one has to attune one's own life to the life of other beings – humans, animals and spirits. This included behaving in non-intrusive ways, learning how to collect field data while respecting people's autonomy and taking responsibility for people who agreed to share their experiences with me.

To understand the contemporary Orochen's ontology of luck, I spent several months throughout all seasons living with hunters and reindeer herders in their taiga camps and villages. This experience increased my knowledge and skills regarding the performance of daily chores while also teaching me how to establish and maintain trust with people. Trust meant interacting with them while respecting their autonomy, which is very important in any luck-generating practice. Successful collaboration with Orochen would have been impossible without maintaining sincere friendship ties, sympathy and relations based on reciprocity. This close relationship has continued until today, when the recent advance of mobile communication technology even into remote villages enables me to chat with people any time and receive news about those I care about.

I started my undergraduate studies at the Department of Biology of Vilnius University in Lithuania, inspired by my childhood dream of spending a lengthy period in the wilderness. This dream grew out of my childhood fascination with Native American cultures, sparked by the romantic books of Grey Owl.[1] My continuing attraction to indigenous cultures convinced me that I should try to combine the study of indigenous people with their environment, so I decided to change departments and become a member of the first cohort of sociocultural anthropology students in the then newly established programme at Vilnius University. I would like to express my deepest appreciation to my anthropology teachers Romas Vastokas, Prof. Emeritus of Trent University in Canada, and Prof. Victor de Munck of the State University of New York at New Paltz. They encouraged my interests in native cultures and supported my studies, first at Copenhagen University and then in the MRes and PhD programmes of Aberdeen University, diligently reading drafts of my project proposals and research papers and also offering very important moral support. My book reflects their friendship and dedication to Lithuanian anthropology as they trained students in a field that was previously undeveloped in Lithuania.

My studies of the reindeer herders and hunters of Zabaikal'ia would have been impossible without the support of Profs. David G. Anderson and Andrzej Weber, who employed me in the Baikal Archaeology Project at Aberdeen University, Scotland. The project provided a stipend that allowed me to learn the skills of social anthropology from excellent teachers at the Department of Anthropology of the North at Aberdeen University from 2003 to 2007. My supervisors, Prof. David G. Anderson and Dr Alex King, commented both generously and critically on the multiple drafts of my PhD thesis (completed in 2009) over several years, for which I want to express my profound gratitude. I also want to thank scholars based at Aberdeen University who offered valuable comments in the early stages of various writings related to the dissertation: Dr Martina Tyrell, Dr Rob Wishart and Dr Joe Vergunst. A heartfelt thank you for many inspiring discussions in the kitchens of student flats and at numerous conferences and seminars goes to my student colleagues and friends at Aberdeen University, especially Vladimir Davydov, Veronika Simonova, Tatiana Argounova-Low and Mariia Nakhshina, as well as Remy Rouillard (McGill University). Last but not least I would like to thank Prof. Tim Ingold for his charismatic presence in the department, which inspired many students intellectually as well as spiritually.

I wrote this book with the support of a grant from the Lithuanian Science Council (MIP-103/2012). The Wenner Gren Foundation for Anthropological Research (7260), the University of Aberdeen School of Social Sciences, the Committee for Central and Inner Asia at the University of Cambridge and the UNESCO Lithuanian committee supported various stages of my fieldwork in Zabaikal'ia over the 2004–2012 period. Special thanks are due to my colleagues and hosts in Irkutsk and Chita, who provided me with necessary documentation and overnight stays: Prof. Artur Kharinskii, Dr Victor Vetrov, Dr Aleksei Yankov, Prof. Oleg Kuznetsov and Dr Evgenii Ineshin. The book also benefited from insightful and critical comments from the examiners of my thesis, Dr Virginie Vaté and Dr Peter Jordan. Virginie also generously sent me additional extended comments, including a translated review of my article by Prof. Roberte Hamayon, which proved extremely useful. I also express my thanks to Dr Otto Habeck (then at the Max Planck Institute for Social Anthropology, Halle) and Prof. Piers Vitebsky (Scott Polar Institute, Cambridge) for supporting the writing of this book by hosting me at their institutions.

My fieldwork in the taiga of Zabaikal'ia would have been a hard and often impossible challenge without the support of the extended Zhumaneev-Aruneev family. I want to acknowledge the much appreciated friendliness of many other Orochen/Evenki lineages of Zabaikal Province (formerly Chita Province) and Buryatia: Taskerov, Aruniev, Urpiulov, Dushinov, Kirilov, Naikanchin, Dogonchin, Torgonov, Mordonov, and Ulzuev. I still feel a deep emotional connection with many of them and am lucky to be able to keep in constant communication by phone with many people, especially Aleksei Aruneev, Nikolai Aruneev, Iura Aruneev, Olga Zhumaneeva, Tamara Naikanchina and Nadia Zhumaneeva. I have been meeting them in my dreams, and they keep encouraging me to come back to their villages and the remote places in the taiga for one more hunting trip and a cup of tea. The hospitality, generosity, and friendship shown me by many local families have touched me profoundly. With this book I wish every hunter I met and hunted with 'the best hunting luck'.

I especially want to thank my family, who have supported my education in all possible ways, allowing me to read academic books in peace instead of joining them in household and farming chores. Finally, there are people without whom my interests and skills in native cultures would not have led me to the enjoyment of fieldwork in the remote taiga. I want to give a big hug to each friend with whom I was able to share my stories of fieldwork success and misfortunes, especially Tauras, Darius, Benas, Ate, Laimis and Vaidas. My thanks go also to my wife Rėda and my daughter Upyna, who supported the final stages of writing with their love.

I thank CCI press for the permission to use some material previously published in my chapter 'Contested Health in the Post-Soviet Taiga: Use of Landscape, Spirits and Strength among Orochen-Evenki of Zabaikal'e (East Siberia)' from *Health and Healing in the Circumpolar North: Southeastern Siberia* (CCI, 2011), ed. D.G. Anderson. I also thank the *Journal of Ethnology and Folkloristics* for permission to use parts of my articles 'Hide Tanning and Its Use in Taiga: The

Case of Orochen-Evenki Reindeer Herders and Hunters of Zabaikal'e (East Siberia)', 4(2): 97–114 and 'Making a Home in the Taiga: Movements, Paths and Signs among Orochen-Evenki Hunters and Herders of Zabaikal Krai (South East Siberia)', 6(1): 9–25.

Notes

1. Grey Owl was the name Archibald Belaney (1888–1938) adopted when he took on a First Nations (Ojibwa) identity. Born in England, he migrated to Canada and rose to prominence as a notable author and conservationist. Three of his books were translated into Lithuanian.

A Note on Transliteration

This book transliterates Orochen Cyrillic and Russian Cyrillic words with the Library of Congress Romanization standard. Russian and Latin terms appear in italics after the abbreviations Rus. and Lat. Orochen and Buryat terms, also italicized, follow Oro. and Bur. Many Orochen terms are now widely used by local Russian-speaking people in Zabaikal'ia and have entered their everyday vocabulary. Local speakers of Orochen wrote words down for me in Cyrillic in the Orochen language to represent the subtleties of local dialects. I have chosen to transliterate these as they are used in everyday language rather than following the standardized dictionary of Tsintsius (1975). Orochen words rarely have an iotized e, and thus the Romanized character e can be expected to represent an э in Evenki or in Orochen-derived Russian words. The standard for soft signs is respected. Russian plural forms are transliterated, as are Orochen plural forms. The following English translations will be used to designate formal units and administrative territories, social roles, and items of daily life.

krai, oblast'	- province
raion	- district
region	- region
komersanty	- entrepreneurs
panty	- velveted antlers
kamus	- leg pelt
obshchina	- clan community
kolkhoz	- collective farm
sovkhoz	- state farm

Luck, Spirits and Places

This book aims to investigate the persistence of Orochen-Evenki[1] reindeer herders' and hunters'[2] ritual knowledge, discursive and embodied practices, movements in the taiga and interactions with various places in the taiga as part of daily strategies driven by the anxious desire to attract and sustain luck and well-being. The prominent Russian émigré ethnographer Sergei Shirokogoroff (1929: 331) noticed during his fieldwork in the early twentieth century that among Tungus in pre-Soviet times any visitor was always asked certain standard questions: 'What animal tracks have you seen? Have you had a good luck-*mahin* or have the spirits sent you anything?' The final question concerned the visitor's health. Shirokogoroff (ibid.) adds that the questions regarding animal tracks and good luck were always met with detailed answers. When documenting the remnants of religious practices among the Evenki of Soviet Buryatia, the Evenki ethnographer Shubin (1969: 172–173) stated that although hunters had ceased to maintain the memory of shamans and were mostly atheists, nevertheless even young people were still 'not free of their belief that the success in subsistence practices still depends on the good will of spirits and they continued to perform traditional rituals'.

As a student of anthropology I hoped to be able to investigate how the new political regime and the market economy in Russia had affected the Orochen's shamanic ritual behaviour and perception of landscape in the taiga. However, the Orochen of the Zabaikal'ia had suffered some drastic reprisals during the Colonial and Soviet times. After the years of brutal Soviet collectivization and persecution of religious practices, no tradition of ritual specialists such as shamans survived in that region. Only a few individuals strove to develop their capacity to heal people by attending training sessions during shamanic gatherings that were held in the Aga Buryat Autonomous District, located in the south of the former Chita Province. As part of the revitalization of indigenous identities and the mobilization of communities, local indigenous leaders have started to conduct public ritual performances 'in the Orochen way' at the funerals of their relatives and indigenous festivals supported by the administration.

To my surprise, various rituals and divinations resembling those described by Shirokogoroff are also creatively re-enacted by the Orochen. Orochen subsistence life is replete with concern about luck (Oro. *kutu*, Rus. *udacha* or *fart*, deriving from Latin *fortuna*), health and the goal of restoring lost relationships with spirits who are responsible for humans' success and well-being. Although Shirokogoroff (1935: 187, 207) described Tungus rituals as a 'shamanic art to control spirits', he also stressed that every hunter must know the simplest methods of 'managing' spirits and avoiding their harmful influence. During my fieldwork I found out that this knowledge of how to pursue subsistence activities through interacting with spirits inhabiting the landscape, obtaining luck and securing one's wellbeing is highly valued again today.

The demise of the Soviet state entailed the collapse of a centralized system of resource redistribution. One important response to new opportunities provided by new laws was the privatization of collective property by local villagers in order to appropriate territories for subsistence and to increase their reliance on taiga resources (for neotraditionalism see Pika 1999). This created a feeling of uncertainty and shortage and led to competition over resources. In an unstable and unpredictable economic environment, anxiety over luck has become a crucial concern for Orochen that shapes their interactions with other humans, animals and spirits as well as with places in the taiga. My ethnographic study will describe the efforts and strategies of the Zhumaneev-Aruneev kin group of hunters and herders in securing their subsistence and territorial base in the taiga and the village in the face of the complex social, economic, ecological and political changes that have affected the Zabaikal Province (former Chita Province).

Anthropologists have aptly noted that in the Western view, the notion of luck or fortune implies the idea of a chance-like incident that is accidental, infrequent, uncontrollable, bounded to individuals and often decontextualized (see Da Col 2012). To the Orochen, luck or *kutu* is based on the morality of humans' and nonhumans' interaction in their living environment. Hence, *kutu* must be analysed with regard to networks of relationships that involve different agents such as humans, animals and spirits; material objects and places; and practices of exchange. Humans can maintain social relations with 'other-than-human persons' and attribute to them all the qualities that human beings have (see Hallowell 1960). Furthermore, humans and nonhumans (material objects, places, animals and spirits) have a 'living energy' (Oro. *musun*) that can impact their health and ability to move or influence other beings (see Vasilevich 1969; Varlamova 2004). Animals and spirits perceive reality in the same way humans do, and it is said that sometimes their strength (Oro. *chinen*) to perform various activities exceeds that of humans. Therefore, nonhuman beings, whether animals or spirits, are believed to have a 'soul' (Oro. *omi*), that can manifest itself through intentionality, volition and cognitive abilities.

The loss of *kutu* (or any other element such as *omi*) by a human can result in the poor performance of any daily task, the loss of one's 'life energy' and passion for life, and even idleness, illness and death. A *kutuchi* (lucky) person is one who is able to enact his skills and knowledge in practice, always succeeds in hunting, is able to feed a family and relatives and remains healthy. Such a person successfully manages relations with domestic animals used in subsistence activities, like reindeer, horses and dogs. Hence, *kutu* is an intrinsic component of human personhood and emerges from humans' interactions with nonhuman beings, animals, places and spirits. It can also be shared with the people with whom a person cooperates and thus helps to sustain kin or wider social relations. *Kutu* can increase and decrease throughout the life course and according to a person's behaviour. In the absence of *kutu*, however, it is impossible to sustain life. The fluctuation of *kutu* is evidenced by the supply of game, which is plentiful at times and at other times limited by the master-spirits who control the animals' rebirth. Every hunter is given what is needed, and no hunter should exceed the number of animal souls allocated to him or her by selling meat or hunting for pleasure. Vorob'ev (2013) describes how the Evenki of Chirinda, who turned from reindeer herding to hunting wild reindeer, believe that any hunter who has killed a large number of wild reindeer should stop for a while, or else that luck (Rus. *fart*) in hunting will end. Hence, the author attributes the 'few remaining taboos' among the Evenki mostly to their beliefs concerning luck (ibid.).

In Russian ethnographic literature, such as the comparative studies of Tungus, Manchu, Turkic and Mongol-speaking groups of Siberia and Inner Asia by Mikhailov (1987), Alekseev (1975), Gurvich (1977), Zelenin (1929) and Petri (1930), the 'master' (Rus. *khoziain*) is at the same time described as a spirit (Rus. *dukh*) or animal that rules over certain places, or a spirit that resides in manufactured objects. According to these authors, such a master-spirit (Rus. *dukh-khoziain*) could be in charge of different geographical locations such as a watershed, hill or lake, or of celestial objects like the sun or the moon, which influence both wild and domestic animals and even the destiny of humans. The place ruled by the master-spirit is viewed as his household, where he can control the animals' procreation and rebirth, and influence almost all spheres of human life, including travelling, dwelling, storytelling and interacting with animals.

The Orochen I stayed with also have vernacular notions of *odzhen* (Oro.) or *khoziain* (Rus.) – during our conversations both terms referred to a master of all kinds of spirits, humans and animals. In Tsintsius' (1975: 437–438) Tungus-Manchu dictionary the Evenki word *odzhen* is translated as 'owner' or 'master' (Rus. *khoziain*), 'ruler' (Rus. *nachalnik, pravitel'*) and 'master-spirit' (Rus. *dukh khoziain*).[3] Today the Orochen believe that reclaiming taiga territories from the state obliges them to establish cooperation with the local master-spirits. Orochen hunters and herders obtain luck (Rus. *dobyt' udachiu/fart/ talan*) through their maintenance of successful relations of cooperation with the master-spirit of a certain place. Orochen acts of cooperation between humans and master-spirits, such as offerings of tea, bullets, coins, matches or other items – have been described since the early colonial encounters (Mainov 1898: 206, Georgi 1779: 13, 38).

Luck can be obtained (Rus. *dobyta*) from master-spirits, but a person can also catch it (Rus. *slovit'*) with the virtuoso use of knowledge and skills in harvesting game animals. The latter are referred to as *dobycha*. People who experience a lack of success in hunting in a certain area can use the following words: 'What can I do there, there is nothing to catch' (Rus. *A chto tam delat' tam mne nechego lovit'*).[4] Unlucky people express their situation with the phrase 'I could not find luck' (Oro. *Kutuia davdachav bakami*). Similarly, Alekhin (2001: 132) cites an Evenki hunter's teaching: 'You must catch luck, while it is available' (Rus. *udachu lovi, poka est'*). Indeed, obtaining luck would be impossible without the hunter's efforts, expressed through the hunter's movements, predictions, behaviour and emotions, as well as discursive strategies intended to maintain the environment where luck can be acquired. Hunters and shamans plead for luck, make offerings, skilfully seize luck (i.e. souls) from the master-spirits, and use various means to avoid misfortune, performing these efforts in rituals like the *sinkelevun* and *ikenipke* described by Soviet ethnographers (Vasilevich 1957; Anisimov 1951).

Master-spirits (Oro. *odzhen*) share the animals with the hunter. Orochen hunters often say that the master-spirit does not give but rather shows animals (Rus. *pokazyvaet zveria*) to the hunter (see also Alekhin 2001: 132). Therefore, they also say that a hunter must be able to overcome individual animals and attune himself to different places in the taiga to catch luck. The master-spirits are entertained by skilful performance in hunting a particular animal and will most probably be generous thereafter.[5] Furthermore, the hunter must be modest and assume the position of a person in need who is willing to maintain reciprocal relations. Hunters entice the master-spirits to provide them with game by telling stories of prior hunting successes before setting out on a hunting expedition. In doing so they entertain spirits that may be generous to people and send them luck (see Zelenin 2004: 27, 1929: 123; Potapov 2001: 115).

It has long been known, however, that most hunters' luck is limited by the master-spirit's effort to maintain a balance of animals in certain places. The idea of the master-spirit's control over animals' rebirth and humans' hunting success is widespread in the literature on circumpolar peoples (see Ingold 1986: 243–276; Jordan 2003: 123–125, Kwon 1998: 119, Hamayon 1990: 365–372). Hunters may be unlucky for lengthy periods and not succeed in killing animals. In such situations, they have to be content with what the master-spirit gives them and live from what others share with them. Enduring misfortune, however, can be seen as an affliction caused either by malevolent spirits or humans, or by a violation of taboos, that can be very dangerous for a human's health and life.[6]

The flow of luck can be predicted through dreams, omens and divinations, and luck can be acquired through rituals or through sharing, besides being 'caught' by the skilful performance of hunting and herding. Orochen believe it is important to make good use of the flow of luck, as one lucky incident attracts another, whereas one misfortune tends to attract other misfortunes.[7] Hunters strive to obtain and preserve their luck by making daily offerings to the master-sprits and by showing respect to animals through the proper way of hunting, proper treatment of the animals' bones and certain discursive strategies and bodily movements. In order to sustain luck, a person must hunt only for his or her own needs and take any animal that encounted, without preferences for certain species. Hence, it is said that one should take what is given by the spirits, but not more than one is able to consume. Luck can also be sustained through moral behaviour like showing respect and sharing (Oro. *nimat*) with other humans and nonhumans. From this perspective, luck is a virtue and a moral precept that guides a person to lead a proper life and shapes his or her daily behaviour.

Hunters and herders see such interactions as the proper way of making a living by creating symmetrical relations of reciprocal sharing with other humans and nonhumans. For the Orochen, luck must be redistributed among relatives and friends, since this practice will serve to generate future luck (see also Hamayon 2012). The sharing of luck includes the sharing of meat and other animal products, the transfer of hunting skills and knowledge, and the organization of joint hunting expeditions. It involves people living in the same camp, people of the same clan and people who participated in a hunting expedition or were encountered en route. Among various forms of help and support, *nimat* (sharing) is described by many ethnographers as a cultural rule or norm that is crucial to the process of hunting.[8]

The lucky hunter shares the meat first with all other hunters who participated in the hunting expedition and then with his relatives in the village. In some small villages like Bugunda, meat was parcelled in a special communal shelter and shared among all seven households. Usually the children participated in delivering meat to each house. Even people encountered on the road by the hunters are seen as part of the environment of luck, so meat was shared with them too in the taiga camps on the hunting trip, although the same people would not receive a share in the village. All beings, including birds like ravens, receive their share when met in the taiga during a lucky hunting trip (see Shirokogoroff 1929: 44). People who like to hunt alone and thus avoid sharing are considered malevolent and called *stramnye*.[9]

Sharing includes local forms of hospitality: anyone visiting a household in the village is always invited to drink tea (Rus. *chaevat'*), which also means getting a full meal of soup, meat and sweets. This form of sharing is generally observed in all the villages of Zabaikal'ia, though it does not usually include a direct offering of meat. Thus people who lack meat at least have a chance to eat meat by joining others in a meal. In some cases, people say directly, 'boil meat, I am going to come for food' (Rus. *vari miaso, pridu kushat'*). Hence, sharing also recognizes the right of others to maintain their well-being. The idea of *nimat* also includes various forms of cooperation and the sharing of tools in joint subsistence activities, as well as selling groceries on credit, lending out various items or making presents. In his report on the Orochen of Buryatia, Neupokoev (1928: 21) notes that rich reindeer herders would give two or three reindeer to those who lacked animals or lost them in an epidemic, and that reindeer were also given as a gift after recovery from an illness or a period of bad hunting luck. A gift could be given as a matter of respect between individuals or clans, but also as support to the poorest families (Shubin 2007: 23). Moreover, giving gifts among hunters can be seen as a way of sharing luck. As Shubin (ibid.: 25) notes, after receiving a gift a hunter, if in good health, was required to embark on a hunting trip for large game. Sharing also includes taking 'purchase orders' (Rus. *zakazy*) from others when travelling to cities or villages. On such occasions, a hunter or herder would ask a person to bring needed items from the village or city, implying his or her own readiness to do similar favours on another occasion.

By sharing with other humans and serving as a conduit for luck, a person sustains his own luck. Nevertheless, one must take precautions so that luck is not 'given away' accidentally. To avoid this, meat should not be passed from one person to another by hand; rather, the person asking must be the one to pick it up. Rastsvetaev (1933: 34) notes that an animal killed by a lucky hunter was left on the ground to be butchered and transported by those who were supposed to receive a share. In many cases the hunter's wife would butcher, divide and then deliver the meat to relatives. A hunter who kills more than one animal and is willing to share the second with other hunters must take at least one of the animal's hind legs for himself. Hunters say that this is what wolves do – eat a leg of a reindeer they have killed in order to sustain their luck.

Lost hunting luck can be restored by taking part in the hunting expedition of a 'lucky hunter'. Such cooperation may occur between people with close ties, such as relatives, friends or comrades (Rus. *naparniki*), when an exchange relationship has been established. In this case, the desired results are achieved through establishing a productive network and creating a 'positive sense of relatedness' with other beings (see Foucault 1980: 119). Master-spirits are believed to be generous to those who have not accumulated a large baggage of sins and are really in need. Hence, hunters not only take a 'lucky boy' along on a hunting trip to elicit the spirits' generosity; they also take very little food, meaning that hunters may eat almost nothing while spending weeks in search of animals. It is said that spirits take pity on those with an empty stomach. During hunting trips, hunters exchange opinions about other hunters' abilities to bring luck or failure, also relating how other hunters' sins in the taiga have affected the hunting luck of the whole group. As one hunter said, 'I will never go hunting with Vasia, as he always takes big bags of potatoes to eat. How could we then be lucky?' Hunters who had brought about failure or who could 'spoil the place' were referred to as *pakostnoi* (Rus. *pakostit'*, spoil), which is one of the most negative things that can be said about another person.

Some say that villagers have begun to compete for resources by using 'black activities' (Rus. *chernota*) to spoil another person's well-being, health or luck. Adverse actions by other humans and nonhumans can influence luck, which one can 'lose' (Rus. *poteriat'*) or 'spoil' (Rus. *napokostit'*) as a result. Most villagers stress that the *porcha* (spell) and *zglaz* (evil eye) are very widespread in post-Soviet villages. *Porcha* is understood as a conscious magical attack to cause illness in another person. *Zglaz* is seen as a negative influence on human activities that a person with 'bad energy' or 'bad luck' unconsciously passes on to another. Therefore, it is said that to avoid harm one should not allow one's belongings, animals, children or activities to be praised, since some people's words can attract misfortune. Only when a curse or evil influence is neutralized can luck be easily gained.

In an environment of shortage and competition for resources, hunters believe that the taiga suffers from constant overhunting and the sinful behaviour of humans. They see animals as 'taken' by 'poaching' or only in order to gain monetary value.[10] Orochen hunters and herders trying to succeed in the post-Soviet context have occasionally resorted to aggressive practices of domination when harvesting game animals. This can happen on certain occasions, for example, when somebody experiences constant misfortune or wants to increase his or her wealth. Usually the Orochen regard such behaviour as negative and mention it with reference to the notion of *ngelome* ('sin', don't do it, bad, terrible, Rus. *grekh*) or 'poaching' (Rus. *brakonerstvo*) (for the Katanga Evenki, see also Sirina 2008: 128–132, for the Surinda Evenki, Alekhin 2001).[11] A sinful person may also let meat spoil, waste game animals, treat animals' remains disrespectfully, use 'wrong' ways of hunting or refuse to either share or trade meat. It is very dangerous to commit such sins as plundering storage platforms – especially platforms or mortuary sites linked to the deceased – or steal offerings from ritual sites. Any form of stealing or using something that belongs to someone else, including things and places used by others (especially a deceased person) is considered *ngelome*. Furthermore, as Alekhin (2001) noted, any kind of aggressive behaviour towards wild or domestic animals was also considered a sin by the Evenki of Surinda.

Many Orochen tell stories of how the baggage of personal sins resulted in disability and death to people and even whole families. Local spirits often intervene to drive hunters away from certain places by attacking them in dreams, sending a bear into their path or making strange noises that madden or disable the hunter. Once frightened by a bear, a person may lose luck, suffer protracted loss of health or even die. Some stories tell of a foolish hunter attacked by a spirit who sent reindeer that pushed him out of a river basin and chased him back to the village. In another case, a bear attacked the hunter in dreams and made him ill. The vernacular concept of 'poaching' among hunters and herders contrasts with formal regulations that define 'poaching' as hunting without a formal license. The Orochen perceive poaching as an 'unequal contest' and a sin committed when a hunter uses overly elaborate hunting equipment, wastes game, makes animals suffer, acts disrespectfully towards animals and their remains, or leaves a place of butchering 'untidy'. Any of these actions may spoil the luck of other humans and animals. Hunting is regarded as a gift when luck has been obtained and animals are hunted and later consumed or disposed of with respect, but it can become dangerous when a hunter harvests animals yet refuses to engage in reciprocity with humans and nonhuman beings. The Orochen consider competing with an animal and outsmarting it in a 'contest of equals' (Rus. *na ravne*) the proper way to hunt and the proper way to acquire luck without threatening a hunter's relationship with the master-spirits of various animals. During the contest the hunter should not show emotion (Rus. *azart*) but be persistent when hunting for game, especially when trailing a wounded animal.[12]

Any kind of sin may provoke an aggressive reaction by animals sent by the master-spirits or by 'malevolent spirits' (Oro. *arenkil*, sing. *arenki*) of deceased people that roam the taiga.[13] A 'sinful person' (Rus. *greshnik*) lacks the support of the master-spirits and therefore is highly vulnerable to such evil attacks. *Arenkil* can attack humans who refuse to share. Constant misfortune, illness or long-term loss of luck may signal a curse from malevolent spirits or souls sent by powerful humans (like shamans), which can cause disease and even the death of family members. Luck can also be either 'spoiled' or affected by *arenkil* that are accidentally encountered in the taiga (Shirokogoroff 1935: 137–138; Tsintsius 1975: 51). The Orochen identify the *arenkil* with the souls of hunters or herders who did not reach the world of the dead because they died suddenly or accidentally, or were not escorted by the proper rituals.[14] These souls had to remain in this world and became malevolent. These spirits are considered to be always hungry for human souls and eager to diminish people's 'living energies' or luck, so someone who encounters such a spirit may fall ill or even die. Old campsites, ritual sites or places where tragic incidents have occurred can be inhabited by *arenkil* and therefore can affect the lives of contemporary humans.

Today the risk of encountering such spirits is increased, as various rituals of respect were neglected for half a century during the Soviet era. Alexandra Lavrillier (2003: 103), who carried out extensive fieldwork among the Evenki (Orochen) of Amur Province and southern Yakutia, similarly notices that the local Evenki communities of Amur Province explain their poor economic conditions as due to their failure to honour their spirits. Buryats in Mongolia also attribute their current misfortune to spirits who have returned to seek revenge for the abandoning of ritual practices (Buyandelgeriyn 2007). The Orochen avoid places thought to be infused with misfortune and manifestations of *arenkil*. People often take precautions by leaving offerings or cleaning themselves with smudge sticks when moving through the taiga with their reindeer so as not to lose their luck and to avoid encountering misfortune.

Not only is luck the outcome of human-nonhuman interactions, but it can also be emplaced and affected by various material objects that have their own agency. Such agency may manifest itself in certain environments and situations and thereby influence the activities of humans. Any crafted items, cloth or tools, but also camps, paths or tracks on the ground are seen as extensions of a human's or a spirit's personhood. In the Orochen lifeworld, all living animals who dwell on the land, leave or hide tracks, harvest resources or build dwellings are said to create 'living places' (Oro. *bikit*) (for *bikit* see Tsintsius 1975: 79). Hunters often use the word *bikit* to describe the living place of an animal such as a wolf, bear, sable, squirrel, rabbit or reindeer (or a group of animals).[15] Knowledge of these places is gained by observing the movement of animals or examining their marks and tracks. Over time, the hunters thus eventually glean information about an animal's personality, character, social life and preferences. They adjust their movements to the animal's *bikit* to create an environment where a person's luck in herding and hunting can be realized. Hunters compete with an animal by hiding their intentions, movements and emotions through observance of prescribed ways of behaving and talking. Hunters are aware that either animals or the place itself will respond to their actions.[16] Hence, while hunting, hunters regularly readjust their movements and camping practices in order to 'fix' animals in the landscape and achieve the best possible hunting luck. Luck is achieved by successfully overcoming an animal through certain ways of walking, talking, and either leaving or hiding tracks.

Humans can also emplace their own luck or misfortune in different places when leaving tracks on the land and building camps. In this way they establish their own 'living places' or *bikit*. A human's *bikit* is maintained through daily walks and the use of certain paths, camps or storage platforms. Creating new ritual sites for carved idols or decorated trees also serves to generate luck for one's living place in the taiga. By modifying of the physical condition of objects or places, a person can emplace it with one's own 'living energy' and luck. One of the old ways to protect a person's well-being involved 'placing his or her soul' inside a certain object called *omiruk* (Oro. *omi-* soul). This object could be a doll made from bone, wood or iron, and it is said that 'if one's soul is placed inside another item, then one may be wounded but will recover quickly' (Vasilevich 1969: 225).

In her study of the Evenki and Eveny, Lavrillier (2012: 116) used the term *onnir* meaning a 'spirit charge' or a spirit's 'imprint' or the effect of its 'imprint': 'humans are thought to leave their imprint on hunting and herding tools, on the land they walk, on the clothes they wear, on the meat they take when hunting, on skins they tan, on the items they sew, on the reindeer they herd, ride or treat for illness and so forth, and on all the ritual gestures they perform' (ibid). Similarly, a hunter can place his or her 'energy' inside objects by making tools. These items then become independent agents, affecting anyone who uses them in a positive or negative way. A new user of a tool may either bring his or her own identity to such items or inherit its destiny from the previous user (see for example Varlamova 2004: 60).[17] A close family member or friend, with whom a relationship based on exchange and sharing has been established, may acquire luck by using the tools of a lucky person.

Those who succeed in establishing a cooperative relationship with the master-spirits are likely to sustain their well-being for as long as they continue to live in the area. People described such experiences of luck, together with the ensuing moral responsibilities toward the master-spirits, as placing one's 'energies' in the places people use for their subsistence. Indeed, recognizable traces left by former reindeer herders and hunters on the land, such as mortuary scaffolds, storage sites, camps and trails, can be seen as imbued with the agency of ancestors, which can be harmful if treated without respect. Places, objects and their nonhuman constituencies can stand as agents of their own right, mediating 'energies' of former users. These places and objects may thus affect the activities of people and animals by the simple fact that people and animals use these places (see Vorob'ev 2013: 46). Living and acting in a place for a long time and experiencing luck there brings a new identity to that place, imprinting it with new experiences.

The proper treatment of domestic reindeer, each of which has its own individual agency, also reinforces the interdependent and intimate human-animal-landscape interaction. Hence animals like reindeer are not seen simply as property, but also as the embodied expression of a person's social relations and spatial interactions, which are infused with ideas of cooperation and luck. As humans constantly compete with and attune themselves to game animals and strive to catch luck, they also must be skilful enough to herd domestic animals and attune their daily practices to the reindeer's needs. 'Reindeer luck' can be also achieved through proper interaction with animals when attracting them to the camp for regular visits or using them as transport in hunting. The loss of a herd is considered a great misfortune affecting a person's health and living energy. Hence, elders say that 'without reindeer, one has no face' (Oro. *Ororver sokordenesh, badeves sokordenesh*). In a similar vein, they add, 'no reindeer, no Orochen' (Oro. *Ororver achin, Orocher achin*). Selling or killing reindeer therefore often means the loss of luck. For this reason, moral rules require that reindeer can be exchanged with other herders or killed only as an offering to the spirits.

In the Russian and the Soviet understanding, hunting practices of indigenous peoples were reduced to technical activities, without acknowledgment of a connection to religious beliefs, which were seen as superstitious relics of the past anyway (see Potapov 2001; Petri 1930). Most of the recent research conducted among Siberian indigenous communities has focused on the indigenous economy of reindeer herding and the constraints imposed by the Soviet and post-Soviet state, whereas research on hunting practices or the combination of hunting and herding remains scarce.[18] At the same time, recent field reports document that many indigenous communities of herders and hunters have given up herding in recent years in favour of hunting or even fishing (Takakura 2012; Vorob'ev 2007, 2013).

The ontology of luck and its connection to hunting skills and techniques, place-making and discursive strategies has been little explored in studies of hunting societies in Siberia and North America. In her analysis of the ethnographic record, Hamayon (2012) argued that in pre-Soviet Siberian societies luck implied the mode of obtainment rather than of production. Hence, game and other things, be they material (such as rain or good pastures, for herders) or immaterial (such as love, fertility, health and success in other domains), cannot be produced since they are limited in quantity and uncertain in availability (ibid.: 101).

In the few existing studies on hunting communities like the Khanty and Yukaghir or groups that combine hunting with reindeer herding like the Eveny and Sakha, the theme of luck remains very marginal or else the term is completely omitted (see Jordan 2003; Vitebsky 2005; Willerslev 2007). Luck is mostly described as a moral imperative based on the hunters' positive relations with other humans, game animals and master-spirits, which is also a common trope in many studies of subarctic hunters in North America (Feit 1994, Ridington 1990, Nelson 1983). In Vitebsky's monograph on Eveny hunters and herders, we find that hunting luck was achieved when animals offered themselves to a worthy hunter at the behest of the master-spirit called Bayanay (2005). Hunting constituted an engagement with the master, owner or ruler of animals more than with the animals or places themselves, since animals were seen as the master's spirit's 'incarnations, manifestations, or refractions' (Vitebsky 2005: 262). The previously underdeveloped themes of the 'materiality of luck' and loss of fortune because of a curse were addressed in recent ethnographic studies of the cattle-breeding Buryats of Mongolia and China. Empson (2011) described how fortune was retained in material forms: it could be harnessed as an inner force persisting in herds or the land, and could also be conceived in kin relations, especially with children. Swancutt (2012) described how the rise and fall of fortune involved efforts to improve or fix it through rituals, divinations and innovative magic remedies.

The most elaborate description of hunting luck among North American subarctic hunters is provided by Richard K. Nelson (1983) in his ethnography of the Athapascan Koyukon. For the Koyukon luck is not a skill or quality, but rather an 'essential element' in the spiritual interchange between humans and spirits that is based on a moral code (ibid.: 26–27, 232). Luck as a 'nearly tangible essence' heavily affects every phase of Koyukon subsistence that is based on the constant interplay between humans with a certain measure of luck and the spirits of animals (ibid.: 358). Nelson (ibid.: 232) also adds that luck is a 'finite entity' that can be retained, lost, transferred and recovered when interacting with other humans and animals. 'Even equipment for hunting and trapping enters into this spiritual interchange, where the behaviour or event associated with a particular trap (or trapping place) may influence its luck for catching animals' (ibid.: 141). In his detailed ethnography, however, Nelson focuses mainly on indigenous hunters' technical adaptations, like their hunting and trapping skills and their knowledge of animals.[19] In many ethnographic studies of North American subarctic indigenous societies, hunting luck is seen as the outcome of a satisfactory and positive relationship and is often guided by reciprocity (see Ridington 1988: 105; A. Sharp 1986: 258).[20] According to Firket Berkes (1999: 84–87), the Chisasibi Cree are to show respect for animals in several ways : the hunter maintains an attitude of humility during the hunt; the animal is approached, killed and carried to camp with respect; offerings are made and the animals is butchered and consumed, and its remains disposed of, with respect. At the same time Berkes describes hunting success as a cyclic, fluctuating and limited phenomenon: 'it peaks with age and experience and then declines since success is passed on to a person's sons and other hunters' (ibid.: 82).

In this book, I approach luck in the active mode by showing the dynamics of hunters' and reindeer herders' interactions with other beings, humans, animals and spirits. Various examples illustrate how certain tactile and bodily techniques serve to enhance luck and well-being. For the Orochen, success in subsistence activities, health and well-being also relies on the creation of objects and places as containers of luck. They pursue various strategies to escape misfortune, remove a curse or perpetuate the experience of luck. The success of such strategies relies on cooperation but does not exclude domination. To understand the Orochen ontology of luck, I will present connected ethnographic case studies that show how luck is obtained and preserved in daily subsistence practices as well as through the interaction among humans and nonhuman beings. The book will show how the anxiousness for luck permeates people's practical activities, discursive strategies, practices of place-making and spatial experiences in the taiga and the village. To this end, I analyse the assemblages of skills and kinds of knowledge, empathy and awareness that people use to obtain and contain luck when competing with animals and other humans or moving through the landscape. I also show how weather predictions, the adjustment of campsites to the shifting environment and the creation of networks of cooperation and exchange with different people serve to realize subsistence opportunities.

Success is also contingent on various rituals, healing practices, divinations and practices of domination. The use of a combination of domination and cooperation in order to achieve success in subsistence may have been influenced by the complex post-Soviet political and economic environment based on the overexploitation of resources, a black market economy and a history of the state's massive penetration of Orochen cultural practices and subsistence. However, I argue that these ambiguous interactions shared by other Siberian, Inner Asian or Canadian subarctic groups. The book re-examines commonly held ideas found in countless ethnographies of hunters and gatherers that have provided iconic descriptions of how animals give themselves up to hunters as long as they are treated with respect. To the contrary, I will demonstrate that interactions between humans, animals and spirits, as well as with material objects and places, are based on complex relations that involve cooperation but also contests with other beings, as well as domination, which creates experiences infused with anxiety, ambiguity and risk.

Outline of the Book

The chapters address the vernacular notion of luck through a series of interrelated ethnographic case studies. Chapter 1 introduces the field site in the Tungokochen District of Zabaikal Province and describes the local identities and contemporary way of life in a post-Soviet village that is marked by competition over taiga resources. It also describes how the state dominated the lives of indigenous people in the region through early colonial policies, administrative changes and Soviet reforms. It introduces the most important members of the extended family of reindeer herders and hunters I stayed with and describes their characters and ways of subsistence. It underlines the skills, knowledge, adjustment and respect for autonomy one must develop to maintain the environment of luck and build mutual trust.

Chapter 2 introduces the book's main ideas and presents linguistic, semantic and ethnographic insights into interlinked concepts that recur in the text, such as luck, strength, soul, mastery, movement and sharing (Oro. *nimat*) as well as nonhuman beings like animals, malevolent spirits (Oro. *arenkil*), master-spirits (Oro. *odzhen*) and living places (Oro. *bikit*). I demonstrate how luck is not achieved simply because of the master-spirits' goodwill, but instead emerges from a complex process of competition during which it must be obtained and then secured. This process involves the enactment of practice-based knowledge and skills as well as empathy, which generate success in the hunter's and herder's daily interactions with animals, spirits and places. It also involves predictions, divinations, dreams, use of various amulets and practices of sharing that attract and sustain the flow of luck. I demonstrate that the desired results can be achieved not only through a positive relationship of hunters and herders cooperating with the master-spirits, but also using various forms of domination referred as sinful behaviour, and clandestine practices too.

Chapter 3 describes how people act either cooperatively or more autonomously according to their experiences of luck and trust, which is crucial to understanding the existing relationships in local subsistence practices. In this context, I describe how luck can be channelled through the sharing of tools, knowledge and skills, and is reflected in cooperative relations. Hunters' and herders' storage practices reveal how they adapt to an insecure socioeconomic environment through accumulation, autonomy and concealment of wealth, although such accumulation of goods, as the opposite of an ethos of sharing, may endanger the possession of luck.

Chapter 4 describes how movement is semantically, practically and metaphorically linked to ways of catching luck. Walking is considered an important skill, an expression of physical strength and a moral value that ensures success in subsistence. I describe the connection between walking and the hunters' and herders' competence in hunting and herding, and contrast it with the pejorative colonial concept of the 'Walking Tungus'. Walking, along with the use of signs and paths, is key to both the success of cooperative endeavours and the autonomy of hunters and herders living in remote taiga areas.

Chapter 5 describes how hunters and herders catch their luck in hunting in what is seen as a dynamic personal competition between the hunter and an individual animal. Luck is viewed as contingent on the hunter's adjustment to the animal's living place (Oro. *bikit*). Reading and interpreting tracks is one of the most important skills in the interactions between animals and humans during hunting and herding. For the Orochen, the habitats of game animals are not just patches of the environment but vibrant places to which humans must attune their senses and movement when hunting for a certain animal. Hence, hunters and herders adjust their daily activities and camps according to their awareness of both wild and domestic animals and spirits living in the vicinity. The experience of luck and well-being when using certain taiga places conveys to humans a sense of mastery of their own living place (Oro. *bikit*).

Chapter 6 examines how luck is achieved through the successful prediction of, and influence upon, the weather. I show how hunters adjust their movements and camping sites according to their knowledge of the weather and the seasons to ensure that they make the best use of certain hunting areas and certain animals. Orochen temporality cannot be described as a fixed and abstract calendar; rather, it is a flow of intertwined incidents situated in places to which a people have to adjust their activities in order to succeed in their subsistence activities.

Chapter 7 describes hunting and herding luck in relation to humans' ambivalent interaction with both domestic animals (reindeer and dogs) and predators (bears and wolves) in the face of a shortage of and competition for land in the post-Soviet environment. The Orochen perceive their interactions with domestic animals like reindeer and dogs as cooperation based on a person's competence, reciprocity and respect for the animal's agency as well as the animal's autonomy. Reindeer herding and dog breeding are closely connected with hunting. Therefore, these economic strategies can be seen as a coherent, interdependent mode of subsistence that relies on an integral system of skills, knowledge and notions of personhood. In a context where interactions with both wild and domestic animals are based on a person's intimate engagement with them and their living places, there is no clear-cut distinction between wild and domestic animals.

Chapter 8 describes how vernacular ideas of health and wellbeing are connected to the use of the landscape. Various old and newly established ritual sites have become important sources of knowledge, health and strength since shamans' absence as communal intermediaries during the past half century. It focuses in particular on how rock art sites have become important sources of luck and well-being for the Orochen of Tungokochen, serving as a continuous monumental manifestation of the Orochen cosmology.

Chapter 9 offers concluding remarks on some overarching ideas addressed in the chapters and discusses these in relation to the ethnographic literature on hunters' and gatherers' ideas of luck, reciprocity and domination. In this chapter I argue that both modes – cooperation and domination – can be understood as reciprocal relations that guide hunters' and herders' enacted and emplaced strategies for interacting with different beings and maintain hunting success and well-being.

Notes

1. The ethnonym Evenki was chosen by the Soviet state as an administrative category in the 1920s after the end of the civil wars. It was used as a unified reference to many scattered groups in Siberia and the Far East that spoke dialects of the Tungus-Manchu language group.

2. By hunters and herders I mean both males and females hunters. Though I spent most of my time with male hunters, nevertheless most Orochen females that were raised in taiga camps were actively involved into hunting of fur as well as game animals.

3. Among Turkic speakers, *odzhen* means 'mastery' and 'power', referring to a quality of places, spirits and humans (for *eeze* among Altaians, see Halemba 2007: 64–67, for *eze* among Mongolians, see Humphrey 1996: 85–86).

4. The Russian word *lovit'* is usually used in games, when a person throws an object, shouting *'lovi'*- catch it. The word *poimat'* (also translated as catch) is mainly used with reference to trapping or snaring game.

5. Swancutt (2012: 179) similarly states, 'Buryats hold that shamanic spirits and Buddhist gods often express their pleasure when observing a person acting virtuously by sending that person blessings and boons of fortune'.

6. Similarly, Swancutt (2012: 13) notices that the Buryat of Mongolia and China believe that 'the strength of a person's fortune and wilful courage (Bur. *zorig*) can protect the entire surface of a person's body, deflecting curse attacks from penetrating the person'.

7. Orochen hunters often talk about the closing road or closing luck (*perekryt' udachiu*) (see Alekhin 2007: 132).

8. On *nimat* see Sirina (2012: 316–335); Shubin (2007: 21–26); Turov (2000: 48–59), Vasilevich (1969: 69); Rastsvetaev (1933: 30–37); Dobromyslov (1902: 80).

9. The old Russian word *stramnoi* means bad, unacceptable, inconvenient and unpleasant.

10. The idea that hunters are not necessarily ecologists is not new in studies of circumpolar people (see Brightman 2002 [1993]; Krech III 1999; Feit 1973).

11. Hunters and herders hold vernacular conceptions of 'poaching' that clash with formal state regulations defining 'poaching' as hunting without formal permission or license. How Siberian hunters and herders negotiate access to resources with the state by relying on their own moral rules and logics rather than observing formal regulations needs to be further explored in future research.

12. It is also believed that both animals and master-spirits may get very angry when a hunter makes an animal suffer (see also Zelenin 1929: 41).

13. In a comparative Tungusic-Manchurian dictionary, Tsintsius (1975: 122) refers to the *arenki* as an evil spirit, devil, monster or ghost.

14. See also the ethnographic compilation of Evenki rituals for the escorting of souls in Ermolova (2010).

15. Anisimov (1959: 18–20) writes that the Orochen, like many other Siberian groups, link certain places to specific animals.

16. As Anderson (2000b: 234) states, 'their [i.e. Evenki herders'] actions, motivations, and achievements are understood and acted upon by nonhuman beings'.

17. A lost item or using a tool can be dangerous for those who handle it without asking its master. As Nadia Zhumaneeva said, 'the thing wants to return to his master'. She gave me the example of a knife found in the taiga that was later used in stabbing the one who found it.

18. At the late stage of editing of my manuscript, a Russian ethnologist published a monumental comparative monograph (Sirina 2012) on Evenki and Eveny land use, traditional subsistence and worldview. The volume provides a rich archival, historical and classical ethnographic overview supported by Sirina's field experience, which gives a good background and deeper linguistic understanding of many Evenki notions – *nimat, omi, arenki, odzhen, seveki* – used in my book on Orochen people.

19. In his earlier ethnographic work, Nelson (1973: 311) compares the hunting skills of Athapaskans and Eskimo, referring very briefly to their notions of luck and success.

20. Many ethnographies of North American Indian communities mention a type of 'power' associated with 'medicine' – *inkonze* (Chipewyan), *inkone* (Dogrib), *inkon* (Slavey) or *ech'inte'* (Dene) (e.g. H. Sharp 2001: 53–54; Helm 1994: 78; Goulet 1998: 60–82). They describe 'power' as a superior quality that ani-

mals have but humans lack. Humans may just have a little of it or, as among the Dene, are deprived of it at birth (H. Sharp 2001: 46). Although it is believed that people can never become stronger than animals, they may regain 'power' during their lives through interaction with nonhuman beings (ibid.). Generally every person in the indigenous community is expected to find his or her own way to meet animals in dreams or visions and gain 'power' by maintaining a lifelong relationship with an animal-helper (Brightman 2002: 169–170; Tanner 1979: 125–126; Hallowell 1966: 455; Speck 1935: 187–188). For the Dene Tha, as for most American Indian people, a nonhuman being encountered in a vision or dream becomes a person's guide for life, helping in hunting and warning of misfortune to come (Goulet 1998: 78–80). This 'power' relationship is described as a matter of respect and exchange. Animals are believed to constantly monitor the actions and words of humans for signs of respect or disrespect towards them. For a detailed translation and analysis of *inkoze*, see Smith (1998: 429; 1973), Rushforth (1992: 486), Ridington (1990).

CHAPTER ONE

People I Lived With

Community, Subsistence and Skills

Indigenous Identities

The nomadic hunting and reindeer herding Orochen communities in-habiting the northern taiga of Zabaikal Province in Eastern Siberia are known in the early literature as Vitim River Tungus or Nerchinsk Tun-gus. Tungus is an old colonial name for the scattered Tungus-Manchu-speaking groups of hunting and reindeer herding people who today call themselves Orochen (pl. Orocher), Evenki (pl. Evenkil) or Eveny. Today, the Orochen also use the term Tungus to refer to horse and cattle raising groups known as Barguzin Tungus (Buryatia) and Shilka Tungus (Zabaikal Province).

Today the indigenous people of the Tungokochen District refer to themselves as Orochen or Evenki, depending on the context. The term Orochen, as they call themselves – 'reindeer people' (Oro. *oron* 'reindeer') – is used mostly in daily life, while the term Evenki is more likely to be used in public and political discourses by officials and indigenous political leaders. The Orochen are members of a Tungus-Manchu-speaking group (of the Altaic language family) of reindeer herders and hunters inhabiting the basins of the Vitim, Lena, Kalar, Olekma, Aldan and Zea Rivers in the eastern part of Siberia.[1] They also include the reindeer herders of Barguzin in Buryatia. Linguists L. J. Whaley, Lenore A. Grenoble, and F. X. Li (1999) argue that the Orochen language should be treated as a distinct linguistic variety rather than a dialect of the Evenki language. Vasilevich (1969) distin-guished between two different dialects of the Orochen language that are found in Zabaikal'ia. Speakers of the eastern dialect live in the ad-ministrative districts of Kalar and Tungiro-Olekma; southern-dialect speakers, in the Tungukochen District of Zabaikal Province. The Vitim River Orochen, who today live on both sides of the Vitim in Buryatia and the province of Zabaikal, speak the same dialect, maintain kinship relations, share the same clans and continue to intermarry and engage in exchange practices. Although Tugolukov (1962: 18) maintained that the Kalar Orochen do not speak the same dialect as the Tungokochen Orochen, are more 'Yakuticized' than the latter and even have a history of hostility, my own local kinship diagrams show that marriage relations between the two groups date back to the late nineteenth century.

Early explorers and Tsarist administrators applied the old colonial name Tungus to the contemporary Evenki and Eveny in their reports. The first knowledge of the Vitim Tungus people who lived on both banks of the Vitim River comes from records of the military expedition of Golovin and Glebov, who followed the Vitim River from its junction with the Karenga River in the seventeenth century (see Dolgikh 1960: 38). While hunting and herding reindeer in pre-Soviet times, the Vitim Tungus roamed the basins of the Vitim River's tributaries: on the right bank, the Konda, Karenga, Kalakan, Kalar and Yumurchen Rivers in Zabaikal Province; on the left bank, the Tsipa and Muia Rivers in Buryatia. Elders still remember that names of rivers were important markers of group identities and that hunters referred to themselves according to the rivers they used for subsistence, like *karengan* (a person from the Karenga River basin) or *nerchugan* (a person from the Nercha River basin). We also find that the Tungus of Zabaikal'ia were distinguished according to their means of transportation early on in reports by Pallas (1788: 328). Nowadays people refer to themselves either as Orochen, people with many reindeer, or as 'Murchen' – 'horse Evenki' (Bur. *murin*, horse) who raised cattle and horses.[2]

Today, most Orochen live in villages and continue to hunt game and herd reindeer in remote areas of the Vitim River basin. Orochen of Buryatia and Zabaikal Province differ according to the administrative units delimited by the Vitim River. They refer to each other according to their respective administrative units either as 'Bauntovskie' and 'Chitinskie' or as 'Tungokochenskie' and 'Kalarskie' Evenki. Kinship relations are actualized in public celebrations of Aboriginal Day.[3] Although I spent most of my time with hunters and reindeer herders of the Aruneev-Zhumaneev kin group from the Chilchagir and Kindigyr clans, I had opportunities to communicate with many families representing various kin groups (see Table 1.1).

The Orochen language is known and spoken with varying degrees of fluency in the villages. Most young Orochen speak only Russian.

Table 1.1 | *Representation of Orochen and Murchen clans and families*[4]

Evenki Clans (Orochen)	Families and their base villages (Zabaikal Province and Buryatia)
Chilchagir:	Aruneev (Tungokochen), Basaulov (Rossoshino), Kopylov (Ust' Karenga), Dimitrov (Bugunda), Semirekonov (Bagdarin, Mongoi), Naikanchin (Bagdarin, Rossoshino, Tungokochen), Molokov (Mongoi, Dzilinda), Dogonchin (Bagdarin, Dzhilinda)
Shamagir	Shireulov (Usugli), Kutonchin (Tungokochen), Chernykh (Ust' Karenga), Dushinov (Tungokochen, Usugli)
Kindigyr	Zhumaneev (Tungokochen), Nerguneev (Ust' Karenga, Tungokochen) Torgonov (Bagdarin);
Turuyagir	Urpiulov (Ust' Karenga), Garponeev (Ust' Karenga, Usugli), Ainchin (Yumurchen Krasnyi Iar), Unaulov (Ust' Karenga), Malkov (Zelenoe Ozero)
Sologor	Kirilov (Bugunda, Tungokochen, Zelenoe Ozero)
Laksikagir	Taskerov (Ust' Karenga), Kantaulov (Rossoshino), Lakushin (Zelenoe Ozero, Tungokochen)
Murdocher	Mordonov (Bagdarin, Rossoshino)

Evenki Clans (Murchen)	Families (villages of Zabaikal Province and Buryatia)
Khamnigan	Otkhondoev, Epov, Morbinev (Tungokochen); Ulzuev, (Usugli, Shilka, Zagulai)
Galdiogir	Baranov, Romanov, Turakin (Bagdarin)
Chongogir	Mironov (Bagdarin)
Tepkogir	Vachelanov (Bagdarin, Kevekta River)

Others who know the Orochen language do not speak it in the presence of non-Orochen; all of my conversations were therefore conducted in Russian. By the end of my fieldwork, I had learned many Orochen words, which helped me follow simple conversations in Orochen intermingled with Russian.

Zabaikal'ia

Zabaikal'ia lies at the intersection of Siberia, the Far East and Inner Asia. Local geographers often refer to it as the 'centre of Eurasia'. Zabaikal'ia (Zabaikal Province) is a vast territory stretching eastward about 1,000 km from the eastern shores of Lake Baikal to the confluence of the Argun and Shilka Rivers. In the north, it starts in the high mountain ranges of Patomskoe and Severo-Baikalskoe (Sakha Republic) and extends south for another 1,000 km to the borders of China and Mongolia. The name Zabaikal'ia, which means 'the area beyond Lake Baikal', reflects a Eurocentric colonial view of the region. In the Russian Empire the region served as a support base for exploration for minerals, silver and gold, which began in the seventeenth century when Cossacks explored and militarized the region by establishing a system of forts. The Chinese, Japanese and Korean empires struggled with Russia for control of the region. It became an important part of the Soviet Union with the increasing exploitation of iron, nickel, molybdenum, copper, titanium, aluminium, zinc, cobalt, and brown and hard coal until the demise of the Soviet state (see Geniatulin 2000: 34–36, 156–159). For centuries, the local population of Zabaikal'ia also supplied the European and Far Eastern markets with the fur of sables, rare natural medicines and nephrite (a kind of jade). Zabaikal'ia became an administrative unit of the Russian Empire in 1851. Much earlier, however, its name had played an import-

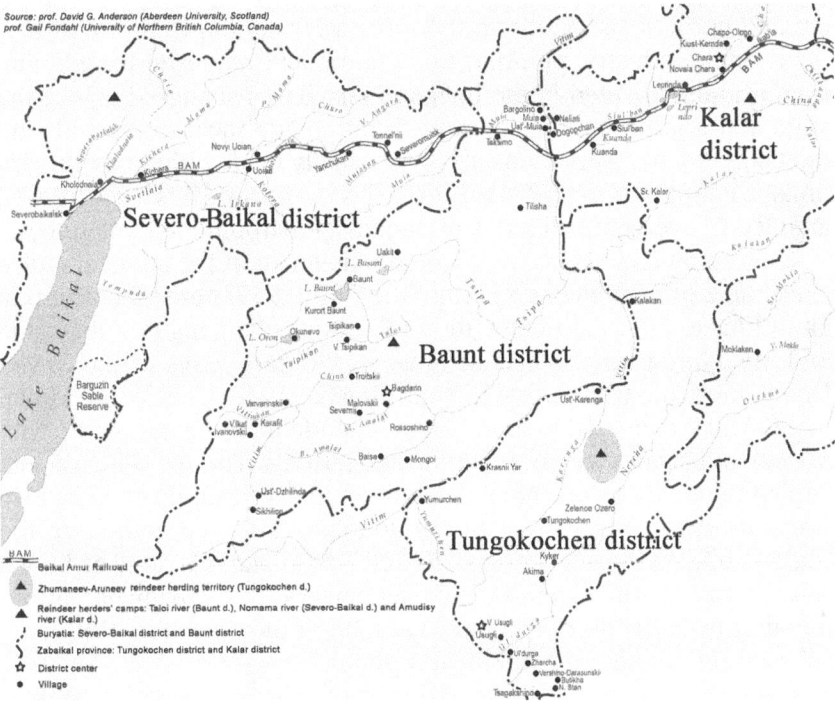

Map 1.1 | *Sketch map of research sites in Zabaikal'ia*

ant role in popular and scientific literature as well as local discourse. Zabaikal'ia's territory covers the former Chita Province (Chitinskaia Oblast') and the Aga Buryat Autonomous District in the east, as well as the Republic of Buryatia and parts of the province of Irkutsk (Bodaibo District) in the west. In the spring of 2008, Chita and the Aga Buryat Autonomous District (Aginskii Buriatskii Avtonomnyi Okrug) were consolidated into a newly established administrative region that was renamed Zabaikal Province (Zabaikalskii Krai).

Today, as in Soviet times, villagers of various origins proudly call themselves 'Zabaikal'ians' (Rus. *zabaikal'tsy*). They point to the demanding local environment they live in, which is characterized by extreme temperatures, river floods and forest fires, and the region's violent history. This idea is encapsulated in the saying that 'God created Sochi and the devil Mogochi'.[5] This identification also alludes to being born and raised in a remote, harsh, peculiar area of a vast country ruled from a centre located in Europe. Indeed, healthcare experts refer to the region, especially its northern part, as 'an extremely unfavourable place for human health' (see Mikheev 1995: 35). Zabaikal'ians' bodies are said to experience stress for 215 days per year, which sometimes causes an immune deficiency (ibid.: 36). Hunters and herders also mention the threats emanating from the former Soviet state industry, pointing to certain places exposed to radiation from uranium located in the hills, military bases scattered across the taiga and a large number of mines that pollute local rivers and ruin the taiga. Such observations are then usually made light of by the optimistic counterargument that those who are born in this area are well adapted to overcome all kinds of negative environmental influences.[6]

The region has also been an infamous location for political exiles since the eighteenth century. Shirokogoroff (1919) noted that Russian and Chinese officials' persecution of Tungus shamans in Zabaikal'ia and Manchuria started at that time. In the early days of the Soviet Union, the region supported the anti-Bolshevik so-called White Movement, which managed to found an independent Far East republic with the city of Chita as its capital in the early 1920s. The republic was occupied by Soviet troops after a lengthy military struggle in 1922 (see Brennan 1999). Because of the prolonged resistance, people of the region suffered heavy repressions after the establishment of Soviet rule. People say that *zabaikal'tsy* have always lived somewhat autonomously from the state and have been 'their own masters' (Rus. *sam sebe khoziain*) under any political regime.

Many Orochen men who served in the Soviet army recall that their comrades saw them as somewhat nonconformist people with anarchistic tendencies. Servicemen from Zabaikal'ia were not only given the derogatory nickname *semenovtsy*[7] but also suffered abuse and humiliations at the hands of Soviet officers. Thus Soviet army service, which in the popular understanding has been called 'a school of manhood', also reinforced a person's identity and sense of local belonging. Hence, a common principle of *zabaikal'tsy* is contained in the adage 'When they call you a Semenov person, you have to be proud; when they calls *guran*, you have to hit him in the face' (Rus. *za gurana mordu biut, za semenovtsev gordiatsa*). People of Zabaikal'ia often say, 'We are all *guran*',[8] alluding to being part of the local (i.e. 'demanding') environment. In recent centuries the region's inhabitants, along with its indigenous population of Buryat and Evenki, have been a varied mix of people of Asian and European origin. Today's Zabaikal'ians still contrast their region with the centre, saying, 'they live in Russia, we live in Zabaikal'ia'. Most people in the northern villages, although of various origins, use many vernacular Orochen words when speaking about hunting or geographical features. A real *zabaikalets* is also often identified by the specific local dialect.

Unpredictable Travel

The Evenki ethnographer Elpidifor Titov (1926a: 2) reported that the only way to reach the Orochen of the Vitim region was to travel by horse-drawn sledge in winter by way of the villages of Akima and Kyker. The situation is little changed today. The only gravel road to Tungokochen village, built just after the collapse of the Soviet Union, stretches about 150 km north across the taiga from the district capital, Verkh-Usugli. The road poses a challenge for vehicles and people in all seasons, and the traveller must be ready for unexpected incidents at any time. A successful trip hinges to a large degree on the driver's knowledge and skill in crossing rivers, avoiding pools and mud holes, and detouring through the forest to skirt flooded sections of road. One should not be surprised to make several stops on the road for small repairs or to visit ritual sites called 'shamans'. These ritual sites, which are located in mountain passages and can be seen from the road, consist of an idol or decorated tree surrounded by empty bottles, cigarettes, toys and pieces of cloth left as offerings to the local spirits. Passengers usually take a short break and leave coins, cigarettes, food and pieces of cloth. They also relieve themselves under common-sense rules that discourage urinating in front of the car lest 'the road be closed' or travel luck vanish. Even the state-run buses that connect different villages and are always full of people stop en route to greet the spirits or at least signal in their honour when passing such sites. People always use the opportunity to throw cigarettes, candies or coins through the window as offerings for the master-spirit who is responsible for one's luck on the road.

Today, most Orochen of the Tungokochen District live in scattered villages established by the state in Soviet times. About 315 Orochen inhabit the six villages of Tungokochen, Verkh-Usugli, Ust' Karenga, Zelenoe Ozero, Iumurchen and Krasnyi Iar. The villages vary in terms of their distance from the district capital and the difficulty of access. Economic difficulties and the administration's inability to sustain local institutions led to the near desertion of the three latter villages in 2011, with only a few families of passionate indigenous hunters living in some of the remaining buildings. To sustain their villages today the villagers of Tungokochen and Ust' Karenga must make huge efforts to support local specialists, secondary schools and day-care centres for preschool children. Many Orochen have relatives on the other bank of the broad Vitim River in the Baunt District of the Buryat republic. About 510 Orochen live in the Baunt District, mainly in the five villages of Bagdarin, Rossoshino, Ust' Dzhilinda, Mongoi and Varvarinsk. With 128 and over 200 inhabitants, respectively, Tungokochen and Rossoshino are the biggest Orochen villages. Only in Rossoshino do they form the majority of the population. Orochen of Zabaikal Province living in the districts of Tungokochen, Kalar and Tungir-Olekma do not have any special indigenous status. The Baunt District, however, has special status as the 'Evenki National District' in the Republic of Buryatia (re-established in 1992). Therefore its Orochen population is regarded as receiving more benefits from the Republic of Buryatia.

Tungokochen village, established in 1932 near the Karenga River, was created through the consolidation of several collective farms and the relocation of some families from Khulugli village and the former district capital of Kalakan (see Fondahl 1998: 66). Further populating the village were employees of the local administration and school system, farmers of Tungus-Cossack origin relocated from the Nerchinsk District (Zabaikal Province) and some Orochen hunters and reindeer herders.[9] The village served as the capital of Tungokochen District between 1939 and 1977 as part of a larger project to civilize indigenous people and populate the remote northern part of Zabaikal Province. In Soviet times the village had an airstrip, a small gasoline-power plant, all-terrain vehicles, grocery and general stores, a hospital, a public bath (Rus. *bania*), laundry facilities (Rus. *prachechnaia*), a kindergarten and boarding school (Rus. *internat*), and even a one-room hotel.

Most people were employed on state farms specializing in horse, reindeer and cattle herding, agriculture and hunting. As residents of a northern village, villagers received subsidies in addition to their salaries. Up to the mid 1990s, all villages of the Tungokochen District were well connected by airplane, which then was the primary means of transportation in the remote region. Villagers remember when they could fly by helicopter or small plane (AN-2s) twice per day to any village in the Tungokochen District. They could also 'catch' helicopters used by the forest department and the health service that flew between villages and the city of Chita. Recently, aviation has been discontinued because of the high cost of gasoline and maintenance. Specially maintained aerodromes fell to ruin or were dismantled piece by piece by the villagers. Nowadays helicopters fly to villages only when somebody's health is at risk. Someone who wants to travel further to remote villages like Ust' Karenga (200 km), Zelenoe Ozero (150 km), Krasnyi Iar (120 km) or Iumurchen (100 km) 'must never plan their trip in advance', since all-terrain vehicles (ATVs) run between villages without any schedule. Winter is the exception, and for four months the frozen rivers become highways for the constant travel of villagers, entrepreneurs known as *komersanty*, fishers and hunters. After the collapse of the Soviet Union, all the northern villages of Zabaikal'ia lost government subsidies and gasoline supplies, often becoming unable to generate electricity for the entire day. Villages also suffered the closure of nursing stations and schools while shops and collective farms were privatized. Soon the Zabaikal provincial administration stopped the costly charter of helicopters and planes to remote villages. Even telephone service was discontinued, and people had to rely solely on sporadic radio connections and the telegraph to send and receive messages. Tungokochen managed to maintain some of its infrastructure, so it has become attractive for people in the small scattered villages. Tungokochen and Ust' Karenga have succeeded in reorganizing their infrastructure and adapting somewhat to the new market conditions, although the hospital in Tungokochen has been closed since 2012.

I had to leave the region every three months to conform with Russian visa regulations. Finding my way to and from the hunting and herding camps was always a challenge. The camps were usually located 140–200 km from Tungokochen village. The availability of different ground transport was always limited by the peculiar geographical and environmental conditions and, probably even more, by people's motivation, which was linked to trust and to previous experiences of success. At the beginning of my fieldwork, I had to take any travel possibility that was available, slowly increasing my knowledge of different opportunities and constantly trying to negotiate with people for whatever means of transport was available at the time. Nowadays potential passengers must be very proficient in gathering all kinds of information regarding people's movements and the availability of transportation in order to reach their destination. This information can only be gained through cooperation among villagers. One may also drift downstream by boat or travel by motorboat during the spring floods, ride on horseback or even walk. Each of these ways of travelling hinges on one's success in collecting information about the movement of others, predicting the weather and traversing rough stretches of taiga. Several times I ended up walking 30–90 kilometres to reach a village or camp. Indeed, as I will show in chapter 4, for all hunters and herders walking along different routes is an important way of travelling to their camps. Some hunters travel on foot to and from their fur-hunting territories in remote and difficult-to-access areas all the time. In general, walking is a highly valued skill that one must rely on constantly in in the taiga. Even for someone riding a horse or reindeer, the peculiarities of the landscape can make it necessary to walk part of the way.

Villagers and hunters use a variety of powered vehicles to travel in the taiga. In Soviet times, when villages and collective farms were well supplied with gasoline, most villagers had access to diesel-powered vehicles and all-terrain vehicles (ATVs) for their private needs. It is said that hunters used such gasoline-powered vehicles even for hunting a roe deer. Today only a few ATVs are left, including old military tanks (model BMP) and Soviet cargo trucks (ZIL 60, ZIL 80 and UAZ) that local traders use to transport goods and local hunters use for travel. A BMP, a military tank built in 1958, was the vehicle mostly used to connect Tungokochen village to other remote, roadless villages. The tank, with its gun removed, was acquired from the nearby military base by a local entrepreneur (nicknamed 'Roubdes' after the shortened version of 'one rouble and ten kopeks') and used for transporting people between villages, and goods to local stores. Such ancient vehicles were also widely used for hunting, fishing trips and transport of building materials for cabins. The tank was driven with extreme skill and at the considerable speed of up to 60 km per hour across swampy, rocky and forested terrain, crashing through trees on the way and giving passengers an extremely bumpy ride. A two-day trip in that vehicle is far from a romantic journey through the wilderness: exposed to exhaust and the constant noise of the engine while squeezed in among lots of goods and vomiting dogs, a rider is left with a headache for several days. These trips always included stops at rivers and log cabins, where the drivers would sprinkle vodka for sake of luck. Swallowing a big shot of vodka on an empty stomach and spending the rest of the trip asleep was considered the only way to relieve the hardship.

The drivers of ATVs, who are usually also their owners, are prepared for any repairs in the taiga, as these vehicles break down regularly. Acquisition of spare parts depends on networks of reciprocity that extend to the city. Since the maintenance costs of these all-terrain vehicles and trucks are very high, villagers usually try to combine several tasks when driving them across the taiga. Hunters and fishermen share meat or the cost of gasoline, and they might also transport passengers, groceries or building materials for log cabins to hunting sites, or militiamen to remote villages. Hunting teams also may invite a knowledgeable and 'lucky hunter' (Rus. *fartovyi okhotnik*) to act as a guide and make his trained dogs available for the whole group. As I will demonstrate later, such cooperation included not only the sharing of expenses but also the exchange of trust, competencies and experiences of luck.

Villagers say that any means of transportation has its limitations in the taiga. Since tanks have difficulty crossing the rocky ground of the highlands, the villagers mostly use it when travelling in the lowlands. Most hunters use other vehicles to travel to their winter trapping sites in November, because the areas that were covered with hummocks of grass in the summer become relatively flat when the raised water level creates ice that weighs down the grass. Only when the rivers and soil are frozen can cargo trucks can be driven across the taiga, crossing frozen swampy areas and rivers on the way to the remote hunting territories scattered across the taiga. In the summer the villagers also use a special tractor with big tires called a 'swamp vehicle' (Rus. *bolotnik*) to access haying sites in swampy areas. The high cost of transportation limits a hunter's autonomy by forcing him to rely on a network of local cooperation and interdependence. Despite the need to cooperate by sharing travel expenses, long-term cooperative relations are always threatened by experiences of misfortune and mistrust.

Weather prediction is crucial when planning a trip. The accessibility of remote taiga places depends on certain weather conditions and requires seizing any available opportunity for travelling. The Tungokochen District is characterized by a continental climate with strong seasonal extremes (see Table 1.2). High mountain ranges in the north prevent warm, humid air masses from reaching Zabaikal'ia.

This creates a harsh climate with tremendous fluctuations in atmospheric pressure and temperature extremes from –60° C in winter to 40° C in summer. The highest mountains and the rocky hill outcrops are often covered with larch and pine trees. Because the permafrost reaches quite close to the soil's surface, excess water is not absorbed; hence the ubiquitous wetland environment, even after a short period of rain. Precipitation averages 300 mm in the river valleys and rises to 600 mm in the hills. About 50 per cent of the precipitation falls in July and August. Snow is not unusual, even in early autumn or May. Winters in the northern part of Zabaikal'ia are sunny and windless, but also cold and long. Temperatures are above freezing for just fifty to eighty days throughout the year. Most rivers stay frozen from mid-October to early May (160–180 days). As noted, frozen rivers are crucial for travelling to remote villages by car or truck. In the summer rivers tend to be shallow, fast and rocky. Since the permafrost prevents rain from being fully absorbed by the soil, rivers can rise quickly, making crossing difficult. Floods are common in springtime because of ice blockages, melting snow and rain. Tungokochen village was destroyed by river floods several times. Such remote settlements were established by Soviet bureaucrats unfamiliar with local conditions. Spring is generally cold, arriving in April and lasting until mid-June, and there is a short but warm summer from mid-June to mid-August (Table 1.2). It is said that Tungokochen District is even more severe than the Magadan Region, which is famous in Russia for its harsh environment (see Mikheev 1995).

Table 1.2. | *Average temperatures in Tungokochen village, 2004–2005 (data provided by Tungokochen meteorology station).*[10]

	Average Minimum, C°	Average Maximum, C°
July 2004	4.4	8.3
Aug. 2004	21.5	3.7
Sept. 2004	–14.8	–1.5
Oct. 2004	–10.3	7
Nov. 2004	–22	–5.5
Dec. 2004	–37.8	–21.8
Jan. 2005	–34.1	–17.7
Feb. 2005	–37.2	–14.5
Mar. 2005	–23.4	–2.2
Apr. 2005	–10.2	6.5
May 2005	–2.3	14.7

Subsistence in the Taiga

With the collapse of most centrally funded economic activities in the villages, the taiga itself, with its abundance of game, became the main source of both food and cash income for many local families. Villagers rushed to the taiga in search of anything valuable enough to be sold, bartered, or used for their own needs (e.g., see Table 1.5). Many people became hunters, visiting the taiga constantly and learning new skills by joining expeditions organized by experienced hunters. As I was told, everyone started to dream about large game animals, especially musk deer valued for their glands, which can be easily traded to China. At the same time different exotic animals' parts and pelts became a staple currency in the context of a shortage of cash and a 'wild market' (Rus. *dikii rynok*) (see Anderson 2000c). Siberian musk deer glands, bear gall bladders and bear paws (Fig. 1.1), and moose lips are highly valued as medicine and sold to China by local traders called *komersanty*. The taiga has become crowded with people competing for different resources.

Ust' Karenga, which is the second largest village inhabited by Orochen (some seventy of them) lies in a rather remote part of Tungokochen District. It has survived only because of its location near the confluence of the Karenga and Vitim Rivers, which means fish can be harvested in its immediate vicinity, from both rivers. It also offers good access to remote areas of the taiga that were unaffected by state industry. Its villagers started to experience a new kind of life in the middle of the taiga, where they can watch wild animals from their windows and encounter predators like bears when herding horses or cattle close to the village. Indeed, people of remote villages often speak of themselves as living not in a village but in a wider area: a river basin or a region of several river basins. It is said that Tungokochen and Ust' Karenga are 'still alive' because of the bountiful taiga and some local people's employment in the educational, administrative and healthcare systems. Although the regional administration implicitly encourages local people to abandon their villages, people claim that nobody is willing to leave. It is also said that the Tungokochen hospital's small staff of nurses and doctors is still working only because they enjoy 'hunting in the taiga'. Hunters and herders often say that hunting, fishing and roaming the taiga make them feel independent of the city's market economy. It gives them a feeling that they are 'masters of their own' (Rus. *sami sebe khoziainy*) – the alternative for them would be 'a miserable existence in a small city apartment'.

Figure 1.1. | *Bear paws cut for trade to China.*

Most villagers generate cash income from hunting fur-bearing animals in winter (November–February). They are also able to hunt enough game for their own year-round food supply. Each hunter supplies his family, which is based in the village, and his extended network of relatives with game. Parts of game animals are also used as important sources of various medicines and materials for the making of gear, footwear and clothing, all of which are also important trade items. Fur-bearing animals and large mammals are mostly encountered in areas that are 50–100 km from the villages. They include moose (Lat. *alces alces*), elk (Lat. *cervus elaphus*), brown bear (Lat. *ursus arctos*), wild boar (Lat. *sus scrofa*), wild reindeer (Lat. *rangifer tarandus*), roe deer (Lat. *capreolus capreolus*) and Siberian musk deer (Lat. *moschus moschiferus*). Rabbit (Lat. *lepus timidus*) is considered a minor kill; nevertheless, fur hunters often live on rabbit meat for the whole winter since the animals are very easy to snare. The rocky forested areas at the upper reaches of the rivers are rich in sable (Lat. *martes zibelina*), the most valued fur-bearing animal, and squirrel (Lat. *sciurus vulgaris*). Hunters also trap weasel (Lat. *mustella sibirica*), ermine (Lat. *mustela erminea*), lynx (Lat. *lynx*) and wolverine (Lat. *gulo gulo*).[11]

Villagers visit the taiga all year round for hunting. Domestic animals like horses and dogs are raised and trained especially for transportation and hunting. Horses of so-called Yakut breeding, which in

Soviet times were raised for meat production by collective farms in Zabaikal'ia, have become the main means of transportation in the taiga, as most Orochen have ceased to herd reindeer. Most villagers use horses to transport the kill from the taiga when there is no snow on the ground. Between November and February, many village-based hunters move to more remote hunting areas in order to harvest fur-bearing animals. They reach their hunting grounds by foot, by boat in early autumn or by vehicle when the rivers are frozen. The hunting grounds are located in the uplands; often the hunters have built several log cabins there and move from one to another with their gear when snaring, trapping or tracking sables and squirrels.

Almost all former state-farm managers have become traders (Rus. *komersanty*), establishing enterprises for fur trading, berry harvesting and forestry. In Tungokochen, some of them have leased various taiga areas from the state and hired local hunters to harvest fur for them. *Komersanty* have also started to supply groceries to remote villages, often handing out hunting supplies in advance and transporting hunters to remote places with the expectation of buying all their furs for the lowest price. Thus entrepreneurs now commonly compete over fur trading and land use, offering clever hunters the opportunity to sell their furs to the entrepreneur who offers the best price. In this context, trade activities in the villages depend heavily on hunters' success, since the goods and materials used for hunting are typically advanced to the hunter by the entrepreneur and paid for in spring at the end of the fur-hunting season, when all the fur has been traded. Most men who hunted fur-bearing animals in ascribed territories during Soviet times have retained their 'master right' to use these places in the post-Soviet era.

Today, however, hunters have to cooperate with other hunters or entrepreneurs to harvest resources and organize their activities, as hunting in remote places requires economic investment (fuel and groceries) as well as different kinds of knowledge about how to hunt. Companionship and friendship play an important role in herders' trading or bartering with entrepreneurs or dealing with the local administration. Since the collapse or decline of most state-funded institutions, many goods can be obtained only on the black market through interaction with people who trust you. Obtaining such resources at a low price requires entering into semi-legal transactions in various networks of reciprocity. Urban networks have helped local entrepreneurs to procure even a tank from a military base to use for transportation. Rifle parts and the gunpowder used for making cartridges have become valuable among hunters.

Table 1.3. *Annual round of levels of hunting activity, 2005–2006*

	Musk deer (Oro. Mekchia)	Moose (Oro. Boiun)	Bear (Oro. Amikan)	Roe deer (Oro. Givchan)	Elk (Oro. Kumakan)	Wild reindeer (Oro. Mongotu)	Wild boar (Oro. Murduk)	Fur-bearing animals
Jan.	Intensive hunting activity	Incidental hunting when roused by noise made by travellers			Incidental hunting: roused by noise made by travellers	Incidental hunting: Encountered when hunting sable	Incidental hunting: animals have no fat	Intensive hunting activity
Feb.	Intensive hunting activity	Intensive hunting activity			Intensive hunting activity	Encountered accidentally when hunting sable		Intensive hunting activity
Mar.		Intensive hunting activity			Intensive hunting activity			
Apr.		Intensive hunting activity			Intensive hunting activity			
May		Intensive hunting activity	Intensive hunting activity	Intensive hunting activity	Intensive			
June		Intensive hunting activity	Intensive hunting activity	Intensive hunting activity	Intensive hunting activity			

July	Intensive hunting activity	Intensive hunting activity	Intensive hunting activity	Intensive hunting activity			
Aug.	Passive hunting: animal is involved in mushroom eating	Intensive	Intensive	Passive hunting: animal is involved in mushroom eating	Intensive		
Sept.	Intensive hunting activity	Intensive hunting activity	Intensive hunting activity	Intensive hunting activity	Intensive hunting activity		
Oct.	Intensive hunting activity	Intensive hunting activity	Intensive hunting activity	Intensive hunting activity	Intensive hunting activity	Passive hunting, animal approaches herders' camp in the rutting season	
Nov.	Intensive hunting activity		Intensive hunting activity	Intensive hunting activity	Intensive hunting activity	Incidental hunting	Intensive hunting activity
Dec.	Intensive hunting activity	Passive hunting: loud walking on snow		Passive hunting: loud walking on snow	No hunting: bad quality meat in the rutting season	Encountered accidentally while hunting sable	Intensive hunting activity

People say that their lives have come to depend not only on exchange and cooperation with other humans and nonhumans, but also on taking advantage of any opportunity. This often means acting aggressively against others (human or nonhuman), engaging in covert practices or refusing cooperation. In the context of shortage and competition over land and resources, hunting and herding grounds quite commonly suffer plundering by people from the villages. Whereas formerly the 'law of the taiga' required leaving salt or sugar when taking something from a storage platform or cabin, nowadays 'everyone takes what is left unattended'. Storage platforms, cabins, traplines and snares are under constant threat of being appropriated, destroyed or stolen. Free-grazing reindeer and horses may be killed for their meat if left unattended. Lawlessness reaches even more drastic levels, such as setting fire to a rival's hunting grounds or cabin. Armed skirmishes have resulted in the 'disappearance' of numerous people in the taiga, and even in open murders. Individuals' activities in the taiga or the village often lead to accusations and conflicts over the use of sites and resources. Therefore, hunters and herders employ various defensive ritual or discursive strategies, or keep their activities and cooperation hidden in order to guard their hunting territories and their well-being.

In Buryatia I witnessed how the competition over resources among hunters, villagers, and *komersanty* also involved groups of special paramilitary forces working for the *komersanty*. Groups of young men who had served in the Russian elite military forces (OMON) were hired and equipped with Kalashnikov rifles to track and drive off people searching for nephrite (Rus. *okatysh*) in riverbeds. These mercenaries regularly travelled by ATV from the capital Ulan Ude to the remote areas around the nephrite mines, destroying the camps of 'thieves' and tracking down groups that attempted to 'steal' nephrite. The nephrite stone hunters, who were nicknamed *varavaiki* (Rus. *varavat'* – to steal), were mostly young, village-based Evenki hunters who came on horseback from all over the rural Baunt District in the hope of earning some cash. The Evenki hunters still considered themselves the masters of their former reindeer-herding territories. The struggles among different groups may also involve the police and the environmental agency, which may harass hunters and herders by demanding to see hunting licences or rifle documents.

Today all hunters, especially those who live in remote places, can indeed be considered poachers because of their inability to register their guns or obtain hunting licences. There are various reasons for this – they may be unwilling to visit cities or may be denied permission because of a former prison sentence or medical technicalities.

Hunters often hide from villagers and officials when returning to the village with game. They also hide their storage sites, called *labazy* (sing. *labaz*), and conceal their future plans for subsistence activities in the taiga to avoid plundering or problems caused by officials. I was told about a well-known rule that a 'too finicky state official [police-man or gamekeeper] does not live long'. Today officials are elected with the support of various informal networks of interests hoping for better access to public resources like gasoline or wood for building. In this competitive context, people involved in the administration of the remote taiga villages seek help by consulting with all kinds of ritual leaders, such as lamas from Chita's Buddhist monastery (Bur. *datsan*), Orthodox priests or Buryat shamans in Aga, in order to se-cure their health and avoid harm caused by their rivals' malevolent magic activities.[12]

All state farms were liquidated and turned into joint stock enter-prises after the collapse of the Soviet system. Hence, anyone who had been involved in farm work had a chance to get compensated in live-stock and privatized vehicles. Reindeer and horses were for the most part divided among individual herders at the collective farm and those groups of herders who had started to cooperate by consolidating their activities along clan lines. New economic and self-government poli-cies designed for the aboriginal people of Russia required the provin-cial governments to allocate lands to clan communities in 1992. These clan communities would herd reindeer, fish, harvest fur and cut hay in the former reindeer herders' farming areas, in designated traditional clan territories or on the former collective farms' hunting allotments. Some community leaders drew up kin diagrams by questioning elders, established kinship-based links to various hunting grounds formerly owned by various clans and negotiated with officials and villagers over their 'master rights' to certain areas. In Tungokochen village, the head of reindeers' community Nikolai Aruneev (1994) published each clan's former migration sites in the local press, describing in detail the places used by different clans in the past. Other Orochen claimed the land by pointing out that they had hunted there for de-cades during Soviet times. The remote valleys of the Vitim River basin became disputed between different hunters, herders and entrepre-neurs, each striving to use them for their subsistence. Today, Orochen point to their ancestors' graves and old dwelling sites scattered over the landscape in order to indicate their 'mastery' of the area.

Today there are about thirty-two clan community enterprises in the Tungokochen District, including several reindeer-herding enter-prises run by people hailing from Tungokochen and Ust' Karenga villages. Reindeer herders and hunters have mostly continued their subsistence activities on the farm's territories in newly re-established camps, letting their reindeer graze freely in the taiga. As one herder said, 'the taiga was returned from state control to the reindeer herders and hunters'. However, former collective-farm pastures and hunting territories leased by indigenous enterprises are the subject of constant negotiations with city-based entrepreneurs and the regional administration. After the repeated reduction of their territories, the Tungokochen herders nowadays continue their herding and hunting activities in neighbouring areas through cooperation agreements with the local owners. They may also hunt in rough, remote areas rarely used by other hunters, as they have the advantage of the use of reindeer on their hunting trips. In the 1990s all hunting and reindeer herding communities underwent reorganization. Many reindeer herders slaughtered or sold their animals after privatization, leaving the enterprises and giving up herding, having failed to cope in the competitive post-Soviet environment. Some people lacked the skills and knowledge to live in the taiga independent of external support and in the context of the 'deformed reforms' of land claims (see Fondahl 1998: 98). Fondahl (ibid.: 98–117) describes the particular challenges such as lack of funds (no operational finances), functional constraints (issues of what constitute traditional activities), competing activities, cultural and spatial marginalization, partial tenure and blatant resistance to indigenous land allotments.

Reindeer herders dwell in remote taiga areas near treeless hills, up to 100 km from the villages. Herding can be seen as an example of extreme autonomy, as it means living in a remote, roadless taiga area, relying on just a few supplies. The herders ride reindeer and use them to transport gear and supplies for their mobile camps and steel traps for fur hunting in the winter. Herders are able to move quickly from one river basin to the next, establishing new camps in the highlands in a relatively short time. Thus they can harvest animals in various river basins. Reindeer can easily carry a hunter's kill from any mountainous place in the taiga. And since they can graze on lichen in the highlands and on grass in the lowlands, they can be used in various environments.

Hunting and herding grounds can also be destroyed by forest fires. Most large villages are surrounded by burned areas. According to the Tungokochen Forestry Department, burned territories comprise about 17 per cent of the district. Taiga fires are caused by military activities but are also a result of wild market competition in the post-Soviet era: hunters burn stretches of the taiga in search of valuable shed antlers, which they collect and sell to China via *komersanty*. The white antlers are easily spotted on the burned surface. However, the burning also destroys the hunting grounds of other hunters as well as reindeer pastures. Thus, forest fires influence people's patterns of migration and land use.

Moving between Categories

Experiences of struggles over land and resources have been familiar to the Orochen reindeer herders since the early seventeenth century, when the Russian Crown claimed all of Zabaikal'ia and the Orochen were forced to pay tribute in furs. The Orochen of Tungokochen District delivered their tribute at Fort Nerchinsk in Eastern Zabaikal'ia and therefore became known as Nerchinsk Orochen. The people known as Barguzin Orochen paid tribute to officials at Fort Baunt in western Zabaikal'ia (see Belikov 1994: 13–24). Although the *yasak* was officially designated as protection tax, it was not unusual for the tribute to be collected by force. For this reason, the tax collectors were often met with resolute resistance. There were also permanent conflicts between indigenous people and Russian colonists over land and the extraction of resources (ibid.). In fact, in the early nineteenth century a governor from Irkutsk declared that indigenous peoples had no land rights at all. This policy led to the appropriation of Orochen territories by newcomers (Fondahl 1998: 42).

In 1822 Alexander I issued a special decree, 'Ustav ob upravleninii inorodtsami', to mediate the constant conflicts between settlers and indigenous Siberians and also allow for the more efficient collection of state taxes. The tsar's adviser, Mikhail Speranskii, authored a statute according to which the Orochen were accorded the special status of '*inorodtsy*' (indigenous people; literally people of different birth; aliens). Indigenous councils headed by Orochen clans had 'master's rights' to certain designated clan lands. The Orochen of the contemporary Tungokochen District were subject to the Council of Urulga (Rus. *Urulginskaia Stepnaia Duma*), based in Eastern Zabaikal'ia. Similar councils were established in the Baunt District for local clans of Kindygir, First Chilchagir, and Second Chilchagir. These administrative subdivisions were also designed to control the collection of tribute and taxes from indigenous people. They remained active up to the beginning of the Soviet era. The statute also divided the indigenous population of the region into settled (Rus. *osedlye*), nomadic (Rus. *kochevye*), and wandering (Rus. *brodiachie*). The Orochen way of life was seen as backward, and they were therefore classified as 'wandering Tungus' (Rus. *brodiachii Tungus*) in administrative documents and ethnographic literature. The 'wandering Tungus' were described as having no ties to land or understanding of the 'mastery of the land' (see in Orlov 1858b). Considering their way of life therefore a relic of the past, the state called for an end to nomadism. Government officials with little knowledge of the local way of life were entrusted with far-reaching decisions on the classification of indigenous groups (see Slezkine 1994: 84 notices).

Ironically, some local Tungus-speaking groups that were referred to as 'wandering people' and accorded the lowest status were thereby made into 'wanderers', against their wish. People had to retreat to remote areas (such as Manchuria) in order to escape from state repression. These aggressive policies in the latter part of the nineteenth century coincided with a programme to convert the indigenous population to Christianity. Both aimed to change indigenous religious beliefs and ways of life (Tugolukov 1962: 19). In the early eighteenth century, an Orthodox monastery and a big church were built in Nerchinsk to advance the conversion of aboriginal people. The state gave the church parcels of land and the right to establish villages for deportees and converted aboriginal people there (see Zhukov et al. 2003: 21).[13] In the nineteenth century, missionary activities in the region became more centrally organized. In 1852, the mission of Zabaikal'ia was established under the Irkutsk Orthodox Eparchy. Along with conversion, the mission's aim was to strengthen government rule over the indigenous people (ibid.). From the mid-nineteenth to the early twentieth century, the building of churches and monasteries increased rapidly throughout Zabaikal'ia. By the end of the twentieth century there were about 300 churches, 300 chapels and four monasteries in Zabaikal'ia (ibid: 22). Missionary activity in the region also steadily increased (see Fig. 1.2), and by the beginning of the twentieth century about 130,000 Buryat had been baptized (ibid.: 21). According to the Baunt Aboriginal Administration (Bauntovskaia Uprava Inorodtsev), all Evenkis were Christians by 1892 (Shubin 2001: 25). Christian Evenki had to pay tribute to the Church. According to special state laws, one could be imprisoned or deported for fifteen years for refusing to practice the Russian Orthodox faith (Zhukov et al. 2003: 21–22).

Some elders in Tungokochen say that although clan councils ruled certain territories in the late nineteenth and early twentieth centuries, their grandparents 'lived everywhere' between Yakutia, Aga and Barguzin while trading, hunting and bartering with relatives. As Fondahl (1998: 33) aptly noticed, the Evenki understood such land ownership

Figure 1.2. | *Christianization of Orochen of Nerchinsk County, early twentieth century. Photo by A. K. Kuznetsov, Archive of Chita Museum of A.K. Kuznetsov.*

quite flexibly and saw boundaries of such territories as 'exceedingly permeable'. It must be kept in mind that the divisions, names and limits of the actual territories of the Tungus-speaking people of Zabaikal'ia were both obscure and ambiguous. Oral histories, local archival documents and ethnographies all suggest that Orochen families shifted from one clan council to another in search of a 'better life'. They often had to change their subsistence strategies after losing their reindeer to disease or other ecological hardships caused by newcomers (see Kozulin 2004: 105–106; Shubin 2001: 75; Tugolukov 1962: 22). In the harshest years, hunters went to work at trading posts, herding horses or cutting hay, and settled down. Sometimes Orochen would again acquire reindeer and return to the taiga immediately, leaving their houses in the settlements empty (see Shirokogorov and Shirokogorova 1914: 133–134).

Outside incursions into their hunting territories, the expansion of the gold mining industry and frequent forest fires forced some indigenous groups to abandon their territories and search for less disturbed areas. Some Orochen groups migrated farther south into the taiga of Manchuria. People from the region ruled by the Nerchinsk council migrated west to lands administered by the council of the Baunt District. As Tugolukov (1962: 20) noted with reference to the ill-defined system of land use in that period, 'it sometimes happened that several hunters would gather at a single site and other territories were abandoned'. This also shows how people adapted to the shifting environment and struggled to live in autonomy by resisting state aggression and migrating to new territories or cooperating with local traders.

By the end of the nineteenth century, a new wave of miners, political exiles, and criminals had joined the workforce in the remote taiga to mine gold. They brought along their cattle and horses, hunted for game and set fires so as to leave only dry trees standing to be used for firewood. According to Titov (1926a: 10), the newcomers would often burn large stretches of taiga, thinking that the trees kept moisture in the soil and thus impeded agriculture. He described the newcomers as behaving like 'plunderers' (Rus. *razboiniki*) in the taiga and said they 'did not act as if they were stewards' (Rus. *vedut sebia ne po khoziaiski*), killing every animal they met without concern for the season or animals' lifeways (ibid.: 10). Newcomers would also come to Orochen camps, disturbing the reindeer with their dogs and by hunting on their ranges. In the late nineteenth and early twentieth centuries Russians and Orochen were in constant conflict over the use of resources and territories. More and more newcomers threatened the local herders' pastures and hunting areas, harvested fur-bearing animals, hunted for game animals without caring whether the reindeer killed were domesticated, and plundered Orochen caches. According to Tugolukov (1962: 19), it was also not unusual for newcomers to use Orochen cabins in the taiga.

After the October Revolution, Zabaikal'ia was a base for White Tsarist troops into the 1920s. The White Army, supported by Cossacks and Japanese military forces, recruited indigenous hunters and requisitioned all their food or other belongings for the army's needs, shooting those who resisted (Belikov 1994: 65). Local guerrilla supporters of the Communist revolution fought against them and likewise requisitioned resources from the local population. This motley array of political movement activists – Bolshevists, Menshevists, Esserovtsy, Anarchists – helped establish an autonomous Far East Republic in 1920 with Chita as its capital (Brennan 1999). Although the Far East Republic proclaimed the indigenous people's rights to autonomy, Orochen clans were denied ownership of land and had no alternative (i.e. not land-based) means to make a living (ibid.: 66).

After a few years, the Far East Republic ceased to exist and became part of the USSR. Titov (1926a: 10–11) noted that issues of ownership became hotly contested in the aftermath of the October Revolution, which propagated new ideas like 'land for all people' (Rus. *zemlia narodu*). Titov (ibid.: 11) described the Orochen 'mastery of land' as linked to local skills attuned to remote places and 'the animals' lifeways' (Rus. *nravy zverei*) as well as 'attention and intelligence' (Rus. *vnimanie i ostroumie*). These skills contrasted with the newcomers' practices, which were based on domination and ideas such as 'the strongest one is master' (Rus. *kto silnee, tot i khoziain*) (ibid.).

Under Soviet Rule

Under early Soviet rule, the Orochen were given some rights of self-government within the framework of the National Districts (*Natsional'nye Okruga*). Orochen clans were reassigned new territories for hunting, herding and pursuing other 'traditional activities'. The Orochen of Chita had a special ethnic status within the Vitim-Olekma Evenki National District (in existence from 1931 to 1938), which embraced the districts of Karenga, Kalakan, Kalar and Tungir-Olekma. It was later reorganized several times, so that the Niukzha River territory included parts of today's territories belonging to Sakha Republic and Amur Province. The Orochen of Baunt retained their native councils (*Tuzemnye Sovety*), and in 1925 these were integrated into the administration of the newly established Baunt Indigenous District (Bauntovskii Tuzemnyi Raion), which was part of the Buryat-Mongol Autonomous Soviet Socialist Republic. Again, the Vitim River served as the boundary between the two administrative units. Groups of hunters and herders that lived near the river were required to rearrange their patterns of land use according to the new district boundaries.

According to the report on Burnarkomzem's expedition to Buryatia (Ekonomicheskii-Geograficheskii ocherk ekspeditsii Burnarkomzema) (1934–1936), the Orochen mostly hunted fur-bearing animals like squirrel or sable and large game like moose and elk in the taiga. Before Soviet rule, each family owned an average of fifteen to twenty reindeer. Some rich Orochen owned up to two hundred reindeer, large herds of horses and even cattle. Members of extended families and kin units jointly herded the domestic stock. Reindeer were mostly used for transporting goods (e.g., camping gear, meat and fur). They were slaughtered only when incurably ill or lame, or as a sacrifice for ritual purposes. People could also ride reindeer. Thus reindeer, being well adapted to moving in the local environment in all seasons, made people highly mobile.

Under Tsarist rule, indigenous people had enjoyed some land use rights to ensure a steady supply of fur to the government. But the Soviet state strove to regulate Orochen land use, subsistence practices and even beliefs in a more organized, more radical way. The Orochen National Districts were abolished at the end of the 1930s. The rapid and brutal collectivization that followed included the confiscation of the indigenous livestock that had been indispensable for hunting, and of tools, turning them all into collective property. Indigenous people were pressured to join collective farms (*kolkhozy*) and cooperatives (*kooperativy*). Soviet planners also aimed to change the Orochen social structure by introducing the clan-based communities to new forms of property and radically different economic practices, turning them into labour-based collectives (*kolektivy*) (for a similar history for the Evenki of Taimyr, see Anderson 2000a: 187–200). As a form of resistance some Orochen slaughtered or let loose all of their reindeer. As they had done in the past, some Orochen moved to remote taiga areas in other regions hoping to maintain their autonomy and way of life. Others migrated with their herds to the northern part of Mongolia or China to escape the reach of the Soviet state. Many families who tried to avoid contact with state authorities and refused to join the new sedentary communities were hunted down by the Stalinist secret police (NKVD).

The politics of sedentarization went along with collectivization. Indeed, as Fondahl (1989: 63) notes, no modern state is enthusiastic about nomads within its boundaries, since the state tends to interpret their autonomy as rebellion. As Vladimir Kozulin, a former chair of the Communist Party in the village of Bagdarin, put it, 'the Orochen people were sedentarized in order to be taught a new, more advanced mode of life'. In the newly established villages there were a few Russian families with white-collar professions in education, administration and trade. Orochen families employed on collective farms were assigned to newly established villages built for indigenous people in the taiga. Orochen women were usually employed on the village's collective farm and trained in agriculture, fur farming, and livestock husbandry. They lived with their children in small wooden houses. Some Orochen women worked together with male reindeer herders and hunters, visiting their family members in the villages only seasonally.[14] Boarding schools for Orochen children were also established. Thus women and children, even in remote villages, often were separated from the nomadic life they had lived and lost their skills and knowledge crucial for subsistence in the taiga.[15] Nowadays, the generations who lost these skills and their traditional relationship with the land find it difficult to use the land for subsistence after its reappropriation from the state (Bloch 2004). Vitebsky (2002: 182) aptly noted that the removal of Evenki reindeer herders from their land also implied a withdrawal from social relations, causing traumatic experiences that still affect the current generation.

The policy of collectivization and sedentarization went hand in hand with the suppression of religious practices. Local ritual specialists, referred to as 'shamans', and other community leaders were arrested, imprisoned and sometimes executed, while any public and overt ritual practices were abolished and persecuted. Across the taiga military troops hunted down shamans, who were jailed, brought to court and often executed. All shamans of the Orochen families of Aruneev, Selezniov, Kopylov, Taskerov and Urpiulov were arrested. Only a few shamans returned to their homeland, their health broken after long prison terms. Many other people, including successful hunters and herders, were also subject to repressions intended to break their resistance.

A well-known story in Tungokochen village tells how some Orochen started guerrilla activities against Soviet oppression.[16] Vasilii Aruniev, with a few others, attacked and killed some state officials after his father, a shaman, was arrested and killed by the secret police. Today Vasilii is known locally as a 'famous bandit' who fought against Soviet oppression. His brother Gilton Aruniev, who later became a secretary of the Communist Party, remembers how as a child he was taken from his shaman-father's camp by the NKVD and left at the village boarding school. Like many children from the taiga camps, he was severely beaten and threatened with death when he attempted to escape to the taiga with some other Orochen children. These children, who often knew no Russian and were not adapted to village life, suffered many humiliations in boarding school. This experience was common among Orochen children born and raised in herders' camps until the end of the Soviet period. Most boys quit school as early as possible, after the seventh grade, and returned to their hunting lifestyle. World War II took the lives of many Orochen hunters and herders because the NKVD impressed young men into the army straight from their herding camps. Young Orochen men had great difficulty adapting to army service. As one man told me, 'a hunter could easily deal with a bear in the taiga, but he had a hard time dealing with the collective or *diedovshchina* [hierarchical] relations in the army.' According to Olga Taskerova, the inability to adjust to army life and the lack of school education were commonly diagnosed as *oligofreniia* (imbecility) by Soviet medical doctors. Many Orochen men thus lost the right to own a rifle – an indispensable tool for subsistence – and thus became even more socially marginalized and vulnerable. Some were even killed in gunfights with the local the militia when the latter tried to confiscate illegal guns.

When Orochen religious practices were suppressed in Soviet times, the idols used in rituals were hidden in caches and worshipped in secret to avoid persecution. Some people left their ritual items at mountain passes, visiting them only when migrating to their hunting grounds. Public ritual practices ceased to be performed in the open. Nonetheless, simple ritual activities for perpetuating hunting and herding luck continued to be practised during the Soviet era (see Arbatskii 1978). At the same time, the Soviet state introduced new official celebrations such as Reindeer Herders' Day (Den' Olenevoda) and the New Year in place of traditional rituals. These festivals, which often lasted several weeks, usually included the consumption of large quantities of alcohol and regularly led to violent altercations. Koester (2003: 43) aptly notes that to express honour and group membership, indigenous people of Siberia had to fulfil their 'obligation to receive in the form of accepting drink'. These drinking practices often led to violence and caused the deaths of many Orochen in the villages and taiga camps.

The indigenous collective farms initially employed many Orochen because they were well versed in fur animal trapping and reindeer herding. These newly established economic units were given the best lands, while those individuals who had not joined them were prohibited from using the land. In the early Soviet period, Orochen observed 'age-old patterns of respect for *obshchina* territories' (Fondahl 1998: 62); therefore, decisions about where to hunt and to herd reindeer remained with the Orochen. Elders still remember how hunters held meetings just as they had in 'the old times', announcing to each other the areas where they would hunt. People could choose their hunting areas from a large territory and easily move on another place in case of failure. At the same time, they respected other Orochen's rights to traplines or hunting areas.

During the first decades of collectivization, people who owned up to twenty private reindeer, the maximum allowed by the state, were allowed to live on land just outside the villages, continuing their migratory way of life when hunting and herding. In later Soviet times, collectivized reindeer herds sometimes numbered up to two thousand head. These herds were under the supervision of collective farm specialists who had been trained at the Institute of Hunting Affairs (Okhotovedcheskii Institut). According to Tugolukov (2004: 343), out of the 537 Orochen living in Tungokochen village in 1958, about 264 worked on collective farms as hunters and herders. Reindeer herding was organized according to the recommendations of committees (Rus. *komisii*) of specialists like geographers, biologists and veterinarians who had little first-hand knowledge of the activities involved. Domestic reindeer were herded by indigenous brigades (Rus. *brigady*) of reindeer herders, more or less equal in terms of status and the distribution of responsibilities, whereas the old way of herding (conducted by families) was replaced by units of mostly male young herders working in shifts. One woman (called a 'tent worker') was attached to each of these units to work as cook, seamstress and laundress (Fondahl 1998: 70). The family unit, which had traditionally cared for reindeer, was destroyed by the collectivization of herding practices. Men worked in the taiga camps for the whole year, while the women stayed in the villages.

High targets set for increasing the size of reindeer herds and raising meat productivity were part of the Soviet planned economy. Elders say that 'no one was master of a reindeer herd, but anyone could be punished for the loss of reindeer'. The economic success of collective reindeer herding was evaluated in terms of the income generated from the sale of meat and skins (Fondahl 1989: 73–74). The provision of transportation for geological expeditions, miners and workers of the Baikal-Amur Magistral (BAM) railroad project was an important source of cash income for state farms and reindeer herders (ibid.). Meanwhile, new villages and *kolkhozy* 'deemed too small to be economically viable' were consolidated soon after their establishment (Fondahl 1998: 66).

By the end of the 1970s, all *kolkhozy* in Zabaikal'ia had been reorganized into state farms (Rus. *sovkhozy*) and state hunting enterprises (Rus. *gospromkhoz*) in order to generate more profit. For instance, the Kirov *kolkhoz* and the 28th Party Congress collective farm in Tungokochen District were consolidated into the new Tungokochenskii reindeer herding state farm in the 1980s. All reindeer were moved from the former collective farm pastures to newly chosen pastures in the river basins of Kotomchik and Siligli. The new herding territory was equipped with base camps, log houses and fenced areas for reindeer. However, some reindeer were lost when the herd was moved to the new pasture. According to Gena Kirilov, some reindeer returned to their previous pastures 'because reindeer are attached to their birth-place'. Most decisions were made by local managers, who followed the recommendations of specialists from the Land Use Committee in Bratsk. Some elders say today that the reorganization and relocation of reindeer herding was very detrimental to both reindeer and herders and damaged the Orochen mastery of the land with policies of seden-tarization and collectivization. The implementation of Soviet policies premised on profit and state control of economic practices caused a constant loss of reindeer during the next few decades, and reindeer herding ceased to be seen as profitable.

Furthermore, the reorganization of farms had divided land into allotments assigned to individual hunters for trapping fur-bearing animals. Indigenous hunters say that this was the death knell of the Orochen's control over their activities and territories, because all the allotments went to nonindigenous hunters. Orochen hunters lost ac-cess to their previous hunting grounds and had to confine themselves to the newly delineated hunting territories. As Gena Kirilov remem-bered, 'formerly, hunters were mainly Orochen; they were masters of wide areas.... After reorganization, many nations started to use the taiga and the taiga lost its masters'. The economic practice of hunting was now separated from reindeer herding and managed by the differ-ent state farms. In this context, a state farm that administered hunt-ing did not pay reindeer herders for the use of their reindeer, which further diminished the role of reindeer and the status of herders. This irrational economic policy was also a cause of decline in the overall number of reindeer.

At the same time, a large number of nonindigenous people turned to hunting and trapping. Hunting was allowed everywhere in the taiga, and hunters using log houses and salt licks could be encoun-tered anywhere. Many state administrators and military and militia of-ficers from nearby bases also turned to hunting. People say today that at this time animals were overhunted by nonindigenous people who had access to state resources like ATVs and even helicopters. Hunting and collective-farm reindeer herding were also under constant threat from mining activities, the BAM railroad and Soviet military bases. It was not unusual to force the subsidized reindeer herds on the collec-tive farms to leave their pastures to make space for industrial state projects. Many reindeer-herding camps and hunting sites suffered from neighbouring Soviet military ranges (Rus. *voennyi poligon*), for-estry and geological expeditions' camps, and meteorological stations. Crashed army rockets or careless exploration expeditions regularly caused large forest fires. Uncontrolled fires usually burned not only trees, but also the soil, leaving behind a rocky countryside that took decades to recover.

The Zhumaneev-Aruneev Reindeer Herders and Hunters

The largest part of my research was conducted in cooperation with Orochen hunters and reindeer herders of the Zhumaneev-Aruneev family in the Tungokochen District of Zabaikal Province (see Fig. 1.3). The first group I lived with was led by the village-based hunter Aleksei Aruneev. A leader of many joint hunting groups, Aleksei spent most of his time hunting on horseback in the taiga around Tungokochen village. The second group was led by Aleksei's brothers Nikolai and Yura Aruneev, owners of a large reindeer herd who wandered and hunted in the remote region of the Kotomchik and Bugarikhta River basins (Tungokochen District). I spent a few weeks in Buryatia visiting reindeer herders led by Vitia and Olga Mordonov and Oleg Prokop'ev-ich Dandeev, a relative of the Zhumaneev-Aruneev family. They were employed as reindeer herders for the Dylacha clan community in the Baunt District. These families helped me understand the varieties of Orochen adaptations to the post-Soviet environment. Despite differences between their lifeways and levels of integration into village life, these three families maintained relations with each other, not only exchanging reindeer and knowledge, but also sharing a common anxiety over luck. Below I want to introduce each of three families I lived with in more detail.

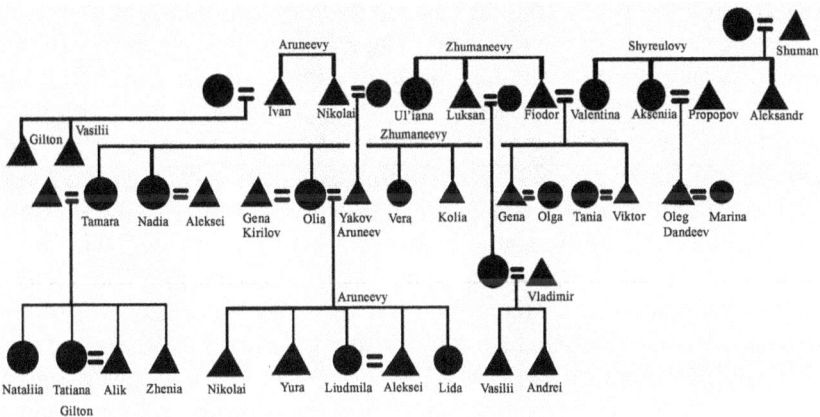

Figure 1.3. | *Kinship chart showing the main families*

Village Hunter Aleksei Aruneev

The main hunter with whom I lived is Aleksei Aruneev (b. 1967). I met him in Tungokochen village when I was searching for somebody to guide me to the Zhumaneev-Aruneev family reindeer herders' camps. I was first introduced to Aleksei when others pointed him out as a 'lucky hunter' and the only one knowledgeable enough to take me to the remote herding camps on horseback. When I first approached him to ask him to become my guide, he invited me to eat bear cub meat after his return from a successful hunting trip but said nothing about whether or not he would help me. Aleksei kept observing me while I visited his house daily. After more than a week, he finally invited me to join him on a trip to the Muishin and Taloi River basins for autumn rut hunting and suggested I should wait for a better time to travel to the reindeer herders' camp. Our hunting trip was successful; we managed to bring home several roe deer. After spending a week in the village I was invited to join him on a second hunting trip to the Muishin River basin. This trip also included a visit to the rock art site of Dukuvuchi, an important ritual site for many Orochen of the region (see Chapter 8). Aleksei recalled how his grandfather had taken the ethnographer Aleksei Arbatskii to the Dukuvuchi rock art site about twenty years ago. This hunting expedition was another success: we enjoyed excellent weather, the horses did not lose much weight and we managed to bring back a moose and many squirrels. This fact indicated that we were well received by the master-spirit and that I did not bring bad luck to the group. Soon Aleksei proposed that I move to his house for a longer period.

Aleksei comes from a large and prosperous family of Orochen hunters and reindeer herders that used to live on both banks of the Vitim River. After the early death of his father, Iakov Aruneev, in the 1970s, Aleksei was raised in reindeer herding camps and travelled with his grandfather, Fiodor Petrovich' Zhumaneev (b. 1906), a famous hunter and collective farm leader. Fiodor was often called 'the last nomad' (Rus. *poslednii kochevnik*) of the Tungokochen District. He lived a nomadic life and hunted in the area with his herd of thirty reindeer until his death in 1992 at the age of eighty-five. Throughout his life his family's main mobile dwelling was a canvas tent, although he also had a house in Tungokochen village. As a schoolboy Aleksei spent every summer, as well as substantial parts of the other seasons, in remote camps, learning hunting and herding skills from his grandparents, mother, older brothers and uncles. He started learning how to hunt as soon as he 'learned to walk' and killed his first moose at the age of eleven.

Hunting has remained his main occupation, so he spends considerable periods of time in the taiga. As an adult, he has also been employed in a collective reindeer brigade, working together with his mother Olga Zhumaneeva (b. 1937), his stepfather Gena Kirilov and his brothers Nikolai and Yura. When the herders had the opportunity to privatize the brigade's herd soon after the collapse of the Soviet Union in 1992, Aleksei received his share of reindeer and continued his herding way of life, working for the Boiun clan community. The community included several reindeer herders and was led by his elder brother Nikolai. In 1999 Aleksei decided to change his life. He gave up drinking after visiting a shaman in the former Aga Autonomous District of Zabaikal Province and married Liuba Aniutina, a primary school teacher of Russian-Tungus origin. He sold his share of the privately owned reindeer herd and bought a house in Tungokochen village.

When visiting Tungokochen village, I always stayed with his family, which consisted of his wife Liuba, his two preschool-age daughters Kristina and Yulia, and Liuba's two teenage children from her first marriage. The family lived in a small log house about the size of a hunting cabin (about 15 m²), located in the centre of the village. Aleksei's wife maintained a garden of potatoes near the house, and four cows were kept for milk and meat. As an employee in the Military Forest Department (Voennyi Leskhoz), Aleksei spent most of his time in the taiga as a lookout for forest fires and also hunted reindeer and fur-bearing animals. Therefore, he typically prepared for another hunting trip soon after returning to the village. He was not very interested in village pastimes like watching TV or listening to the radio; rather, he always followed the 'call of the taiga'.

Aleksei hunted large game in spring, summer and autumn, moving through an area with a radius of 100 km from Tungokochen village every two to three weeks and camping in taiga shelters. He seemed to prefer travelling with other former reindeer herders with whom he had established long-term cooperation in joint herding experiences as members of the same brigade. For hunting trips, Aleksei chose his grandfathers' migration places in the basins of the Muishin and Taloi Rivers, where he had spent his childhood. He had built some shelters there and also experienced the support of local master-spirits. Aleksei also visited places that belonged to relatives and friends and hunted in cooperation with them in the winter. Nevertheless, he never stated that he preferred one place over another. His decision on where to go was determined by certain omens that appeared either in the environment or in a dream, and by his knowledge of animal tracks that he had found in certain places in the past. Therefore, I could never predict where we might move next for hunting or how and what we would hunt next. He spent the long winters in his brother's herding territory in the Siligli River basin, trapping and tracking fur-bearing animals together with other hunters and exchanging groceries, meat and ammunition with his reindeer-herding relatives (see Map 4.1).

Aleksei was known for his competence in hunting (Table 1.5), and other hunters were constantly inviting him to join them on hunting trips in order to 'bring his luck' to the hunting group. He spent some winters in a fur-hunting area in the Siligli River basin mainly tracking, trapping and camping throughout the basin, even reaching the basins of the Kotomchik and Nercha rivers. Most of the mobile Orochen had ceased to herd reindeer, so Aleksei owned a few horses and several dogs used mainly for his own hunting needs. His main activity was hunting fur-bearing animals in the winter, which brought cash income to his family while the meat fed his relatives, colleagues from the Forestry Department and neighbours. When staying in the village, he walked around every morning to visit neighbours and share news. Aleksei acquired his awareness of village activities by listening to the sounds of ATVs, observing moving cars and people through the window or in his backyard and thus finding out about various opportunities involving movement and subsistence practices. He did so in

Figure 1.4. | *Aleksei Aruneev skinning a moose.*

much the same way that someone would gain knowledge about subsistence opportunities in the taiga by being aware of the movements of domestic animals or changes in the weather and adjusting one's activities accordingly.

Aleksei was short and wiry, and despite having chain-smoked strong cigarettes since he was a teenager, he performed what to me were amazing physical feats, carrying heavy logs for firewood or walking long distances. In the village such acts were probably what had earned him the nickname Pikha, derived from the Russian word *pekhota*, literally, 'infantryman'. Almost everyone was known by one or several nicknames, while their Christian names and surnames often remained unknown outside of their family. Local nicknames reflected upon a person's 'place' in the community, often referring to personal characteristics.[17] After I had participated in several hunting trips and people had come to know me, they also gave me the Orochen nickname, always spoken with laughter, of 'Mangi', a cosmological being that can be described as a giant, cannibal or monster.

Aleksei had little interest in such issues as 'Evenkiness', and though he was fluent in the Evenki language, he did not use it in the village.[18] Therefore he was sometimes called a 'Russified Evenki'. Nevertheless, he knew how to sustain hunting luck and took dreams and rituals seriously, having observed the latter while migrating with his large family of herders and hunters during his childhood. Aleksei, like most village people, was concerned about any incident that might bring either misfortune or luck. He was keen to show me various ritual sites and make me experience signs of luck myself, rather than giving detailed verbal explanations of how success can be achieved. His stories about hunting were typically told in certain environments far from the places where the incident had occurred in order to avoid attracting misfortune.

While staying with Aleksei, I was introduced to many hunters with whom he cooperated in different seasons. My successful cooperation with Aleksei was the key to entering into close relationships with many of his relatives from other villages. I had the closest relationships with his aunt (who was in her sixties), a seamstress named Tamara Naikanchina, her hunter son Zhenia (b. 1983) and another aunt and storyteller named Nadia Zhumaneeva. Both aunts were familiar with the life of hunters and herders and had spent substantial time living in herders' camps. Like many other village-based Orochen, they were willing to comment on stories that I brought with me from remote taiga camps. I also had constant interactions with Aleksei's cousins Andrei Malkov and Liuba Urpiulova and their families, the elderly hunter and herder Gena Kirilov, and the elderly uncle Gilton Aruniev, all of whom lived in Tungokochen village.

Like many village families, Aleksei's family owns horses, which enable them travel without relying much on others or having to pay for gasoline or vehicle repairs. Formerly, the Orochen in Tungokochen District used horses for riding and carrying goods when travelling to remote trading posts or searching for scattered reindeer in the taiga. Today, villagers ride horses to the sites of hunting and hay cutting from spring to autumn and let them graze freely during the winter. Aleksei uses his horses mainly for travelling to various hunting sites during the snowless part of the year and transporting the hunted game back to village. A few hunters ride on horseback when trapping fur-bearing animals even in the wintertime. Local horses are interbred with the Yakut breed. They are short, sturdy animals that survive by living in herds and migrating to particular valleys on their own during the long winter. Horse herding is based on the same skills and knowledge as reindeer herding and hunting. A horse owner must be able to track his animals up to 30 km from the village and catch them so he can use them for hunting.

Since most hunting sites are located in the upper reaches of mountain valleys, they hold only a few fields with juicy grass for the horses to graze on. When planning a trip to the uplands by horse, one must first find oats, which are always in short supply in the villages. Feeding horses oats keeps them strong and healthy when carrying loads on the long taiga journey. Without oats as a staple, a horse can get very thin in a few weeks of travel and may even die. Horse riding in the taiga is risky and exhausting for both human and animal. It requires much skill and knowledge of the animal as well as of the locality. A horse gets exhausted quickly walking on the muddy, swampy ground caused by melting ice in spring and autumn. After frosty nights, the horses can slip and injure themselves on the thin ice that covers the ground even in early autumn. Therefore, horses are ridden mainly on paths and to locations that are suitable for grazing. Riding is always combined with walking. When the hunter is on foot, the horses either follow or are left in the taiga camp. Nevertheless, horses remain very important to hunting for most of the villagers, who also use them to carry supplies to their winter hunting log cabins in early autumn. During that time they hunt mainly on foot in the area around the cabins while trapping in the nearby lowlands.

The second family I lived with in the taiga, known as the Boiun clan community, was headed by Aleksei's brothers Nikolai (b. 1959) and Yura (b. 1960) Aruneev, and Aleksei's mother Olga Zhumaneeva

(b. 1935). Nikolai, Yura and Olga, together with several visiting relatives and friends, roamed the taiga hunting fur-bearers and game with their herd of five hundred reindeer and rarely visited villages. The area the reindeer herders used for grazing was located about 200 km from Tungokochen village. Because of the rough terrain, the lack of radio connection and the unpredictable movements between camps, it was hard to reach the herders from the villages. They lived in canvas tents equipped with an iron stove and moved every two to four months between seasonal camps in the Karenga River basin near the Kotomchik, Bugarikhta, Poperechnaia and Bazarnaia Rivers.

The Boiun clan community and their herding and hunting territories were officially recognized by the government. Established by twelve reindeer herders in 1992, the clan community consisted of the Zhumaneev-Aruneev kin group and friends. It underwent several reorganizations when the government reduced the herding territory in several steps from 420,000 to 100,000 ha, whereupon some reindeer herders left the community because it made no monetary profit. At the time of my fieldwork, the community no longer formally existed: it had not been re-registered and had no formal ownership rights to its territory owing to multiple disputes between herders and local officials. The reindeer herders' actual herding and hunting territory also included the territories of other hunters from Ust' Karenga and Zelenoe Ozero villages. The Boiun clan gave some areas that had been damaged by forest fires to relatives to be used for fur hunting in winter.

Their hunting and herding grounds are in the coniferous taiga, where trees cover the hills and ridges from a minimum altitude of 800 m to as much as 2,000 m. The highest rocky peaks of these hills often form mountain chains reaching above the treeline; they are covered with reindeer-attracting lichen (mainly Lat. *cladonia*) and scattered bush-like Siberian dwarf pine (Lat. *pinus pumila*). Meanwhile the middle and lower parts of such hills are mostly covered with coniferous forest. The taiga of open larch (Lat. *larix gmelini* and *larix dahurica*), pine (Lat. *pinus silvestris*) and birch (Lat. *betula pendulus*) forest gives way to wet, open lowland fields of 'hummocks', some of which are covered with willow (Lat. *salix*) bushes, rhododendron and islands of coniferous trees. These areas serve as spring and summer reindeer pasture. Reindeer herders have also cultivated the landscape through burning, creating the open marshy fields that Orochen call *kever* (Rus. *kochki*), which are suitable for reindeer grazing (Fig. 1.5). A *kever* is burned in the springtime to stimulate the growth of fresh grass (see Brandisauskas 2007). Fresh grass (Oro. *irgekta*) growing on

Figure 1.5. | *Burned hummocks in a field (Oro.* kever).

semi-spherical hummocks is an important spring supplement to the reindeers' diet. Maintaining open fields is also important for observing reindeer movements. Nikolai always burned the *kever* meadows in the vicinity of his camp but not those farther away, saying that those fields should be left for berries. The burning of fields can also create a landscape that is attractive to reindeer, encouraging a large reindeer herd to stay in a relatively small area. Controlled burning of bushes or dense taiga around hunting cabins also creates places where one can more efficiently hunt game animals. Controlled burning has become an important practice, clearing brush and last year's dry grass, and stimulating fresh grass growth after the long winter. Fields with fresh grass are said to attract animals to the area and thus enhance opportunities to gain luck in hunting. Villagers, herders and hunters also burn patches of land to protect their hunting territories and living places from forest fires. Burning all the dry wood in early spring is believed to help prevent large forest fires during the summer dry period.

The herders used more than ten camps scattered across a few river basins, so one could hardly predict where the Zhumaneev-Aruneev group would be found. The summer camps were established near the lower reaches of rivers or at confluences of large rivers. Winter camps were located near treeless hills. There were also special autumn and spring camps equipped with corrals to hold mating and calving reindeer. The herding and hunting area was well equipped with storage platforms and man-made salt licks that were constantly maintained by the herders, as were smudge fires to protect reindeer from mosquitoes during the warm period of the year.

In spring the family looked after calving reindeer to protect them from predators, often rounding up the herd and keeping females and calves in specially built corrals. As summer turns to autumn, reindeer start to migrate to the higher locations of the river basin, and the herders' camp is usually moved close to the smaller rivers in the foothills. They must work hard to cut reindeer antlers before the mating season to keep reindeer from hurting each other. At this time castrated animals are closely examined and given medicine to facilitate healing. During the mating season, cows and calves are often enclosed at night and let out for the day, and the herd is carefully inspected so that 'wild bulls don't steal females'. As soon as the rivers freeze hard, camps are moved to the bottoms of treeless hills near small tributaries. Reindeer graze on lichen above the treeline and roam freely in the uplands throughout the cold period. Salt is given to reindeer to lick in all seasons but mostly during the winter, to encourage them to visit the camps. Reindeer herds can be left with a minimum of supervision during the fur animal hunting season.

The Zhumaneev-Aruneev family did not use reindeer for commercial transportation and had no regular trade relations with village people. The family's main cash income came from the sale of squirrel and sable pelts. Special parts of animals, such as dried antlers, tails or penises, were sold to traders in Chita for export to China. All the money was spent to acquire and transport camping and hunting gear, ammunition and supplies to the remote herding and hunting grounds. Despite owning large herds, the reindeer herders of Tungokochen did not rent their reindeer to other hunters or entrepreneurs. Large reindeer herds were also kept to maintain the large territories allotted for herding and hunting, and to live independently of the cash economy (see Fig. 1.6).

Mobility in the taiga relied on the use of reindeer for transportation. Reindeer are most needful of their herders' attention in the late spring calving period and early autumn mating season, but they can graze without much care during the winter. In summer, reindeer stayed close to camp to take advantage of the smudge fires that protected them from insects – they are fairly vulnerable to mosquitoes. In fact, herders in summer camps constantly maintained smudge fires to lure reindeer to the camp. When herders use reindeer for transportation, they take a midday break to build a smudge fire to pro-

Figure 1.6. | *The reindeer herd owned by the Zhumaneev-Aruneev family*

tect themselves and reindeer from mosquitoes and allow the reindeer to rest at the peak of the day's heat. Elders may ride reindeer when hunting fur-bearing animals. People said that squirrels or sables formerly could be shot without dismounting from the reindeer. Others mostly walked with animals transporting meat, supplies or camping equipment in the summer. Herders even used the term 'riding' (Rus. *ekhat'*) in everyday conversation to man walking with a leashed reindeer. Hunters who used reindeer for subsistence were known as the most productive hunters from early Soviet times and remain so today. In Ust' Karenga and Baunt villages, even entrepreneurs supported reindeer herding, as hunters mostly hunt in barely accessible river basins. The Orochen hunters who used reindeer were known as the most successful hunters, bringing much-valued fur to the *komersanty*. Although reindeer were more and more being used as a tourist attraction by the reindeer herders of Baunt District and Severobaikalsk in Buryatia, these domestic animals remain an unbeatable means of transportation when hunting or travelling in remote areas.

The Arumeev-Zhumaneev family regularly hunted wild animals for food and fur-bearing animals for cash. They used about forty well-trained reindeer, mainly castrated males, as cargo animals to carry canvas tents, kettles, an iron stove, personal bedding and supplies when moving from one camp to another. The family used any available reindeer for a trip but preferred well-fed animals, and each animal carried only a minimal load, in order to preserve its health. The large size of the herd provided opportunities to select and train young reindeer as pack animals. Game could be hunted anyplace, because animal carcasses could be transported from remote and rough taiga areas in any season. Reindeer are well adapted to moving through snowy, rocky or swampy areas. As one hunter told me, 'a reindeer walks wherever its snout points' (Rus. *vezde idet kuda mordoi stoit*). The family hunted fur-bearing animals in areas of the Nercha River basin whose use had been negotiated with other hunters and entrepreneurs. They usually used reindeer when travelling to a hunting area to transport all the camping gear, iron traps and supplies. The reindeer allowed hunters to change their hunting camps often, moving into the highlands of any river basin.

Reindeer can transport all camping equipment, as well as the carcasses of hunted game animals and furs, without slipping on icy surfaces as horses would. Supplies like frozen and canned vegetables, rice and macaroni are carried between caches by reindeer the year round. Meat and personal belongings are also transported from one storage platform to the next when the camp is moved. Reindeer are considered very docile animals; when leashed, they follow the hunter anywhere he or she walks. I was surprised to see a reindeer walk, breaking dry wood and branches, through a dense forest of trees and bushes while transporting a moose carcass. In addition, a reindeer can graze in any lowland or upland place where it is left by the hunter. Thus reindeer allow hunters to establish camps anywhere they wish to trap or hunt. Using elaborate ways of packing and special bags, herders can transport anything on the narrow paths in the taiga. With reindeer, hunters can stay many weeks in any given area without returning to their caches. It took a few hours to unpack the goods loaded on a reindeer, set up camp and erect a canvas tent. In winter the hunters moved to their remote fur-hunting places with all their camping gear and supplies loaded on reindeer, setting up a new hunting camp every four to seven days while covering large areas when trapping or tracking animals. A hunter used five to seven reindeer, each animal carrying a 30–40 kg load. Immediately upon arriving in the hunting camp, the hunter put bells on the reindeer (Oro. *botolo*) and constrained its movements with a piece of wood called *moonmokan* (Rus. *potaskushka*). This animal could find food even in the rough uplands and eat snow for its water supply without needing running water. The hunter could find his or her reindeer again by following the tracks of its *moonmokan* in the taiga, and transport his gear and supplies to another hunting area. Most indigenous hunters believe that reindeer have many advantages over horses in the taiga (Table 1.4).

Although reindeer were killed for meat in Soviet times, Boiun reindeer herders believed that killing a reindeer just for food or money would bring misfortune upon the herd. A reindeer was only killed as a sacrifice to the master-spirits in rare cases such as a herder's illness, ritual requirements or public festivals and feasts. Families exchanged reindeer with other herders of the Dylacha community in Baunt District to 'freshen the blood of their herd'. Interbreeding between domestic and wild reindeer was also tolerated as 'freshening the blood' (see Fondahl 1989: 94). Introducing a wild reindeer bloodline into the herd lessens herders' dependence on trading relations with other groups of herders. Nikolai sold reindeer in 2005 to his relatives and friends in order to re-establish a new herding community in Baunt District, and again in 2007 to Yakutian reindeer herders. Nikolai's grandfather Fiodor Zhumaneev used to say to his relatives that 'without reindeer, the Orochen lose their luck and strength'. His son, Yura, states that reindeer give joy to his life and 'it is life itself' for him because it gives 'energy and health'.

Table 1.4. | *The use of reindeer vis-à-vis horses as transport in hunting.*

Horse (Oro. *murin*)	Reindeer (Oro. *oron*)
Horse riding in the taiga requires much investment. Hay must be prepared in the summer for autumn and spring, and extra oats must be bought to feed the horse during autumn hunting.	Reindeer are easy to maintain in winter, since they drink by eating snow and can graze in any area of the uplands. They do not require imported forage.
Horses are less obedient; they will not follow on a leash in the taiga.	Reindeer can follow anywhere where humans go in the taiga.
Horses stumble frequently when walking through fields of hummocks (Oro. *kever*). Because they are very clumsy walkers in swamps and mud, some hunters believe that certain areas can injure or even kill an animal.	Reindeer have stable footing when walking through fields of hummocks or snow and therefore can walk fast carrying a load. They walk well in swampy areas because their hooves have a large surface area that gives them greater stability on muddy or slippery surfaces.
Horses are limited primarily to permanent routes and level surfaces.	Reindeer can travel on any surface, climbing and going down steep mountain slopes.

Table 1.5. | *Variety and seasonality of animals killed by two Aruneev family groups based in different settings.*

2004–2005	Meat supplied by two hunters (Aleksei Aruneev and Gena Dushinov) and shared in the village.[19]	Meat supplied by two taiga-based hunters (Nikolai and Yura Aruneev)[20]
Sept.	1 bear, 2 elk, 1 moose	1 wild reindeer, 4 moose, 1 bear, 2 slaughtered domesticated reindeer
Oct.	3 moose, 1 squirrel, 1 boar,[21] 1 rabbit	2 wild reindeer, 1 moose
Nov.	1 boar, 1 roe deer, 4 rabbits, 25 squirrels	4 wild reindeer, 53 squirrels, 3 rabbits, 1 partridge, 1 domesticated reindeer[22]
Dec.	1 slaughtered cattle calf, 12 squirrels, 8 rabbits	1 moose, 23 squirrels, 3 rabbits, 1 capercaillie, 1 partridge
Jan.	12 rabbits, 6 squirrels	1 lynx, 4 rabbits, 28 squirrels, 2 partridges
Feb.	3 capercaillies, 3 squirrels, 5 rabbits	1 roe deer, 12 squirrels, 3 rabbits, 1 moose, 2 partridges
Mar.		
Apr.		3 capercaillies
May	1 roe deer	1 moose, 2 capercaillies
June	1 moose, 1 roe deer	3 roe deer
July	1 bear, 3 boars, 3 roe deer	1 elk
Aug.	1 moose	1 moose, 1 elk

Reindeer Herder Nikolai Aruneev

Nikolai Aruneev (see Fig. 1.7) was the most prominent reindeer herder of this group. He graduated from the Fur College in Irkutsk and studied at the Irkutsk Ranger Institute for four years. His last year of studies coincided with the collapse of the Soviet Union, so he left school to establish the Boiun (Moose) clan community. He privatized the herd in cooperation with other reindeer herders of the collective farm. The clan community was established as a herding and hunting enterprise on the lands of the privatized Tungokochenskii state farm, with grazing areas located in the Kotomchik and Siligli river basins. Villagers often referred to Nikolai as the district's 'saviour [Rus. *spasatel*'] of

Figure 1.7. | *Nikolai Aruneev transporting a moose carcass and his camping gear by reindeer.*

reindeer'. Indeed, the clan community led by Nikolai survived several crises caused when some reindeer herders left the community, taking their herds with them. Nevertheless, Nikolai managed to double and even triple the size of the herd owned by his family using a clever strategy of constant control of the reindeer's movements and adjustment to the reindeer's needs, maintaining a safe living environment, trading domestic reindeer and breeding them with wild reindeer.

In addition, Nikolai was able to procure fur-trading and grocery supplies in the cities and villages at the best prices. Not only was he familiar with such details as the shades of fur colour, but he also knew how to handle local officials, traders and his extensive networks of acquaintances. Villagers often referred to him as '*khitryi*' (cunning) because he had managed to conceal some of his plans and activities from other people, including his kin. The Zhumaneev-Aruneev family were very hard-working herders who became the biggest reindeer owners in Zabaikal Province. Nikolai, like some of his relatives, was also widely known as a skilful and knowledgeable hunter who in Soviet times had been awarded many medals and diplomas of honour for his hunting achievements for the state farm.

After the Soviet Union's collapse, Nikolai became also acknowledged as an articulate political speaker for the local Orochen communities. At one stage of his life, he combined his activities in the taiga with being the chair of the Evenki Association of Tungokochen District and also a ritual leader. Indeed, at the beginning of the 1990s he became very interested in elders' knowledge about the use of land, old rituals and beliefs, and local reindeer herding history. He published several articles in local newspapers laying out Orochen clans' rights to various taiga territories. Many of his roles in the community were also combined with his 'shamanic' practice. It is not exceptional for a descendent of shamans to feel a need to continue some of their fathers' or grandfathers' legacies. Nikolai's grand-uncle Ivan Aruneev was a well-known *nimnanivki* (shaman) in the Amalat region (Buryatia), while his grandmother Valentina's father Shuman was one of the most powerful shamans among the Nerchinsk Evenki (see Sem 2002). He furthermore called his grandfather Fiodor's uncle Seleznev shaman. Nikolai honoured spirits that had been neglected and ancestors at rock art and shamanic burial sites, feeling that misfortune would befall him if he failed to do so. Many shamans' descendants hold similar ideas in Siberia today (see Vitebsky 2002: 191–193).

Nikolai led public rituals, which he himself had often re-created, at Orochen festivals like Aboriginal Day (*Den' Aborigena*).[23] He sought knowledge and inspiration from elders, shamans from the Aga region and even early ethnographies. He was one of several people who enthusiastically re-established or created new ritual sites near the main travel routes and mountain passages (Oro. *dovan*) leading to the taiga. Nikolai was among those who strove to calm the *arenkil* spirits and establish relations with the master-spirits. He hoped to make them work to his benefit by helping him to develop his shamanic abilities. He was inspired by his own and other people's extraordinary experiences at certain places, and by contact with local elders and shamans from Buryatia, Yakutia and the Aga Autonomous District. The tangible ritual sites Nikolai established throughout the landscape also served to signal his cooperation with the master-spirits to others, helping to protect his hunting and herding areas from 'plunderers'.

Nikolai's extraordinary knowledge was often expressed in the constant flow of jokes and 'half-truths' he told to people in the taiga and villages. Indeed, joking and laughing was common among many Orochen in the village. Nikolai was likely to connect any hunter's failure to the manifestation of spirits (Rus. *dukhi*), hinting about the hunter's 'sin' (Oro. *ngelome*) as the cause of misfortune. In his stories and sayings, Nikolai often switched from laughter to a straight face, telling the others, 'Why are you laughing? How can you doubt? Ask others!' (Rus. *kak tak ne mozhet byt', ty chto dumal, sprosi u drugikh)'*. This way of speaking, combined with his achievements in hunting and his knowledge of the taiga, often put him in a difficult position with the non-native villagers, who treated him with a certain reserve. Nikolai's stories always evoked the villagers' superstitions in some way, since many of them had been touched in a similar way by the accidental death of a relative, complete failure in their subsistence activities or terrifying hallucinations. Similar to the Darxads of Mongolia, talking based on jokes and half-truths was a way for Nikolai to assert his knowledge of 'shamanic nature'. Pedersen (2002: 135) called this way of communicating the manifestation of 'an incomplete shaman' who was stuck in the process of becoming a full-fledged ritual specialist. Humour and 'lies' is one way that this 'amorphous nature' manifests itself in the practices of such individuals (ibid.).

Nikolai's humour was a 'safe way' of delivering messages about spirits, asserting his power and securing his territorial claims and well-being by trying to influence others. Indeed, stories and jokes are a powerful tool in a context where most people, their status and education notwithstanding, are equally concerned about escaping misfortune and maintaining luck when they attend visiting shamans from Aga or Buryatia. Sometimes Nikolai stated directly that one activity or another would bring death to anyone who violated taiga laws and failed to show respect to the master-spirits. This made people believe he could bring misfortune to others by uttering such words. This kind of discourse was also called shamanizing by villagers, since speaking about spirits meant attracting their attention. Bad thoughts can be dangerous, so a hunter may make a grass doll, infuse it with his bad thoughts and then destroy it, thus to 'punish the bad thoughts' (see also Varlamova 2004: 70). Elders say that spoken words can cause much damage since words can kill and be killed. Varlamova (2004: 59–63) states that among the Amur Orochen words have *musun* – a power that may have its own life – and therefore words can 'run' (Rus. *ubegat'*), 'fight' (Rus. *borotsa*) and 'stumble' (Rus. *spotknutsa*).

Stories and warnings carried by jokes have always been part of the pedagogy of the hunters and herders that was taught to me. They preferred jokes to elaborated verbal guidance on how to do something correctly. Humour is an important way to teach about wrong behaviour among many Northern hunting societies (on the Taimyr Evenki, see Anderson 2000a: 120–121; on the Kluane of Canada, Nadasdy 2003: 100). Nikolai maintained the same playful manner throughout my stay with him in camps and villages, giving elaborate answers to my questions about the life of animals and landscape features or trying to help me to memorize certain Orochen words. Although he enjoyed sharing stories with me and with all other villagers, he was very selective about what to say about nonhuman beings and when to say it. He was aware that words can bring misfortune when future plans mentioned aloud are heard by sentient human and nonhuman beings. Nikolai concealed his hunting and herding plans from other villagers and even other herders, often giving misleading answers to their questions, as he aimed to avoid negative magic influence on his success. Such overt and covert ways of talking, together with the performance of rituals and the establishment of tangible ritual sites, recall Anisimov's (1936: 111–112) description of mastery as shamans' building of a symbolic fence to protect the clan's well-being against outside influence.

Nikolai's Family: Yura and Olga

Nikolai's brother Yura and his mother Olga were committed, hard-working reindeer herders and hunters who mostly shared Nikolai's awareness regarding nonhumans. Yura was known as a skilful and knowledgeable herder who could manage the reindeer herd alone whenever Nikolai was in the city. He constantly walked the landscape rounding up reindeer and studying the movements of predators. During the critical periods of reindeer calving in spring and the mating season in autumn, Yura lived separately from other herders in remote camps, taking care of groups of reindeer that strayed from their grazing territory. In spring, he chased groups of reindeer for several days in order to return them to the herd. Like many other elder Orochen females, Olga Zumaneeva was acknowledged as a good hunter and herder, hunting squirrel and sable as well as large game during the winter (see Fig. 1.8). Hunting was typically performed by both sexes among the Orochen. Olga had spent all her life working at the *kolkhoz* reindeer farm and was an excellent hunter like her mother and grandmother. She taught her hunting skills to her sons and nephews as well as a niece. It is not uncommon for young Orochen boys to learn to hunt birds and snare rabbits from their grandmothers or mothers and only later join the adult male hunters. I spent most of the time sharing a tent with Olga Zhumaneeva and was surprised by her passion for long walks as well as her hunting success. In addition, Olga Zhumaneeva, like most Orochen women of her age, was a master seamstress of footwear (Oro. *emchure*) and skin carpets (Oro. *kumalany*) and provided the men with handmade hunting gear. All reindeer herders preferred to cut wood by hand rather than chainsaw, relying on the skills of elders when building their conical tent *chum* and sledges. These

Figure 1.8. | *Olga Zhumaneeva with hunted squirrels.*

skills in the 'old ways' of doing things by using locally available materials were probably based on the need to perform all kinds of tasks in the taiga, in autonomy from village supplies, rather than on an interest in reviving a 'traditional lifestyle'. In the taiga, the majority of my companions were male hunters, since the females involved in hunting and reindeer herding were elderly and few. Most of my interactions with Orochen women happened in the villages.[24]

Any hunter and herder, regardless of gender, was also well skilled in such traditional crafts as skin tanning, the making of fur clothes and footwear, the use of birchbark and the building of various kinds of shelters. Barbara Bodenhorn (1990) deconstructs several stereotypes linked to gender roles in hunting that are widespread in anthropology of hunters and gatherers. She shows that in Inuit society, hunting cannot not be considered a purely male activity (ibid.) and also stresses the interdependence between females and males in both the practice and the symbolism of hunting. Similarly, Varlamova (2002: 36–138) underlines females' role in the hunting rituals of the Amur Orochen. She points out that Orochen women often leave gifts to a master-spirit in mountain passages to safeguard the lives of their husbands or families and to have 'a good trip' (Rus. *dobryi put'*) (ibid.). Men, by contrast, ask for hunting luck in a much briefer manner (ibid.).

Learning Skills

While staying in the taiga camps and villages, I learned crafts and skills from members of both sexes and various age groups: processing skin and sinews, producing various kinds of leather footwear and making birchbark bowls (see more in Brandisauskas 2011). Many of the skills I learned were not just a way of getting to know people but also a matter of personal necessity, since having proper footwear and shelter, and knowing how to make fire and properly boil water are crucial for survival in the taiga. At the same time, participation in such crafts often was the only way to get to know elder women and men who were knowledgeable about many aspects of Orochen daily life. My own apprenticeship stories often stirred the memories of my new companions and served as conduits to valuable information about their experiences. Female elders also enjoyed seeing my involvement in their own activities, sometimes joking and laughing, other times praising me by saying 'your woman will not recognize you since you have become a full-fledged Orochen' (Rus. *tvoia baba neuznaet tebia, sovsem Orochenom stal*). My involvement in these practices also served to boost trust in me among many Orochen hunters and herders.

My daily life in the taiga consisted mostly of taking part in hunting and herding while continually moving around via all sorts of transportation, as mentioned above. This included walking fifteen to thirty kilometres daily in search of animal tracks and gaining knowledge about animals, or engaging in less regular seasonal activities such as collecting berries, burning patches of grass, poisoning wolves or salting special hunting sites. The people I lived among always shared their living space with me. In the snow-free period we usually slept in various kinds of easily dismantled shelters made from wooden poles covered with canvas. Only sometimes did we stay in permanent shelters made of wooden frames and larch bark panels. In winter we mostly used a canvas tent of four square metres and carried a handmade wood burner along. In some cases we stayed in larger wooden cabins fitted with the same kind of stoves.

Experiencing my own luck and misfortune, I shared in the responsibility for different outcomes of our joint activities. In camp I did such daily chores as collecting firewood and ice, fetching and boiling water for tea and cooking food for the dogs. I was doing what is known as the 'work of teenagers' (see Shirokogoroff 1929: 286). I was implicitly shown the best ways to get accustomed to life in the taiga on my own, learning how to build a shelter or how to select and prepare different kinds of firewood. In most cases, the learning process was stimulated by extremely cold conditions. I typically learned to perform certain tasks the 'right way' by emulating my Evenki hunting partners, sometimes asking them questions. The hunters and herders expected me to learn through my own activities and experiences of luck rather than from verbal instruction (see also Shirokogoroff 1929: 288). Most hunters and herders say that nobody ever taught them how to do things the 'right way', since 'everyone was busy working'. The hunter Yura Epov described his learning process as a practice where skills and knowledge were generated through bodily enactment: 'I used my eyes to observe, my head to make decisions and my hands and legs to do things myself'. Hence, the term 'teaching' (Rus. *uchit'*) was never used regarding hunting skills; instead it was replaced by the word 'drag' (Rus. *taskat'*), referring to one's enactment of knowledge in practice, as in 'my uncle used to drag me all over the taiga'.

My hunting and herding activities in the taiga were conducted in silence throughout the day. People were either too busy hunting and herding or too exhausted to speak. Hunters do not value filling silence with talk during the day and often signalled what they expected me to do with simple hand gestures. Despite my friendship with Aleksei Aruneev, he often answered my questions about obvious issues with the short Russian phrase '*a ia khui znaet*' (fuck if I know). Reindeer herders would typically talk more willingly with each other at the end of the day, telling about their experiences, various animals' ways of life, weather predictions, the landscape and signs. At that time they were also slightly more responsive to my questions. This way they also shared their knowledge about activities that that were mostly performed alone with other hunters. People could talk for half an hour at night, sitting near the fire and warming their backs. Before going on a hunting trip, experienced hunters were happy to tell stories about their struggles with powerful animals like sable or moose. These stories, spiced up with details of the actions of both contestants, were also told to persuade the master-spirits that the teller was a worthy hunter and thus to gain luck.

Although the hunters and reindeer herders knew me well, they told me things they considered important in their own way, and only in those situations and locations that suited them. They seldom answered my questions in a way I anticipated or at the time that I asked the question. For instance, sometimes a question about how to interpret certain elk tracks might be answered a few days later in the village over a cup of hot sweet tea or smoking a cigarette. Specific incidents and individuals were mostly discussed far away from the places where the former occurred. Similarly, the ethnographer Suslov (see in Batashev 2007: 99) describes his 'difficulties of communicating' with the Evenki of Tunguska in his expedition diaries (1926–1927) and states that the Evenki usually talk about events indirectly (Rus. *inoskozatelno*), and only when there is some kind of spatial distance from the object they are talking about. Suslov (ibid.) points out that Evenki believe spirits can hear them, recognize their personality and get angry at them (Rus. *gnevo ego [dukha] ne budet predela*). When hunters tell a story, they prefer to tell it once without repeating it. Hunters and herders also believe that words cannot convey truth about events and often run the risk of being misleading or causing misfortune. Truth is rather attributed to well-performed action, whereas talk about things often tends to be 'lies' (Oro. *ulal*). Indeed, my wrong interpretations of animal tracks were often followed by the exclamation '*ulok*' (liar). Brody (1982: 175) also notes that some hunting people make no distinction between an error in judgment and telling a lie in the context of how 'the information about the land and its animals can make the difference between life and death'.

Many former collective farm workers talk about their hunting luck as passion by using the Russian word *azart* (thrill). However, in the Orochen hunters' explanations these emotions tend to be expressed through talk, movement, rush and much shooting, as well as in conversations after the hunt. Such behaviour is considered improper. It is said that one should neither express happiness about hunting luck nor show disappointment in case of misfortune. Concealing one's emotions, activities and plans from others is part of the hunters' strategy of achieving luck. Hunters were aware that nonhuman beings understood spoken words and reacted with emotion or anxiety, which could threaten the hunter's luck (see also Zelenin 1929). Often questions about future plans, predictions or success were answered brusquely with '*ne budem zagadyvat*' (let's not give orders/forecast the future').

Hunting luck – *kutu* – can be acquired by hiding one's tracks and movements as well as one's emotions, trying to outwit the game. In addition, people tried to secure luck by keeping the plans and results of their hunting trips from others, including state officials and *komersanty*. The police and the environmental protection inspector may also threaten hunters' well-being since most lack hunting licenses or hunt out of season. Concealing one's plans from others in the face of mistrust, violence and the possibility of magical spoiling of one's luck is analogous to the way people seek to mislead malevolent spirits. In various ethnographies we find accounts of how the Orochen change or conceal their names by using nicknames, after certain critical incidents or in order to sustain their luck and protect their well-being, to mislead malevolent spirits (Shirokogoroff 1929: 266, 284; Tugolukov 1962: 37). By observing the hunters I became aware of how they were observing my own actions and later commented on them. People spoke to me in a rude manner when hunting had been unsuccessful. They also left me alone in the taiga and made me learn through extreme experiences. In this way I learned how to behave, talk and touch things in the environment as my informants did, and how to study life in the taiga in non-intrusive ways. In most cases, my integration into the hunters' society resulted from experiences of good luck shared by our whole group. I tried to learn when and where to ask questions, what items could be touched and what actions taken in different situations to sustain luck. Among the Orochen, personal autonomy requires respect for the autonomy of others, so hunters and herders are expected to allow others to take advantage of their opportunities to accumulate luck.

Self-Reliance in the Taiga

Success in subsistence activities and the acquisition of luck is impossible without maintaining autonomy in the taiga. Autonomy is based on various skills and kinds of knowledge about how to survive long winter hunting seasons and sustain one's well-being in remote areas. Each winter most hunters leave their villages to hunt animals for fur, living in tents or log houses in remote parts of the taiga for up to five months. Success in subsistence thus depends on one's ability to live on one's own. For this reason, Orochen pedagogy teaches that one should be skilled in all kinds of crafts and also in curing disease.

Successful living in the taiga hinges on the ability to use a wide range of available resources. The Orochen's success in the post-socialist economy revolves around their ability to take all available opportunities to harvest taiga resources, and to manufacture their own gear and clothing from hides. Various kinds of gear, rifle parts and building materials like tent covers, for instance, were acquired from a crashed rocket from the nearby military base. Herders and hunters strive to learn, rediscover and rely on traditional knowledge of crafts in order to be independent from goods imported from the city, making but little effort to be connected with the state. David G. Anderson (2006a) aptly noted that the way of using all kinds of available resources is a continuation of the Orochen's 'dwelling intuition', of how people make a home for themselves in the same way as they did in the past.

The collapse of centrally funded economic activities in the villages made hunters and herders rely on the old ways of doing things, including the production of gear, camp equipment and storage. Hides tanned by hand in the traditional manner became even more important in the production of various items for daily use, since many store-bought items like canvas and cordage were in short supply in the taiga and rather expensive. The interest in the 'old ways' of making things is a way people seek to accommodate to a harsh environment by using everything that is available and striving to be less dependent on the cash economy. Shirokogoroff (1935: 93) described the knowledge and skills of gear making and hide tanning as a complex of Orochen adaptation to the local environment, where hunters and herders are able to use whatever material is 'found-at-hand' for their clothing, household and subsistence (see also Vasilevich 1969; Mazin 1992). Mazin (1992: 110–113), who overviewed pre-Soviet Orochen material culture, remarks that Orochen knowledge and skill in tanning and handicrafts started to disappear with the influx of newcomers in the beginning of the twentieth century. In recent decades, however, in classes and workshops initiated by indigenous activists in secondary schools or 'houses of culture' in the large villages (Rus. *dom kultury*), elders teach children to process hides and to manufacture various items from buckskin. Orochen intellectuals see old handicrafts as a way to maintain an indigenous identity. Such materially embodied skills and knowledge serve as representations of the continuation of Orochen 'culture' (Rus. *kul'tura*) that are well received and supported by the state, as evidence by exhibitions of various Orochen crafts during festivals at the district level.

In the Soviet period, the practice of hide tanning was preserved mostly by elders. With the establishment of collective farms, the indigenous brigades (Rus. *brigady*) of reindeer herders received supplies of food, gear, clothing and footwear for their work in remote taiga camps. In Tungokochen County, collective farm planners even built permanent wooden houses of several rooms, equipped with saunas, so the reindeer herders would 'have a comfortable rest' in remote herding areas.

Orochen dress was considered backward in the villages. Russian-style clothing was preferred, especially the padded cotton jackets known as *fufaika* – which, ironically, was initially prison garb – that became the most popular item of clothing in both the villages and the taiga. Even today, the Orochen, who are a minority in most villages in Zabaikal'ia, often feel uncomfortable wearing clothing made from hides, whereas the *fufaika* retains its popularity.

All goods imported from China were considered to be for one-time use only (Rus. *odnorazovye*). Given the shortage of high-quality goods in the taiga, most hunters and herders of both sexes started to tan hides and manufacture buckskin for footwear and clothing suited to life in the taiga. Many hunters claimed that one would not survive the winter in the taiga without proper footwear. When I brought heavy felt boots to a reindeer herders' camp, I was told that I would have no hunting success in them because they were cold, noisy and too heavy. I tanned many hides, made sinew threads, fashioned three pairs of footwear for myself, and wore them every day during my fieldwork.

An Orochen handcrafted tanned hide (Oro. *manivcha*, Rus. *polovinka*) has a soft, porous quality achieved through treatment with liver of wild animals, physical manipulations and rotten-wood smoke. Such tanned hides, with the hair and epidermis removed, can be called buckskin. They are made from the hides of animals like deer, elk, moose, roe deer or musk deer. The fabric of such buckskin has the same quality as factory-made leather. It is soft, light, warm, strong, durable, breathable and washable. Gear and footwear made from buckskin can easily be repaired or reused to manufacture other items for various purposes.[25] The use of proper footwear, clothing and gear is crucial to a person's health and well-being in the taiga and indispensable for walking long distances, spending nights in taiga camps and adapting to the local landscape and fluctuations in temperature.

Many Orochen in their fifties said that they had never been taught how to tan hides, but most of them had observed their elders, parents or grandparents do so during the Soviet period. Indeed, many elders born in pre-Soviet times were known as highly skilful tanners, and hides were widely used in the manufacture of clothing. During the severe shortage of cotton material in the taiga in the harsh years of World War II, most hunters and herders made their clothing themselves from buckskin. Olga Zhumaneeva, for example, remembered that her family manufactured musk deer buckskin for underwear that was cotton-like in texture.

Today's elders remember that everyone knew how to tan hides in a variety of ways. The well-known Orochen craftswoman Tamara Naikanchina from Tungokochen village told me that she had never been taught how to tan hides; rather, she had attended medical school in Krasnoyarsk. When she retired from her job, she started sewing a special kind of shoes – *untakar* (locally known as Rus. *unty*) and rugs called *muruko* (Rus. *kumalan*). 'My mother never had time to teach us', Tamara told me, 'so we learned by observing and trying to imitate her work'. Today, hide tanning is again practised by men and women of various ethnic backgrounds. Some kinds of work, like moosehide tanning, are done predominantly by men, whereas hide softening is mostly the province of children or women. Although everyone had their own knowledge and experience in hide tanning, some patterns were common across the northern part of Zabaikal'ia. The Orochen said that just as they remember every place they visited in their childhood, they know how to manufacture every item that they saw in their childhood. Every Orochen family has inherited old hide scrapers and special tools for hide softening that are nowadays shared and used again.

Hunters and herders generally used self-made canvas tents equipped with iron stoves, spending little time in log cabins. They also collected and stored certain animal parts that could be turned into food or gear. Elders remembered that in Soviet times the Orochen would leave many parts of animals in the taiga. Today, however, any part – hide, genitals, tail – of a moose or deer is useful and can be traded, exchanged or exported to China.

Figure 1.9. | *Gena Kirilov softening moose skin.*

Hunting success also depends on a person's ability to walk and transport goods through swampy areas, across rivers and up steep rocky hillsides. Because walking in the taiga is such a crucial activity in reindeer herding and hunting alike, footwear made from tanned hides has become a highly desired item. In winter, hunters preferred to wear the light, warm footwear called *emchure* in Orochen, made from depilated, grained, softened, smoked hide. Indeed, in the winter young hunters often complained that they could not hunt successfully because of their inappropriate footwear. The successful hunter Aleksei Aruneev told me that he managed to wear out one pair of *emchure* per year. Indeed, the the *emchure*'s rawhide sole has to be repaired almost every week. The hunters have developed elaborate techniques of repairing footwear by sewing different patches.

Aleksei's footwear also had pieces of leather attached to the sole that served as a tread. This is important, as hunters and herders have to carry heavy loads long distances on their daily winter walks. They usually carried a small kettle (Oro. *kolokochan*) and cups for the midday break, along with some bread (Oro. *kiltera*), sugar (Oro. *oloke*) and tea (each hunter brings his own supply) in backpacks locally called *poniaga* (a bag tied to a wooden frame). Fur hunters also carry a rifle (Oro. *paktyravun*), a bullet bag (Oro. *tauseruk*), a knife (Oro. *koto*) and a special belt (Oro. *chimka*) with a toggle on one end that is used to carry squirrels. A backpack was used to carry several iron traps in winter. Most of the gear was made from hand-processed hides. People said that clothing and gear made from hides are durable enough to be worn in the taiga, where there are many areas of thick underbrush. Furthermore, unlike cotton clothing, hide clothing was never damaged by the hunted animals' blood.

The hides of animals like moose, reindeer, elk and musk deer were used to manufacture various items for hunting and herding. Moosehide was preferred for clothing and footwear. In autumn or winter, moose-leg hides, called *kamus* (Oro. *oso*), were used to make the warmest footwear (*untakar* or *unty*), which was very popular among villagers and city people in Zabaikal'ia. Some old-style *unty* were soled with the depilated autumn hides of bull moose, taken from the animal's neck (Oro. *kukuio*). Others had rubber and wool soles attached by skilful village cobblers. About six to eight *kamus* were needed to make a pair of *unty*. The hair was left on the hides, and they were thoroughly softened, oiled and smoked. In some cases they were tanned with liver. It took two to three days to make the *unty*. In the final stage they were handcrafted and attached to a sole made from modern material. Such footwear cost up to 3,000 roubles (US$120) in the villages and up to 5,000 roubles (US$200) in cities.

The Orochen manufacture the same kinds of gear that were used in the early Soviet years. Today hunters wear buckskin pants (Oro. *urki*), long leggings with the foot attached (Oro. *aremus*), jackets made from roe deer pelts (Oro. *kaidak*) and reindeer pelt jackets (Oro. *mukulmi*) in the coldest period of the year (from late December to late January). All clothing, gloves (Oro. *kokolda*) and shoes were made with the seams on the outside, while the former have the hair side on the outside. A cap (Oro. *aun*) was usually made from rabbit or squirrel fur, the feet of a musk deer or a newborn reindeer (Rus. *pyzhik*). Hides harvested in autumn were also used for knife sheaths (Oro. *unoki*), axe cases (Oro. *topku*), bullet bags (Oro. *tauseruk*), belts (Oro. *buso*) and special belts for squirrel fur (Oro. *chipka*). The latter were usually made from fleshed and depilated hide that is softened and smoked.

Softened pelts of reindeer, deer, bear and wild boar were also used for mattresses (Oro. *girkovun*) and sleeping bags. Light reindeer hide (Oro. *boiuksu*) is humidity-proof and warm and served as a mattress in autumn, spring and summer, whereas bearhide (Oro. *amikaksa*), considered the warmest and softest, is mainly used as a mattress in winter. Hides could also be used as blankets (Oro. *sun*). A special rug called a *muruko* (Rus. *kumalan*) made from a winter reindeer pelt (Oro. *dori*) is used to cover reindeer or decorate the tent and is highly valued in the villages and cities. Orochen women usually manufacture *muruko* in the summer. Today, the *muruko* plays an important role as both a representation of local handicraft skills and a source of cash income. Moosehides taken in the rutting season are the thickest – solid and tough – and therefore well suited for whips and straps. Neck hide (Oro. *kukuio*) is usually taken for socks, while straps are made from circular cutting. Reindeer harnesses (Oro. *tynaptyl*, Rus. *podpruga*), bridles (Oro. *usi*, Rus. *uzda*) and durable bags (Oro. *potol*) are also manufactured and used for transporting meat and camping articles by reindeer or horse. Some *potol* are made from *kamus* (Oro. *oso*), others from moose, wild reindeer or elk hides with the epidermis remaining.

Hides can be tanned in any season. However, I saw tanning most actively performed in summer and autumn before the fur-hunting season, when the weather conditions were favorable. The reindeer require little attention in summer, so hunters and herders have much leisure time. Moreover, summer hides make the best buckskin for clothing. It is a process with several stages that required special tools. First, the hide must be carefully stripped of flesh, dried and then stored for some time. Flesh and epidermal hair are removed with a special tool, and the hide is rubbed with liver, then softened and finally smoked. The so-called *U* tool, a short bent scraper, is used to remove the hair and epidermis, and for fleshing. The *chuchun* (Oro.) scraper, with a straight head and 'teeth', is used to smooth the hide. It also helps to remove leftover flesh and dry the hide by friction. This tool also contributes to stretching the hide and making it softer before the final softening by hand takes place. The *chuchun* is also used to press or hold the hide when it is cut. A rope attached to a *chuchun* turns it into a *chuchuvun* (Oro.) tool. Nikolai used the bent iron leg of a bed with a rope attached to make such a tool. Hunters often tie the *chuchuvun* rope to their feet and soften the hide with pressure from one foot. Another softening tool for processing large hides is the *ongnachevun* (Oro.), a U-shaped wooden tool used for initial hide softening by pressing the hide with the heel. The main softening tool is a *talki*, which is made from carved larch wood. There are two types: one is short, about a metre in length, and is used for *kamus* softening; the other, about two metres long, is used to soften moosehide. The *kedera*, made from a scythe (Rus. *litovka*), can be used for scraping remnants of flesh or liver from the hide.

The collapse of Soviet collective farms provided Orochen with a rewarding environment in which to privatize reindeer, access land and use a variety of taiga resource. Hunting and herding of reindeer provides meat and fur as well as different sub-products, such as hides, antlers and other parts of the animals, that also bring value in both trade and production of gear and medicine. Furthermore, indigenous intelligentsia made hide tanning and craftwork into an important identity marker and representation of Orochen identity at festivals, conferences and political meetings. In the Soviet period, most reindeer herding brigades were supplied with gear and food supplies, but today they have to rely on their own stocks, supplies and crafted equipment. Orochen success in the post-socialist economy therefore revolves around their ability to seize opportunities to harvest different taiga resources and to produce self-made gear and clothing from hides. They strive to learn, rediscover and rely on their traditional knowledge of crafts, aiming to maintain their autonomy from goods and resources imported from cities while expending little effort to connect with state powers. In describing the historical and geographical context and the local people's and communities' adaptations to the post-Soviet environment, I have also described my stay with Orochen hunters and herders, which was inseparable from learning taiga skills like hunting and herding, hide tanning and daily household chores. It also included learning non-intrusive ways of being in the taiga, asking questions, building trust, respecting people's autonomy and gaining luck.

Notes

1. For more on Orochen, Murchen, Evenki and Khamnigan see Sirina (2012: 43–57).
2. Murchen derives from the Buryat word *murin* 'horse'. Tungus Orochen also use the term Tungus to refer to horse- and cattle-raising Murchen people 'like the Buryat people', such as the Evenki from the Barguzin (Buryatia), Shilka and Nerchinsk (Zabaikal Province) regions. Shubin (2001: 80), who conducted fieldwork among northern Baikal groups of Evenki that had few reindeer or none at all, notes that they were referred to as 'walking Tungus' (Rus. *peshie*).
3. Aboriginal Day is celebrated by indigenous people all over Siberia and the Far East on 9 August, which is the International Day of Aboriginal People. This celebration replaced Reindeer Herders' Day, which existed during Soviet times.
4. Unless otherwise stated, all information represented in tables is from my interviews and field observations.
5. Sochi is a famous Soviet-era resort on the Crimean Peninsula. Mogochi, a city in the eastern part of Zabaikal province, is known for its harsh environment and gulags.
6. People of Zabaikal'ia like to refer themselves as being strong and well adapted to consuming huge amounts of alcohol while still staying healthy.

At the same time, people involved in state apparatus often remark that indigenous Orochen are unable to cope with large amounts of alcohol because of genetic limitations.

7. Grigorii Semenov, a controversial general and *ataman* (military leader) of the White Cossacks, was based in Zabaikal'ia.

8. *Guran* is a Tungusic word for male of roe deer.

9. Orochen also use the term Tungus to refer to Evenki people that raise horses and cattle 'like the Buryat people', for instance, the Evenki from the Barguzin (Buryatia), Shilka, and Nerchinsk (Zabaikal Province) regions.

10. I measured temperatures myself while I was living in the taiga, comparing these data with the data from the meteorology centre of Tungokochen village. It was always five degrees colder in the taiga camps than in Tungokochen village.

11. In addition to large game, fur-bearing animals like lynx and squirrel are a welcome addition to the diet. Most hunters would say that sable, wolverine, wolf and fox are not edible. However, when food is in short supply they may eat any animal they can find.

12. Villagers of different ethnic origin in the rural areas of Northern Zabaikal'ia hold common ideas linked to spirits, health and healing with the Orochen (see Basharov 2003).

13. 'Nerchinsk katorga' had been famous as a place of exiled people (including political activists) used as labour power in local mines since the eighteenth century.

14. I was told by the elder Nadia Kopylova from Ust' Karenga that most elders who spent their whole life in the taiga usually changed places by moving the canvas tents they lived in, sometimes to the backyard of their own family's wooden house.

15. See Vitebsky and Wolfe (2001: 81–95) on gender roles in Siberian reindeer herding.

16. See more examples of Orochen resistance in Fondahl (1998: 76, 81); on the Tungus uprising, see Pestrev (1994).

17. On names and nicknames, see Sirina (2012: 171); on nicknaming among the Poligus Evenki, see Ssorin-Chaikov 2003: 159–162).

18. Like his brothers Yura and Nikolai, Aleksei did not know any Russian when he started boarding school at the age of eight.

19. The meat was shared by all the hunters who participated in the hunt and their relatives in the village.

20. Some small animals were killed by the elder female hunter Olga Zhumaneeva. The meat was consumed by three to six hunters.

21. Boars are rarely shot around reindeer herding sites because they live in the lower reaches of big rivers that are usually not visited by reindeer herds.

22. Three male reindeer were killed as payment for transportation.

23. Nikolai was very interested in ethnographic studies and questioned elders and shamans about reconstructing and performing different rituals in the taiga and the villages.

24. Most Orochen hunters and herders in their forties or fifties were unmarried. This gender imbalance and split as an outcome of women retreat from traditional indigenous spaces such as taiga and tundra, are well documented in a number of ethnographies (see Lyarskaya 2010; Povoroznyuk, Habeck and Vaté 2010).
25. Hunters and herders can make footwear from old buckskin trousers and knife sheaths from old footwear.

CHAPTER TWO

Luck, Spirits and Domination

Linguistic, semantic and ethnographic analysis of the Orochen vernacular term *kutu* reveals the complexity of a notion of luck that embraces
interconnected ideas of movement, energy, strength, soul and mastery. The term *kutu* can function as either a noun (Oro. sing. *kutu*, pl.
kuty, kutymungi 'my luck'; Rus. *moe schast'e*) or as an adjective (Oro.
kutuchi beio 'lucky human'). For the Orochen being alive means having a soul (Oro. *omi*), which can manifest itself as movement, strength
(Oro. *chinen*) or energy. Among some Orochen groups of Zabaikal'ia
and South Yakutia the term *kutu* is semantically linked to or stands for
both 'soul' and 'power' (Oro. *musun*) (see also Titov 1926b: 85; Vasilevich 1957: 173-175). In Turkic languages, the term *kut* also refers to
concepts of 'living power', 'soul', 'spirit' and 'prestige' (see L'vova et
al. 1989: 72–80). We also find that the Orochen idea of *omi* is translated among Mongols as 'breathing'. Indeed, among Turkic peoples
breathing is another important metaphor for being alive (ibid. 1989:
83, 86). In this context, the Evenki and Turkic-speaking people do not
refer to 'breathing' and 'moving' as limited only to humans and animals, but also attribute it to plants and geographical features (ibid.:
89–90; Vasilevich 1969: 228).[1]

According to Vasilevich (1957: 166), the Evenki living near Vi-
tim-Oliokma used the word *kutu* (or *sinken*, depending on the dialect)
not only for human fortune, but also for material objects such as special amulets that attract luck or contain souls. Shamans of Zabaikal'ia
used special items like a *kuturuk* (Rus. *dushekhranilishche*- placing
of souls), a rug made by the Orochen from wild reindeer skin covered with drawings of animals, in rituals for obtaining hunting luck or
healing reindeer (see Vasilevich 1957: 175–176; Mazin 1984: 91–93).
Some Orochen stories I recorded tell of a strong human who could
not be killed, partly because his strength was located inside an *omiruk*

(Oro. *omi-* soul) (see also Voskoboinikov 1965: 335). Some hunters and herders still have a doll *omiruk* made by their parents after their birth (see Fig. 2.1). However, destruction of one's *omiruk* is believed to be very dangerous for that person. One family told me that their son's *omiruk* was destroyed by a flood in the village of Rossoshino shortly before his tragic death. Various objects can be beneficial for the one who made and used them, but harmful to other users.

Being Alive

A person has to compete with game animals to catch and sustain *kutu*. Local hunters say that 'being alive' and 'skilful' means being in 'motion' or 'moving', which is also described as having an *omi*.[2] Among the Orochen such a lucky person has *chinen*, which refers to 'spiritual strength' (Rus. *dukhovnaia sila*), 'energy' (Rus. *energiia*),[3] 'capability' (Rus. *umenie*), 'physical strength' (Rus. *fizicheskaia sila*) or 'strength of movement' (Rus. *sila dvizheniia*). Indeed, we find in Tsintsius' dictionary (1975: 396–397) that the term *chinen* is translated as 'might' (Rus. *mosch'*), 'strength' (Rus. *sila*), as well as 'strong person' (Rus. *bogatyr'*) and 'chief' (Rus. *vozhd'*) (for more on *chinen* see Titov 1926b: 112, 171).

Figure 2.1. | Omiruk *dolls belonging to the Dogonchin family (Baunt District).*

The Orochen believe that one can pass one's *chinen* (also referred to as 'energy') to different objects, or to places and other humans, and that these objects can in turn affect other people who use them. The ethnographers Vasilevich (1969) and Varlamova (2004) described how some Orochen groups saw different places, material objects, phenomena and nonhuman beings as well as spoken words as potentially having *musun*, which is referred to as 'power' (Rus. *sila*), 'energy' (Rus. *energiia*) and 'movement' (Rus. *dvizhenie*).[4] According to Vasilevich (1969: 227–228), the oldest meaning of *musun* was 'strength of movement', a quality intrinsic to all environmental phenomena. We know from her descriptions that rain, wind, clouds, rivers, and all other objects that were seen in motion can be referred to as *mususchi* – that is, possessing and exercising *musun*. Vasilevich adds that the Evenki perceived even geographical features like mountains as moving (as in the case of falling rocks) and therefore called them *mususchi* (ibid.).

These terms, she explains, developed at a later stage of Evenki religion's evolution and referred to personalized entities such as humans, strong master-spirits, capable storytellers or shamans. Vasilevich regarded this as the transformation of archaic beliefs into shamanic practices (ibid.). Her interpretation probably arose from the doctrine of social evolution, which permeated all Soviet ethnographic works at that time. The Evenki folklorist Varlamova (2004: 59–60) identifies *musun* as 'psycho-energy' (Rus. *psikhicheskaia energiia*) or 'life energy' (Rus. *zhivaia energiia*) that is intrinsic to many inanimate objects. She describes how the Orochen of Amur's interactions with different objects containing *musun* might bring people luck and good health. Since *musun* could be shared, certain items like hunting trophies or presents were seen as sources of *musun* and were often collected and used by hunters as purveyors of luck. Varlamova furthermore noted that negative human action could kill the *musun* of certain objects (ibid.).

According to the Orochen, spoken words can become 'placings' that convey 'good' or 'bad' energies and can be used to influence certain situations (on the power of words across Siberia, see Zelenin 1929). Words can also serve to either destroy or generate *kutu*. In order to sustain *kutu*, the Orochen say, one should be called by a nickname rather than a 'real name', since the real name contains a person's strength or soul (Rus. *dusha*) (see also Kureiskaia 2000: 5). The elder Yulia Semirekonova once remembered how a shaman called her Aiulchik (male name) in order to mislead a malevolent spirit that made her ill. In fact, many ethnographies have documented how Orochen change or conceal their names by using nicknames to mislead malevolent spirits (Shirokogoroff 1929: 266, 284; Tugolukov 1962: 37; Kureiskaia 2000). As Weiner (1991: 31–32) notes, language is not merely a neutral tool useful for describing a world 'out there', but constitutive of the world itself. Hence, Varlamova (2004: 61–63, 71–72) shows how words and speech can be seen as *musuchi* (objects with *musun*) and as such have the potential to either cause damage or bring help, unless the *musun* of these words can be neutralized.

Yulia Semirekonova, who was among the main informants of the famous Russian folklorist Voskoboinikov and a storyteller herself, told me that her clan used to invite an elder from the Zaguneev clan who could tell an epic (Oro. *nimngakan*) for three days. Everyone took part in such storytelling, getting involved emotionally and singing songs together with the storyteller. People participated in storytelling events to empower themselves by taking part in the contest related in the story. Elders say that some people were even healed or received special healing powers by taking part in the narration of an epic. As Yulia Semirekonova concluded her statement about storytelling, 'this was the way we used to obtain luck in any difficult situation'. To elaborate on Kwon's (1993: 67–80) arguments, while these stories were told to convey information that hunters needed to find their way in world, the act of storytelling also served as important source of empowerment and a way to attract luck.

Past conflicts among kin or a curse may continue to affect the lives and well-being of their descendants. Thus every single member of the extended family of an Orochen man who helped the NKVD eliminate a shaman either died young in various tragic incidents or led lives marked by prison sentences, rapes and illness. According to Smolyak (1991: 173), the Tungus-Manchu speaking Ulchi see *musu* as a 'living line' that connects very close relatives; therefore every member of family has a very similar *musu*. If the *musu* is in good condition, then all relatives are healthy and have good hunting luck. Hence, a skilful hunter and a person recently recovered from illness can both be referred to as lucky. If a family constantly encounters misfortune and illness, then the *musu* must be fixed in a ritual performed by a shaman.

Catching Luck

In the Orochen storytelling tradition, strong and skilful humans achieve luck through contests with various other beings. Ethnographic studies of the Evenki describe various communal rituals for obtaining luck during a bad hunting season or before the start of the hunting season, performed either by the hunters themselves or by shamans (see Va-silevich 1930, 1969: 238–239; Anisimov (1949, 1958). These rituals, known as *sinkelevun* or *ikenipke,* served to catch the souls of domestic or game animals, and even of sick children (on the Nercha and Bar-guzin Evenki, see Shirokogoroff 1935: 310–311). Anisimov suggests a linguistic interpretation of the word *sinken* 'hunting luck' that links it to the idea of 'imitation' (1949: 167), hence *sinkelevun* could be se-mantically translated as 'searching for hunting luck' or mean 'imitat-ing luck' or 'obtaining hunting luck'.

Anisimov (1949: 179–181) recorded the details of such rituals performed by group of hunters and a shaman of the Podkamenaia Tunguska Evenki near a sacred rock called *bugady* in 1937. During one ritual the shaman had to travel to the upper world and meet the master-spirit of various animals. Once the shaman had persuaded the master-spirit to give up some animals, the shaman caught their souls with a rope and brought them back, whereupon the animals' souls were released in the clan's hunting territory. If the game harvested in the clan's hunting territory still was not enough, the hunters asked the shaman to undertake a second journey. This was considered a very difficult task, as this time the shaman had to take animals away from the master-spirit by overcoming the master-spirit and grabbing the animals' hair-souls from the master-spirit's bag. After the shaman's return, the hair turned into animals.

In other instances the shaman, imitating a reindeer or moose, was caught by the group of hunters, thus securing luck for the commu-nity (see Novik 1984: 152). Vasilevich (1969: 248) describes how the Evenki of the Aldan River performed a ritual stealing of the souls of domestic reindeer during an epizootic illness in their herds. The sha-man had to travel to the upper world to meet the main spirit Seveki and seize the reindeer's souls. When he returned to camp, a group of men with ropes were waiting to catch the reindeer. The shaman was caught, harnessed and then brought to the conical tent called a *chum.* He jumped around and shook his body, releasing the reindeer's hair-souls, which were carefully collected and placed in a special bag. In this way reindeer luck was secured, which also provided good health for the herds. Similarly, Empson (2011: 70) described how the Buryat of Mongolia today conceive of luck (referred to as *hishig* 'fortune') as something that circulates outside the subject but can be harnessed and carefully contained in certain forms to secure the growth of peo-ple, animals and things. Hence, the Buryad take a piece of an animal, like tail hair, that mediates the animal's agency and keeps it in the household to invite further good luck for the herd (ibid: 108).

Other parts of the *sinkelevun* ritual as described by Anisimov (1949) included dances, improvisations and appeals to the game animals. The main dance was performed by a hunter who imitated the lead animal. His role in the ritual dance was to lure animals to the clan's hunting territories. Such a ceremony for catching luck could also include the staging of a hunting expedition. In this case, the hunters manufactured miniature items representing various parts of the landscape that were attractive to reindeer, such as burned areas, fields, bushes and other attractive features of grazing areas. Dolls representing the animals' offspring were also made from willow branches and placed in the landscape. During this preparation, elders told stories and folk tales. Next the hunters made miniature bows and arrows and started searching for tracks of the game, finding its feeding grounds and carefully approaching it. Finally, the game was shot. A domestic reindeer was slaughtered as an offering, its skin hung on a pole for the master-spirit and its meat consumed by all participants. Since evil spirits would attempt to chase and attack the hunters by following their footprints, they had to escape by passing beneath the splayed legs of a wooden idol called a *chipikan*. This part of the ritual was also performed to cleanse the hunters. Finally, the legs of the *chipikan* were tied together, thus closing the passage to the spirits, and gifts were offered to the idols.

The acquisition of hunting luck or of souls hinged on the hunter's or shaman's skill in interacting with the master-spirits or bird-souls (Vasilevich 1969: 238–239). Interaction could include pleading with the master-spirits to send game or stealing pieces of the animal's hair (Anisimov 1949: 186). Shubin (2007) also described how a hunter threw a rope outside of the conical tent *chum*, thus performing the catching of an imaginary animal and of luck. In Vasilevich's (1969: 238) description of rituals the same elements appear in various ceremonies designed to catch luck and souls and secure them in a special bag to ward off future misfortune. Nikulshin (in Maksimova 1994: 138) reports that a shaman's ceremony could transfer disease to a reindeer, whereupon the animal was killed in a staged hunting expedition; thus the disease too was killed. When misfortune continued and the people could not discover the cause, they simply moved to another hunting territory, believing they would escape malevolent spirit dwelling there (ibid.).

The contest between humans and nonhumans played an important role in the Evenki ritual of *ikenipke,* which was performed among the Evenki of Sym until the beginning of the twentieth century (Vasilevich 1957: 151–163). An elaborate ritual performed in the spring, *ikenipke* ('imitation of life', 'playing for life', Oro. *ike* 'play') lasted eight days and featured singing, competitions and divinations as well as hunters' performance of chasing moose (ibid.). The goal of the staged contest during the ritual was to obtain luck and well-being (for current re-enactments of this ritual among the Evenki of Amur, see Lavrillier 2003). The tropes of respect and the contest were also important elements of the bear-hunting ritual among many Evenki groups (Turov 2000; Vasilevich 1971). Competitions among people during such rituals can also be understood as creating 'equal and harmonious' relationships, perpetuating partnerships and helping to acquire luck (for Turkic people of Siberia, see also L'vova et al. 1989: 125–128; Hamayon 1996: 61–66).

Although proper hunting should be based on the notion of an equal contest between hunter and prey, sometimes a bear is killed in its den, where it is unable to offer much resistance. In such cases the hunters may enact a struggle with a straw doll of a bear to avoid misfortune and calm the master-spirit. Vasilevich (1969: 237) gives a description of a bear killing ritual that included a boy wrestling with a straw bear made from branches, or else from the real bear's bones. Although Vasilevich (ibid.) suggests that this ritual symbolizes man's victory over the animal, I would rather argue that it dissolves the status of relationship. Wrestling with a straw doll of the bear may be better understood as demonstrating a man's competence and worthiness to use the bear's body (and thus to kill the bear). Seen in this way, the wrestling is a way of reducing the dangers inherent in the act of killing. In fact, wrestling with relatives was formerly a common pastime among the Orochen I knew and was still practiced by the older generation. Elders in the village of Tungokochen told me about a certain ceremony practised by some hunters when two friends or relatives meet after not having seen each other for a long time, they often wrestle (Rus. *boriatsa*). Kureiskaia (2000: 4) observed that when two Evenki hunters met in the taiga they would rub their backs together to share their luck. Wrestling is also an important 'ritual of luck' in other parts of Siberia (Vaté 2005: 57; Hamayon 1996). Contests between friends or relatives are an opportunity for enacting skills and capabilities, which can serve to share luck.

Many hunting stories and fairy tales told by Orochen elders contain the idea of a contest between various animal species. We find animals competing with each other, trying to outsmart their opponents alone or in cooperation with other animals in tales called *nimnakanil* (for tales see Vasilevich 1936: 158–161; Voskoboinikov 1965: 70–103). According to Anisimov (1958: 18–19), the Evenki believed that a master-spirit could compete or trade with other master-spirits in charge of nearby places (see also Shirokogoroff 2001: 125). Hence, when game was scarce in a particular area, hunters knew that a master-spirit had lost all his animals in a contest with another master-spirit (Anisimov 1958: 18–19). Gurvich (1977: 150–171) described a special type of Evenki epic from Yakutia called *soning* or *sine*, translated as 'strength', that told of a skilful hunter who could provide his whole clan with meat and overcome various challenges when competing with various nonhuman beings.

Analysis of the hunters' and herders' everyday skills and everyday knowledge, which have been attained through multisensory awareness and empathy, is important for understanding how luck is caught in contests with animals. According to the hunters and herders, both humans and animals possess a sense of volition and rationality, cultural knowledge, the skills to read tracks and predict each other's intentions and actions, and the strength or luck to perform different tasks. Hence, animals are seen as independent actors that can react to human activities and thoughts and are able to respond to the hunters' actions.[5] Hunters and herders have to attune their awareness to animals moving in various places when they want to acquire hunting luck and succeed in their subsistence quest. This is always a two-way street, as both humans and animals react to each other's behaviour. Animals are active participants in their relationship with humans and possess their own agency (see also Nadasdy 2007: 30).

Orochen hunters often refer to a lucky hunter (Oro. *kutuchi*) as 'capable' or 'skilful' (Rus. *umelyi*). Such a person is said to be able to express his or her knowledge through actions rather than words. In Canadian indigenous societies 'power' is also described as linked to a human person's experiences and knowledge gained through practice (see Goulet 1998: 33–36; Ridington 1988: 104; Rushforth 1992: 483–500). According to Goulet (1998: xxix), a Dene with religious or mystical experience is best described not as a believer, but as a 'knower'. 'True' knowledge is not seen as transferable. Rather, it is learned from one's own practice and experience (see Rushforth 1992: 488).

Luck in subsistence practice is achieved through contests, by relying on knowledge that is generated through a human's active engagement with the environment, and in processes of learning and processes of 'enskilment' (Ingold 1996: 38–40). In a number of circumpolar ethnographies anthropologists have elaborated on the concept of 'enskilment', suggesting that it represents a process of fine-tuning a person's perception and actions based on one's 'multisensory awareness' (on awareness, see Lee and Ingold 2006; Ingold and Kurttila 2000; on enskilment, Pálsson 1994). Smith (1998: 413) suggests that all kinds of Chipewyan hunting knowledge can be described as empirical, experiential, holistic and 'supra-empirical', based on 'melded thought and action' and 'holistically interacting senses'. He proposed the term 'bush sensibility' to describe the experience of successful hunters. According to Smith (ibid.: 418), 'bush sensibility' also conditions humans' and nonhumans' inextricable engagement in a 'complex communicative interrelationship'. The description of knowledge as being both linked to one's experiences and fine-tuned in practice is suitable for understanding how Orochen catch luck in their subsistence activities. Hence, Orochen knowledge of competing with animals can be compared to Scott's (2006: 60–61) remark that 'semiotic and phenomenological, ontological and epistemological aspects of perceptions are immanent, simultaneous, and mutually reinforcing in our experience and understanding of the world'.

The notion that knowledge is acquired through empathy is important for understanding the Orochen's ways of predicting animal movements. Empathy can be framed as the 'perceptual entering at the home of others, laying aside your views and yourself in order to enter another world without prejudice' (Rogers 1975: 4). It aims to understand the experiences of others instead of taking them as one's own (as in sympathy).[6] Empathy is the way humans and animals gain knowledge about other beings and achieve hunting results. However, hunters' desire to learn about their game through empathy also arouses the animal's awareness and enables it to gain knowledge about the hunters themselves. The notion of communication via empathy is important for understanding how humans coordinate their activities with other humans in their subsistence practices. It also stipulates relations between animals and humans.[7] When hunters show their interest in a wild animal, they often also stimulate the animal's interest and enable it to respond to their actions. Aggression means losing the master-spirits' support and luck and thus making hunters vulnerable to attacks by bears or malevolent spirits.[8]

Predicting and Containing Luck

The contemporary Russian ethnographer Alekhin (1998) mentions the term *nengo*, used among the Evenki of Surinda. *Nengo* describes various strange events that a hunter observes in the taiga, such as the weird behaviour of a bird, that may foretell an incident, usually an undesirable one. *Nengo* may also refer to the last words of a terminally ill person, which are seen as way of forecasting the future (ibid.).

Similarly, the Tungokochen Orochen performed a special divination as part of mortuary rituals. Typically, a fire was kept burning all night near the mortuary scaffold; then, in the morning, people could foretell the future by the tracks of animals in the ashes.[9] Bear tracks, for example, indicate a coming illness or the death of a relative. Orochen hunters and herders say that both luck and misfortune can be foretold from various signs and dreams or in rituals that involve divinatory elements. The old hunter Bultai told me he had met an eagle sitting on a branch right in front of him before the death of a close relative. A white partridge alighting on a tree after it has been flushed from the ground is also interpreted as a bad omen. Hunters say that even one's body may send out signals that foretell luck or misfortune. They maintain that everyone has to find their own way 'to foresee their luck'.

Anna Taskerova from Ust' Karenga village told me that flying sparks can be understood to express the fire's wish to comfort the feelings of a hunter who has had trouble hunting. Accordign to Chulan Kirilov from Bugunda village, 'if a person does not know if he is right or wrong, the fire always can tell him by making certain noises'. In such cases, as Andrei Dogonchin from Karaftit village said, '*togo sinkerideran*' – 'the fire sends you a message' or 'the fire is shamanizing'. For this reason, he said, some people will even put dry wood on the fire and sit closer to it in order to try to understand the fire's voice. Sometimes a person will tell his troubles to the fire aloud and listen for its answer. According to Aleksei Aruneev, sparks hitting a person is considered a lucky omen (Rus. *fart varozhyt*) for a hunting trip. At other times hunters and herders observe the fire and its noise in order to figure out if a particular site is bad or good as a long-term campsite.

Some hunters only occasionally have dreams that foretell the future, but others link every hunting trip to an omen seen in a dream.[10] Hunters said that as a source of knowledge, dreaming was as important as seeing or hearing. A person must therefore align her or his activities with the knowledge thus gained so as to either acquire luck or escape misfortune. According to Aleksei Aruneev, seeing a drunken man in a dream is a sign of bad luck. He would usually postpone a hunting trip after having had such a dream. Indeed, on several occasions I had to wait for several days before going hunting because many bad signs and omens made hunting inauspicious or the 'route to hunting closed'. Nikolai Kirilov could even gain knowledge of the definite location of game. He told me once that acquiring knowledge of different incidents was 'like looking through a window into the world'.[11] Bultai from Bugunda village, who was known as a very good dreamer, could communicate with animals in a dream and even entice them to move to certain places. As soon as he awoke, he would go to the spot he had dreamed about, meeting the animal he saw in the dream on the way. The prophetic dreams of reindeer herder Nikolai Aruneev typically contained images of Buryat people, blood or horses. Dreams may also serve to predict a change in the weather that is crucial for hunting. Once, Nikolai Aruneev saw dead people walking north with a reindeer in a dream, which forecast a change in the weather. Disease is also predicted in the interpretation of dreams (Voskoboinikov 1965). If one sees blood in a dream, illness is imminent. A person who gains knowledge about animals in a dream must take the opportunity to go hunting in order to sustain his luck; otherwise, good omens will cease to appear.

Anisimov (1949) told of the Evenki belief that hunting luck could be also obtained in special rituals, when the hunter would shoot a miniature replica of an animal with an arrow from a specially made bow. Missing meant he would not have hunting luck and should not go on a hunt. In case of misfortune, a hunter could try again, putting a dog figure into the 'taiga' and trying once again to hit the miniature representation of the game, thus trying to gain luck with the help of a dog (ibid.). Hamayon (2012: 103) notes that 'thus playing is experienced as the testing of an omen's luck or capacity for luck in the future, and believing in this test is held to help one jump at opportunities'.

The most widespread divination practice among hunters in Zabaikal'ia involves the use of animal parts. Pavel Naikanchin from Rossoshino village told me about a common ritual where a hunter burns the foot of a partridge killed at the beginning of a hunting trip in the fire; red colour on the foot is held to predict good hunting. If blood is found in the beak of certain birds, one should aim to kill a bird. The *daludavi* (Oro. *dalu* 'scapula') ritual is also well known among the Orochen and several other people of Inner Asia and Subarctic North America (see Speck 1935). *Daludavi* is performed by both men and women, using the scapula of a roe deer or musk deer. The scapula must be carefully cleaned of meat after it is boiled; then it is heated next to a fire. Hunters wait and see if dark spots appear on the scapula. If they do, success in hunting is almost guaranteed. Skilful diviners can even distinguish between various species of animals depending on the size of a spot. The cracking and breaking pattern of the scapula helps to forecast various details such as an animal's tracks, locations or the weather (see Fig. 2.2). As Pavel Naikanchin says, 'the scapula is like a map that can tell the hunter what to do. One can also predict where a hunted animal can be found, which direction to move or what weather to expect'. It is said that not every hunter has the skills to

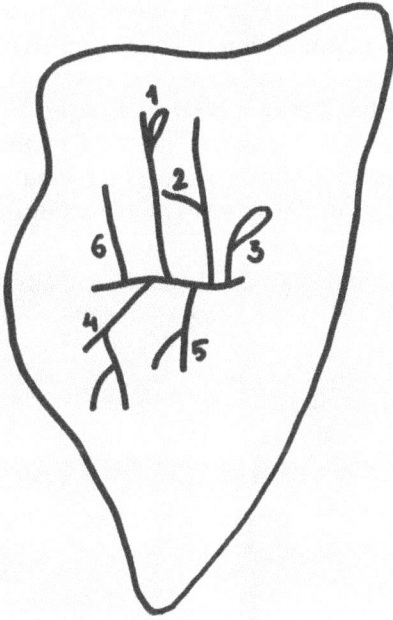

Figure 2.2. | *Sketch representing fragmentation of a scapula (Vasilevich 1969: 243). 1. and 2. Long straight lines with a circle: luck and killing an animal; 3. Short line with circle: unpleasant event, a bad day after killing; 4. Curvy line: unlucky trip or encountered person; 5. Forked line: good travel, weather and encounters; 6. Nice day: good weather.*

divine with a scapula, but every family has a skilful hunter who is capable of it (see Fig. 2.3).

If a hunter foresees an opportunity, he must continue to act in a normal way and show no hurry or emotion. The hunter Aleksei Aruneev paid attention to the way he got dressed. Putting socks on inside out by mistake may bring misfortune to a hunter. Some hunters believe in wearing clothing stained with animal blood because luck attracts luck. Other hunters bloody their knives before leaving camp for hunting. An assemblage of various animal parts, often coloured furs or certain rare items, is seen as a way to contain luck or make it persist. Many ethnographic accounts mention the practice of collecting amulets (Anisimov 1958: 24–25; Vasilevich 1957: 175–178; Rychkov 1917: 80–81). Parts of animals' limbs and jaws are collected, strung on a sinew cord and kept in a bag. As Anisimov (1949: 168) notes, such collections of amulets were sometimes larger than a wooden idol. Elders recall the past by taking these amulets, with various furs and pieces of fabric of different colours attached, from their bags. Orochen hunters and reindeer herders also believe that pieces of animals – the fur of sable (red is especially valued), the claws and feet of predators and birds, the incisors of musk deer, the upper jaw of a moose with the teeth attached, or a moose tooth amulet called *gainakta* – attract luck in hunting.

Like many hunters in the village, Aleksei Aruneev took his small amulets with him on a hunting trip, smudging them with the smoke of *senkire*. Small amulets are kept in the bullet bag or a coat pocket. In wintertime, Nikolai Aruneev carried the legs of a sable in his pocket, leaving them at a mountain pass or near a river at the end of the hunting season as an offering to the master-spirits. Olga Zhumaneeva also collected claws and pieces of fur. Hunting amulets have a highly

Figure 2.3. | *Aleksei Aruneev divining from the shoulder blade of a roe deer.*

personal value. Nikolai said, 'my mother and other elders collect various things but never give us any detailed explanations how they use them ... it certainly brings her luck (Rus. *na fart*)'. In some cases, these amulets are kept hidden and only rarely shown. The Orochen may smudge their bundles of amulets and make offerings of vodka. They also ask animals not to hide their trail or to meet the hunter on his way, or they invite the animals to come and visit their friends. Anisimov (1949: 167) describes how the amulet was tossed in the air and then grasped by the hunter; this way 'luck has been caught'.

Formerly, one or several of idols *seveki* were respectfully carried along on a family's migrations in the taiga. It was believed that the *seveki* would help in acquiring luck in hunting or herding, so the idol was also referred to as 'master' (Rus. *khoziain*, Oro. *odzhen*). It was usually stored in the rear of the tent, which is called the *malu* and is known as the 'master's place', or in the main room of a log house. There were many rules and restrictions concerning the use and location of *seveki* in the tent and outside of the tent. The family of Nikolai's Aruneev's stepfather Gena Kirilov kept their three *seveki* out of reach of the dogs so they could not smell them, and women were not allowed to step over them.[12] If the idol had been taken outside the tent, it was usually returned from the rear part, which is considered cleaner than the front entrance. The same procedure was followed when bringing the carcass of a highly respected animal like a bear or sable into the tent. It is said that if a spirit gets angry and seeks revenge on the hunter it will not find the entrance this way. In the time of Soviet repression of shamanism, some hunters kept their wooden idols in remote caches and continued to visit them to pray before the hunting season. The hunters smudged the idols with smoke at remote storage platforms or left them on mountain passes, visiting them when passing by. Today, such idols are either inherited or newly manufactured and are considered sources of shamanic knowledge, ritual performance and empowerment for the owner.

A ritual interaction with the *seveki*, who was also called 'master of the taiga', was an extraordinary event. A calm day would be chosen for the ritual. The idol was unwrapped from its cloth cover and placed on the ground. According to Nikolai Kirilov, food was then cooked and the *seveki* was fed with hot meat, tea and cigarette smoke. It was given a piece of an animal's heart or head, which hunters consider the most valuable pieces. Paying close attention to the environment was part of performing this rite, as 'anything might speak'. Fire might make a crackling sound, which predicts luck, but the rite had to be stopped when a strong wind starts to blow. The hunter might, in an elaborate dialogue with the *seveki*, describe his or her need for hunting luck and well-being.

In the case of absents of luck, the idol might also be suspended by a rope so that its answers to the hunter's yes or no questions could be told by the way it swung. In talking with the *seveki*, the hunter might use kinship terminology when appealing to the *seveki* or invoking an established relationship based on exchange. He or she might promise to pay the *seveki* back in some way in the case of future success. A hunter might feed the *seveki* with fresh blood after a successful hunt to give thanks and ask for further help in the future. Orochen also described how hunters would try to coerce and persuade the *seveki* to provide them with game. Some hunters might even make demands in a loud voice, chanting *bukal mindu boiun* ('give me a moose'), for example.

Misfortune, Mastery and Domination

In villages people often complained that they had lost their luck because of somebody's negative actions (Rus. *pakostnost'*). Village hunters said that luck could be 'stolen' or 'dragged off' (Rus. *fart utashchenyi*) right in the village. This happened when a woman crossed your path carrying empty water cans as you were leaving the village for a hunting trip. Hence, 'empty cans can take away all your luck'. When I was visiting an elderly female hunter in a remote village in the spring, she complained to me that it had been an extremely unsuccessful winter. She had shot only a few squirrels because of a visit from another woman who 'spoiled' her (Rus. *naportila*). This woman had offered her a magically spoiled bowl, and she later sensed that her luck had ebbed away since she accepted the present. It was said that the loss of luck is likely to last for an entire season, and that others could take the luck that was lost. In this way competing hunters could improve their own prospects in the struggle over resources. Nikolai Aruneev says that no one should ever give ammunition or a rifle away to a non-kin person. It was also not appropriate to give away the head of a killed animal. One should not give meat with one's own hands; rather, the recipient should pick up the meat. Luck could be accidentally passed away in transfers such as these. Somebody's urging or demanding that something be given to a hunter against his or her wish might also cause the hunter to lose luck.

One autumn day as Aleksei, Orochen hunter Sopka and I were leaving Tungokochen village for a hunt, we met a woman who stopped and asked, 'are you going to the taiga again to harvest meat?' This was said to be a bad question (or bad words), spoken by a jealous person. Hunters remember many such incidents. In this case, Aleksei explained, this incident was the cause of our misfortune. One can steal luck by walking around another person's house or tent when the other is getting ready for hunting. It was said that taking a circular path 'closes one's path' (Rus. *zakryt' dorogu*) (see also Sirina 2002: 225). According to a hunter nicknamed Andera, 'if you see a fox crossing your path, you better return to the village and go to the sauna, since going hunting would be useless'. Indeed, in many Orochen *nimnakans* (tales) the fox is described as an animal that can harm any other animal.[13]

The hunter Nadia Taskerova told me that during her deceased husband's life, she had respected all his items. She would avoid stepping over guns and even over his clothing and did not make *emchure* for him when she was pregnant or menstruating (on Orochen menstruation prohibitions, see Shirokogoroff 1929: 260). A hunter would smudge a tool with rhododendron smoke to ensure its 'good performance'. Hunters said that different personal items such as rifles could also carry misfortune from having been 'spoiled' (Rus. *naporchenyi*) by others. Aleksei sometimes called out in Russian *ruzh'e prostrelialsia*, meaning that his rifle had started to shoot badly because of a negative influence. Such a condition was diagnosed when a hunter did not manage to kill an animal when shooting at short range, or when bullets failed to bring an animal down and it escaped despite being badly injured. In that case, hunters recommended cleaning the gun with a certain kind of grass (Rus. *son trava*).

Acts of gift-giving and cooperation with the master-spirits notwithstanding, hunting could be unsuccessful for weeks. It was not unusual for people to return from a hunting trip with a story of complete failure. The hunter would say something like, 'I was shooting from a short distance at an animal that was standing still and it still escaped. Then I trailed the badly injured animal for three days. Both the animal and my dog disappeared.' In such cases of misfortune, people may decide to poach or use aggressive rituals to coerce the animals. All the hunters I hunted with had sometimes acted aggressively against animals.

Hunters often put much energy into swearing when an animal does not collapse right away after it has been hit. Negative words powered with a person's 'energy' can be used to force the animal to give in.[14] Animals can even be punished for not letting themselves be caught easily in order to achieve better hunting results in the future. Vladimir

Torgonov told me how to punish a 'stubborn wild animal'. He learned it from his father, who once took a stick and started to beat the dead animal, blaming it for refusing to be killed and also berating it 'in order to gain future luck'. Hunters also spear an animal's ears and pierce their eyes, so 'that the animals would not be able to feel the hunter' in the future. Some hunters cut off the legs of a squirrel right after it was killed, so 'it would not run so fast'. These are examples of hunters' aggression against their game, when they try to 'weaken the animal's power' instead of competing with it in a 'contest of equals' (Rus. *na ravne*).

Shirokogoroff (1935: 187, 207) describes mastery as the 'shamanic art of controlling spirits' yet also adds that every hunter must know the simplest methods of 'managing' spirits and avoiding their wrath. In a similar vein, Anisimov (1963) speaks of 'mastery' as shamans' ability to dominate spirits in order to achieve desired results in healing or fighting malevolent spirits in rituals to protect their own clans. Hence the Tungus shamans can be 'persons of either sex who have mastered spirits, who, at their own volition, can receive spirits into themselves and use their power over other spirits in their own interests' (Shirok-ogoroff 1935: 269). The shaman masters spirits by performing rituals in which he coerces, cheats, manipulates and even threatens them (ibid.: 187–207, 2001: 125). If a weak shaman who receives a spirit into his or her own body fails to master that spirit, then the spirit will most likely become the master and destroy the shaman (ibid.: 207).

Shirokogoroff (1919: 102–103) also describes how even spirits who have been mastered by shamans can still be dangerous for them:

> Once a shaman was attacked by spirits. His appeals to those spirits that were mastered by him were unsuccessful. Then the shaman decided to use a serious remedy: he made a small placing and placed the malevolent spirits in it (he did not know the exact spirit) and then stabbed at the plac-ing with his knife. When he returned home and approached his tent, he became crazy and stabbed himself to death with his knife.

Shirokogoroff (ibid.) explains that the spirits took revenge on their shaman-master by moving from the 'placing'[15] into his body and caus-ing him harm. He notes how spirits mastered by shamans can act in dominant mode against shamans and points out that this hap-pens quite often, as when spirits try to turn away luck by frightening hunted animals (ibid.). Spirits fooling a shaman is a common trope in other ethnographic descriptions (see Anisimov 1963: 104). The most vivid examples of domination over spirits are also found in Anisimov's (1963) article. He describes shamans as mastering spirits in a way that resembles military training and combat: the shaman fights against foreign spirits or powerful shamans of other clans and protects his own clan from attacks by hostile spirits (see Rychkov 1917). The shaman is thus represented as controlling and commanding spirits, skilfully manipulating them by building a 'special fence' (Oro. *maril*) (see Anisimov 1963: 105–112) out of his own spirit helpers for use in the ritual struggle with other powerful beings (ibid.). When treating a patient possessed by an malevolent spirit sent by a shaman of a hostile clan, the shaman has to fight those spirits and try to force them out of the patient's body (ibid: 104):

> Then the shaman, annoyed, once more threw himself on the drum. It sounded loudly in his hands, deafening the disease-spirit with abuse and threats. The shaman gathered all his spirit-helpers. These surrounded on all sides the disease-spirit residing in the person. The shaman began an account, fascinating for its fantastic content, of the battle between the shaman's zoomorphic spirit-helpers and the disease-spirit. The latter hid itself in the contents of the stomach. Then, the most cunning of the shaman's spirits, the goose, pushed his beak into the patient's stomach and with it caught the cause of the disease. The shaman and his spirits celebrated. The joyful, deafening sound of the drum rang out. The clansmen attending the ceremony sighed with relief, but the joy showed itself to be premature. The disease-spirit tore itself from the goose's beak and threw itself in the direction of the onlookers. They were stunned with horror. However, another of the shaman's spirits, the splintered pole symbolizing the shamanistic tree, was in the runaway's path. The pole seized the disease-spirit, squeezed it into its wooden body, and under guard of two wooden watchmen came over to the shaman.... The shaman's spirits, as followed from his songs and actions, were surrounding the captured disease-spirit in a dense ring, showering it with the most malicious jokes, ridicule, profanity, and threats. The spirits pinched it, nibbled at it, pulled at its legs, spat; the most irritated of them urinated and defecated on it, and so on. The tent rang with the sound of the drum, exclamations, and the wild cries of the shaman imitating the voices of his spirit-helpers.

In cases of loss of luck or hunting failure, Orochen hunters and herders might try to coerce not only animals but also spirits and even wooden idols (Oro. *seveki*). Shirokogoroff (2001: 126) described how the Orochen could attempt to destroy certain spirits. They made mannequins and persuaded the spirits with offerings, deceit and promises (Rus. *ugoschenii, khitrosti i obeshchanii*) to enter the placing. Then the idol with a spirit would be destroyed. Every Tungus hunter knew the simplest methods of 'managing' spirits by enticing them to enter such carved placings or other specific objects (see Shirokogoroff 1935:

149–150, 187, 207). As Vasilevich (1930: 58) observes, hunters may dance with a *seveki*, persuasively singing, 'I will give [the animal] to my children'. If the hunt is still unsuccessful after all, the *seveki* may be called a 'stingy being' (Rus. *zhadnye, prizhymistyi*).[16] If the rituals are unsuccessful, hunters may toss the *seveki* into the air and try to read the future from the way it lands. Landing facedown is interpreted as a sign of bad luck. According to Vasilevich (ibid.: 60), such divinations could also include beating the idol. However, aggressively coercing the *seveki* is considered dangerous since the angry spirit may seek revenge.

In some cases even animals can become a target of aggression. The elder Vladimir Torgonov remembered how his father once mistakenly killed a pregnant animal – a musk deer (*kabarga*) – which was a great sin. Blaming the animal for this misfortune, he grabbed a stick and started beating the dead deer to punish it. The Evenki of Khabarovsk even know a special way of achieving success through a beating, called *kongkonokhin* (Varlamova 2004: 70). Varlamova (ibid.) recorded the following story by the Evenki elder E. N. Solov'eva:

> Last year my son became disturbed [Rus. *maials'sia*] and could not hunt (Rus. *dobyt'*) anything. When he was leaving on a hunt I asked him, 'bring me some dry grass'. I made a male and female doll from it. Then I ordered him, 'take them along and feed them with some food. Tommorow take a wooden stick and walk up to them. Then beat [Rus. *otlupi*] them with the stick saying, 'don't do anything bad to me!' He beat the dolls well and this year he had a good harvest. My grandfather used to do this. It is only because my son was indeed in great difficulty that I did it.

Places, Spirits and Monsters

Anthropologists and archaeologists have stressed that the human perception of locality cannot be seen as passive, universal and abstract, but is rather a dynamic cultural process that involves an experientially grounded mode of human habitation (see Bender 1993; Bender and Wiget 2001; Hirsch and O'Hanlon 1995; Ryden 1993). Ethnographies show how personal knowledge, experience and life histories are linked to people's intimate attachments to certain places. According to Basso (1996: 55), the Western Apache hold that places are animated by the stories people tell about them and places animate the ideas and feelings of people. Landscape is represented in a set of 'mental images' conveyed through place names filled with moral stories of events that occurred in the past but still convey meanings to people in the present (ibid.). Such senses of place tend to be constructed through positive values and emotions described as 'moral teachings', 'wisdom', 'sharing' and 'respect' (see Ingold 2005: 399–410; Legat 2007). Local wisdom is created by accruing multiple 'lived experiences' that people connect with such places (see Basso 1996: 54). Ethnographic examples from various parts of the world have likewise demonstrated that indigenous people interact with ancestors and spirits through the landscape.[17] Such spirits, as inhabitants of the land, are seen as contributors to humans' well-being, providing food, guidance, and security (Ingold 2000: 142). Indeed, descriptions of indigenous people's interactions with places usually describe them as positive experiences and only rarely include references to violence and domination. However, social scientists also stress that people's experiences of space are not neutral or devoid of social context or conflict (see Harvey 1989: 238).

Orochen place-making is the outcome of a dynamic social and cognitive process that invests the location with meaning based on personal experience. I follow Casey (1996: 13–52), who proposed that place could be seen as the most fundamental form of embodied experience – the site of a powerful fusion of self, space and time. Orochen arrive at their knowledge of the landscape through active, practical, perceptual engagement with the dwelt-in world that is also built on the sociality of a manifold field of relationships with humans and nonhumans (see Ingold 2000). The landscape is also invested with meaning through narratives and mnemonic representations that shape present-day human activities.[18] Humans can sense the presence of master-spirits through their sight, smell, hearing or other embodied experiences. Certain caves, lakes, rocks and rock art sites are experienced as places with master-spirits to whom one attends, all the while engaging in social interactions. Hunters and herders often encounter the master-spirits when visiting these places. They vividly describe the master-spirit as a peculiar being that lives in different places. Local traditions also include stories linked to observable manifestations of master-spirits or places where the presence of spirits can be heard or felt. People point to remains of a 'master' found in the earth, a type of mammoth called *seli*.[19] Master-spirits can communicate with people at rock art sites by showing different drawings to those who are attentive. Hunters, herders and villagers see master-spirits as either bringing benefits or hurting people. The interaction with the spirits of different places reflects a person's emotional experiences, conditions critical incidents in life, evokes reciprocal relations and leads to experiences of either luck or failure. These nonhuman beings, fused with places and placings, can also foretell a person's future in terms of her or his life course, luck or reproductive success.

Interactions between nonhumans, places and humans create a 'sense of place'. The notion of 'sense of place' refers to an individual's or group's ability to experience and develop knowledge of particular settings based on combinations of use, attentiveness and emotion (see Casey 1996: 13–52). An Orochen hunter's sense of place depends primarily on his experience of luck or misfortune. Places associated with past humans and spirits also condition the daily experiences of hunters and herders. These experiences can shift through ongoing interactions among different people. In this context, the landscape is also experienced as being in a constant state of becoming. Recent post-Soviet policies have led people to reappropriate state territories, triggering competition over land among state officials, entrepreneurs and indigenous people. This situation also impacts peoples' experiences of places. Hunters and herders employ covert and overt discursive strategies and activities of aggression and cooperation to achieve success in subsistence as they struggle with local entrepreneurs and state officials. In this context, new forms of ritual performance have become an important means to appropriate the local landscape and claim mastery over it.

Ethnographers of Siberia have extensively described so-called 'sacred places' linked to 'spiritual power' or 'a spirit pantheon', where indigenous people perform rituals in order to acquire luck and maintain their well-being (for Altaians, see Halemba 2007: 39–49, for the Siberian Khanty, see Jordan 2003: 139–145). In Zabaikal'ia, we also find references to different places as 'shamanic': there is a 'shaman stone', 'a shaman pass', 'a shaman tree', 'a shaman hill' or 'shaman's drawings'. These sites are ascribed a special agency to act on humans' and nonhumans' lives and activities. Recently, some of these places have ceased to function: a rock art site may stop 'drawing'; springs with healing water or 'stone medicine' known as *mumio* may move to another place or hide from other beings.[20] Caves where people used to gain hunting luck through visions have also lost their power because geologists explored or excavated them, and ancestors may cease to inhabit a certain area when forest fires destroy physical signs of their presence, like graves. Indeed, various malevolent beings that existed in Evenki cosmology for centuries are continuously experienced and animated in contemporary storytelling. Today, these narratives link various tragic events, past policies, personal misbehaviour and loss of memory with current Evenki misfortunes.

A great number of tragic events, deaths, drunkenness and disabilities occurring in Orochen communities in Zabaikal'ia have left significant marks on the local landscape. The impacts of these events shape current experiences and memories of indigenous people, particularly those living in remote villages. Today, Evenki hunters and herders believe that many old, empty reindeer herders' camps and unattended mortuary sites, as well as various tragic places scattered throughout the taiga, have become sites that manifest the malevolent nonhuman beings. As in the years when ethnographer Sergei Shirokogoroff (1935: 137–138) conducted his fieldwork among Tungus (Evenki) in the Zabaikal'ia and Amur Province, today, people today believe that various 'bad places' continuously demand new victims and affect the well-being of various kin members and the community as a whole. The Orochen link all their current difficulties not only to an unpredictable post-Soviet economic environment but also to loss of memory of past tragic places combined with neglecting of interaction with spirits and ritual places during Soviet times.

Today, Orochen aim to reconfirm their relations with the landscape and the sentient beings that inhabit it. Primarily, they strive to calm forgotten and untamed local spirits and garner their support in dealing with current misfortunes or disabilities. Lavrillier (2003: 103), who carried out extensive fieldwork among the Evenki of Amur Province and southern Yakutia, similarly noticed that the local Evenki communities of Amur Province say their poor economic conditions are explained by their failure to honour their spirits. Likewise, Buyandelgeriyn (2007) noticed that the Buryats of Mongolia also attribute their current misfortunes to spirits who have returned to seek revenge for the abandonment of ritual practices. Hence, by talking about spirits, locating them in the landscape and contacting them through rituals, the Evenki aim to remaster taiga territories as well as their own destinies in an unpredictable socioeconomic environment. Today, local people talk extensively about widespread poaching activities, enormous humans' gluttony for resources and the current environment of competition between hunters in which taiga ethics may be ignored, animals are disrespected and hunters' and herders' storage sites occasionally plundered. In this context, local Evenki also refer to the profusion of revengeful and malevolent spirits (Oro. *arenkil*) as well as cannibal beings (Oro. *diaptygil*).

While working in the area in 1917, Shirokogoroff (1935: 121) stated that the relevance of these malevolent spirits (Oro. *arenkil*) was minor, though they could bring some small troubles. The current appearance of cannibalistic or monstrous features among various beings and their linkage to tragic events and places symbolizes Evenki's experience of the contemporary socioeconomic environment as unpredictable, even dangerous.[21] For the Evenki of Zabaikal'ia, various malevolent beings can be met anywhere in the taiga and can take the shape of a human or an animal. They can threaten someone in dreams and inflict physical and psychological damage or even kill a person. They are thought to influence hunting and herding success, health and well-being. When talking about malevolent beings, the Evenki of Zabaikal'ia describe events that occurred in the remote past but easily link them to their present life and extraordinary experiences in the taiga.

Hunters, herders and people based in villages all talked constantly about their vivid experiences with malevolent beings and humans that they meet in taiga and villages. They referred to these spirits as *arenkil*: monsters (Oro. *mangil*) and cannibals (Oro. *mangi, diaptygil*). Contemporary and Soviet ethnographers and folklorists also widely documented the persistence of storytelling about malevolent beings among Evenki living in various regions of Siberia. Such a being can be referred to as *arenki, molkosh, melkun, bugadyl, main* or *mekachony* among different groups of Evenki (see Simonova 2013: 259–274; Vorob'ev 2013: 46–47; Alekhin 2000; Maksimova 1994: 102; Simonov 1983: 104; Vasilevich, 1969: 222). In ethnographies these spirits abound at sites of tragic events, mortuary places and abandoned dwellings, or can be met anywhere in the taiga and even villages. Some Evenki folklore tales also depict cannibals (Oro. *changit, mangi* or *diaptar*) (see Vasilevich 1949; Varlamova 1996; Gabysheva 2012; Varlamov 2011).

The Evenki have often seen various historical tragedies like epidemics, the overhunting of their living territory and fights among different Evenki clans as connected with the activities of malevolent beings, shamans or spirits (see Anisimov 1963). Today as in the past, the Evenki of Zabaikal'ia Province experience the contemporary taiga as full of such angry, malevolent beings (Oro. *arenkil*) that significantly influence the success of subsistence activities and personal well-being. In the works of Shirokogoroff (1935: 138–165), there is no clearly established terminology and hierarchy of spirits based on their role, and the essence of various spirits can be seen ambiguously as both malevolent and benevolent. *Arenkil* can be described as the souls of hunters or herders who did not reach the world of the dead because of sudden or accidental death or because their souls were not ritually escorted there (ibid.: 137–138). According to Shirokogoroff (ibid.), these souls had to stay in this world being malevolent. It was believed that *arenkil* can even be powerful enough to be 'masters' of certain mountains or small regions (ibid.: 139).

Arenkil wandered the taiga and, according to Shirokogoroff (1935: 149–150), along 'roads' by which they entered and exited different placings either independently or upon being invited or enticed by humans. Any geographical location, tree, animal, human, artefact or part of an organ could become such a placing for the spirit (ibid.: 149–150, 160). The *arenkil* could influence a human mind and could also cause serious illness or lead hunters or a hunted animal astray (ibid.: 139–140). Their activities also encompassed lesser mischief like misleading humans in the forest, laying false tracks, frightening hunters and herders with lights in the darkness or making spooky noises.

> The *arenki* have no body. They are very numerous in the forest and marshes. However, sometimes they penetrate to the store houses erected near the wigwams. They stay in rotten hollow trees, sometimes even in living trees. When the Tungus cut down such a tree they may hear screams of *oniu* – i.e. 'painful' from these spirits. Such an accident is sufficient for causing a serious illness with a fatal outcome – the people lose their minds and die.... As a rule they are numerous near graves. The *arenki* may be seen in the form of light, usually bluish or reddish, also sometimes moving, but when people approach them they move farther away. They whistle. They produce an echo. Generally speaking they are mischievous. ... They are always hungry for their food they depend upon the people's generosity. (Shirokogoroff 1935: 139–140)

The Evenki of Transbaikal'ia often describe and know *arenkil* as always hungry, wishing to consume human souls or reduce their 'life energies' (Oro. *musun*) or luck (Oro. *kutu*). Having encountered such a spirit, one may fall ill or even die. Therefore, these beings are not simply mischievous but potentially very dangerous. As prominent reindeer herders once declared, 'all through the taiga, spirits started to act with violence' (Rus. *dukhi budorazhut po taezhnym debriam*).

During sable hunting season in the winter of 2004–2005, the prominent Evenki hunter Aleksei Aruneev and I stopped to smoke a cigarette on a road passing a pine-covered hill on the western banks of the Levyi Kotomchik River (see Fig. 4.1). Aleksei pointed to a hill he called Pine Tree Hill (Sosnovaia Sopka) and said it was a very unlucky (Rus. *nefartovaia*) place that should be avoided. He typically smoked cigarettes while travelling on foot, but on this rare occasion he abstained due to the location. He told me his brother had once injured his ankle when he did not stop there to show proper respect. Aleksei also said he never crossed the river to visit that hill, even though sable and musk deer abound there. He decided to abandon the site, saying it was 'really bad to go there' (Rus. *stram poiti tuda*). In the past, Aleksey had never had any hunting luck there, though many times he tried to appease the local spirits by feeding them (Rus. *nosil ugashchenie*). His relative Yura Aruneev also told me about several tragic, spooky incidents that had occurred in the area of that hill. Several years earlier, a spirit had caused him great distress when he decided to camp near the hill. The *arenki* made his dogs and reindeer go crazy, and he heard voices and a domestic reindeer herd passing the place. Furthermore, a visiting relative had been stabbed by a reindeer herder during a drunken skirmish in that place. The elderly father of the deceased even tried to kill the spirit by setting fire to the forested hill; however, the spirit is still active there.

Some reindeer herders sought the counsel of a female shaman in the Aga Buryat Autonomous District, who told them to look for the remnants of an old mortuary site presumed to be located near the hill. Local hunters and reindeer herders believed the soul of an Evenki shaman buried there was continuously causing trouble for people who camp or move around. Reindeer herders Nikolai and Olga regularly used to sprinkle tea in the direction of this place when camping at distant reindeer herders' camps. They hoped to locate a mortuary platform and then establish positive relations with the place so as to use the area for reindeer herding and hunting, as they lacked good reindeer pastures and wanted also to use the river basin for reindeer grazing. Hunters who do not manage to establish reciprocal relations with a local spirit often leave the area. Similarly, Shirokogoroff (1935: 87) described how some Tungus felt a certain place should be avoided because of the presence of spirits until other Tungus reported that they felt nothing. If a spirit's activity was not noticed, 'the original safety of the place is restored' (ibid.).

Quite a number of Tungokochen villagers, reindeer herders and hunters had stories of encounters with *arenkil*. These nonhuman beings could talk to people, ask for cigarettes or food, tease dogs, steal different items, disorient people and even drive humans and animals insane. People said that *arenkil* are hungry for human food (especially liver) and attack humans who refuse to share with other beings. Furthermore, in some cases the *arenkil* might be eager to turn living humans into souls; hence, even encountering *arenkil* in a dream is considered a bad sign meaning illness. People say that without the support of master-spirits, a person is extremely vulnerable to such malevolent spirits.

Orochen I lived with also refer to some nonhumans as cannibals (Oro. *changit, mangi* or *diaptygil*). Similar to *arenki,* these beings are considered to be extremely dangerous, very hungry beings that are both anxious to consume food or vital body parts of humans, such as the heart, liver or intestines, and thirsty for blood or one's 'life energy'. Elder hunters and herders from Tungokochen, Zelenoe Ozero and Ust' Karenga villages told of how, during the Soviet years, they had encountered hungry beings that looked like humans in the taiga. Such human-like beings were regarded as cannibals and called *bamlak* (i.e. beings of the Baikal Amur Railroad, BAM) and were associated with prisoners and workers labouring at industrial sites in Transbaikal'ia. The elder Olga Zhumaneeva warned me that in the taiga one can still meet dangerous and very hungry *bamlak* who can bring serious harm. In the past, such meetings in the taiga had been plentiful. These stories can be linked to the widespread storytelling in Siberia about prisoners escaping the gulags who used to take one colleague to be consumed as food on their long trip across the taiga. Indeed, many areas in Siberia are marked by instruments of Soviet policies of domination, such as labour camps, prisons, and railroads or roads built by political and criminal prisoners and deportees sent to Siberia from all over the Soviet Union. Evenki of different regions say that some of the indigenous villages and roads were constructed directly over humans' bones. The description of *bamlak,* sometimes called *diaptygil* (Oro. *diaptar* 'eat'), can be seen as an outcome of the fusion of repressive state policies and existing Evenki cosmologies. Ethnologists Archakova and Trifunova (2006) also noticed that Siberian Eveny attributed various features of cannibalism to the state officials associated with domination or danger, such as the tsar's tax collectors and military personnel. In a similar vein, Cossacks who used to bring wine to the Evenki of Amur in order to weaken them also had similar images of cannibals (ibid.).[22]

In her book, Ulturgasheva (2012) also reports that 'wandering spirits of the dead', called *arenkael* by Eveny, are associated with the repressive policies of the Soviet Gulag. In this way, stories related to malevolent ghosts are symbolically associated with suffering, violence and the deaths of prisoners. The Eveny's *arenkael* were originally forest spirits, but today these spirits are present in village buildings, thus transforming perceptions of locality and affecting present Eveny experiences of life lived in a cursed place (ibid.). In a similar vein, Simonova (2013) reports that among Tungus-Evenki living in the northern part of Lake Baikal, various malevolent beings have become very active not only in the taiga but also in villages as well as former abandoned industrial sites. Hence, abandoned places have connections with the idea of governmental violence and the devastation of formerly prosperous places that consigns people to an unstable life. Gordillo (2004) aptly notices that such spatialized memories and experiences of indigenous people are active forces in the production of various monstrous beings and meaningful places. Furthermore, the environment of competition for resources leads people to believe that in a context of scarcity, this feature of cannibalism can be realized by any malevolent, greedy or revengeful being, be it animal, spirit or human (see cannibal shamans in Stépanoff 2009).[23]

Various stories about dangerous beings told in the camps of Evenki reindeer herders and hunters have the aim of instilling a sense of fear as well as awareness of possible danger. Narratives linked to the monster-cannibals usually tell of skilful humans who escape monster-cannibals. Such stories provide the audience with emotional inspiration and implicit suggestions of the various possible ways of escaping danger, such as by creating different obstacles for the monster to follow or other ways of misleading or deceiving the monster. Furthermore, these stories can teach moral ways of behaving in the world, such as reciprocal relations while interacting with other humans, nonhumans and places. A good example of the fusion of fear, morality and awareness is found in the Evenki game called Channit-Khalganchuluk. As the explorer Klitsenko (2009) documents, the game was recently re-enacted and played by children of Surinda village in Evenkiia. Channit-Khalganchuluk is a one-eyed, one-legged, one-armed monster represented by a specially dressed Evenki child. For the game to start, the smartest child is chosen to play the key role of the monster-cannibal in a fair way. The monster has to catch a 'caravan' made of children and choose any child to be eaten. A dialogue established between the monster and an individual player helps to depict what is right or wrong. As Klitsenko (2009) aptly notices, this game helps children make moral judgements and identify sinful behaviour (*ngelome*). The aim is also to develop the children's awareness of signs that predict future misfortunes. Such signs are known as *nengo* among the Evenki (see also Alekhin 1998: 79–80).

The morality of stories linked to monsters, ghosts and cannibals always refers to the violation of normative rules or ethics. People believe that accidental disrespect to the spirits and ritual sites, along with theft of different objects from old storage platforms or mortuary scaffolds, has caused disabilities for many people. Greedy people can potentially die tragically and become *arenkil* themselves. Disrespect and greediness linked to hunting and use of other resources often turns people into victims who either lose luck or health, or remain troubled by spirits or anxious about something until their death. Among the Algonquin language family groups, images of a nonhuman being called a *windigo* are continuously animated in narratives linked to aggression and cannibalism. The *windigo* is described as gigantic human-like creature or spirit who wanders in the forest and has a heart of ice (Ferrara and Lanoue 2004; Mermann-Jozwiak 1997: 45; Teicher 1960: 7). This being has the desire to eat human flesh and also displays qualities of selfishness 'to the point of becoming monstrous' (Mermann-Jozwiak 1997: 45). A human can be transformed into an malevolent spirit or monster through misbehaviour or through possession, witchcraft and extreme starvation (Podruchny 2004; Brightman 1993: 137–159; Ridington 1990: 160). For Ridington (1976), the phenomenon of humans turning into the cannibalistic monsters known among Algonquians and Athabaskans as *wechuge* was no simple psychosis, but a social sickness linked to the influx of strangers and mixing with peoples who did not know the taboos associated with sacred bundles. In other cases *wechuge* can be associated with strangers who threaten internal social cohesion and the disruptive influence of contacts with Europeans.

Similarly, Feit (2004) describes how among the Cree, 'other', White men are associated with the being *atuush* (similar to the *windigo* described above). The *atuush* is a cannibal monster that lives in the forest and occasionally captures people for food or keeps them as slaves. Today, *atuush* is used as a metaphor among the Cree to describe the moral delinquency of any person (ibid.). Hence, the image of *atuush* is about antisocial behaviour stemming from self-interest, irresponsibility and exploitation, or about the commodification of humans' relationship with the environment in the context of growing conflict with Euro-Canadians over various development projects (ibid.). According to Feit (2004: 123), the *atuush* can be overcome by going into the forest and reuniting people, spirits and the environment. Similarly, both nomadic and village Evenki believe that performing rituals of respect and reciprocity and returning to nomadic life might help to calm the forces located in the landscape and even get them to act on the behalf of people in the taiga and the villages.

In an unpredictable environment, various malevolent beings embody threats and violence that have occurred in the past or present and have a continuously negative affect on the current life of humans living in the area. Today, these beings have become displaced from the taiga and localized in villages, buildings or neglected industrial sites, but they also can still be met wandering the taiga. All these landscape features, infused with bad memories, tragic events and spooky manifestations, shape the Orochen experience of place. Orochen strategies of dealing with these beings include the revival of memory of past tragic events as well as storytelling. This includes being aware of old and neglected camps, storage platforms, mortuary scaffolds or rock art sites. Orochen strive to appeal to these spirits by engaging them through ritual and creating reciprocal relations.

Various malevolent beings that existed in Orochen cosmology for centuries and that have attributes of gluttony and in some cases anthropophagy, today, are continuously experienced and animated in contemporary Evenki storytelling. Orochen link the influence of malevolent beings with dominative state policies and tragic events, ruptures of ethical norms and personal misbehaviour. Telling and participating in the storytelling empowers Evenki to exert some of the predictability over their lives and subsistence and promote awareness of potential dangers at the same time teaching appropriate moral behaviour and judgements.

In this chapter I aimed to show that luck does not flow simply from the master-spirits' goodwill as outcome of reciprocal relations; rather, it is achieved by humans through complex processes of competition with an animals and spirits. Furthermore, maintaining luck requires much skill and knowledge, for luck must be predicted, dreamed, attracted, caught, shared, secured and contained by interacting with other humans and nonhuman beings (animals, spirits and places) as well as crafted material objects like amulets or wooden idols (Oro. *seveki*). By these means, people often tend to risk and gain desired hunting results through various forms of domination, which are also regarded as clandestine practices and sinful behaviour that call for spirits' revenge. These practices are often linked to the gluttony of humans, state powers or high-ranking officials on a continuum of displaced fields of relations between humans, nonhumans and the landscape.

Notes

1. Siberian ethnography features examples of shamans blowing air into a patient's mouth in order to retrieve his soul (Vasilevich 1969: 240).
2. The Evenki of the Sym River call the wagging of a dog's tail *omimi*, translated as 'external soul manifestation' (Maksimova 1994: 83).
3. The leader of reindeer herders Nikolai Aruneev, who was thoroughly familiar with New Age literature, preferred to use the word *energiia* (see also Zna-

menski 2007: 354). Indeed, *energiia* was a word well known to all villagers because it had been used by the formerly popular healer Kashpirovskii, who performed on Russian television in the early 1990s.

4. Alekseev (1975: 32) similarly elaborates on *ichi* 'mystical power' among the neighbouring Yakut. He also refers to *ichi* as the property of the *khoziain* (ibid.).

5. Images of animals reflect knowledge of an animal's agency and personal experiences of the interactions between humans and animals as sentient beings, which are supported by a person's empirical observations (see Scott 2006: 60–61).

6. Sympathy aims at making another's experiences or state of mind one's own. On the difference between sympathy and empathy, see Wispe (1986).

7. On communication via empathy, see Vreecke and Van der Mark (2003). On animals' empathy and emotions, see Damasio (1999).

8. Ulturgasheva (2012) points out that a 'volatile soul' and a weak connection between soul and body make a person vulnerable to attacks by predatory spirits.

9. The famous Russian explorer Potanin (1883: 697) described the same Orochen ritual as performed near the fireplace before leaving camp. A kettle was put on the cleaned ashes, an elder told stories and afterwards the hunters would lift the kettle and search for animal tracks (ibid.).

10. See the early records on Zabaikal Orochen dreaming in Nirguneev (1928: 44) and for the Enisei Evenki in Rychkov (1917: 266–267).

11. Nikolai told of how, when looking into a pool of water in the taiga, he had seen images and heard sounds that told about critical events in his family.

12. Such bundles also include the furs of various animals, which are smoked and used for predicting hunting luck.

13. I mainly refer to *nimnakans* told by the elder Agafiia Dandeeva from Rossoshino village (Buryatia) to Vladimir Torgonov and Anna Naikanchina between 1992 and 1998.

14. Swearing is described as an important ritual practice for banishing spirits among Zabaikal'ia Russians (on mastery and swearing, see Basharov 2003: 12).

15. According to Shirokogoroff (1935: 191–197) placing (Rus. *vmestilishcha*) a Tungus (Evenki) notion, which means a material object (idol, crafted item, place) or alive being (tree, human or animal) inhabited by the spirit or humans' soul.

16. Orochen elder Vladimir Torgonov remembers that *seveki* is not the best word to call a dangerous person.

17. For Australia, see Morphy (1995) and Myers (1986), for Papua New Guinea, Kahn (1990), for Canada, Hallowell (1960).

18. On histories of disease and places, see Vitebsky (199; on memoryscapes among Inuit, see Nuttall (1992: 38–58); on storytelling and local landscape in the Yukon Territory, see Cruikshank (1998).

19. The Orochen tell a story, which is also known to many Evenki groups, that the landscape was created by the struggle between a mammoth (Oro. *seli*) and a giant snake (Oro. *diabtar*) (Anisimov 1958: 134–135; Mazin 1984: 20–21; Vasilevich 1936: 280).

20. *Mumio*, locally called 'stone oil' (Oro. *delaniuksa*, R. *kamenoe maslo*), is a well-known medicine harvested from cracked rocks that is believed to strengthen a person's metabolism.
21. In their storytelling, Khanty employ an image of a large man with an iron stomach and big cap who is able to eat everything he encounters (see Novikova 2014: 182). This new negative image evolved out of Khanty interactions with oil companies to replace the earlier images of villains in traditional folklore (ibid.).
22. King (1999) also shows how among the Koryak, images of vampire shamans (*kalaw*) can be seen as culturally appropriate symbols and metaphors for describing current difficulties or people who refer to officials draining of public resources for personal economic wellness. In the stories of Koryak people, *kalaw* can 'prey upon other people, draining their spiritual energy or life force in order to gain extra power or maintain unusual youth and prolong their life' (ibid: 59). Today, in the present insecure economic environment, people are divided into victims and *kalaw*: 'Koryak administrators and managers are analogous to vampire shamans draining the vestiges of a vital force from a now-dead corpse [Russian economy touched by crisis]' (ibid: 64).
23. Similarly, Vasilevich (1968) noticed that during healing rituals in the past, Evenki shamans could eat humans' souls as well as spirits.

CHAPTER THREE

Sharing, Trust and Accumulation

My process of being accepted into hunting expeditions and becoming a trustworthy person involved different stages and was not much different from how local hunters establish relationships. At first all my activities were under constant observation, and I was not allowed to touch certain hunting or harnessing tools or take photographs. Trust was attained through the shared experience of spending time with people and learning how to perform daily chores. At the beginning of my fieldwork, when I spent some time with hunters from Ust' Karenga village, I was surprised to find that our hunting results were somehow considered contingent on my participation. I was reported to be an 'unlucky' person (Rus. *nefartovyi*) because on each trip I participated in, it rained constantly and we did not encounter any hunted animals.

My second round of involvement, with hunting groups from Tungokochen village, was marked by success – which, I believe, was a very important factor in my being accepted on further hunting trips. During rutting season, we managed to kill two moose, four roe deer and a rabbit in a relatively short time. I was taken to a rock art site in Dukuvuchi, and hunting luck stuck with us. Moreover, the weather was continuously sunny and cold, and thus very suitable for travelling. Our horses never stumbled because the soil surface was frozen, and we killed various small animals every day. We ultimately managed to get home without being seen by other villagers or running into state officials.[1] Our horses and dogs were healthy and returned in good condition. With each successful hunting trip, the shared experience of luck integrated me further into the circle of hunters. Finally, Aleksei stopped calling me *mata* in Orochen, that is, 'the person from afar' or 'stranger', and started referring to me as 'friend' (Rus. *drug*) before the other members of the hunting group and the village community at large. His wife then acknowledged me in public, saying, 'Well now, you are a lucky person' (Rus. *odnako, ty fartovyi*). Thereafter Aleksei would even wait for me to join a hunting trip when I was away from the village. The elder hunter Chulan Kirilov told me that in the past, Orochen hunters took young boys along to cook and help out, selecting them with regard to their 'ability' to bring luck or failure to the hunting group. Only 'lucky boys' (Rus. *fartovyi malchiki*) were invited to participate. Only after one year of fieldwork did Aleksei suggest that I use his hunting tools and dogs on my own hunting trips.

Hunting in remote taiga areas required considerable resources and gear, such as means of transportation, petrol, dogs, ammunition, traps, stoves, tents, footwear and provisions. For this reason hunters were likely to organize joint hunting groups, pooling all available resources. These cooperative arrangements tend to be based on kinship relations, but the wide range of skills and tools required in hunting always calls for the inclusion of unrelated individuals. Hunters would say that the 'taiga has ears and eyes', and therefore any individual's action, speech, thought and previous hunting history have some influence on their present-day success. Any participant in a hunting expedition can have an effect on the hunting luck of her or his companions. Thus, alongside mastery of certain skills, trust and previous experiences of luck are the main requirements for building a hunting group.

In this chapter I will describe how people act either cooperatively or independently, according to their previous experiences of trust and luck. I will elaborate on two forms of cooperation among local hunters: friendship (Rus. *druzhba*) and companionship (Rus. *naparniki*). I will suggest that they are based on different levels of sharing and exchanging favours as well as different experiences of luck. Feelings of trust or lack of trust shape the way herders and hunters organize their camps and storage platforms in the taiga and influence the dynamics of cooperation between individuals. Reindeer herders secure access to their camps and caches and provide for their future in the unstable post-Soviet environment by hoarding goods.[2] Nevertheless, hoarding and refusing to share accumulated goods, animals, skills or knowledge with relatives also entails the risk of eventually attracting misfortune. Hence, refusing to share with kin or close friends is seen as the opposite of *nimat* (see Introduction) and can be considered a sin (Oro. *ngelome*) that is likely to endanger one's luck.

Sharing Luck

For the past two years, Aleksei Aruneev had hunted sable, squirrel and other fur-bearing animals in the Siligli River basin in the company of Yura Epov, a hunter of Tungus-Russian origin. Yura, who was also called Gluhar' (Capercaillie), was a former collective farm driver and owned a truck that hunters loaded with their winter hunting and camping gear, including their dogs, for the trip to the remote winter cabins. Yura's brother Misha worked as the driver for the administration of Tungokochen village, so if the truck was too expensive to use he could always use the administration's UAZ van to help the hunters move. As most hunters do, Yura and Aleksei called each other *naparnik,* shared the costs of gasoline and split the killed game. However, so-called black gold – sable fur – was collected individually by each.

Naparnik relationships are easily threatened by lack of hunting success, as one member of the hunting party may be accused of spoiling the luck of the whole group. Such misfortune need not necessarily be caused by a person's incompetent performance or lack of skills. Nonhuman beings seeking revenge on a person will bring bad luck to the people that person cooperates with. This makes *naparnik* relationships even more unstable. *Naparnik* relationships between people can be considered pragmatic and therefore more easily threatened than those built on kinship or friendship ties. Hunting relationships may indeed be limited to a single transaction whose failure means the end of such cooperation.

Another form of cooperation, *druzhba* – literally 'friendship' – is based on mutual aid and unselfish sharing and allows access to different resources and knowledge for the perpetuation of luck. In *druzhba,* neither the expenses nor the outcome matters. Exchanges among *druziia* (friends) are not necessarily equal and are often referred to as aid, sharing (Oro. *nimat*) or a treat (Oro. *kundulo*). Some hunters even collect their fur into one pile called 'the common pot' (Rus. *obschii kotel*), which is then divided among *druziia.* A hunting trip's outcome depends on the group's luck. Usually, cooperation among *naparnik* hinges on a calculation of benefits for both parties, whereas *druziia* entails a network of reciprocity based on sympathy and mutual interrelatedness. It differs from *naparnik* in the degree of trust. In *druzhba* relationships, as opposed to *naparnik* relationships, failure does not endanger the friendship. A successful friend can share his luck and give it to another hunter through joint activities.

Oleg Taskerov from Ust' Karenga village told me that once he lost his luck when hunting musk deer and was unable to kill an animal for a substantial period of time, although he came very close to it. Later attempts to snare animals also brought no results. Finally, Oleg asked a friend who had luck in hunting musk deer to help him get his luck back (Rus. *vernut' fart*). Hence, friendship (Rus. *druzhba*) implies a long-lasting relationship where hunters exchange not only resources but also luck.

In cases of *druzhba,* not even lack of hunting success can endanger the mutual relationship. Sharing luck is not considered dangerous: friends can share without risking the loss of their own luck. According to Nikolai, though, sharing with strangers or *naparniki* entails some risk of 'giving luck away'. The risk increases when the giving is done in response to pressure or demands. Hence, some hunters never use their hands to offer pieces of meat to someone who has approached the house and asked for meat. Instead guests help themselves to chunks that are placed on the floor. This keeps luck from being 'given away'. To that same end some hunters never shared cartridges, and the head of an animal was never given away. In the local ways of cooperation, differences between the economic benefits of the market economy, local practices of sharing and ideas of luck became blurred. Also blurred was the contrast between transactions known as gift exchange among relatives in so-called traditional societies, and commodity exchange among socially distant individuals in so-called modern societies as described by Sahlins (1972). In local cooperative relations, the two forms have different implications that include notions of sharing, exchange, trust, and economic benefits and create a different quality of relationship among actors.

I usually brought a large quantity of goods to the taiga to share with the hunters, sometimes having received an 'order' for particular items. Mostly I had to decide on my own what to give to my friends. Such participation in a circle of reciprocity among friends and relatives is also linked to the idea of exchanging luck. The items I brought were often considered to bring luck (Rus. *fartovye veshchi*). People believe friends can bring luck by giving each other various kinds of tools or gear, whereas demanding or receiving items from people with a bad reputation is likely to entail risk and danger for the recipient. Some hunters also claim that generosity must not be insisted upon because a direct order can be understood as a form of coercion that may cause misfortune for both parties.

'Being My Own Master': Accumulation and Mistrust

Reindeer herders would not be able to maintain their remote herding and hunting territories and camps without large amounts of supplies that they take twice a year to storage sites scattered across the taiga. In the herders' community, Nikolai Aruneev was the main organizer of supplies via his fur trading in Usugli or Chita. Nikolai, who in the taiga wore mostly worn-out clothing layered with patches, changed quite noticeably into a well-dressed man when in the village. He usually got a haircut first and then exchanged his taiga clothes for a clean, well-fitting ensemble, becoming a completely different person in a black leather jacket and polished shoes with a leather briefcase under his arm like the head of a collective farm. Twice a year Nikolai would come to Tungokochen village and spend two weeks visiting various households to exchange news, which is crucial in contexts where there is no telephone service or regular mail connection. The exchanging of news and telling of jokes and tall tales was also a way of maintaining his relationships.

In the city, Nikolai stocked up on provisions, traded his furs and acquired the items he needed for his camp. He usually got good value for his furs. All the items he purchased at various stores were transported to his camps in a large vehicle with a driver that he hired in the city of Chita. He usually bought gear from the storage rooms of state institutions connected with reindeer herding, such as geological expeditions that the herders had worked for. Reindeer medicine and wolf poison are in short supply nowadays, and good contacts with institutions that were established in Soviet times are still key to getting access to these valuable resources. To ensure successful transportation, Nikolai typically tried to avoid interacting with people in the villages on his way back, especially after a large purchase of groceries (see Table 3.1).

In autumn 2004 Nikolai Aruneev had his goods transported by truck from Chita to his camp. On the return trip the truck was loaded with reindeer meat, *kamus* and a variety of peculiar animal parts, such as penises and soft velveted antlers (Rus. *panty*), that are highly valued as alternative medicine, along with dried antlers, which also have a high market value. Each chunk of meat from four reindeer bore a tag with the address of the recipient in Nikolai's *naparniki* network in the cities. As the truck driver told me, Nikolai tried to increase the meat's value by constantly stressing that reindeer meat had medicinal qualities and was even useful for 'cleansing the body of the negative

Table 3.1. | *The variety of groceries imported to the storage platform in autumn 2004.*

Products	Quantity	Expected period
Flour	1,000 kg	6 months
Macaroni	120 kg	6 months
Sugar	150 kg	6 months
Salt	500 kg^3	6 months
Rice	100 kg	6 months
Tea	120 packs (100 g each)	6 months
Cooking oil	48 bottles (1 litre each)	6 months
Butter	10–20 kg	6 months
Fat	10 kg	6 months
Candy	12 kg	6 months
Dry Soup	50 packets (90 gr each)	6 months
Dry Milk	10 kg	6 months
Spring wheat	50 kg	6 months
Onion	5 kg	6 months
Garlic	5 kg	6 months
Potatoes	50 kg	6 months
Soda	4 kg	12 months
Dry yeast	0.5 kg	12 months
Cabbage	10 kg	6 months
Canned vegetable soup	24 cans (500 g each)	6 months
Spices	Some	6 months
Ketchup and mustard	Some	6 months

influence of radiation'. The veterinarian in Tungukochen generally received one piece of meat in return for writing a license for meat transportation. Another went to the head of the administration, while many others were circulated in the city-based exchange network that Nikolai had built up over a decade of trading fur and negotiating with officials about various reindeer herding issues. Finally, the driver was happy to have received his own winter's meat supply upon returning from the taiga camps.

All goods brought from the city to the taiga were deposited in specially built caches. Storage sites that were important in Soviet times are neglected today, and others have been established or re-established for storing or hiding valuable goods. The Zhumaneev-Aruneev family used three caches built near their long-term camps after the collapse of the Soviet Union, as well as several former collective farm caches that had been repaired. Some of these caches are located close to the main Kotomchik base camp, three are near the Poperechnaia River winter camp and four others are scattered in the vicinity of seasonal campsites at the Bugarikhta, Bukteni and Siligli Rivers and in a remote winter hunting site in the Nercha River basin. Groceries and other goods are often moved from one cache to another by reindeer. Thus the remote camps are supplied with supplies easily accessed at a cache close by.

Siberian storage architecture and its seasonal, functional use have received considerable interest in the Russian ethnographic tradition (Turov 1974, 1975; Vasilevich 1961; Sirina 2006: 138–143). Evenki cache-type structures are described as seasonal storage platforms designed to store winter or summer gear, meat, berries and dried fish. The caches also hold broken items like old guns, bowls, fur clothing or ritual items (see Arbatskii 1981, 1982). For some authors, like Turov (1975), the structural variety and specialization of these storage facilities demonstrates the development of more elaborate Evenki economic and spatial practices. The Orochen elder Chulan Kirilov from Bugunda village still remembers that in pre-Soviet times most caches were built near the main trading routes to store items for trade. The traders travelled from the city of Nerchinsk to remote areas to trade with the Orochen, and the local reindeer herders and hunters visited these trading routes to offer fur, berries, cedar nuts, birds, and meat in exchange for sugar, flour and ammunition. The Orochen visited these platforms while hunting and herding reindeer, transporting their goods piece by piece from one storage site to another in their hunting and herding areas. Elders say that these caches were well known and accessible to anybody. The Zhumaneev-Aruneev family's storage system demonstrates how hunters and herders creatively adapt to socioeconomic realities like mistrust, the shifting market economy and an environment of shortage. Anisimov (1936) describes how, in times of inter-clan warfare, storage caches that held various goods and were located in areas of different seasonal activities served as reserve bases and even strongholds. Today these storage platforms once again form a buffer against resource shortages, enabling people to maintaining their autonomy in the face of short-term shifts in the resource supply.

The family's newest storage site, built near the fur hunting camp of Poperechnaia, is a large platform on four legs with a rectangular log frame and a ˜span roof. It was built after the collapse of the Soviet Union and subsequent shift in reindeer herding from collective to private ownership. Together with an experienced reindeer herder named Gena Dushinov, Nikolai's stepfather, Gena Kirilov, built the platform in the early 1990s to store the gear of the newly established Boiun reindeer herders' community. The wooden structure was elevated on the limbless boles of four larch trees that that had measured six metres in height when they were green. Three metres off the ground on these posts, the log structure held eight square metres of storage space. The supporting trunks were rooted and could therefore be expected to steadily support the platform for a long time. The roofing was initially made from several layers of larch-bark sheets flattened with a pole (Oro. *triovka*). Later, newly acquired tar sheets replaced the bark. This example illustrates the Orochen's tendency to use building materials based on their availability, as they do with any resource (see also Anderson 2006a: 2).

The system of caches and platforms is perfectly suited to storing goods of any kind in the taiga. They are well protected from the rain and damp. The Zhumaneev-Aruneev family's caches were filled with a large variety of items: ammunition, gasoline, military winter and summer outdoor clothing, footwear, new cold-weather cotton jackets (Rus. *fufaiki*), gloves, caps, canvas for tents, plastic sheets, traps, salt, cigarettes, vodka, blankets, sleeping bags, some reindeer medicine, a radio, three nicely adorned pairs of footwear (Rus. *unty*) made from *kamus*, two pairs of buckskin footwear (Oro. *emchure*), extra fishing nets and wool fabric for lining boots. In addition to the permanently stored goods, they usually contained hunting trophies, tanned buckskin, rawhide and dried animal skins. I found that a cache also contained plants, peculiar parts of birds (the clawed feet of sea eagles and owls) and oddly coloured furs used as amulets to attract luck. In the fur-hunting season, fur pelts were stored in a cache far away from the trapping camp. The caches near the Kotomchik base camp and the Poperechniaia River contained a mixture of goods useful for different seasons and were mostly used for long-term storage.

Near the main winter camp on the Poperechnaia River, two large caches built in late Soviet times were located about three hundred metres from the camp and from each other. In the 1990s a third cache was built in the same area about six hundred metres from the camp and hardly visible from there (see Map 5.4). The large number of caches scattered throughout the taiga illustrates the nomadic lifestyle of a group of hunters and their ability to exploit a fairly large territory. Most caches also hold various tools and equipment that became available with the collapse of the centralized system of state distribution. Such use of storage sites is a good example of how herders strive to secure their future by accumulating various goods in the same way they have done throughout history (see Turov 1975). In the unstable, insecure socioeconomic environment, the goods stored in remote caches are fundamental to the herders' autonomy.

Furthermore, the family's storing strategy shows how the reindeer herders creatively adapted structures from Soviet times to their own way of life. In Soviet times, a *baza* was the territory of a collective farmhouse built in the 1980s to provide hunters and herders with more comfortable living conditions in the taiga. Volodia Balakhshyn, a former official of the Tungokochen reindeer herding farm, told me that these houses were designed as permanent dwellings, a 'place for reindeer herders and hunters to rest comfortably after work'. The *baza* was divided into two big rooms, one assigned to herders and the other to hunters. Each room was fitted with a durable, heavy metal stove for heating and cooking. In addition, a sauna and a small shelter for a diesel electric generator were built next to the house. In more recent times the *baza* had been rearranged and outfitted according to the specific needs of the reindeer herders. The house was rarely lived in for lengthy periods, and the electrical generator was never used. Since the log house was located at the end of the taiga road, it served as an initial storage area where all incoming goods were kept.

The *baza*'s space was organized in the same way as a short-term camp. It contained different activity zones around the log house: a corral, several campfires, drying racks, open meat storage platforms (Oro. *delken*), a cache. In the second room of the log house, which was used as a storage space, three elevated platforms were built. A meat storage pit (Oro. *ulatki*) was dug beneath the floor. Personal belongings hung all over the walls and from the low ceiling. When most of the gear was transported to another cache farther away, the *baza* was used as a storage site for all kinds of less valuable or 'disposable' stuff and various by-products of hunting such as skins, furs, sinews and some antlers. In the winter of 2004–2005, hunters and herders made multiple visits to the *baza* and to nearby platforms while transporting goods to the area by reindeer. Some goods were stored at sites farther away from the base camp. Two caches near the *baza* at the Kotomchik River contained smaller quantities of the same kinds of items as the cache at the Poperechnaia River.

Caches located near the base camp were known by the names of their owners, for example 'Yura's cache' or 'Nikolai's cache', and were used for storing fur (Fig. 3.1). Farm officials encouraged the hunters to build such individual storage places in order to hoard hunted fur individually and increase hunting productivity through competition

Figure 3.1. | *Nikolai Aruneev inspecting his fur in the cache.*

among hunters.[4] Today, some of the Zhumaneev-Aruneev family's storage caches are accessible to all members of the family. Some visiting herders have also stored their personal belongings there along with items belonging to family members. The accumulation and storage of resources can be seen as a successful adaptation to the post-Soviet environment, replacing supply mechanisms once centred on the collective farm. Yura Aruneev constantly repeated to me during my research, 'I am my own master and do not need to report to anybody' (Rus. *ia sam sebe khoziain i ne daiu otshchetu nikomu*).

Hunters move some of their supplies by reindeer each time they migrate from one camp to another, while still keeping an eye on their main storage sites. In the post-Soviet environment the lack of trust has shaped the way reindeer herders establish and use their storage sites. All the Zhumaneev-Aruneev family's storage platforms are located near important campsites so that the reindeer herders can attend to them regularly. According to Aleksei Aruneev, 'villagers always take what is left unattended'. The most important caches are built far from the camping area, in the dense forest (Oro. *siikhi*), so that even in wintertime they are hardly visible. The specially made ladders for accessing the platform are carefully hidden. Several times I tried to check the content of a cache when walking alone in the taiga, but did not manage to find the ladder to climb. The most highly valued privately owned goods were not stored there but at other sites – located 'farther away from the others' eyes' (Rus. *podalshe ot chuzhykh glaz*), as Nikolai said – that I was never shown. It was not easy to locate the storage place when standing in the camp. As Dobromyslov (1902: 79–80) noticed, 'although there is a reindeer track, there are no footprints of people [Orochen] leading to this cache. ... Nobody knows when one visits this cache except the master of the cache'.

In Soviet times, the Kotomchik River log house (Rus. *baza*) was seen as place of comfort, but today it is not considered a safe place to store valuable goods. Its location is well known and it is easily accessed by villagers. Indeed, villagers have already once plundered the house, carrying off some tools and bags of flour on horseback. The base house was a 'public place' where the herders met with truck drivers and administrators. Villagers who were not related to reindeer herders were usually not allowed in a herder's camp. Reindeer herders stayed at the house just for a few nights, taking steam baths and inspecting their stores while migrating with their reindeer. It would probably be impossible to maintain a reindeer herd and store goods if the herding territory were not located some distance from the villages (e.g., seventy kilometres from Ust' Karenga and two hundred kilometres from Tungokochen).

The Zhumaneev-Aruneev family group allowed their relatives, who were former reindeer herders, to hunt in areas of their territory that are close to the villages and are not used for herding. Hence, Nikolai's brother Aleksei Aruneev, his uncle Gilton Aruniev, and his cousin Andrei Zhumaneev used a hunting territory in the south. The territory of the former reindeer herder and kinsman Gena Malkov from Zelenoe Ozero village and Gena Garponeev, who still owned seven pack reindeer and used them for hunting, lay to the east. In the north was the hunting territory of Lionia Unaulov, a herder from Ust' Karenga village. These men usually used to spend part of their time in the reindeer herders' camps working together with the Zhumaneev-Aruneev unit. In the north-western part of the territory, the former reindeer herders of the Taskerov family from Ust' Karenga village continued to hunt. Hunters and herders often shared goods with their neighbours, who formed a kind of trustworthy screen for reindeer herding activities and the storage of goods.

The Zhumaneev-Aruneev family took various measures to make their platforms inaccessible to scavengers like ermines, sables, mice, bears and birds. All the posts were stripped of bark, thus making them hard for animals with claws to climb, and the platform rims extended beyond the posts, preventing access even if an animal did manage to climb a post. Moreover, Nikolai Aruneev cut down the nearby trees to keep scavengers from jumping onto the cache from above. 'Animals are very creative' (Rus. *yolki da nu kakie oni nakhodchivye*), he often told me. I have indeed seen evidence of how ermine destroy stored goods they find on the ground or on an open platform.

The reindeer herders tell many stories of how caches can retain the agency of a deceased owner. They also relate personal experiences of how violations of caches led to punishment like loss of hunting luck, incapacity, bear attacks, the appearance of spirits and even death. During Soviet times some people kept their idols hidden in caches, regularly feeding and smudging them. Nadia Taskerova, who was a shaman's daughter, considered these caches a safer place to store idols than a camp. Turov (1975: 198) notes that the Evenki built special caches for sacred items that served as protection for the hunting territory. Nikolai told me how stolen personal gear of Orochen, be they dead or alive, can cause much harm. Such stories are told also for strategic purposes.

In the 1980s anthropologists debated storage in terms of evolutionary models that divided 'primitive' societies into hunter-gatherers, pastoralists and agriculturalists. Some scholars argued that hunter-gatherers are distinguished by their lack of storage (Lee and DeVore 1968: 12). Others distinguished several types of economic systems that existed among hunter-gatherers, pastoralists and agriculturalists. 'Delayed return' systems require an investment of labour into resource extraction and storage (Woodburn 1982: 433–444). 'Immediate return' systems (which exist in only a few hunting societies) are based on sharing and immediate consumption (ibid.). Woodburn (ibid.) noted that the majority of these societies practice a 'delayed return' economy and that storage forms the base of the transition to sedentarism, social stratification and higher population density. Ingold (1983: 561) criticized this approach, suggesting that more attention should be paid to 'social storing', in which storage is concomitant with social relations of distribution. Ingold (2005: 405–406) also pointed out that immediacy, autonomy and sharing were important idioms in multiple ethnographies describing the distinct sociality of hunters and gatherers. In this context, he argued for elaboration on the ideas of autonomy, trust and sharing, examining them in the local context unbiased from Western understandings (ibid.). With the Aruneev-Zhumaneev family, I found that autonomy from state resources was maintained by the avoidance of sharing in a context where trust is lacking.

Nikolai generally wanted the villagers to know as little as possible about his trading activities and his property. Hiding one's intentions regarding trade helps one avoid requests to share goods, which are veiled demands that are difficult to refuse. When we once hired a vehicle from Tungokochen village to transport goods, the driver kept demanding various goods for the next half-year, even though he had already been paid in cash. In addition, he called Nikolai's household stingy after he had visited his base camp. Nikolai believed that such stories worked as curse that could cause him misfortune. Keeping his trading activities hidden was an important way of securing his well-being and luck. Indeed, no one knew exactly how much Nikolai earned from his fur trading or how much he spent on supplies. In the villages and to me, he would often talk about his complete failure and his misfortune, always blaming administrators and the government. Just as shortages of goods led to hoarding in Soviet times, living in an unstable market today requires that everyone avail themselves of all possible opportunities to accumulate important commodities.[5] Thereby, uncertainty and lack of trust continuously shape the family's hoarding practices and their organization of storage in the post-Soviet environment. The case of the Zhumaneev-Aruneev family shows that hunters and herders strive to accumulate animals and equipment as well.[6]

Burch (1988) describes the sharing and accumulation of wealth among the Canadian Inuit, suggesting that their strategies rely on a combination of competent production, clever trading and wise management. According to Burch (1988: 107), a successful person was known as an *umiliak,* translated as 'rich man,' and enjoyed high social status. Nikolai Aruneev also had the status of a rich man in the community, a fact that is nevertheless acknowledged with a certain sarcasm and with reference to his 'stinginess' (Rus. *zhadnost').* Reindeer herders are known to have always camouflaged or disavowed their possessions and supplies. Even after I had lived with the family for a year, I was always told that they owned no more than 300 reindeer, even though I had personally participated in the counting of up to 500. In pre-Soviet times, the richest reindeer herders owned herds of up to 300 head that were used for riding and transportation. Many men were involved in the herding and used the animals for transport. The Zhumaneev-Aruneev family used only a few reindeer for riding and transportation, despite the large size of their herd.

Managing the large herd was indeed difficult for Nikolai and Yura, the only two brothers who stayed in the taiga, after their mother Olga Zhumaneeva passed away in 2010. Other relatives in the village refused to support them, accusing them of accumulating too much wealth and not sharing it. The brothers were furthermore accused of being unwilling to support their relatives with taiga goods like skins, sinews and pelts. They themselves expressed reluctance to train younger relatives by letting them stay in their taiga camps and sharing equipment, skills and knowledge with them. Last but hardly least, the herders refused to share the reindeer they had inherited from their mother with their relatives in the village. In 2012, several groups of reindeer ran off to the Olekma District beyond the Nercha River basin. The herders returned home after having spent almost two weeks unsuccessfully chasing them in the taiga. This meant the loss of almost half their herd, which they had managed to increase from 150 to up to 500 over the past twenty years. Similarly, Empson (2012) demonstrated that for the Buryat of Mongolia the improper accumulation of too much fortune and too many animals in the new market regime invites its polar opposite: misfortune. Indeed, when Nikolai was bitten by a tick (Oro. *daikta,* Rus. *karpishka*) and infected with encephalitis and his brother was almost killed in a bear attack, villagers and relatives attributed these incidents to their unwillingness to share their taiga resources and wealth with other people.[7]

This case study demonstrates how the Zhumaneev-Aruneev reindeer herders adapted to an insecure socioeconomic environment by accumulating and concealing wealth while also taking the risk they might lose luck by challenging the ethos of sharing. Supplying, storing and securing goods for the future and being 'independent' from external social and economic constraints was one way to maintain personal autonomy in the insecure environment. Meanwhile, the idea of sharing stands as important value that is crucial to understanding how people built social relations based on cooperation, exchange and luck.

Notes

1. Many hunters avoid not only land use officers but also people who may spoil (Rus. *napakostit'*) their activities with the 'evil eye'.
2. The generation of Orochen born in the 1960s and 1970s remember the Soviet time as a period of stability when everyone had jobs and people drank much less, allowing friendship and collective ties to be better maintained. Bloch (2005) argues that such expressions of Evenki nostalgia for the socialist era are 'a form of critique of the neoliberal logics emerging in Russia today'. Indeed, such nostalgia can be understood as humans' protest against current economic difficulties that are not easily resolvable.
3. Extra salt is used to feed reindeer, as well as to make the salt licks (Oro. *taloi*, Rus. *solianka*) used to attract wild animals.
4. Leacock (1982: 159–169) suggested that among the Montagnais-Naskapi of Canada, fur hunting for commercial purposes led to similar individual storage practices.
5. Such hoarding can be seen as a continuation of the Soviet 'shortage economy', in which access to resources was unpredictable and unreliable (see Kornai 1980: 22).
6. On food preservation and storage techniques in Siberia, see Ziker (2002).
7. In his doctoral thesis, Alekhin (2000: 132) also underlined that contemporary Evenki of Surinda believed master-spirits did not tolerate excess hunting luck.

CHAPTER FOUR

'Relying on My Own Two'
Walking and Luck

Orochen refer to power – *musun* – as 'life energy', which means being in 'motion'. A person with *musun* is also described as having a soul (Oro. *omi*) and possessing strength (Oro. *chinen*) that can be exercised in practice to achieve success. For the Orochen, sustaining one's life means having hunting luck that is acquired through the skills of walking in hunting or herding animals and by being aware of their movements and of possible changes in the environment that may affect all beings. This notion corresponds to Ingold's (2011: 67–68) use of 'being alive' as a metaphor that describes the 'condition of being alive to the world, characterised by a heightened sensitivity and responsiveness, in perception and action, to an environment that is always in flux, never the same from one moment to the next'. The Orochen perceive walking as a valuable skill that is indispensable to becoming a full-fledged hunter and herder. Knowledge gained through walking, multisensory awareness and the ability to skilfully adjust one's body to the environment (see Ingold and Vergunst 2008) are essential to being successful in hunting and herding and making good use of certain taiga places. Walking is also linked to powerful metaphors that concern the hunter's and herder's strength and sense of belonging to the land, and knowledge of signs and paths is crucial to both cooperation among herders and individual autonomy when staying in the remote taiga.

In this chapter, I will explore the daily skills and kinds of knowledge that reindeer herders and hunters use in the practice of walking, leaving signs and using specific routes. Furthermore, I will elaborate on the image of the 'Walking Tungus' (Rus. *Peshyi Tungus*), a widely used pejorative epithet in Imperial and early Soviet literature. Dismissively referred to as 'wanderers' under the tsar, the Orochen today consider their walking abilities to be their main strength (Oro. *chinen*). Hence, I will invert earlier negative images and replace them with analysis of the themes of pedestrian journeying and using forest pathways, which constitute central dimensions of the Orochen worldview and moral code.

The 'Walking Tungus'

As of the seventeenth century, the indigenous peoples of the Russian Empire were classified into 'settled' (Rus. *sidiachie*), nomadic (Rus. *kochevye*) and wandering (Rus. *brodiachie*) groups, according to their pattern of movement. This terminology is rooted in the hierarchical understanding of civilization that dominated Siberian ethnography and geopolitical thinking for centuries. These notions, grounded in early colonial encounters, became administrative concepts with the legislative reforms of 1822, known as the Speranskii Code.[1] The code was mainly intended to improve the governance of the empire's indigenous people, who were called 'aliens', and collect more taxes.[2] The categorization of indigenous Siberians into three classes followed the assumption that the more mobile they were, the more primitive. By this logic, reindeer-herding societies, including the Orochen of Zabaikal'ia, were classified as 'wandering people' (Rus. *brodiashchie*), the most mobile type. Wanderers were regarded as the least advanced kind of indigenous people, and their way of life as one 'without any order' (Sakharov [1869] 2000: 2). The Buryat and Barguzin Tungus of Zabaikal'ia were categorized as 'nomadic people' (Rus. *kochevye*). Nomads were considered to have a 'more predictable' mobile way of life, since they occupied clearly definable territories, camping at certain sites that varied only by season. The last group of aliens, the so-called settled people (Rus. *sidiachie* or *osedlye*), were seen as the most civilized and therefore accorded the same citizenship rights as Russians.

Each category of aliens was identified with a particular policy of taxation and level of self-determination. However, as Forsyth (1992: 156–158) noted, this awkward classification, based on such vague criteria as mobility, 'way of life', 'peculiarity of customs', and 'economic activity' (Rus. *glavnyi promysel*) caused some indigenous groups to be mistakenly charged with higher taxes. As Slezkine (1994: 84) noted, it was up to local officials to decide which category a certain group belonged to. Hence, the so-called 'settled Tungus', also known as 'Lamuchen' (Oro. *lamu* 'sea'), who lived in wooden huts on the shores of lakes, were categorized as sedentary people and ascribed a high rate of taxation, although they were later found to be the 'poorest people' in Zabaikal'ia (see Titov 1926b: 5; Neupokoev 1928: 13–14).[3] According to Shubin (2001: 73–75), this classification exacerbated social hierarchies when people were forced to fulfil the expectations of state officials.

The classification based on mobility and land use was also widely adopted in the early ethnographic studies of the people of Zabaikal'ia. The explorer Cyvan-Zhab Sakharov ([1869] 2000: 2) described the Zabaikal Tungus as people with a distinct way of life he called 'nomadic' and 'wandering'. The Barguzin Evenki were labelled as nomads because they lived in wooden houses in the winter and used yurts in the summer like the Buryat. They kept herds of cattle and some even cultivated crops; moreover, they were baptized into the Russian Orthodox Church. The Tungus people of the Vitim River were called wanderers, since 'they did not have a constant place of abode and therefore just wander with their herds of reindeer from one river to the next while hunting and fishing' (ibid.). Meanwhile, Sakharov (ibid.) also acknowledged certain shortcomings of the classificatory system when remarking that the Tungus people of Kuchitsk, who were thought to be wanderers, most likely were better referred to as nomads.

In order to understand the history of the adjective 'wandering', we must look at the reports of expeditions undertaken by Imperial officials like Orlov (1858a, 1858b), who stated that the term was 'a way of scorning' (Rus. *iz vidov korysti*) the Tungus (1858b: 180). He also remarked, however, that Orochen deserved such appellations since 'they indeed live in the wilderness and have no understanding of a homeland [Rus. *rodina*], no place of abode [Rus. *obshchezhitie*], but are always wandering around in the bush [Rus. *skitaiutsa po debriam*], migrating through forests, hills and places that can hardly be traversed by human beings' (1858b: 180). Furthermore, Orlov (ibid.) colourfully described this 'poor people' (Rus. *bednyi narod*) as being completely dependent on 'the rough taiga' and on the Russians. They were described as begging for crusts of bread from the Russian people during their wanderings. Indeed, popular images of the Orochen depicted them in terms of poverty, pristine innocence and an 'unelaborated culture', with behaviour no different from that of animals (Rus. *podobno zveriam*).[4]

The categorization of indigenous Siberians into settled, nomads and wanderers continued to dominate Soviet policy discourse, sociopolitical literature and ethnographic research. The evolutionary ideas of the early Soviet years were evident in administrative policies of educating indigenous people with the idea of improving their lives. As the explorer Paladimov (1929: 83) suggested, 'there is an extreme need [Rus. *kraine neobkhodimo*] to change the Orochen's way of life from wandering to settled, since their everyday life of hunting, their constant movement, their life in chums in winter and summer – all of this makes them die out'. The reindeer herders' and hunters' nomadic way of life was also of great interest to the Polar Census expedition of 1926, for which a questionnaire was designed to gain detailed knowledge about nomadic people and their patterns of migration (see Anderson 2006b).[5] Soviet state officials also proposed a policy of collectivization and sedentarization in order to overcome the nomadic way of life and 'to bring a positive influence to their economic practices' (see Tugolukov and Shubin 1969).

The ethnographer Titov (1926a) presented a different classification, stating that the so-called mountain Tungus (i.e. wandering Tungus) were people of the 'highest mode of production'. He suggested that walking to remote areas and using reindeer for transportation was a much more productive way of life than either hunting without reindeer or sedentarism (ibid.). Titov (ibid.) referred to so-called settled Tungus or coastal Tungus as 'poor people', as they had lost their reindeer and therefore were considered degenerate. He (ibid.) also identified a third group of Tungus who still had a few reindeer but also built wooden houses, raised cattle and even planted some crops in addition to hunting. Finally, a fourth group, called 'settled-nomadic', was divided into two subgroups: those who moved with reindeer between several hunting cabins and those who did not have any reindeer, but changed their places of residence according to the seasons in order to hunt and fish at big lakes in the summer (ibid.).[6]

Late Soviet ethnography described walking as the way 'poor Evenki' move through the taiga, alluding to indigenous struggles against the 'wild' environment. Vasilevich (1969: 43–45) described the 'settled' (*sidiachie*) Evenki way of life as regularly walking to hunt in remote areas, occasionally taking reindeer along. Vasilevich and Levin (1951) attributed walking to the 'Evenki' economic strategy of reindeer husbandry among the Severobaikalsk Evenki, which they contrast with the more advanced 'Orochen' strategy of husbandry among Vitim River Orochen, where everyone rode reindeer during the migration. Tungus-speaking groups of Zabaikal'ia had already been distinguished according to their means of transportation in the early reports of Pallas (1788: 328). Ethnographic texts refer to the Orochen as 'Reindeer

Evenki' (Oro. *oron* 'reindeer'), who owned many reindeer; the Murchen as 'Horse Evenki' (Bur. *murin* 'horse'), who raised cattle and horses; and finally the 'Walking Evenki' (Rus. *peshie*) who had few or no reindeer (see particularly Shubin 2001: 80).

A range of ethnographers from Irkutsk University also described Evenki subsistence practices (see Petri 1930; Turov 1990; Sirina 2002). They noted that the nomadic way of life is neither random nor chaotic but allows for the exploitation of resources in 'a well-organized' way (Rus. *uporiadochnost'*). The nomads follow seasonal routes that are called 'central roads' (see Petri 1930: 33 and Turov 1990: 132–133). Turov (ibid.: 78) studied the wandering way of life as 'a core of cultural adaptation' that developed over the course of generations. He suggested that the Evenkis' mobile way of life had been conditioned by fur hunting, and that they been more sedentary in earlier times (ibid.: 77). Although Turov (ibid.) in a way rehabilitated the wandering way of life by describing it as a successful Evenki adaptation to the environment, he nevertheless remained caught in the usual evolutionary framework when describing Evenki culture in terms of mobility.

Such stereotypes and classifications always went hand in hand with policies that challenged Orochen rights to the mastery of their land. However, I will refrain from detailed discussion of which of these interpretations is closer or further from the 'truth'. What is striking is that the practice of wandering, walking or moving has been the main criteria of such classifications. For most Evenki groups in the Zabaikal'ia environment, irrespective of their pattern of residence, frequency of migration or use of domestic animals, walking constitutes a crucial element of their subsistence.[7]

Walking in the Taiga:
Skills, Awareness and Competence

For the Orochen, walking in the taiga means moving on foot while transporting one's personal belongings and tools or hunting and camping gear on the back of a reindeer or horse. Hunters and herders have a special word, *peshkov'e*, for the hunting that is done by means of walking. It describes searching for game alone, with or without the help of dogs. As the elder Olga Zhumaneeva once concluded after I talked with her about her life in the taiga: 'The Orochen life is all about walking' (Rus. *Orochenskaia zhizn' – sploshnoe peshkov'e*). Indeed, reindeer herders and hunters regularly leave their camp for daily walks in the taiga, monitoring the movements of their reindeer and of wild animals, and thus gaining knowledge that is crucial to their subsistence.

When I stayed with reindeer herders in remote camps, I usually joined them on walking trips every two to three days, crossing mountain ranges and rivers in order to gather information about animal marks, tracks and signs in various places. Reindeer herders and hunters typically walk about 6 km per hour. When hunting or searching for reindeer, they walk for eight hours per day in both summer and winter. If a hunter is tracking an animal like sable in wintertime, he may even cover a distance of up to 60 km in a day. Hunters talk about their success in terms of walking: 'the wolf is fed by his feet' (Rus. *volka nogi kormiat*).

In the winter, hunters preferred to wear light, warm shoes (Oro. *emchure*) handcrafted from buckskin leather. Almost once a week, the rawhide soles have to be repaired and scraped with a knife. Hunters have developed an elaborate technique for patching leather and rubber footwear.[8] Bootliners (Rus. *portianki*) make boots comfortable in the taiga. They are a square piece of cloth wrapped around the foot to provide a snug fit inside the boot. Ordinary socks often cause blisters, especially if they start to fold. A piece of kersey is used in winter and a piece of cotton fabric in summer. Wrapping the feet with bootliners is a special skill. Not wrapping them in the right way may hurt the foot, which can mean serious consequences for the walker, perhaps even a lengthy incapacitation. Therefore, skilful hunters regularly stop to rewrap their feet and use any opportunity to dry the bootliners, often even building a small rack (Oro. *lokovun*) to dry them beside the fire.

When Aleksei Aruneev hunted large game, he carried a special forked walking stick called a *tyevun*. The *tyevun* is popular among local reindeer herders and hunters and has several uses: for touching animal tracks in order to check their depth and rigidity; for prodding reindeer, for leaning on when leading a reindeer through hummocks and for supporting a gun when shooting. Hunters say that shooting with a *tyevun*, especially at a distant target, is much more successful because it helps to steady the rifle. As mentioned, the *tyevun* also helps to establish the age of an animal's imprint in snow. The hunter will touch the track with the *tyevun* to check the softness of the snow. Sun and wind will harden an animal print over time, so if the snow is soft, then the footprint is fresh. The *tyevun* was among the items that Aleksei believed would 'bring luck'. Therefore, he used the same stick on many trips during the autumn and winter hunting seasons.

I was not really able to walk skilfully until the end of my fieldwork. Effective walking depends on feeling a track and observing the surroundings, but it is also a bodily technique. Although I could easily walk on flat surfaces, I found it impossible to keep my balance when walking through rocky areas and especially in fields covered with hummocks. Below I present a passage from my fieldnotes to describe my own experience of walking:

> We spent about 9 hours from 9 am tracking sable until sundown and we only had a 35-minute break to drink tea and eat some bread, dipping it in sugar. Aleksei planned to kill his first sable 'for luck' [Rus. *na fart*] in this winter season. Aleksei, the dogs and I hiked over three mountain ranges to follow the tracks of sable that ran up and down the slopes, as, I was told, the 'sable was looking for berries'. I guess we must have walked up to thirty kilometres. Now, we are back at our tent on a *golets* [treeless hill] and I feel pain in my legs again and even in my shoulders although I was not given any iron traps to carry. I feel the blood pulsating in my head and I can feel a noise in my ears – it is driving me crazy. Yura said that I look completely drunk and indeed my movement has become uncoordinated. As usual, I will also feel like each of my joints is broken in the morning. For some reason, I was always falling over when walking and trying to keep up with Aleksei. While Aleksei walked really fast, he was still able to notice every detail on the surface including the backs of roe deer that were hiding about three kilometres away. Furthermore, he managed to see different marks on the trees from a distance, connecting them to last year's animal tracks, movements and mastery. He also managed to smoke on his way without slowing down a bit when lighting his cigarette. I was able to pay attention only to the ground in front of me and still had great difficulty walking. I tried to imitate Aleksei's way of walking and noticed that he walked differently in different areas. He never took big steps but mostly walked in fast, short steps. He gave the impression of being bow-legged and was simply made for this way of walking. Imitating him made me feel a little bit safer, but I still have to learn how to balance my body. I hope I will get less tired after learning how to walk correctly. Probably, this way of walking in this terrain must be learned from childhood. Now I know why Aleksei is nicknamed 'Pekhota' [Infantryman].

At the beginning of my fieldwork, Aleksei quickly evaluated my performance in walking with him on our first hunting trip as disappointing. Although I made my best effort to follow him, he had to wait for me time after time. After several hours of walking through the *kever* and a third break, he uttered the following terse comment: 'You will be a fucking bad reindeer herder if you keep moving your legs this way' (Rus. *khuiovyi olenevod budesh, esli tak budesh nogi dvigat'*).

Indeed, no hunter or herder I knew in the taiga liked to wait for those who stumbled. Since this happened to me quite often, I started to understand the reason for their impatience. As mentioned before, you have to hide your presence from animals and spirits in order to acquire hunting or herding luck. Walking briskly away from the village ensures you will spark less curiosity (Rus. *liubopytstvo*) and reduce the likelihood of meeting malevolent people who may threaten your luck by 'closing the way' (Rus. *zakryt' dorogu*). Therefore, it is said that once you start out, you must avoid any delays or stops on the road that may give you away to the animals. Hunters believe that you should never turn back when something has been left at the camp or *zimav'ie* (cabin). On their way to their hunting areas hunters stop only at mountain passes, at special ritual places called 'shamans', to pay their respects by leaving offerings to the master-spirits of that place. You must not delay a group's hunting activities and endanger the others' success. As Anderson (2000a: 121) noted, 'a poor performance [among the Evenki of Taimyr] can also lead to the usurpation of one's intended task'. However, a hunter who knows for certain where a particular animal dwells need not hurry when leaving the camp.

Skilful walking meant moving fast. It also meant making no unnecessary movements, taking no breaks and keeping silent (see Fig. 4.1). Hunting by walking relied on the hunter's multisensory awareness being specially attuned to the movements of animals, even as 'the body and the environment are blurred by movements of both' (Lee and In-

Figure 4.1. | *Aleksei Aruneev walking from a moose kill site to the camp while carrying the moose's leg and pieces of meat.*

gold 2006: 72). We always avoided certain areas, this way hoping to encounter animals unexpectedly. Once I was told that my careless walking downwind of the upper river basin had made all the animals disappear. It was said that if an elk was scared off, it would return after only three or four days, whereas moose would not come back for two or three weeks. As Aleksei taught me, hunters also must approach the tracks of sable from below because the wind often blows downriver at night when the sable is active. The sable cannot smell a hunter's footprints this way. When hunting with members of the Aruneev-Zhumaneev family, I was always pointedly told to avoid wearing clothing that could make noise. My nylon winter trousers were often said to be too noisy. Olga Zhumaneeva once teased me, saying, 'Do not put it on, since when you walk all the taiga moves' (Rus. *vsia taiga sharakhaetsa*). Walking in the snow was always much noisier because of the squeaking snow. Sound also travels much better in cold conditions, when there are no leaves on the trees to muffle sound. Hence, adjusting one's body to the environment is key to effective walking. When walking I sometimes asked Aleksei how many kilometres we still had before us, but I never got a direct reply – I would only be told that there were 'a couple of hours to go'. Hunters do not like to predict their walking time, so he would say, 'We should not try to guess' (Rus. *ne budem zagadyvat'*). This relates to the belief that animals may react to anything that is planned in advance, which may ruin your plans.

Walking through various areas in the course of quotidian subsistence activities generates knowledge and experience. As Ingold (2004: 330) noted, 'through our feet, in contact with the ground (albeit mediated by footwear), we are most fundamentally and continually *in touch* with our surroundings'. In the course of hunting, one must hike up and down hills, crossing long stretches of loose rocks that cover the slopes. The walker must be aware of holes between the rocks that at first glance appear to form a smooth surface. Hilltops are covered with high, soft moss in which an unskilled walker inevitably stumbles. Finally, the large hummocks (Oro. *chiopchioko*) that cover the lowland make walking extremely hard. A walker crossing such a field must be skilful enough to walk fast even in summer, when the fields are covered with grass and the spaces between the *chiopchioko* are barely visible. Walkers may stumble, and risk breaking a leg, by accidentally stepping in the space between hummocks. I was taught to pay attention to the colour of the grass on the hummocks: a darker shade of green indicates that the tuft of the hummock is fresh and offers fairly stable footing. This kind of close observation of the environment permits rather fast walking.

Walking in the taiga is inseparable from reading animal tracks. Hunters carefully touch footprints with their hands or with the *tyevun* to gather initial information. Tracks that are less than three hours old are considered very fresh. Tracks that are between twelve and twenty-four hours old may still be worth following. A fresh track in the snow is always soft. Attention must be paid to the colour of the imprint's surface, the presence or absence of dew on the grass and the track's smell. As Nikolai Aruneev noted, fresh tracks or marks left on trees and bushes smell different from old ones, in the warm period of the year. A hunter tracking an animal must stay downwind of the animal so it does not catch the hunter's scent. Through the constant examination of each other's tracks, hunters and animals are always aware of each other's presence. Nikolai, who used different metaphors when talking about the daily aspects of a herder's life in the taiga, once described his daily walks as follows: 'You can learn everything about animals and people by reading their tracks in the taiga just like you get information from reading a newspaper'. Nikolai claimed to personally know all the animals living in the valley, and to know each animal's history and way of walking and hunting. Tracks may also reveal an animal's sex, age and activity, and tell the hunter where a particular animal spends most of its time when grazing, resting and drinking. Tracks may also give information about how long an animal has stayed in an area and whether it lives there or is just passing through. Herders and hunters tell stories of the social life of the animals of a whole valley. Just by observing the networks of tracks, they can know things like what direction a moose has taken, what the predators are up to and how many squirrels live in a certain clump of trees.

Hunters say that people's tracks and ways of walking show their competence. Chulan Kirilov told me that people who were not born in the taiga 'drag their feet when they walk in the taiga', whereas hunters and herders always step lightly, taking short steps, almost 'like they are running'. The ability to walk long distances when hunting or searching for reindeer is also seen as part of a person's competence. By covering large distances, a herder is thought to gain more information about the reindeer's 'living place' (Oro. *bikit*). A herder who is searching for reindeer usually circles the camp: the wider the circle, the greater the likelihood of locating the reindeer. Yura Aruneev often mocked other herders' inability to walk long distances in search of reindeer. He was known as a person who, according to his uncle Gena Kirilov, 'never gives up following the tracks of animals, therefore he may walk for up to a week to hunt moose or bear, and sometimes he walks for an entire day without stopping'. At the same time, herders

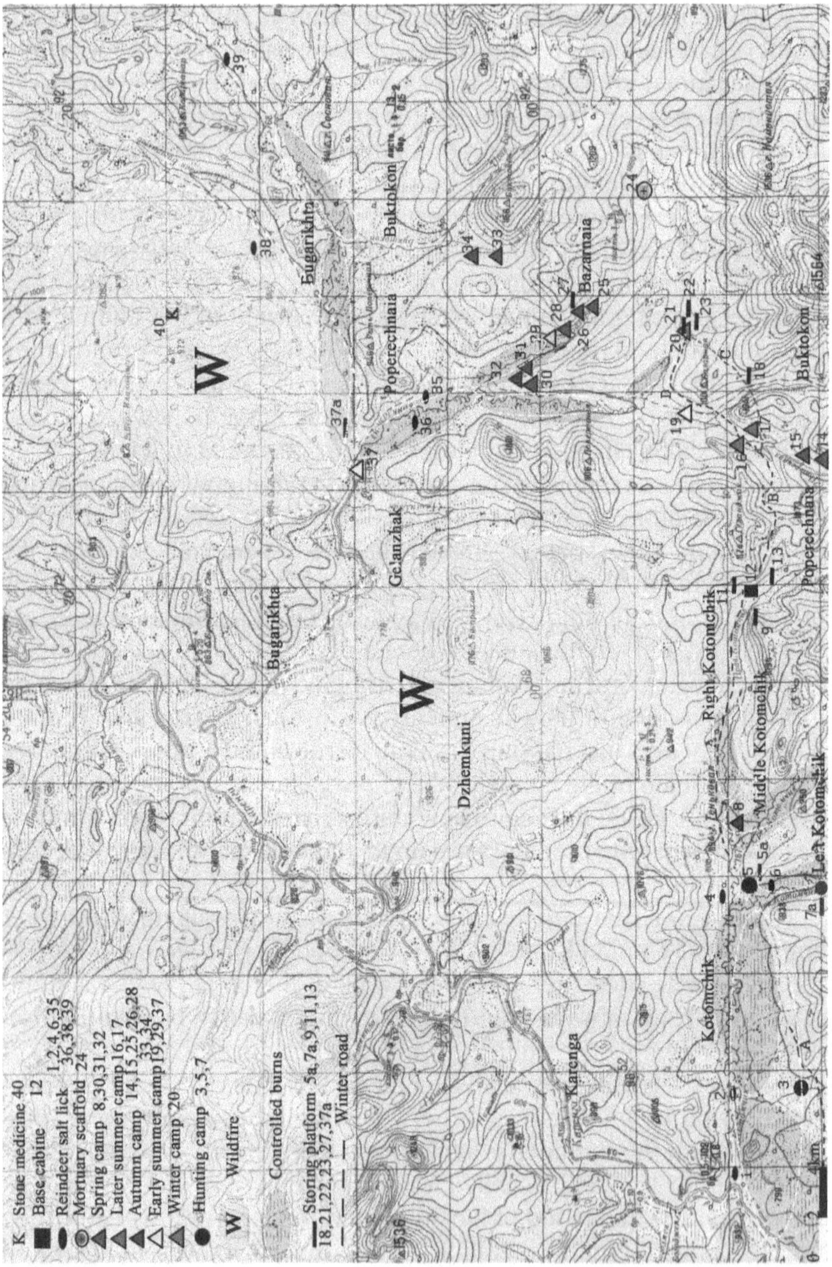
K Stone medicine 40
Base cabine 12
Reindeer salt lick 1,2,4,6,35,36,38,39
Mortuary scaffold 24
Spring camp 8,30,31,32
Later summer camp 16,17
Autumn camp 14,15,25,26,28 33,34
Early summer camp 19,29,37
Winter camp 20
Hunting camp 3,5,7
W Wildfire
Controlled burns
Storing platform 5a,7a,9,11,13, 18,21,22,23,27,37a
Winter road
Bugarikhta
Buktokon
Poperechnaia
Bazarnaia
Gelanzhak
Dzhemkuni
Right Kotomchik
Middle Kotomchik
Left Kotomchik
Kotomchik
Karenga
4km

Map 4.1. | *Aleksei Aruneev's fur and game animal hunting routes, followed for a few weeks in the Siligli River basin in 2005. The outlined walking trajectories are for hunting and trapping fur animals, snaring rabbits, hunting birds and hunting large game animals.*

and hunters see such exhausting walks as a normal part of life in the taiga. People simply say, 'you have to walk to live in the taiga' (Rus. *v taige zhit' nado khodit'*). Being an Orochen is inseparable from walking. The elder Olga Zhumaneeva remembered that during her childhood, she and her siblings were roused early in the morning every day by their father and sent in search of reindeer, whether or not there was a need to find them. She recalled that although children had a hard time waking up, 'nobody could resist their parents'. She talked about walking in a somewhat poetic way, complaining that spending more than two days in camp without walking gave her the feeling she was getting 'spoiled' (Rus. *kisnut'*). Hunters often refer to skilful walking as an important path to success in hunting, proudly proclaiming that the game was 'killed by relying on my own two' (Rus. *dobyl na svoikh dvoikh*).

Signs and Communication

Walking in the taiga is a way of both gaining and leaving information. At the beginning of the twentieth century, hunters and herders used to leave various signs on their routes in the taiga to communicate with relatives who hunted in other river valleys and were met only a few times a year.[9] The hunters and herders of Tungokochen District travelled hundreds of kilometres to the former Aga Buryat Autonomous District in the south and the Kurumkan District in eastern Republic of Buryatia to trade. In Soviet times reindeer herders often hunted or tended their scattered herds independently from each other in the taiga and were separated from their families in the village for long periods. They also visited relatives who lived as far away as Yakutia, which meant walking up to 1,500 kilometres one way. In this context, they communicated with each other using various signs that allowed people to notify others about their plans or about news concerning health, hunting, herding and migration, and to point out sites with plentiful resources or sites of misfortune that were to be avoided. Elders remember that their relatives travelled back and forth across a very large area. Vladimir Lokushin from Zelenoe Ozero village described how he had used signs in the past:

> The Orochen knew each other's plans well in the past; they knew where one would migrate, where you could find your relatives and when and where you could meet them. People would migrate anywhere in the past, they would visit any valley, and therefore there were many people travelling in the taiga. People left signs for each other. They also arranged [Rus.

zakazyvali] meetings. Every clan had its own sign. My father left a cut on a tree in the shape of the young moon and a *kamus*-shaped cut as his mark.

Special signs called *sama*, which are well described in ethnographic accounts, continue to play an important role in the everyday life of both nomadic and sedentary Orochen.[10] A sign may consist of a long pole put on a tripod or leaned against a tree stump. The end of the pole is wrapped with cotton or grass to indicate the direction of migration. As Nikolai Aruneev explained, 'the greater the angle of the pole from the ground, the farther you can expect to travel to your relatives' camp.' A sign may be left by breaking a branch of a young tree at eye level or leaving a piece of moss or grass on the top of a short tree. Nikolai often left me signs on the snow when travelling, since he usually walked much faster than I did.

Members of the Zhumaneev-Aruneev family of reindeer herders, like other village-based hunters, also leave glass bottles containing written notes at crossroads or mountain passes. These messages may inform readers of the presence of predators in the area or the deaths of animals, or they can place an order for ammunition or certain goods from the storage platforms.[11] In this way people can cooperate while herding and hunting without meeting each other. Herders regularly break the ends of branches when travelling by horse or walking with reindeer to mark their path for future use. They also leave signs for other family members or for themselves, in cases when animal meat is left at the butchering site: one's family or other hunters are expected to find a certain place by following the signs. When leaving a kill site, Aleksei Aruneev would break the branches of trees in several places. As soon as he was on his way, he would make a special cut in the bark of a tree. A stick may also be left pointing toward the carcass of a killed animal. Often some of the meat is left to be taken to camp by another relative who is hunting or travelling in the area. After returning to the main camp, hunters also tell their wives or children to go and bring the meat home on a reindeer. Signs help people spend as little time as possible in the pursuit of various activities.

To draw someone's attention to a place in the taiga, people strip the bark off a birch tree or tie a circle of birch bark around a young, growing tree. This sign can be seen from far away, since the brown colour revealed under the peeled white birch bark is very conspicuous. Hunters mark items that are left for other people, for example by stripping off bark close to a mortuary scaffold, expecting that no other people or animals will disturb that place. Indeed, if someone passes close to a mortuary scaffold, the master-spirit may become very angry and cause misfortune for anyone in the area. Nikolai Aruneev once picked up a knife from the ground around an old mortuary scaffold, and since then several visiting hunters have lost their knives at that place because 'the master always takes them in place of his own lost knife'. Warning signs can inform other hunters that a certain site must be treated with respect if one's luck is to be preserved in passing by. Nikolai frequently told me of his own misfortunes, for example, when he lost a valuable riding reindeer (Oro. *evuchak*) because he had unwittingly walked across a burial site. Hunters continue to mark burial sites even when they have long been destroyed. Various signs may also be left on trees to alert hunters to poison left for predators and warn them to take care of their dogs. Hence, signs help to maintain one's well-being and avoid misfortune in the taiga.

Similarly, signs can demonstrate one's master right to certain places, caches or other storage sites. They are believed to entail some kind of protection. Aleksei sometimes left a piece of cloth close to a butchered moose, saying, 'I do this so nobody takes it', believing the cloth to be imbued with a his energy. Vasilevich (1969: 187) describes how Evenki would even carve faces on trees next to their migration routes, expecting them to become the homes of spirits. Such 'placing' served to protect the area. This kind of sign-making thus constitutes a way to create a secure environment for one's subsistence activities.

Some signs are intended to convey more complex information. The local ethnographer Arbatskii told me that the Zhumaneev family communicated by building a small rectangular structure from thin sticks (see Fig. 4.2). He has documented several kinds (A and B) of signs that were intended to draw the attention of hunters when they came close to these structures (C). In the third case, birch bark was wrapped around the stem of a larch tree so that the white colour would be visible. In the second case, a young tree was tied to a stump. Fiodor Zhumaneev would make four or five layers of sticks indicating the number of overnight stays. If there were four layers, it meant that the family would be about eighty kilometres away. The stick inside the rectangle marked the direction of migration, while other signs of crossed sticks would indicate the number of nights spent in camp.

'Living When Walking'

The imprints left on the land by movements of animals and humans in the taiga are called paths (Oro. *oktol*). By using such paths across the taiga, hunters and herders reach distant areas in a relatively short

Figure 4.2. | *Sketch of Fiodor Zhumaneev's signs, drawn by Aleksandr Arbatskii (1981: Appendix): A. Sign of attention (birch bark wrapped on the tree); B. Sign of attention (bent tree); C. Construction representing the direction of migration and number of camped nights.*

time. People maintain these paths by cleaning them and removing dry and green wood. Like rivers, paths are seen to change with the seasons, and sometimes they indeed become channels for water after rainfall. A heavily used path that cuts deeply into the surface often turns into a water channel, especially when the snow melts in May. When water further erodes parts of these paths, they begin to take on a V shape that makes them difficult to traverse for humans and domestic animals. When horses start having trouble walking such paths, the hunters make new paths that run parallel to the old ones.

Well-known *kolkhoz* paths in the taiga are also marked on various maps. They were used by *kolkhoz* workers and are still used today by hunters, foresters and hay-cutters, who are often former *kolkhoz* workers. These paths are very conspicuous because they are deeply carved into the surface of the soil by the ATVs that formerly belonged to the collective farm. In different seasons, the paths are also used for travelling to hunting sites or hay-cutting areas by horse or reindeer. They connect all the important river valleys, log huts and hay-cutting sites. Using *kolkhoz* paths for travelling in the taiga has many benefits but may also create difficulties. One may encounter other hunters or unwelcome officials when following such paths. Therefore, hunters and herders often rather avoided the main arteries of travel, preferring to keep their hunting activities hidden and avoid meeting other people along the way. Orochen hunters believe that someone who asks too many questions about their activities may cause misfortune. Aleksei often used *kolkhoz* paths and returned to the village only after dark.

The movements of a group of reindeer herders and hunters often create a network of paths that are maintained and used by them alone. These paths serve as an observable and intuitive guide to one's activities in various places. They are more or less visible but may be completely indiscernible to the untrained eye. They should not be understood as a straight line, but rather as certain directions marked by sole marks or imprints. The course of a path may change if a large tree or another obstacle happens to lie across it and people start walking around it, or if other physical changes in the landscape make modifications easier than following the original path. Herders create their own paths across mountain passes, which are well known only among a certain group. People feel they can appropriate a place by constantly moving along certain paths in the pursuit of their subsistence activities. They may avoid certain paths that are known to have caused misfortune because of *arenki* dwelling there. Their way of using paths to move across the taiga also illustrates how hunters strive to make their life secure in the post-Soviet social environment of mistrust.

Burned areas of the taiga are known to be pathless. Nikolai says, 'In *diagdanda* [burned areas] even birds do not fly, while animals die in such places if they visit them by chance'. Burned areas are dangerous to move across, as burned trees that are still standing can fall at any time and kill a traveller. Herders always walk fast when crossing such areas. Burned areas cannot be used as reindeer pasture for up to twenty-five years because fire damages the turf, roots and soil.

Since most villagers cannot avoid using the *kolkhoz* paths anyway, they frequently meet on the way and stop to chat. When hunting in the rutting season, people usually stay for ten or twenty minutes to smoke cigarettes and exchange thoughts about the area. Hunters rarely give explicit information about their success in order 'to maintain their luck', but they freely share their knowledge about animal tracks they have seen. Sometimes we passed campsites that were occupied by hunters for a night. Since the number of permanent shelters (Oro. *kaltamni*, Rus. *balagan*) was limited, we would share the camp space for the night, if the occupants were friends. On such occasions hunters exchange news about life in the village and about people who hunt in particular areas. People also share food, especially freshly hunted meat, during such encounters, saying that they also share luck this way. Someone who is in need of some item or information can make camp near the main route so as to encounter a person who can be asked for help or for something that is needed.

Elders say that 'to live means to walk on paths and leave an imprint' (Rus. *zhit'* – *tropy tropit'*). It means that people create places that are infused by their own 'energy' (Rus. *energiia*) and affect a walker's life. Hence, the Orochen believe that walking along paths made by past generations is like receiving the place from the ancestors. One's sense of belonging to the land is grounded in skilful walking and visiting certain places, just as it depends on rituals of cooperation and creation of new networks of paths for the best use of a landscape. Vladimir Lokushin from Zelenoe Ozero village described the interrelation between generations of herders and places by observing that 'a herder's grave is covered with grass and even when it can hardly be seen, his paths are still there on the land and are walked by his children'.

It is said that old paths are traversed by *arenkil* and camping near them should be avoided (see Basharov 2003: 9). *Arenkil* are especially likely to approach people who camp at a crossroads. Nikolai smoked cigarettes as he approached such a crossroads to greet the local master-spirit (Rus. *mestnogo dukha khoziaina*). He told me that once he had hurt his knee after failing to perform this ritual of respect. He always performed elaborate rituals when transporting his supplies by truck to the remote camps. Once Nikolai asked a driver to stop at every river and mountain pass on the way, which the latter found very annoying. Walking, leaving tracks on paths and ritual performance are elements of a person's subtle interaction with the spirits of various places. Successful interaction with spirits and the long-term experience of luck, in turn, create a sense of belonging to a place.

Orochen elders often use the metaphor of paths to talk about their lives. They say that a person who does not sin follows a 'straight path', whereas a poacher walks a 'crooked path' (Rus. *krivaia tropa*), which always comes to an end (Rus. *konets tropy*).[12] It is said that good people die of old age while still actively hunting and herding in the taiga. As the elder Olga Zhumaneeva said, 'I will live as long as I walk' (Rus. *budu zhit' poka khodit' budu*). In the herders' political rhetoric, walking along paths is a metaphor often used in reference to those Orochen who lead a 'traditional life' of reindeer herding and hunting. Mortuary rituals are also based on the idea that the soul follows a path to the 'world of the dead' (Oro. *bunil*). For this reason the Orochen often leave food and tools in the grave. The living are responsible for helping the dead get ready for the trip. A corpse must be dressed in clothes made without ribbons. As Ania Semirekonova explained to me, 'dead people should not stumble [Rus. *nespotykalsia*] on their path'.[13]

Walking across the landscape inevitably leaves footprints and tracks and also involves reading the footprints and tracks of others. In the words of Ingold and Vergunst (2008: 5), 'the movement of walking is itself a way of knowing. ... Walking is as much movement of pensive observation – of thinking as you watch and watching as you think – as it is a way of getting around.' The Orochen also believe that footprints and other imprints of human activities leave a person's energy at a place. Animal tracks convey information about the animal's living place. By walking along paths, hunters and herders interact with master-spirits and ancestors alike, who have left their own tracks and imprints on the landscape. Such interaction requires the performance of rituals of exchange with nonhuman beings. These beings can either endanger humans or provide them with luck, which also shapes people's sense of belonging to a place. Hence, the notion of walking along paths is a strong metaphor that links past and present and refers to a person's morality and success in living in certain places. By inverting the earlier, negative images applied from outside, I replaced them with the positive, emically derived themes of pedestrian journeying and use of taiga paths and signs that are at the core of the Orochen world view, success in subsistence and land use.

Notes

1. For interpretation of the Speranskii Code, see Forsyth (1992), Slezkine (1994: 80–92) and Pika (1999: 35–43).
2. 'Alien' is the translation for the Russian term '*inorodtsy*', which literally means 'foreign people'.
3. Comparing groups that used reindeer and others who did not and were settled, Titov (1926a: 5) suggests that the use of reindeer increases hunting productivity in terms of the fur and the meat of animals.

4. See Dobromyslov (1902: 81–82) and Paladimov (1929: 85–86).
5. The Polar Census was part of the first Soviet All-Union census held in 1926. It surveyed rural households in the Arctic regions, providing basic data on each community's demography, diet, economy, migration routes, beliefs and folklore (Anderson 2006b: 30).
6. Titov (1926a: 10–12) draws the radical conclusion that sedentarization means death (Rus. *vymiranie*) and calls the Orochen's Russian neighbours 'poachers' and 'colonizers' that destroy Orochen lives.
7. Tugolukov's (1969) popular-scientific book 'Pathfinders Who Ride Reindeer' (Rus. *Sledopyty Verkhom na Oleniakh*) presented a romantic image of the riding Orochen. He described them as mobile hunters of Siberia who skilfully hunt from the backs of their reindeer (ibid.). Tugolukov (ibid: 22) also described how Evenki hunters track squirrels, shoot them and even use a stick to pick up the carcass from the ground without ever dismounting. However, the author also underlined that hunters could ride reindeer only in the short snowless season, and that most Evenki of Zabaikal'ia spent their time on foot in their mountainous, marshy environment (ibid.: 22–23).
8. Both summer and winter footwear is expensive and therefore always carefully maintained. In the summer, hunters use factory-made rubber boots imported from China. They complain that Chinese rubber boots last for only a short time, whereas Soviet boots could be worn for several seasons. I was told that a skilful walker manages to use his footwear longer without replacing it.
9. On Evenki signs see Georgi (1779: 36), Mainov (1898: 7), Khoroshikh (1950: 57–59) and Vasilevich (1969: 186–187).
10. Quite strikingly, many signs remain unchanged since the days of the Mainov (1898) expedition. Mainov (ibid.: 7) describes winter signs left by the Tungus when migrating to remote areas: the herders would stick a pole into the snow with its end pointing in the direction of their intended migration.
11. We once found a short note in the taiga that said, 'Bring bullets' (Rus. *privezi patronchiki*).
12. The end of the path means a person's death. People say that the dead take a path that leads in just one direction, but paths on the land never end and can always be travelled both ways.
13. The metaphor of the path, which links place and time, life and death, luck and biography, can be found among many Central Asian people (see L'vova et al. 1988: 71–85).

CHAPTER FIVE

Living Places

Tracking Animals and Camps

Optimal foraging theory proposes that subarctic foragers (e.g. the Cree) see the environment as a 'heterogeneous habitat' or a 'mosaic of resources' that has been termed 'patchy' (MacArthur and Pianka 1966; Winterhalder 1981; Smith and Winterhalder 1992). A patch embraces multiple environmental features that are delimited by physical differences, and contains a distinctive assemblage of fauna and flora (MacArthur and Pianka 1966). According to this assumption, a hunter ranks these patches based on his or her knowledge of the local environment and their productiveness, preferring to visit favourable patches in order to reduce average travel costs for hunting (ibid.). Evolutionary anthropologists (Winterhalder 1981: 90; Smith and Winterhalder 1992: 57) have argued that a Cree hunter's success depends on a strategy called 'rule of thumb'. This strategy can be described as movement between 'highly ranked patches', reading fresh animal tracks and visiting patches only when the prey is known to be around.

In the following I will argue that the Orochen see animal habitats less as patches than as vibrant spaces, called *bikit* or 'living places', to which the hunter has to attune her or his own senses and movement when hunting a particular animal. From this perspective, hunting is a dynamic competition between the hunter and an animal. It can be described as a process of 'fine-tuning one's attention' to the movement of animals in their living places (see also Ingold 1996).[1] The animal's *bikit* is the sustained focus of an animal's seasonal activity. It cannot simply be mapped out as a geographical area. Rather, the Orochen reason, such a space is created by the animal's movements. The hunter may gain knowledge about the animal's character, its social life, strength, sex and even its mood as well as its *bikit* by reading and interpreting its tracks.

Tracking skills, which involve multisensory perception and empathy, are very important in attuning oneself to the animal and overcoming it. Lavrillier (2009) discerned two spheres of habituations among the Amur Orochen: the 'wild world' is inhabited by spirits, while the 'domestic world', which she identifies with the vernacular Evenki word *beiechi* (Oro. *beie* 'man'), refers to the 'realm of humans' and includes 'locations of domestic reindeer' and 'forest roads'. The idea of *beiechi* is quite similar to that of a human *bikit*. It also involves cultural modifications of the landscape by building camps and making tracks in the forest (ibid.). Nevertheless, the idea of a human's *bikit* does not exclude the use of landscape by nonhuman beings. Hence, one must adjust one's activities to the movements and presence of animals and spirits to create a human's *bikit,* which can be described as the outcome of the successful coexistence of humans, animals and spirits. Such experiences of luck are crucial in humans' interactions with animals or nonhuman beings as they create their own 'living places'. A human *bikit* can be identified by cultural modifications of the landscape like paths, short- and long-term campsites, and sites of ritual performance. The *bikit* can shift with the seasons, in response to animal migrations or because of experiences of misfortune.

In this chapter I will also discuss how the needs of hunting and herding influence the choice of the location and composition of camps (Oro. *urikital*). With the help of maps I will show how the Zhumaneev-Aruneev hunters and reindeer herders organize their residential camps and establish a seasonal camp in relation to the animals' *bikit* (living place). I argue that the practice of building camps is shaped by people's awareness of their surroundings and capacity to adapt to shifting environments inhabited by both animals and spirits. Camping strategies combine experiences of places encompassing both past activities and the present aim to sustain luck. I will also demonstrate how hunters and herders establish their camps with an awareness of animals' living places, spirits and experiences of luck. They cooperate with reindeer by adjusting their daily activities to the reindeer's rhythm of life, using or re-establishing long-term residential camps and striving to adjust to the reindeer's *bikit* in order to acquire luck and make the best use of reindeer while hunting. Success is based on a strategy that combines camping, reindeer herding and hunting into an integral subsistence practice. At the same time, though, herders today experience misfortune in herding or grazing because officials have reduced their territory, forcing reindeer to live in one area for too long. I will show that reindeer herders' camps are located at the intersection of various activity zones and have been adjusted, with the help of the hunter's multisensory awareness, to animals' living places in the vicinity so as to offer the hunter the best opportunities for subsistence activities.

A sketch map (see Map 5.3) shows how winter-season camping zones cover areas that lie at some distance from each other. The building of camps allows people to monitor their surroundings while performing daily chores close to the fireplace. Hunters learn most about subsistence opportunities by being attentive to sounds, observing the movements of animals and birds, feeling the wind, observing the behaviour of the domestic animals and paying attention to the nearby fields, ranges and slopes. Campsites are chosen on the basis of past experiences of luck or misfortune. Manifestations of malevolent spirits (Oro. *arenkil*), which happen when duties toward a place's master spirit are neglected, also factor into the choice. All such experiences shape the way people build their camps, always aiming to avoid misfortune.

Animals' Living Places

Hunters and reindeer herders use the word *bikit* when talking about hunting wild animals like moose, roe deer, elk, wolf, bear, sable, squirrel or rabbit. According to Orochen elders, all beings, including wild and domestic animals, have their own *bikit*. Anisimov (1959: 18–20) wrote that the Orochen, like many Siberian people, associate certain places with the images of certain animals. Animal movements and tracks are key to identifying an animal's *bikit*, and hunters need this knowledge to succeed. Hunters gain knowledge about *bikit* mainly by examining animal marks and tracks to learn about the animal's movement. Tracks, scrapes and marks left in the soil, on plants or on trees can be interpreted as evidence of a certain animal's long-term presence in the area. Over a period of tracking and observation, the hunter eventually gleans information about an animal's personality, character, social life and preferences. Using this knowledge, people adjust their movements and camping activities to the animal's *bikit* in order to acquire hunting or herding luck.

I was introduced to the concept of *bikit* on my first hunting trip to the Taloy River basin close to Buryatia, which was organized by the experienced hunter Aleksei Aruneev. My companions Aleksei Aruneev and Gena Dushinov used the term *bikit* when sharing their knowledge of the particular area where an animal was being tracked. With an air of importance, Aleksei would announce the results of his study of tracks – for example, that moose lives (Rus. *zhivet*) in a certain valley. In the evening, after finding a *bikit*, he would give a brief summary of his hunting plans for the coming day, solemnly saying something like: 'We will follow the Siikta River [pointing toward the river valley] since I saw some fresh tracks of three moose playing there. I know they live there. Tomorrow, we have to take both dogs along.'

My subsequent experiences tracking wild animals and working with domestic reindeer taught me how hunters and herders gain knowledge about an animal's *bikit*. I learned the skills needed to find any marks left by animals, like broken branches or tracks on the ground, and to create from them an image of the animal's behaviour (see Fig. 5.1). As we searched for reindeer or hunted squirrels, Nikolai would describe his observations of tracks like this: 'Look, there are the tracks of four moose, they were butting all the way and competing for the good grazing area.... Look, they ran off and met again near the tree line, butting again there.' One old hunter, Chulan Kirilov from Bugunda village, could tell a wolf's mood, its social life, when it last ate, and where it would spend the night just from looking at its tracks and claw imprints. An animal's *bikit* can be seen as an area of constant movement – 'playing', eating and procreating. By leaving tracks, animals show that they are the 'masters of a place'. People believe that some animals are masters of certain places and are due respect. Various signs are left to warn newcomers about camping in these places. Wolves often urinate to leave their smell in various locations. They also break twigs to mark their territory. In the rutting season, moose and red deer use their antlers or hooves to leave marks on trees or on the ground. The elder Kirimbai explained to me that animals may even show their strength (Oro. *chinen*) through the marks they leave on the ground or on trees.

To examine tracks, hunters carefully touch them with a hand or with the *tyevun* to gather initial information. 'Fresh' tracks are less than three hours old, and tracks that are between twelve and twenty-four hours old may be worth following. According to Yura Aruneev, it can even make sense to follow animal tracks that are two or three days old. In such cases, Yura would circle the area to find out whether the animal had left the vicinity or was still around. The Orochen have a special terminology for various kinds of animal tracks. A very fresh trail is called *olokos nongononoptyn*, less fresh prints are called *omukta udia*, and old tracks are *goropty udia*. Yesterday's tracks are *tynivar*; today's tracks, *ositkaptak*; and a trail from the same morning, *tymani*.

Such crucial knowledge is gathered by reading tracks with multisensory awareness, paying attention to their colour and smell, and to the dew on the grass. As Nikolai Aruneev noted, in the warm period of the year the smell of fresh tracks or marks left on trees and bushes differs from that of old ones.

The elder Vladimir Torgonov told of how in the past, powerful hunters would talk about certain sites in a boar's *bikit*, where many animals would meet and spend the night together. Only extraordinarily skilled hunters could find these sites, he maintained. Hunting luck was also acquired through a hunter's skill in lying quietly in wait for an animal for long hours in cold weather. As the young hunter and skilled craftsmen Andrei Dogonchin told me, on such occasions a powerful hunter 'melts' (Rus. *slitsya*) into the landscape in order to be successful. When an animal lives in a certain place for a long time, it is believed to become somehow tied (Rus. *privyazan*) to that place, or as one hunter put it, 'the animal is nurtured by that place'. Orochen hunters and reindeer herders believe that if a predator or ungulate lives in a particular place, it will stay in the area for a while. If a moose is not scared off by predators or killed by another hunter, then one can expect to find it in the same place even after two or three weeks.

When I asked where I should go to hunt roe deer, Nikolai responded, 'they are everywhere and nowhere' (Rus. *vezde oni est', i nigde*). In fact, storage platforms (Oro. *delken*) close to salt licks (Rus. *solontsy*) are considered to be perfectly suited for stalking animals. However, hunters never emphasize this and do not refer to these places as promising. Anyone who visits these platforms with the intention of stalking animals must first find out if an animal regularly visits the salt lick. This requires spending a night sitting in the dark, rain and wind and listening, while hiding one's intentions and movements. Previous generations of hunters have already used the platforms and salt licks as game-stalking sites. The practice of stalking from a storage platform also evokes notions of spirits bothering hunters and of moral obligation. Hunters often encounter malevolent spirits and bears when stalking overnight at salt licks.

Skilful hunting requires a certain form of behaviour from the hunters searching for animal tracks in the taiga while hiding their own presence. The required skills include particular ways of walking through various terrains, adjusting your movements to the weather and seasonal conditions, and paying attention to the wind and the cardinal directions. Hunters always say that you must try to see the game before the game sees you. Some hunters spend much time reading tracks and observing the game before starting out on the actual hunt. As the elder Bultai said, 'If you see an animal – get to know it first, do not start shooting right away' (see also Shirokogoroff 1935: 335). Hunting methods are adapted to one specific animal and its movements in a certain area, rather than to the species as a whole.

Empathy plays an important role in hunting. Aleksei once told me that 'a hunter must feel the animal [Rus. *prochiustvovat' zveria*] and predict where it might go'. I heard hunters saying that a successful hunter has a good feeling for animals in addition to being a powerful walker. Olga Zhumaneeva would offer predictions of animals' behaviour every day by saying something like, 'So cold, uhhh, let's wait for the *tyrgalcha* [sun] ... the sables are curled up now, I saw the footprints showing that they run on the soles of their paws, poor little guys, it is so cold, they do not want to leave their nest in such weather, no way to get them'. The following Nikolai's description of a moose's behaviour demonstrates how complex the knowledge about animals and their habitat can be:

> Now, this moose lives in that *bosoo* [shady slope] of *yanil* [treeless hills] in the daytime, since the snow is covered with ice in the lowlands.... An animal does not feel good in the lowlands, only wolves feel good there who want to follow the moose.... All rivers are covered with ice and it is hard for the moose to walk and drink there, therefore the moose lives in the *bosoo* now. There is still enough soft snow and the animals can safely walk, run, and eat snow there.... It will get warmer in a few days and the snow will melt on *alga* [southern slope], the old moose has already started visiting it in the daytime; there is no wind there, the moose gets less tired using his hooves to get at moss under the snow there. Only at night does he return to the *bosoo* since then *alga* freezes and becomes dangerous.

Similarly, hunters pay attention to mosquitoes in the summertime, calculating how they affect animals: moose may move to hide near lakes, rivers or other open, cold places when mosquitoes are very active. Tracks tell a moose's age and preferences as well as the effect of mosquitoes on its movements. Hunters always approach animals with an awareness of the individual animal's personality, the wind direction and terrain conditions. They react to hearing, seeing and smelling the animal – as Nikolai Aruneev puts it, 'feeling the animal's breath' (Rus. *dyshanie*). Such hunting practices recall Ingold's (1996: 40) description of acquiring practical hunting skills based on observation and imitation: 'rhythmic adjustment or resonance in the relation between the hunter and his surroundings is the hallmark of the skilled hunter'.

To maximize their chances of obtaining luck, hunters and herders also strive to camp close to the game's or domestic animal's *bikit*. Therefore, the *bikit* of reindeer herders and hunters often overlap. The living places of animals are also constructed through human and non-human interaction that is likely to shift with the movements of animals and humans or with changes in the weather. The sketch maps drawn by Nikolai show an animal's *bikit* as linked to a set of interactions with other animals, rather than a stable, bounded territory. Living close to animals' living places is crucial for the subsistence of hunters and herders. Maps 5.1 and 5.2 show the *bikit* of reindeer and moose, respectively, in late winter 2004. Maps 5.1 and 5.2 illustrate the daily activities of hunters and animals in different areas, as well as different sites of interaction of humans and animals on a certain day or season.

The sketch in Map 5.1 shows the *bikit* of reindeer by depicting a Poperechnaia camp location close to a ridge (Oro. *ural*), a system of rivers (Oro. *biral*) in the uplands, and various kinds of elevations like treeless hills (Oro. *yanil*) and mountain ranges (Oro. *toksokol*).

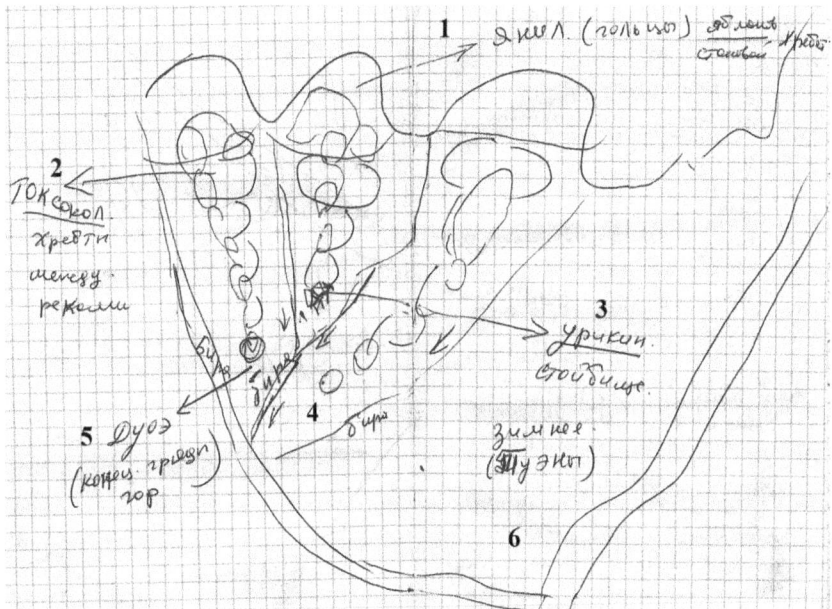

Map 5.1. | *Sketch map of reindeer* bikit *drawn by Nikolai Aruneev.*
1. Treeless hills (Oro. yanil); 2. Mountain ranges (Oro. toksokol);
3. Camp (Oro. urikit); 4. River (Oro. bira); 5. Ends of hills (Oro. duoe);
6. Field of hummocks (Oro. kever).

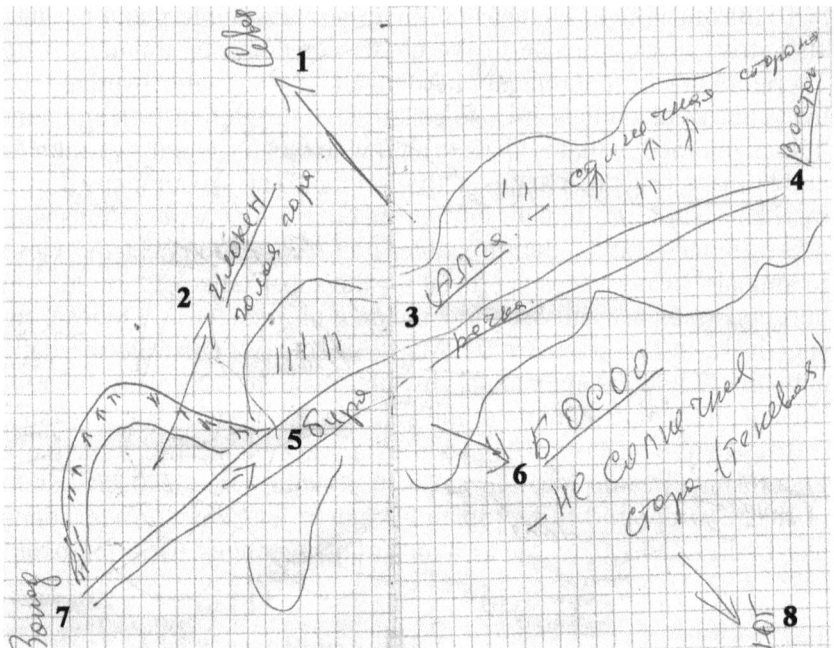

Map 5.2. | *Sketch map of moose* bikit *drawn by Nikolai Aruneev.*
1. North; 2. Treeless hill slope (Oro. iloken*); 3. Southern exposure*
(Oro. alga*); 4. East; 5. River (Oro.* bira*); 6. Shady side of slope*
(Oro. bosoo*); 7. West; 8. South.*

The *toksokol* environment was used by the reindeer herders of the
Zhumaneev-Aruneev family for hunting and trapping sable, squirrel and lynx in late winter, while the *yanil* environment was an important reindeer grazing area used until early spring. On the right
side of Map 5.1, Nikolai left a space identifiable as a wide *kever* field
near the camp. At the time the sketch was drawn, the *kever* had been
visited by groups of reindeer searching for young grass on the root
hummocks. This signalled that the reindeer were about to move and
shift their activities to a nearby *kever* downriver. The existence of an
open *kever* area near a camp is important to herders' observations
of animals' movements through multisensory awareness. The second
sketch map (Map 5.2), drawn to show a moose's *bikit*, details how an
animal that was being tracked moved among different treeless hills
in early spring, when the sun affected snow conditions differently on
each type of slope. The moose moved through southern slopes the
hills in the daytime and grazed on northern slopes at night. The map
shows the living place (Oro. *bikit*) where a moose grazed on young

grass before being stalked and killed without the use of dogs. A good hunter aims to 'fix' an animal to a certain place in order to gain luck.

Contesting Animals

Animals are perceived as nonhuman persons with their own volition and the intelligence to communicate among each other and with humans, learning from them. Nikolai believes that animals and humans are equals in this game-like contest. Other hunters also say that any animal can be extremely cunning (Rus. *khitryi*). Animals and humans compete in a kind of game of hide-and-seek, trying to avoid being scented, seen or heard and trying to increase their knowledge about the other. Animals always react to a hunter's behaviour; therefore, a hunter's actions must be constantly adjusted to the animal's movements, hiding human intentions while moving within the animal's *bikit*. It is said that animals can always tell when a human is carrying a rifle and will hide from an armed individual. The contest between hunter and animal may include the switching of roles between prey and hunter, in which the hunter' intentions must remain hidden to avoid provoking the animal's attack. The reindeer herder Nikolai Aruneev described such interactions in the following way:

> You should not even think badly about animals. They can read your mind and may go to war against you. If you are thinking about hunting a bear, he will start hunting you. He will wait for you or follow you. You should not give away any information or even talk badly about animals to your closest friends. It is best not to mention animals at all. If you find a wolf's den and talk loudly about it, I will go hunting and the wolf will escape for sure; it will shit and it will hide.

When a hunter strives to gain knowledge through empathy about a particular animal, that animal can easily receive these signals, feel the hunter's intentions and react to his or her thoughts. Nikolai tried to convince me that 'if a herder starts to think and talk too much about reindeer sickness, then a wolf will certainly use the opportunity to visit him and prey on this animals'. Therefore, one must carefully hide one's intentions when preparing to go hunting. The act of butchering an animal must also be hidden in order to escape misfortune and not invite the presence of predators in the area.

Upon returning from exploring a *bikit*, a hunter usually calmly drinks tea. Even after seeing fresh tracks or finding a bear's den or moose's *bikit*, she or he just makes small talk after slowly drinking tea while staring into space. Misleading language was not exclusive to hunting preparations. In some cases, a hunter simply misleads others by saying that he or she is 'going to have a look around' or 'going for harvesting of bone marrow' (Rus. *chumugovat'*).[2] One hunter from the village of Yumurchen phrased the seen many fresh tracks of moose thusly: 'I have seen a huge squirrel, we may eat some liver.' Nikolai Aruneev would usually wait until late morning, drinking tea and slowly getting ready for the trip like he was going nowhere particular. The elder Fiodor Zhumaneev would leave camp very early in the morning, when nobody could see him or assume he was going hunting. His daughter Tamara remembers that nobody was allowed to even ask where hunters were going, how long they would be gone or what they were planning to do. Her sister, Nadia Zhumaneeva, told me that 'one should not even look in the direction the hunter went'. As I learned from my own experience, one is expected to find out about other hunters' activities by observing their behaviour or preparations rather than asking questions.

Aleksei Aruneev did not like hunters who visited him to talk about hunting in detail before leaving the village. He would even avoid running into them, swear and say, 'These people just wag their tongues' (Rus. *tol'ko odin iazyk*), adding 'What the fuck kind of hunters are they?' (Rus. *kakoi khui eto okhotniki?*). Aleksei believed that those who make too much fuss (Rus. *suietiatsa*) in the village before leaving for a hunt are usually among the first to return because they have had no hunting luck.[3] Nikolai once vividly told me that 'all animals will run from a talkative person whenever such a person walks by. The animals run away without a chance to track them'. But if all emotions are hidden, one may acquire luck in tracking an animal, even when following a week-old trail. Elders told any young hunter who had killed an animal never to show emotions about the kill – 'neither happiness, nor passion'. Aleksei never told his wife about his hunting success straight away on his return, although she was always very curious. In fact, having had luck, he and his brothers told a story that was the opposite of the actual outcome of the hunting trip so as to secure luck for future hunting trips by not being boastful. By contrast, hunters talked openly about their misfortune, believing that a master-spirit would take pity on them and give them more animals next time.[4]

Nicknaming animals in daily conversation is also part of a hunter's strategy of concealing plans to ensure a successful hunt. By giving them nicknames, hunters aim to mislead the animals.[5] Thus, the Tungokochen Orochen often refer to lynx (Oro. *diukte*) as *nanda* (fur) or as *sekalan* (with ears), to wolf (Oro. *changa*) as *irgichy* (with a tail) and to sable (Oro. *niaka*) as *udia* (imprint). These nicknames are most often used to talk about potentially dangerous animals who may harm people and whom hunters do not want to encounter. Hence the wolf (Oro. *changa*) has more nicknames than most other animals. In the Zhumaneev-Aruneev family wolves were called in Orochen *bagdama* (white one), *kuturuk* (luck-holder), *bamlak* (vagabond),[6] or in Russian 'grey one' (Rus. *seryi*), 'plunderer' (Rus. *razboinik*) or 'dog' (Rus. *sobaka*).[7] Other hunters would even refrain from using geographical references like *uktan* (island of forest surrounded by a field) when approaching certain sites in order to maintain their hunting luck (see also Zelenin 1929: 126).

Reindeer, moose and red deer gain information about their animal kin by reading and following their tracks. Ermine also hunt by following the footprints of bears and wolves in order to 'steal' their kill. An animal may use its own tracks as a regular route. This is why the tracks of sables or rabbits sometimes become deeply carved in the

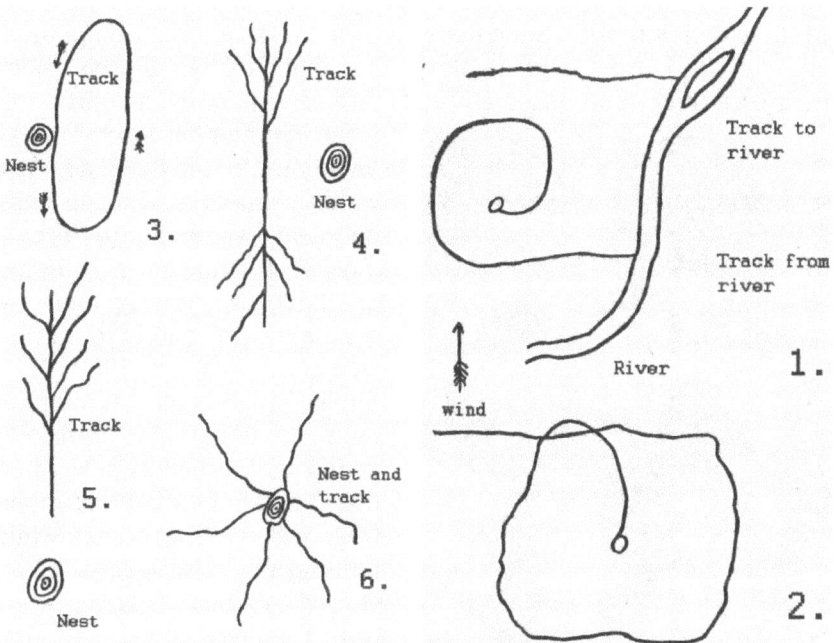

Figure 5.1. | *Tungus sketches representing different signs formed by tracks. 1. Tracks of male moose coming to the river and leaving it for a day's rest; 2. Tracks of a moose before it takes a rest; 3. Tracks of a squirrel moving in circles; 4. Two squirrel paths around the main nest on a tree; 5. Straight tracks of a squirrel from its nest; 6. Tracks of a squirrel leading in all directions. (Petri 1930: 39, 57)*

snow, prompting hunters to set traps along them. The proper reading of tracks and marks on soil and snow, trees and bushes also helps the hunter protect himself against animal attacks. An animal is said to 'communicate' with the hunter through its tracks, leaving information on its 'mastery of place' and its intention to protect it.[8] Vasilevich (1930: 66) notes that 'the Evenki believed that animals leave messages for hunters'. These webs of tracks increase in significance the more the hunter knows about a living place, an individual animal and last year's tracks (see Table 5.1).

Animals also struggle with each other over places, leaving their own marks and signs. People say that no one has enough living space nowadays because of the state's domination over people and animals alike – today only the strongest survive. Hunters say that bears often knock down trees, biting and bruising the trunks with their claws. The animal then rubs its underside against the old trunk, leaving its hair and smell to warn others. Other animals that compete with bears may do the same thing, trying to leave their bite marks higher up the trunk to show their strength. Such marks are called *kikchavkin*. Competitors are likely to leave the place alone after that. Animals always check their own tracks and become much more careful, or even aggressive, when a hunter has left his marks on them. It is said that if a hunter wants to meet a bear, he need only leave some sign by breaking off a branch or stepping on the bear's tracks; then the bear will start searching for him (see also Vasilevich 1969: 217). Similarly, bears alert hunters to their emotional state, breaking young larch trees as a warning that they are in a fighting mood (Fig. 5.2). Leaving tracks while hunting may also lead to being chased by a bear. Nikolai Kirilov from Bugunda village said that wild boars, like bears, have special holes in their scapulae; as soon as a hunter touches the animal's tracks, it feels pinpricks in these 'ears' and becomes aggressive towards humans.

Figure 5.2. | *A larch tree marked by a bear.*

With their constant examination of tracks, hunters and animals alike are always aware of each other's presence.[9] When hiding a trap under the snow by a sable's tracks, our hunting group always took care not to leave too many footprints. Aleksei Aruneev said that the prints of hunters' shoes pique an animal's curiosity, so it may pass by the trap instead of stepping on it. Sable tracks must be approached from downwind to keep the scent of a human footprint from spooking the animal. In winter, hunters hide tracks by sweeping snow over them. When pursued, sable or lynx are likely to move along fallen trees that are not covered by snow, so as to leave no tracks behind. They may also circle around an area, trying to shake predators off their tracks. Animals also often walk in their own old tracks or the tracks of other animals. Rabbit tracks that are deeply imprinted in the snow often become roads for other animals, so it is impossible for dogs and hunters to track rabbits. When animals hide their tracks, hunters may search for hours and finally give up. Once, as I was trailing a wounded red deer with Vitia Mordonov from the Taloi reindeer herding camp, the dogs lost its scent and the tracks because the animal had walked in a river. Such manoeuvring by animals was interpreted as the outsmarting of those trailing them. Viktor Lokushin told the following story about how hunters outsmarted a lynx:

> I really respect the lynx for its braveness, skill [Rus. *masterstvo*] and carefulness when it is approaching others [Rus. *skradom*] and because it is not a greedy organism [Rus. *zhadnyi organism*]. Thousands of times in my life I tried to chase this animal after I found fresh tracks and only a few times did I manag to kill this smart animal. The lynx walks skilfully and silently without squeaking and chirping. It can approach such careful animals as reindeer or roe deer in fifty degrees below zero, in winter, when a little squeak of the snow could be heard at a distance of one kilometre. I do respect the lynx since it will kill a bird or a delicious rabbit and live on it for three to five days, not hunting again until it has eaten all the meat without wasting any of it. It is not greedy. One lynx, which we nicknamed Umurchu, was powerful, it was healthy and cunning and our dogs could not attack it openly so they left it alone and came back after some barking, while the lynx stood his ground and wouldn't even climb a tree. It walked off with easy steps and we never could track it down by following the dogs' barking. Once I got an idea, I put a *botolo* [bell] on a dog and made him a fur coat. When I found fresh tracks of Umurchu I put this on him and unleashed him to let him track the animal.... So the lynx finally was killed after having been hunted for many years. It jumped on a tree when it saw that furry devil and was shot by me.

Many such stories tell of how a hunter, after unsuccessfully chasing an animal, at last found a way to overcome the animal through his

Table 5.1. | *How hunters read animal tracks in summer and winter.*

Summer:	*Manure*	*Other signs*	*Dew or Rain*	*Colour*
	If the manure looks fresh, it is less than 24 hours old.	If a footprint is seen imprinted in lichen (Rus. *yagel*) and the lichen is wet, then the footprint is fresh and the animal has just walked there.	If there is no dew on the grass within footprints in the morning, an animal has just walked there. Such grass does not glitter if the sun is shining.	If small trodden bushes lying on the ground have fresh colour, then the animal has just walked there. If they have darkened, then the animal might have walked there 2–3 days ago.
	If the manure is dry, then it is more than 24 hours old.	If branches are broken and the broken wood is still soft, then the animal has just walked there.	If footprints are washed out by rain or dew, then the animal walked there before the rain.	If the trodden grass is getting dry and of yellow colour, an animal walked there about 2–3 days ago.
	If the manure is completely dry, it means the animal's footprints are more than a couple of days old.	If gum (Oro. *lu*, Rus. *smola*) is dripping from an animal scratch made on the trunk of a larch tree, then it is about 24 hours old. If no gum is dripping, then the animal mark is less than 24 hours old.		

skill. However, hunters are not always successful and may face the prospect of returning home empty-handed. One may try to weaken an animal by means of rituals like cutting off the leg of a hunted sable or cursing it while trying to kill it. Such behaviour can be seen as improper and prone to cause misfortune. Many stories like the following one, told by Viktor Mordonov, have a different ending concerning hunting success. For many years Viktor tried to hunt a clever sable who left large prints. He tried to track it in various ways and also set traps for it. Other hunters were also unsuccessful in hunting this

(continued)

Winter:	Colour changes	Wind	Temperature	Sun
			The lowest temperature can be observed when the sun is setting or raising.	
	If snow in the print is a darker colour than the surrounding snow, the footprint is about 24 hours old.	If the footprint is almost covered with snow, it can be almost one week old.	If the footprint has a hard icy rim and icicles can be seen in it, then it is about 24 hours old or the footprint was left in the night-time.	If the footprint is glittering like glass, then the animal walked in the night-time (it means that it is quite fresh).
	If the footprint's colour is similar to the colour of snow, then the footprint was left today.	If fresh snow is seen in footprints, it can be 10–30 minutes old.	If the footprint is tough, it means it can be older than 24 hours.	If the snow crust is tough and broken into many parts after being touched with *tyevun* or hand, it can be less than one hour old.
	Footprint up to 3 hours old are of a brighter and lighter colour.		If the print is of soft snow, it is less than three hours old.	

sable. After some years he finally managed to find the sable's living place and even his nest (Oro. *gaino*). He set an elaborate snare close to the place, left a capercaillie as bait and took a good hunting dog with him. However, after a few days he found the dog caught in the snare. Meanwhile, the sable had not even touched the grouse, even though its tracks were all around it. Viktor concluded that one must not push too hard when luck proves elusive. In this case, the spirits reacted by taking a dog from the hunter, causing misfortune for him.

Establishing Camps

The long-term use or re-establishment of camps is conditioned by the hunters' and herders' interactions with domestic reindeer and wild animals. Success in tending a large herd hinges on the adjustment of campsites to the 'animals' needs' and to the herder's need of reindeer for hunting. The hunters' and herders' desire to acquire luck in their subsistence practices also influences their choice of campsites (Oro. *urikital*), the camp's setup and the daily ritual interactions in the camp. The camp structure allows the projection of awareness onto a larger area around the camp, revealing its enhanced capacity to use an environment that is inhabited by various animals. Reindeer herders' camps are dynamic assemblages of different zones established by humans using their multisensory awareness to adjust to nearby animal living places in order to get the best access to them. Such camps consist of different camping zones dispersed over the area in some distance from each other (see layout of camp in Map 5.3). The establishment of camps allows people to monitor the surroundings while performing their daily chores around the fireplace. By being attentive to sounds, observing the movements of animals and birds and the behaviour of the domestic animals, feeling the wind and paying attention to the fields, ranges and slopes around them, hunters gain the best knowledge on how to fulfil their subsistence needs.

An Orochen camp must not be pictured as one unified area; rather, camps consist of multiple zones that are spread over a large area. In his ethnoarchaeological study of Dene hunters' camps in Canada, Robert R. Janes (1983: 68–69) describes various camping zones as functionally distinct areas of different activities. Reindeer herders and hunters adjust their camps to the living places (Oro. *bikit*) of animals as part of their subsistence strategy. In this section, I analyse this adjustment in terms of the process of establishing a camp, the structure of the camp and the activities that occur at the camp, using the example of a camp near the Poperechnaia River in the winter of 2004.

I participated in the setting up and using this camp from the very start of my hunting group's stay in it that winter. I observed how it was organized with continuous attunement to the landscape and the reindeer from winter to spring. During the fur-hunting season of 2004–2005, the Zhumaneev-Aruneev family tended their reindeer herd at the Poperechnaia River from early November to the end of April. Then they moved downstream to the reindeer calving camps (Map 5.4: 30). They migrated from one camp to another based on their knowledge of the weather and the usual movements of animals. Herders always make their decisions in accordance with the weather conditions, so the length of the stay at a particular camp was also adjusted to the weather conditions and varied from one year to the next, as a particular season might start two weeks earlier or later than expected. Local reindeer herders in fact seldom use the terms spring, summer, autumn and winter in naming their camps, although the log house has been called the 'winter cabin' (Rus. *zimnik*) since *kolkhoz* times. Nikolai referred to camps using either the name of a river or a certain stretch of it, sometimes including certain activities. For example, he might mention 'the rutting-season camp in the uplands near the Poperechnaia River'.[10]

We chose to spend the coldest period of the year 2004 in a camp built on the slope of a treeless mountain (Oro. *ian*, R. *golets*) called a *duval* (see *Kamenistaia golets* in Maps 5.3: 2 and 5.4). This treeless hill offered tundra vegetation including lichen, an important part of the reindeer diet, and was encircled by two eastern tributaries of the Poperechniaia River. The place was considered the gateway to the whole valley, from where the reindeer's movements could easily be monitored. Like many other campsites, this one was located on a *naminga*, a flat area covered with mature trees, where people felt comfortable enough even in the cold season because it was protected from the wind and warmed by the sun in the daytime. We harvested firewood from the thick forests (Oro. *siikta*) covering the riverbanks. An open field stretched to the camping area. Such fields are common features of campsites.

The campsite featured some permanent storage platforms (Oro. *gula*, Rus. *labaz*) (Map 5.4: 16) and three standing smudges (Map 5.4: 14) used by visiting herders in the warm season. There were also remnants of a fence built in Soviet times (Map 5.4: 6) with some open platforms called *delken* (Map 5.4: 5, 7).[11] Aside from three platforms and a reindeer corral, there was also a spring called *bukta* (Rus. *nakip'*) just two kilometres away. As a source of drinking water, a *bukta* attracts reindeer, which come to lick ice from the *bukta* in the wintertime as it remains free of snow all the time. According to Nikolai, the reindeer who visit the *bukta* always come to the reindeer herders' camp looking for salt. They also feed on a green plant called *sivak* that grows around the *bukta*.

As soon as Olga and I arrived at the campsite, we tied the dogs to the trees in a circle around the camp. Then, as typical for local hunters, the first job was to start a fire (Map 5.3: 9). The new fireplace was built a few metres away from the old one. First, we built a cooking

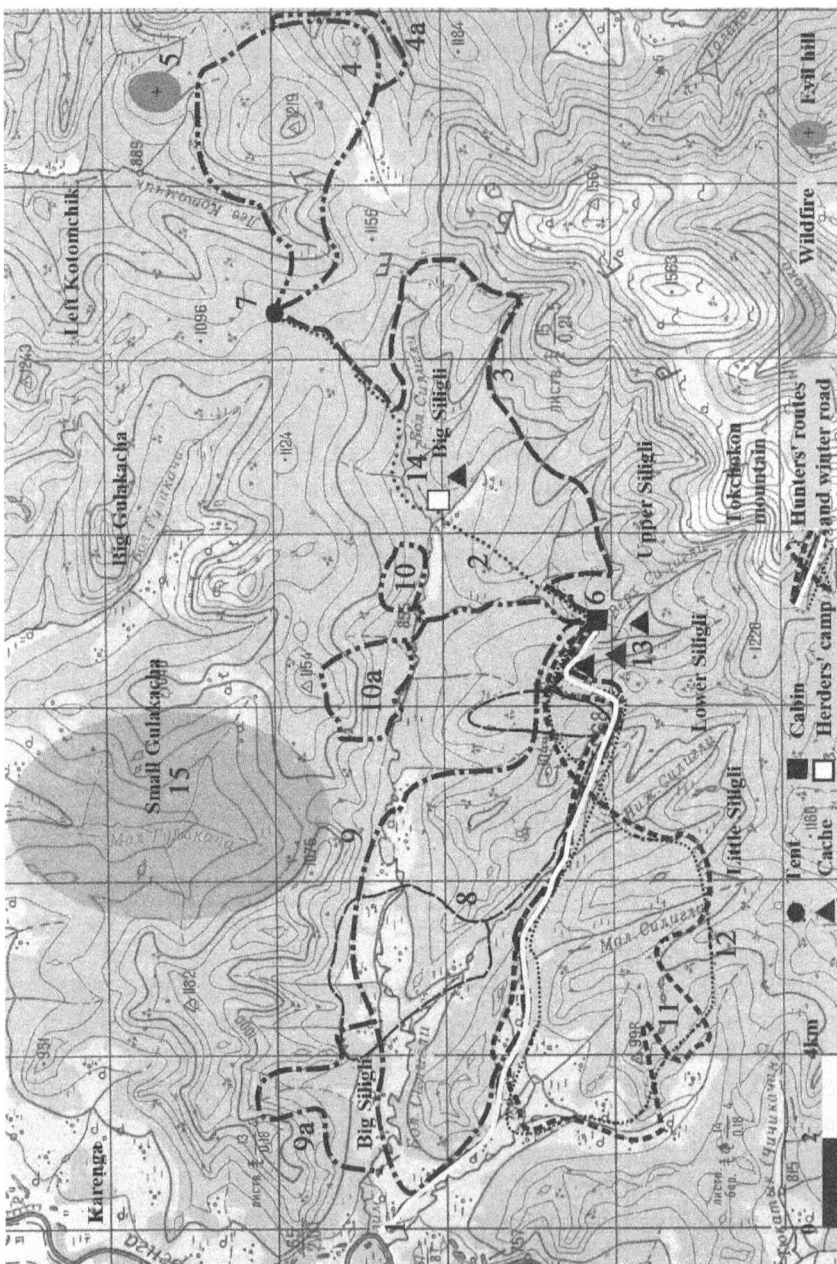

Map. 5.3. | *Map of the Zhumaneev-Aruneev family's camps and other important sites of subsistence. The map represents a preliminary location of established camps that were used in last decade. There is a much greater number of camping sites found in the area where herders can return to re-establish it and build new construction near it.*

rack called a *togan*. It can support a kettle and is usually made from a green birchwood (Oro. *cholban*) pole two to four metres long.[12] One end of this pole is weighted down with a stone (Oro. *dido*), while the other end is elevated with the support of two crossed forked posts (called *choska*) about half a metre in length. A wooden tripod called a *sounang* is also used. Both the *sounang* and the *togan* are usually made from green birchwood, which is resistant to burning.

In the cold period, water is kept boiling most of the time at the outdoor campfire in order to prepare food for the dogs (Oro. *dalavun*) and tea or food for the humans. The zone around the fire, called the *otog*, remains clear of snow due to the constant cooking (Map 5.4: G). Standing at the fire, one could easily observe all the dogs and the reindeer herd. Dogs always barked to alert the hunters that reindeer, wild animals, predators or humans were approaching the camp, so the herders always knew in advance that someone was coming.

As soon as the fire was started, two big kettles were filled with ice for making tea. During the fur-hunting season, water was drawn from two places about 170 and 220 paces from the outdoor fireplace.[13] The ice-fetching site (Oro. *diukulavun*) (Map 5.4: 13) was located at a spot where the ice was sufficiently thick and free of grass, needles and sand. When Nikolai's brother Yura and a visiting reindeer herder, Lionia Unaulov from Ust' Karenga village, arrived from the *baza*, two canvas tents were erected at some distance from each other (Map 5.4: E, H) in order to give each household a certain privacy and each tent sufficient space for various activities and storage. One tent was for the two brothers Nikolai and Yura; the other was for me, the grandmother Olga and Lionia. These two tents also represented different social groups. Many other former reindeer herders said that among the Orochen, different generations live in different tents located some distance from each other. This creates separate living zones called *aranil*, each with its own temporary storage platforms, racks and woodpiles close by. The tents' entrances faced in different directions, but each had a direct view of the reindeer salt lick site, the dogs and the open field by the river. The dogs were kept near the main routes leading to the living area. Every hunter cut grass for his dogs' bedding from a nearby field of hummocks and leashed the animals in a place where they could be watched from the tent.

For the first week, we gathered firewood next to our canvas tents. Later we walked some three hundred metres into the dense forest to harvest firewood (Map 5.4: B). In fur-hunting camps, firewood fuels the handmade iron stoves and the campfires that are usually located outdoors. Hunters and herders usually did not heat the canvas tents at night and put just a little wood into the iron stoves during the day.

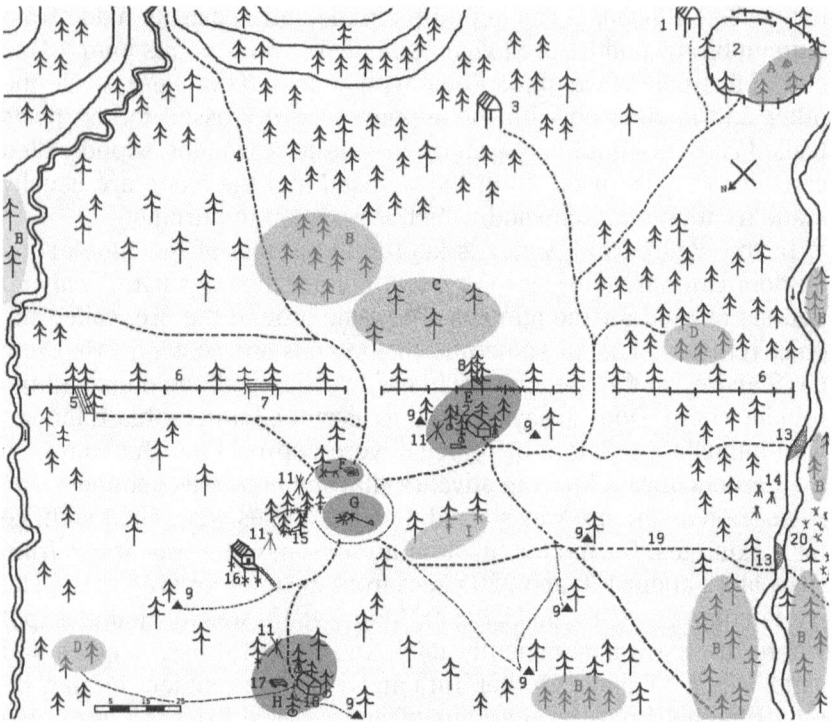

Map 5.4. | *Sketch map of fur hunting camp near the Poperechnaia River (February 2005). The camp is located near a treeless mountain area between two of the river's highland tributaries. The map depicts several daily activity areas scattered over a flat site covered with mature trees. The sketch delineates the main activity area (Oro. aran), including the fireplace tripod (Oro. togan), (G) and nearby areas such as a dry goods storage site (Oro. kurekan) (15), a tripod for storing bundles above the ground (11), and a firewood chopping and storage site (F). Two tent areas (E and H) shown in more detail depict canvas tents, tripods used as racks (Oro. lokovun) (11), horizontal pole racks (Oro. lokovun), a flooring platform (17), a meat open platform (Oro. delken) (5, 7) and garbage sites located near trees' roots (Oro. nelge). Routes that start from dwellings lead to the storage cache (Oro. gula) (1, 3, 16), opne storing platform delken, leashed dogs sites (9), ice harvesting sites (Oro. diukulavun) (13), wood harvesting sites (Oro. umgaun) (C), toilets (D) and reindeer corral (Oro. kure) (2). An area in the reindeer corral (A) is designated for slaughtering and butchering reindeer, burning flesh leftovers as undigested lichen found in intestines (fire is marked) and drying skins. Area C is also a reindeer-marshalling site where mature trees are brushed with salt. The fence (6), built in the Soviet times, separates living areas from reindeer resting sites. In the same area is a summer short-term camp with a couple of smudges (14).*

They usually lit a fire in the stove before going to sleep. After they got into their bedrolls, no more firewood was added to the stove until morning, despite temperatures reaching −60° C. We cut two dry (sometimes semi-dry), mature larch trees every day and carried four to six heavy logs (50 kg each) on our shoulders to the sawing site. The hunters always stressed that camps must above all be located in areas that are rich in firewood. Rather than carry these heavy logs in the next year, Yura Aruneev told me, they would move the camp about three hundred metres to have dry firewood 'close at hand' (Rus. *pod rukoi*).[14] The wood sawing and chopping site was about fifteen metres away from the main fireplace (Map 5.4: G). In the camp we found and repaired an old sawhorse made from a log (about 1.5 m long) resting on four supporting legs. Logs were usually placed waist-high (approximately 1 m), and two people cut the wood with a double-handled saw called a *druzhba* ('friendship'); they also chipped wood with an axe. We spent two to three hours each day sawing, chopping and storing firewood at a site called a *mookit* (Map 5.4: F). Noisy chainsaws were never used for cutting wood, and all this work was usually done in the evening, when the reindeer were away from the camp, in order to ensure that their rest was as comfortable as possible.

The first group of domestic reindeer visited our camp within a few days of our arrival. Their visit was guaranteed by the successful choice of the campsite. With the help of salt, several reindeer were lured into a nearby corral thirty metres in diameter. Four two-year-old male reindeer were chosen for slaughter. Yura shot them in the forehead with a small-calibre TOZ rifle. The carcasses were butchered inside the corral and offerings made to the fire, and by sprinkling rice around the inside of the fenced area (Map 5.4: A). The butchered reindeer were given in payment to the driver, who was waiting at the Kotomchik River base camp. Some reindeer hides were stretched on the corral fence, while others were stretched with a long carved stick called an *ivalda*. According to Nikolai, it was important to do the butchering in an enclosed space so 'the smell of the reindeer's blood wouldn't scare off other reindeer from the camp'.

Throughout the entirety of my stay, our camp was permanently under construction as the different zones were rearranged according to the herders' shifting needs. We regularly visited the base camp, bringing back various products and storing them on the three platforms. Non-perishable goods like flour, dry dog food, salt, sugar, dry bread, candies and canned vegetables were also stored on the ground in an area called the *kurekan* (Map 5.4: 15) which was fenced off with young larch logs tied to mature larch trees. A system of racks (Oro.

lokovun) was constructed for storing a variety of tools, furs and personal belongings. Various bundles were hung above the ground on tripods to protect them from humidity, mice and dogs. Some of these tripods (Map 5.4: 11) stood close to the tents to store gear for daily use (such as footwear or drying *kamus*). Others were located near the *kurekan*, where bundles and bags with personal belongings were hung about one and a half metres above the ground. Some tripods used in the Poperechnaia winter camp held fur bundles about two metres off the ground. The *kurekan* was also used as a rack for saddles (Oro. *lachako*) and reindeer bags (Oro. *potal*) (Map 5.4: see X in 15). Most tools, ammunition and dried meat were wrapped in plastic or canvas bundles and hung on racks placed in nearby trees. All kinds of personal belongings were hung on branches of mature trees and the corral fence. Ammunition bags (Oro. *tauseruk*) were strapped to the tent frame, and guns (Oro. *paktyravun*) were often leaned against nearby trees or tent frames so they could be grabbed quickly, should a bear enter the camp. The domestic reindeer were caught by the salt lick and taken to a special area (Map 5.4: I) where one or more were saddled and loaded with bags. In this special area reindeer halters were tied to trees (see the X marks on trees in Map 5.4: I). Such gear was taken down to be used each morning and tied up again as soon as its user returned from riding a reindeer. People also tied gear for daily use – harnesses, ropes, belts, backpacks, clothes – to mature larch trees close to the tents, platforms and *kurekan*. This way of organizing the camp shows the intention 'to have everything at hand'.

We walked to the base camp on a path across the highlands (Map 5.3: C) that had been broken by Aleksei when he established the clan community. Reindeer herders more or less ignored the lowland route made by ATVs in the Soviet era about twenty years earlier (Map 5.3: D). Indeed, Nikolai mostly avoided anything reminiscent of the marks left by industry on the taiga, as he was convinced that such modern constructions had negative effects on people's lives. We moved all meat supplies from the *delken* of the base camp (Map 5.3: 13) to the *delken* of the Poperechniaia River camp (Map 5.3: 21) within a few weeks. Other *delken* were filled with bags of flour, while small *delken* mostly held the frozen leftovers of reindeer and pieces of a reindeer that had been killed by wolves, which were used to feed the dogs. Smelly bottles of gasoline were placed near such meat to keep scavengers away. Four weeks later, Yura Aruneev built several low platforms (Oro. *ongovun*) (Map 5.4: 17) near his tent. Built from young larch tree poles and about twenty centimetres above the ground, these platforms were used to store provisions like meat for daily consumption and berries kept in birchbark bowls. Some leftovers and cans, bottles or bags were placed in the branches (Oro. *nelge*) of trees close to the fireplace. Some leftovers from slaughtered reindeer, hooves and bones were also left close to the tents (see the O mark under the trees in Map 5.4). This was not a dumping place for garbage, however, but another kind of storage place, since hunters often reuse leftovers, cans and bottles. Nikolai Aruneev explained that such items are placed among tree roots to keep reindeer from cutting themselves on the sharp edges.

All other seasonal camps consist of several isolated functional zones. In the mosquito season, a smudge area (Oro. *samnisal*) holding four to ten smudges (Oro. *samnin*) is built about three hundred metres from the tent. Each smudge consists of a fireplace surrounded by poles that form a cone. Reindeer usually spend half a day resting in the smudge area. Mature larch trees covering the whole camping area and the smudge area give shade to humans and reindeer in the hot summer months. Shade also offers some protection from warble flies and botflies, which are less aggressive in the shade. Nikolai maintained that he preferred a camp on the northern slopes of mountains (Oro. *bosoo*, Rus. *tenevaia storona*) to living in the sunny side of the mountain in the summertime, saying that 'the wind always cleans out the camping area and pushes the bloodsucking mosquitoes out to quieter and more closed places'. Rutting-season camps are usually located close to wet hills and ridges that are rich in mushrooms (Map 5.3: 25, 26, 28, 34, 33). Corrals up to fifty paces in diameter are built to control the reindeer herd, part of which is kept inside the corral every day. Calves are also kept inside in the daytime; their mothers are expected to return to the corral after feeding on mushrooms at night.

Reindeer herders burn *kever* around the camp to create an open, treeless area, which is another key zone for the camp's success. Mosquitoes thrive mainly in in the wet, densely vegetated taiga, whereas open fields have fewer mosquitos and also make it easy to see and hear reindeer moving and attract animals to the camp. The Zhumaneev-Aruneev family builds salt licks in and around their camps to attract both domestic reindeer and wild animals. Large game like moose, elk, wild reindeer, roe deer, bear or boar may visit them at night. Hunters create salt licks (Oro. *taloi*, Rus. *solianki*, Rus. *solontsy*) especially at sites that are easily accessible to them but little known to other people (Map 5.3: 1, 2, 4, 6, 35, 36, 38, 39). Salt licks also appear naturally in places where the soil contains a high level of minerals. The herders regularly salt both the natural (Rus. *solontsy*) and artificial (Rus. *solianki*) salt licks.[15]

No matter where their seasonal camps are located, reindeer herders and hunters spend most of their time in camp close to the fire, where most of the time-consuming work of preparing food for humans and dogs, repairing gear or skinning animals takes place along with daily socializing. The fireplace is always located in a spot from which herders can observe the movements of their reindeer on the *kever* field and keep an eye on the smudging area (Oro. *samnisal*), the salt licks (Oro. *udiumokit*) and the corral (Oro. *kure*) while doing their daily chores. Aleksei Aruneev chose his campsite by paying careful attention to the surrounding area and its wildlife, even if the camp was used for just a night or two. A hunting camp is made in a wooded area close to a hill, quite often at a river junction. The location of our campsites always offered direct access to various areas. Our hunting trips started in the early morning. In rutting season camps we listened to the songs of mating elk, imitated them and hid our presence while doing our daily chores or talking. Aleksei's campsites were located in a kind of 'acoustic corridor' where we heard the whistling of the wind that blew from the uplands at night or from the lowlands in the daytime. From their camp the hunters could tell the presence of animals by the sound they made anywhere in the valley. We were indeed awoken several times in the early morning by the dogs barking about three to five kilometres from the camp. They had caught the scent or sound of an animal, hunted it down and called us to come with their barking. This success in Aleksei's subsistence activities was based on his choice of campsite and its adjustment to the wind direction and the terrain, which kept animals from smelling or hearing it. Hunters time their activities carefully and pay attention to the wind direction while doing their daily chores at the campfire. Cutting wood is very noisy, so they prepare firewood in the evening, after the time for hunting is over. Hunters also teach their dogs to keep silent except to bark at exceptional moments.[16]

When the Zhumaneev-Aruneev family makes camp at an old site, they usually select a new fireplace, although old fireplaces (Oro. *togokit*) are still discernible.[17] Nikolai Aruneev explained to me that every camp has its own spirit, its own energy (Russian *energiia*). Therefore one should not camp at the same site twice, lest the place's *omi* (soul) exert a harmful influence. According to Nikolai, reindeer will be healthy and people will be *kutuchi* (lucky) if they follow this rule. When I was hunting in the Ima River basin I noticed old fireplaces every thirty to fifty metres along a one-kilometre stretch of a *naminga* (a flat, dry area with mature trees along a ridge). Zhenia Naikanchin told me that his grandfather Fiodor Zhumaneev (also Nikolai's grandfather) used to pitch camp about two hundred metres from the previous year's site.

In Nikolai Aruneev's camp there is always more than one fireplace in any season. Iron stoves are not used in the warm period of the year, so two fireplaces are set up outside the dwelling. The main fireplace is usually located close to the larch bark shelter; the second one is five to twenty metres away. The main fireplace is for boiling water and cooking food, as well as for chatting and daily chores like tanning skins or repairing gear. The second fireplace is for boiling additional water that provides fresh tea all day long, and for preparing dog food. It may also serve for smoking meat (Oro. *sirna*, Rus. *kukuro*). In the wintertime, the main fire, maintained in the iron stove inside the tent, is used for frying food and boiling tea. The stove must be tended all day and part of the night because it is essential for providing warmth. In winter many activities are performed inside the tent around this source of warmth. An outdoor fire is also kept for preparing dog food and unleavened bread and sometimes making soup. It took several hours each day to melt ice and produce the approximately thirty litres of boiling water needed to make food for the six or seven hunting dogs in the Aruneev Zhumaneevs' winter camp.

Herders and hunters often talk about the area around the fire that is called *aran,* the site of all human activities that are connected to the fire. *Aran* also refers to the ground for erecting a chum (Oro. *diukiia*, conical skin tent). This site is the central area of the camp, where people spend most of their day doing kitchen chores and handicrafts. Sables (Baunt Oro. *udia*, Tungokochen Oro. *niaka*), squirrels (Oro. *uluki*), rabbits (Oro. *tuksaki*) and other fur-bearing animals are skinned close to the fire. The making of buckskin in winter also takes place at the fire or close to the iron stove in the tent. Hunters mostly return to camp by the end of the day and then do tasks like skinning, sewing, brushing fur and repairing leather footwear at night by the fire. I found myself skinning animals' legs and tanning the hides (Oro. *osi*, Rus. *kamus*) at the fire with others in the long hours of dusk in autumn and winter. Food is always consumed when people sit next to the fire. The fire gave light and warmth, which was important even in the summer because evening temperatures could still drop below zero.

In Nikolai's Aruneev's reindeer-herding camp, fire is considered the manifestation of master-spirits and is always offered the first spoonful of soup, meat or tea before any meal. Usually the person who cooked the meal makes these offerings. When food is shared, the herders also put a piece from their own bowl on the coals. This procedure is followed anywhere in taiga or village by almost everyone in northern Zabaikal'ia.

While butchering an animal, Aleksei Aruneev offered pieces of meat from its various parts to the fire. If a kill is not transported to the hunting camp, it is butchered and left on a specially erected platform (Oro. *delken*, Rus. *labaz*) near the kill site. In the autumn when nights are quite cold, the meat is covered with birchbark (Oro. *talu*). However, hunters always take a piece of meat from the kill site to the camp for supper – usually the liver, kidney, or tongue. Aleksei Aruneev once cut a slice off each part he brought back, heart, tongue, and liver, put them into the fire and said, 'God gave it to us, now we are treating Him.' Thus the fire was fed as a way of giving thanks for a successful hunt. When people cook food in a canvas tent or log house on an iron stove, the doors of the stove are opened and the fire is fed every day. It is believed that this way food is shared with that particular campsite's master-spirit (Oro. *odzhen*, Rus. *khoziain*).

Social activities like drinking vodka in a hut or in the village are always preceded by the offering of the first glass to the fire to honour the master-spirits that rule the particular area. When hunters spend the night in a deceased person's house in the taiga, feeding the *khoziain* is believed to also feed the spirit of the deceased and thus legitimate the overnight stay. This way of asking permission also guarantees a peaceful night and luck in the future. The practice is not known only among native people but is very popular among all Zabaikal'ia villagers, including Russians. Reindeer herders also perform a daily ritual of feeding the fire in the name of the master-spirit and sprinkling tea in the direction they intend to go for hunting.[18] They believe that the master-spirits shares its animals with hunters out of generosity; therefore hunters must also share their kill with the spirits. Spitting into the fire is considered inappropriate and disrespectful. Additional 'sins' include moving firewood with a sharp object – especially a knife, since a nonhuman being may get hurt – urinating on or saying bad things about the fire. Gilton Aruneev told me a story that illustrates the Orochen's perception of fire very well:

> The Orochen say that fire has a spirit that is very similar to that of humans. A couple of Orochen women were sitting around the fire at night softening skins, when suddenly the fire started making noises and shooting sparks. One woman got angry at the fire, grabbed her stick and hit the fire with it. It became silent, but after some time the women noticed a wounded person lying on the ground. There was no more light and warmth in the tent.

The women got very upset and scared and asked a shaman for help. It took the shaman many days and attempts to revive the fire again.

At the beginning of my fieldwork, when we were hunting near the Ima River north of Tungokochen village, I kept asking Aleksei Aruneev about the campsites of his grandfather, Fiodor Zhumaneev. It surprised me that Aleksei, who grew up in that area, could hardly point out any old campsites. Yet at the same time, I noticed that Aleksei remembered every detail from his previous hunting activities. He could recall previous walking routes and animals' tracks perfectly well, but when asked about campsites, he only said, 'my grandpa camped everywhere' (Rus. *vezde stoial*). Later, in the autumn of 2005, as we hunted a bear in Fiodor Zhumaneev's hunting territory near the Ima River, I noticed dozens of old campsites located every fifty metres on a dry area about two kilometres in length. In the morning, as we drank tea in the log house built by Aleksei's uncle Vitia Zhumaneev, Aleksei Aruneev pointed to an elevated area near the house. 'You see', he said, 'when I was eight years old our tent stood there.… My brother Yura and I lived in our own tent and even cooked food separately from my grandpa'. While telling another hunting story he pointed to campsite about a hundred and fifty metres from the previous year's campsite and then to the site of his grandpa's tent, about two hundred metres in another direction. When I started asking him about locations of campsites, Aleksei's cousin, Zhenia Naikanchin, who hunted in Fiodor Zhumaneev's former territory, explained to me that their grandpa had taught him that old campsites become 'dirty' (Rus. *griaznaia*). One should not stay there for a long time but move to another site. Aleksei's grandpa had set up a new camp every season by moving a bit farther from the previous one.

Nikolai Aruneev, who with his herd moves about two hundred kilometres from his grandpa's hunting territory, also changed the campsite or its structure every year. He explained this by saying that every old site has its 'own energy'. Hunters say that if you camp at the same site every year, the place's 'energy of the past' may negatively influence your present life. According to Nikolai, camping in the same spot can cause reindeer disease and predator attacks. Indeed, hunters say that if you have had no *kutu* in hunting at one campsite, you must move to another to 'escape misfortune' (Rus. *izbezhat' bedy*). The short supply of territory and potential campsites, which Nikolai calls 'the outcome of the Chita government's policies, forces herders and hunters to use the same campsites and herding areas for long periods. Under these conditions, Nikolai Aruneev escapes 'continuity with the past' by making his camp in the same place but changing the organization. He chooses a new spot for the tent and starts a new fire close to the old fireplace.

In my time hunting with Ust' Karenga and Tungokochen hunters, I observed that all of them avoided old campsites and started their fires some distance from old fireplaces, even when staying for just a few hours. Oleg Taskerov from Ust' Karenga village once refused to spend the night in a camp that had been established by his now deceased uncle, explaining that he that he did not want to be troubled by *arenkil*. One can run short of campsites rather than risk arousing *arenkil*, which molest people and their animals and bring them disease. Every hunter has stories of encounters with *arenkil* to tell. Gilton Aruniev told me about his experience of camping near a 'singing lake' where Orochen have drowned. The place is shunned because the *arenki* 'sing their songs there'. Everyone also knows about a rock near Usugli that is famous for driving people to jump from its ledge to their death. *Arenkil* talk to people, ask for cigarettes or food, tease dogs, steal different items, disorient people and even drive humans and animals insane. Local herders believe that old campsites hold the energy (Rus. *energiia*) of past incidents and thus influence people's present-day experiences of luck. Such experiences indeed shape the way herders organize their camps so as to acquire luck and avoid misfortune. Shirokogoroff (1935: 88) notes that the Tungus explained their choice of campsite in a similar way by saying, 'This is a good place, there are no bad spirits around'.

In December 2004, I walked with Nikolai Aruneev and Olga Zhumaneeva toward the Siligli River to camp there and hunt for furs. We travelled for three days, crossing several watersheds and four mountain passes to cover a distance of about seventy kilometres from our winter camp at the Poperechnaia River. We constantly made offerings to spirits on the way. While making an offering of rice to the master-spirits and boiling tea after we had crossed the last mountain pass, Nikolai told me we had arrived at our new 'home', where we would stay and hunt for the next two weeks. I was indeed happy to arrive, as I was exhausted from hiking in deep snow and it was getting dark. However, it turned out we still had to walk uphill for more than three hours to reach the intended campsite.

Believing that a *dovan* (mountain pass) marks the border between different basins controlled by different master-spirits, many hunters stop there on their way, dismount and have a smoke. Being entry points to a master-spirit's territory, these sites are important for establishing relationships with nonhuman beings. Various hunters perform rituals like leaving cigarettes, matches, candy, bullets or a piece of cloth when crossing a *dovan* (Fig. 5.3). Old wooden idols (similar to *seveki*) and bowls for leaving food offerings are found at some *dovan*. Traces of past ritual and economic activities and the remains of old camps may signal that 'some master-spirits live there'. Before entering the river basin where his grandfather had built many still present camps and storage platforms, Aleksei would greet the latter, believing that his spirit still dwells there and affects present-day hunters. Nikolai always greeted the spirits with offerings when crossing a river or entering a log house or old campsite. All hunters and herders perform libation rituals of sprinkling vodka in all four corners before spending a night in a log house.

A hunter may experience nothing but misfortune in some areas. When I asked people why they rarely camp near the Buktokon River, Yura Aruneev explained to me that reindeer dislike some river basins despite abundant lichen. 'Reindeer do not like some sites, but always come back to others', he said, adding that the Bazarnaia River basin, where there was less lichen, was very well liked by reindeer, so herders preferred to camp there. Later, his brother Nikolai confirmed that reindeer refused to graze on the Buktokon River and that 'when you force them they will start to get ill'. He added that reindeer herders

Figure 5.3. | *Aleksei Aruneev and Sopka leaving offerings at a mountain pass.*

who migrated to this area in the early 1950s had noticed then that reindeer shunned it for some reason. Nikolai remarked that it was a 'bad place' (Rus. *plokhoe mesto*) and that only in the future might the reason for it become apparent. Therefore, herders simply stayed away from that area. Other places were avoided because of a resident malevolent spirit with whom Nikolai could not establish a cooperative relationship. Nikolai even pointed out areas where he had ceased hunting on my map. However, state politics have so diminished the Orochen's territorial choices that they must force their reindeer to live in a certain area for a long time, even when they experience misfortune there.

Hunters' and herders' set-up and use of camps is shaped by their awareness of spirits, domestic and hunted animals' *bikit*, and experiences of luck. This awareness derives from their personal experiences, their reading and interpretation of wild and domestic animals' tracks, and the adjustment of their spatial activities to shifts in the environment and the movements of predators and reindeer. Catching luck while competing with individual animals also means being in the right place at the right time. The experience of luck when living in certain taiga places endows humans with a sense of mastery of their own *bikit*.

Notes

1. Willerslev (2007) describes how Yukaghir hunters of Northeastern Siberia imitate their prey and take on the animal's identity while hunting it. Thus the hunter perceives the world as the animal does, yet does not surrender his human self.
2. Bone marrow is a delicacy among the Orochen.
3. Similar stories about talking and making noise before hunting can be found among other Evenki; see Vasilevich (1957: 164).
4. A. Sharp (1994: 48) described how Chipewyans similarly present themselves as powerless to others in order to influence their behaviour.
5. On special languages among the hunters of Eastern Siberia, see Zelenin (1929: 113–138).
6. In Zabaikal'ia *bamlak* is a pejorative term for the BAM (Baikal Amur Railroad) forced labourers, who often got into trouble with indigenous people during Soviet times.
7. On interpretations of animals' nicknames among the Evenki, see Petrov (2000: 329–330).
8. Some hunters described walking alongside tracks as an opportunity to 'feel the animal's strength'.
9. For a description of how a sable misled Tungus hunters by leaving tracks, see Shirokogoroff (1929: 84); for descriptions of how squirrels try to outsmart Tungus hunters, see Petri (1930: 39).

10. Some ethnographic studies have classified Evenki residential camps according to seasons: winter (Oro. *tuvekit*), spring (Oro. *nelkinit*), summer (Oro. *dugekit*) and autumn camps (Oro. *bolokit*) (see Turov 1990: 142–145). I use the Orochen's own categorization of such camps according to the main activities and rivers.

11. These abandoned fences were built as part of a collective farm project for the more 'advanced' herding of reindeer in the 1980s. They enclosed areas of up to 25 km².

12. I noticed that hunters always preferred birch to larch (Oro. *irakta*) and was told this preference was based on the birch's resistance to fire.

13. Hunters and reindeer herders constantly consume hot tea in camp. Aleksei Aruneev told me that sweet tea is a mainstay of hunters. Hence, the hunting is said to be finished when the sugar and tea run out, whereas the lack of groceries is never seen as an obstacle to continuing the hunt.

14. The herders had camped in the area for about ten years and were considering moving farther south to camp by the Siligli River near some bald hills called the Tokchokonskii Golets. Fifteen years ago the area had been destroyed by forest fires, but nowadays, the herders maintained, reindeer are increasingly attracted by the recovered grazing areas in the Siligli River valley.

15. Orochen elders call such sites 'dirt' (Oro. *taloi*) since they are always grassless areas of wet soil trampled by animals.

16. A hunter's 'stupid' dog may be the reason that other hunters refuse to cooperate with him, since it could bring misfortune to the whole hunting team.

17. In summer and autumn, the hunters cover all fireplaces with sand and stones when leaving camp, to avoid causing forest fires. The elder Nadia Kopylova from Ust' Karenga village told me that water is rarely poured on the fire, but Aleksei Aruneev often used water or leftover tea to make sure the fire was out.

18. Most Orochen hunters and herders feed the master-spirits by feeding the fire. It is said that 'all spirits eat through the fire' (Varlamova 2002: 129).

CHAPTER SIX

Mastery of Time
Weather and Opportunities

In this chapter I describe the way hunters and herders experience time as a flow of interconnected events and places that change with the weather, the movements of animals and the fluctuations of rivers, all of which entail different opportunities for using the environment. Seasonal changes and weather conditions impact the activities of humans and animals alike. The weather influences hunters' and herders' patterns of movement and subsistence. Successful use of hunting and herding territories hinges on the ability to forecast the weather and adjust one's behaviour accordingly. Therefore, hunters and herders strive to forecast the weather so as to make the best use of the environment and be ready to catch luck. Knowledge of the weather is gained by observing changes in trees and plants, feeling the direction of the wind, reading and interpreting animal tracks and the behaviour of dogs and reindeer, listening to birds and heeding the signals of one's body. During their subsistence activities, hunters and herders 'read' such signs, trying to predict changes, and exchange information. Their constant preoccupation with the weather shapes their perception of temporality. No fixed, abstract calendar of activities exists; rather, flows of interconnected events link to places that human activity has to be adjusted to. In this context a person may acquire luck by using skills and knowledge to forecast the weather, remaining ready to adjust her or his movements to various taiga places and seasons in making use of any available opportunity. People conceive the weather as 'emplaced', that is, as something that can be known only by the daily experience of living in and engaging with certain places. The notion that embodied experiences of the environment and the proper use of the human body in daily activities lead to acquiring luck in sub-sistence indicates a perceived connection between the human body and the environment.

Weather and the Use of Places

In camp and village alike, any hunter's outdoor activity starts with an effort to forecast the weather, which is part of the process of making plans. In the morning, a hunter who plans to undertake a trip with reindeer deliberates over whether the reindeer herd will come to the camp for salt, which is more likely to happen on a cold and sunny day. People say that reindeer adjust their movements to the weather. When starting a seasonal migration or transporting gear from one camp to another, herders and hunters wait for good weather, like a sunny, calm day, in order to protect personal belongings from rain. Knowledge of wind, rain and temperature shifts are crucial to reindeer herding. Car-rying a heavy load while being plagued by bloodsucking insects on a very hot day can even kill a reindeer, some say. 'As soon as one warble fly [Rus. *ovod*] starts to fly, stop walking and have a break', Nikolai advised. A precise weather forecast can help herders avoid the worst insect infestations.

Knowledge about the weather is important for any kind of move-ment, be it travelling to villages, transporting goods, hunting and herd-ing, establishing camps or constructing dwellings. The shifting weather conditions require the constant adjustment of human activities. Most northern villages are located near big rivers, and the changing con-ditions of the river are also linked to the villagers' experiences of time. Rivers pass through different stages, from early spring floods to summer shallows, autumn flooding, first ice and full ice cover. They may flood after a strong rain and present serious obstacles to people's movement, trapping them in their villages or hunting areas. Therefore, trips are always planned according to the knowledge of river condi-tions. In wintertime, the large frozen rivers become roads for transport to remote villages and hunting sites. In summer villagers travel by boat or drive ATVs along the riverbanks to visit other villages departing from Tungokochen. Large vehicles are always in service near Tun-gokochen village, waiting to transport small buses and cars across the river (see Fig. 6.1). Drivers are always challenged to keep a car with passengers steady in a bouncing bus struggling with the current. Such river crossings are dangerous, and deaths from drowning are not rare.

Figure 6.1. | *A passenger bus crossing the Karenga River near Tungokochen.*

Some hunters can reach their winter hunting sites only by boat when the river is ice-free in early autumn or by vehicle after it is frozen solid. Hunters who have been unable to forecast the weather correctly may even fail to reach a remote place, thus losing the opportunity to hunt game or fur for weeks or even months. In such cases, neigh-bouring hunters may use that hunter's territory for their own needs, as long as they do not see his tracks (Rus. *nevidno trop, bez trop'ia*). Hunters and herders can declare their 'master right' to a territory af-ter they have, for several seasons, used certain places for subsistence that were not 'looked after properly' by those who used them before. According to Nikolai, a master hunter has to make regular use of his or her hunting territory by burning patches, maintaining routes, clearing away trees and establishing camps. The Zhumaneev-Aruneev family used several 'neglected' areas that were not officially part of their clan community's territory. Hunters who fail to reach their territory at the appropriate time may find that other hunters have already harvested squirrels, or that squirrels are not yet in the condition to be hunted. Maintaining places for reindeer grazing and hunting game is always tied to a person's ability to choose the proper time to visit these places and use any available opportunity. If you are unable to use a territory for subsistence, your claims are forfeit.

Embodied Knowledge

To refer to the way wrong decisions impact the whole body, Orochen hunters use a popular Russian saying: 'If one has a stupid head, then his feet do not rest' (Rus. *ot durnoi golovy i nogam ne pokoi*). Tugolukov (1969: 92–93) documents an Evenki calendar of months (Oro. *be*, moon) that correspond to parts of the human body (Fig. 6.2).

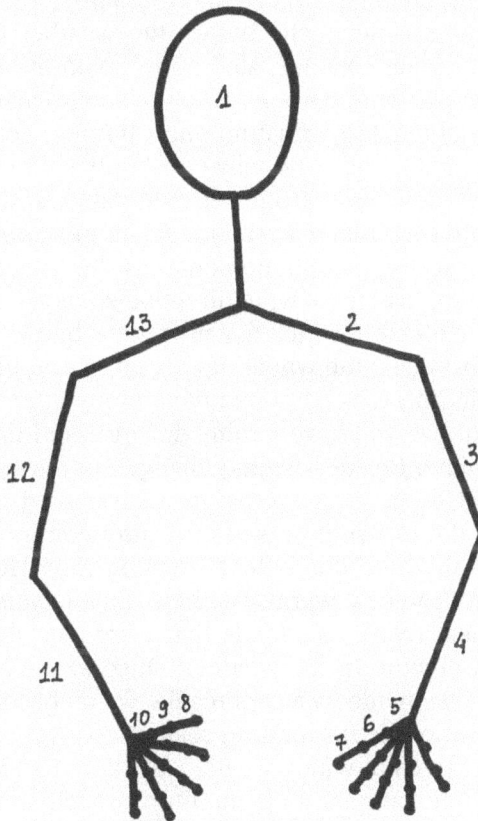

Figure 6.2. | *Sketch of old Evenki calendar (Tugolukov 1969: 92–93): 1. Sonaia – head or start of the year; 2. Evrimira – left shoulder (continuation of year); 3. Ichan – left elbow; 4. Bilian – left hand; 5. Unmui – finger root joints of the left hand; 6. Charatki – middle finger joints of the left hand; 7. Ogikta – finger tip joints or fist. From here, the year progresses to the right side of the body, starting with the fingers of the right hand. The second half of the year mirrors the first: 8. Ogikta 9. Charatki 10. Unmu 11. Bilian 12. Ichan 13. Tukturimira – right shoulder.*

Starting from the head, the first month begins after the spring equinox. Parts of the body are also reference points in such activities as manufacturing gear and measuring distance. Orochen seamstresses use their fingers to measure footwear (on Evenki embodied measuring see Shirokogoroff 1935: 61 and Vasilevich 1969: 185). A short walking distance may be referred to as 'half a leg' (Rus. *s pol nogi*).

Ingold and Kurttila (2000: 189) mentioned Sami reindeer herders' multisensory perception of the weather based on such bodily experiences as hearing, smelling and seeing. Similarly, Yura Aruneev told me he always gets a headache before the weather changes, while another hunter, Lionia Unaulov, said he felt pain in his joints before rain. Changes in the wind (Oro. *odyn*) are also critical cues for taking note of weather shifts and adjusting one's hunting activities (see Table 6.1). In Zabaikal'ia the wind may constantly shift direction. In the daytime it blows downriver from the mountains, and at night (Oro. *idia*) it blows upriver as either warm or cold air moves along the valley. Local hunters describe this phenomenon as the 'mountain's breath'. According to them, 'when the wind direction changes, a change in the weather can be expected, which usually means bad weather'. Aleksei Aruneev would forecast the whole day's weather on his morning trip to the toilet, bringing various phenomena to my attention, saying for example, 'Mangi, we will have a rainy day indeed, I have felt no dew on the grass today'. Besides feeling changes in the weather, Nikolai could also smell them. As we crossed a *kever* field he brought the strong smell of the growing grass to my attention, noting that grass usually smelled just like this before a strong rain. Hunters also say that animals can 'forecast warm weather' (Rus. *teplotu varozhyt*). On our walks we heard various sounds that were considered indicators of an imminent change in the weather. Once at the end of the cold period, a loud noise made by a capercaillie we met was interpreted as signalling the end of the fur hunting season.

Animals react to cold, windy weather by hiding and becoming untraceable, so some hunters stop hunting in such weather. As Zhenia Naikanchin explained, 'animals cannot catch a scent in windy weather and therefore do not feel safe and hide'. Nikolai Aruneev adjusted his daily hunting schedule according to the weather, pointing out that 'as the sable mostly eats berries, it waits for the clouds at the end of day'. Weather shifts affect not only the animals' behaviour but also humans' ability to see, hear and move silently when tracking or stalking an animal. Local hunters state that animals react to weather, feed, migrate, rest, hide, procreate or hunt only under certain conditions. As Nikolai said, 'animals try to acquire the most *kutu* [luck] in

Table 6.1. | *Correlations between weather and hunting activities.*

Meteorological Phenomenon	Snow (Oro. *imanda*)	Rain (Oro. *tygda*)	Wind (Oro. *odyn*)	Hot weather (Oro. *okok*)	Cold (Oro. *inin*)
Influence on hunting	Snow is very welcome in early autumn because it makes animal tracks much easier to see.	Rain is good for hunting because it mutes the noise of walking.	Wind is unwelcome, since all animals hide from it among rocks in the hills or in narrow valleys.	When it is hot, animals hide in the dense forest (Oro. *siihi*).	Hunting is difficult in the cold because walking is noisier and animals can hear the hunter from far away.
	In deep snow, dogs are unable move fast enough to trail animals.	Animals prefer to graze in the rain because it is cooler and fewer mosquitoes are around.	Small animals always hide in windy weather.	When the sun is shining in springtime, hunting is easy because the animals are grazing.	When the temperature is very low, sables and squirrels hide.
	Spring snow has a crust once its surface melts, so walking is very noisy. It is easier to track animals on skis.	It is uncomfortable for hunters to walk in the rain.	It is hard to approach an animal because it can smell you with the shifting wind.	All animals walk on *kever* in the springtime when it gets warmer, so this is a good time for hunting.	Cold weather in summertime makes for better hunting because mosquitoes are fewer and walking is easier.
	Hunting on the snow in winter is very difficult because the snow glare hurts your eyes.			When the winter grows milder, animals start moving around and you can start trapping fur-bearing animals.	
	Fresh snow in winter makes hunting easier by making tracks easier to read.				

their subsistence activities, just like humans'. Acquiring hunting luck depends heavily on a person's ability to foresee how certain weather conditions will affect animals' movements. It also hinges on the ability to adjust one's movements to those of the animals.

People also pay close attention to the weather when they use horses and cattle or cut hay for the winter. Weather is understood as a local phenomenon that can be experienced and known only by those who engage with local places. Environmental conditions can be different in the lowlands and highlands, and even from one river basin to the next. People trust only knowledge derived from the observations of environmental signs. Official weather broadcasts are therefore often objects of ridicule. This attitude is illustrated by a popular joke, which was told to me several times by different people:

> A shaman was asked by two hunters to forecast the coming winter. The shaman promised them a cold winter after he performed divinatory rituals and therefore the hunters left early for their hunting territories. Since the shaman had some doubt about his forecast, he went and asked a meteorologist. The local meteorologist predicted a cold winter since he had seen hunters leave early for hunting.

In the villages, hunters and herders who spend most of their time in the taiga are often asked about their observations concerning the weather or seasonal conditions. They may be asked to share their observations of the blossoming of certain flowers and the behaviour of birds in certain areas. Hunters also discuss the weather among themselves, guessing and weighing their observations about the coming weather against each other. Talking about the weather is thus not a matter of polite small talk but an important part of shared activities in perpetuating luck and partnership. Indeed, the biggest part of a hunter's everyday conversation concerns experiences of the weather, the observation of environmental features and 'signs' in a *bikit*. By sharing such knowledge, hunters coordinate their activities and adapt them to each other's plans. Such exchanges take place almost every night in reindeer herders' and hunters' camps.

Good hunters must be skilled enough to 'read the taiga' (Rus. *prochitat' taigu*) with an eye to weather shifts. Such information can be gleaned from changes in colours and in the texture or shape of certain objects. Weather can be predicted by observing the sky, trees, snow, wild and domestic animals. One must pay constant attention to the environment. Celestial bodies like the sun, moon, clouds and stars are important indicators of weather shifts because they are easily observable in the clear weather that prevails in the region. Everyone, it is said, knows that 'if the sun is setting behind a cloud, the next day will be cold. If it is shining brightly before sunset, there will be many clouds on the next day'. A special colour or aureole around the sun or moon may also indicate a change in the weather. If it is warm at sunrise or a certain circle around the sun (Oro. *sekalacha*) can be seen, colder weather can be expected. If the sun is shining brightly in the morning, a cloudy day can be expected after midday. One must pay also attention to the brightness of the sun. During a trip in the taiga, Nikolai Dimitrov shared his observations with me and other hunters and gave some explanations:

> If I see the sun turn red before sunset, I expect a strong wind at night or for the whole next day.... If I see an aureole around the moon in the evening, I expect a cold day.... If the sky is bright and stars glitter at night, I can expect a cold day.... If the clouds are like feathers, it will be a cloudy day or it will rain or snow.

Such knowledge may be combined with observations of domestic and wild animals, which are believed to have good knowledge of the coming weather. I heard it said that 'when a goose is flying low you can expect snow and cold soon, while dogs usually sleep curled up when cold weather is coming. When dogs eat grass, then expect rain'. When Nikolai Aruneev observed his reindeer jumping and playing, he took it as a sign of a cold day. He also said that reindeer rub their antlers against larch trees before a warm day. People who stay in camp can forecast the weather by observing the fire, coals and ashes. The elder Olga showed me 'how smoke may give a message'. If it rises slowly and stays close to the ground, you can expect a cloudy or rainy day, while glowing coals in the campfire are interpreted as a sign of a cold day ahead. One very cold winter morning as we were cutting ice from the river, she also pointed out how the tops of young larch trees were leaning against each other. She took this as the first sign for the coming of warm days. Every hunter knows a simple method to predict weather shifts from his knife blade: if it is dark, expect bad weather. A bear's skin is considered to be the perfect barometer: the colour and texture of the hair change and sometimes it becomes slightly wet before the coming of bad weather.

The experience of time and weather is not limited to observing the signs of weather changes. Hunters must sometimes wait weeks for good hunting conditions, so bad weather is seen as misfortune or as a punishment for sinful behaviour. Malevolent *arenkil* spirits may punish a hunter by sending a fog to make him lose his way. Many mythical stories tell of how good weather and seasonal shifts are the outcome of contests between among powerful beings. Oral traditions tell of the monster *mangi* or a 'powerful elk' who stole the sun (see also Vasilevich 1936: 282, Anisimov 1959: 12–13). The Orochen of Tungokochen referred to the Milky Way as the ski tracks of a hunter who chased that 'monster' and brought back the sun. Formerly hunters enacted this story in rituals called *ikenipke* by chasing reindeer or elk and ritually killing them in order to ensure well-being and luck (see Novik 1989: 23). People can influence the weather by coercing nonhuman beings. It is said, for example, that destroying a crow's nest will bring long-term rain.

It is also said that idols must not be taken from their bundles in bad weather, wind or rain, since they may be disempowered by bad weather. Furthermore, as the storyteller Yulia Semirekonova from Mongoi village said, when telling an epic the storyteller has to be sensitive to the environment. When birds fly over the place, the story must be interrupted and the storyteller must hide her or his face so the birds cannot 'steal' the epic's power. Elders remember that the telling of an epic could also influence the weather. Bogoraz (1919: 54) described how Chukchi storytellers used stories to calm storms, finishing them by saying: 'I have just killed a storm'. Most Orochen hunters know the simple method of calling for snow or rain by shaking a bearskin outside the tent (see also Sirina 2008: 124). Hunting after snowfall is easier, since animal tracks can be seen clearly, but people would laughingly add that this activity may also attract a bear, which is not a fortunate event at all.

Local Seasonality and Calendars

To interact with state officials, traders and tax collectors, and to celebrate church holidays, the Orochen require a certain degree of knowledge of the European calendar. The ethnographic literature on Tungus and Evenki therefore mentions various local calendars among the so-called 'settled Evenki', ranging from embodied representations to carved wooden markers.[1] Mazin (1992: 63) notes (drawing on Vasilevich [1969]) that many ethnographers have nevertheless had difficulty in connecting the Evenki perception of time to a calendar, since 'none of the elders could describe the calendar or give the names of the months in a certain order or link it to the contemporary calendar'. I would suggest that this is not due to memory loss among the indigenous elders but rather the expression of a peculiar perception of time that does not necessary align with the European conception. Smoliak

(1989), who worked among the Tungus-speaking Ulchi of the Amur Province, noticed a great variety of temporal categories linked to natural phenomena even among a single group of Ulchi. She aptly remarked that most calendars are the outcome of early ethnographers' interactions with indigenous people, when the former arbitrarily aligned the indigenous with the European Christian calendar, while the Ulchi tried to adjust their time-reckoning to the Russian example (ibid.).

Experience of time in the taiga is connected to a person's prediction of various events. The successful use of luck in various contexts is based on a person's ability to combine experiences and observations in an effort to foresee (Rus. *prosmotret'*) changes in the environment. Shirokogoroff (1935: 64) notes that 'the knowledge of small details could so far that e.g. the Manchu people, for example, were able to predict the day of the break-up of the ice on big and small rivers with an approximation of four or five days, which they may predict several months before the fact takes the place'. Orochen hunters and herders experience time as constant changes in the environment and weather that create various interrelated events and opportunities with regard to subsistence. The Tsar official Orlov (1858b), who travelled in Siberia at the end of nineteenth century, described the peculiar Orochen perception of time as follows:

> In general, the Tungus people do not pay much attention to counting time. They recall events from the past by relating them to certain sites on their migrations or to specific events like illness or the death of a reindeer and do not much care about the precise year and time. ... These new Christians never observe church festivals but always remember an occasion of luck in killing valuable animals. (Orlov 1858b: 23–24)

The perception of time among hunters and herders relates to weather shifts that cause changes in the behaviour of animals and human subsistence practices, rather than to the observation of 'standardized and abstract global coordinates of time' (Huber and Pedersen 1997: 579). The perception of the flow of time as activity recalls Harris's (1998: 74) study of the rhythmic manner in which social life and the seasons relate to one another. Rephrasing Harris, Orochen people's activities can be described as attempts to master their movements by constantly monitoring seasonal variations (see also Smoliak 1989).

The local hunters and herders perceived changes in the environment as leading to further changes, events and actions. Although some hunters claimed that accurately forecasting the weather has become trickier today since 'nothing remains in its proper place and is always shifting' (Rus. *vse ne nasvoih mestah, vse meniaetsa*), Nikolai Aruneev still maintained that 'everything in the taiga depends on one another' (Rus. *vse v taiga zavisit drug ot druga*). Once warm weather arrives and the snow starts melting on the slopes, herders must be much more attentive because the sun awakens the bears. Vladimir Torgonov, a speaker for the Baunt Orochen community, told me the elders believed that the sun hides in the *chum* accumulating warmth during the winter, then spreads much of this warmth in spring. With the onset of warm weather, the first grass appears on the *kever* and the reindeer start to migrate to the calving grounds. This event is called *charulin* (time of the tree sap) because the sap is starting to rise in the trees. Hunters said it gets hard to walk at that time because buckskin footwear (Oro. *emchure*) gets wet in the melting snow. As the snow melts, patches of the slope begin to appear. This also means that herders have to move to their camps from the lowlands to the uplands, following their reindeer. Crows (Oro. *turanil*) return from the south at this time, staying close to humans and 'helping to foretell *kutu* [luck]'. Elders respect the crow as a messenger, and Vladimir Torgonov says that the period of 'extreme cold' (winter) ends with the crows' reappearance. This event is called *turan* (crow), because the crows are hatching their eggs. Soon the reindeer herders are busy taking care of reindeer calves and fighting predators. By the end of this period, the larch needles have turned green and the bushes have started blossoming.

According to Nikolai Aruneev, the call of the first cuckoo announces the coming of the warm period. This period corresponds to the end of the reindeer calving season and is the best time for hunting large game. Moose have become fat enough to be hunted. At this time the first mosquitoes start attacking reindeer and humans, so the reindeer herders maintain smudge fires in their camps to protect their reindeer from mosquitoes and thus more easily control the herd. At this time, berries ripen on the branches and animals graze in the river bottoms close to *kever* fields and lakes, searching for fresh grass. Hunters may go to the marshes to hunt large game. Reindeer herders clean lice larvae off their animals' antlers. Birds start teaching their fledglings to fly. Smudge becomes more and more important to protect reindeer and humans alike from the swarms of warble flies (Rus. *ovod*, Oro. *irga*) that arrive with the rising temperature. Andrei Dogonchin, a hunter from the Baunt District, called this period *irgalaka*, the period of the active warble flies. By the end of *irgalaka*, reindeer and all other ungulates have grown fat on mushrooms and berries. In the upland camps, herders build fences and live inside with their reindeer during the mushroom season, called *irkin*. At this time the reindeer start to lose the velvet of their antlers, and reindeer herders begin cutting off the dry antlers to keep them from rotting. People also select reindeer for castration and transport.

The end of the warm period comes with a rich harvest of bilberries. The first frost (Oro. *iksen*) marks the end of the blossoming of nature. There are fewer mosquitoes and more dew in the morning, and the nights get longer and colder with brightly shining stars. Birch leaves are the first to turn yellow. At this time birds gather into flocks to get ready to fly south. Yura Aruneev stated that for him, autumn started with the onset of the reindeer's rutting season, called *sirudian* (Rus. *gon*), when hunters must keep an eye on their reindeer to protect them from wild reindeer bulls that try to 'steal' female reindeer. Villagers start to pick loganberries (Rus. *brusnika*) and blueberries (Rus. *golubika*) for the winter. It is much easier to pick berries with a special birch bark bowl when they are frozen and dry. As soon as the larch needles begin to fall, elk and moose start their rutting games. This is the most exciting time of the year for hunters, who now leave their camps and villages for the autumn's rut hunting. They take along a special tool for imitating the call of a bull elk. Skins are tanned and smoked at the end of this hunting season, since autumn skin is considered best for winter footwear (Oro. *emchure*) and gelded reindeer are not bothered by the smoke. The last remaining birds, like geese and ducks, leave for the south. Lakes and rivers are now completely covered by a thin layer of ice.

Hunters and herders say that their experience of winter does not correspond at all to the 'month of December' or the 'snowy period'. What matters to them is that the water disappears from the rivers in the uplands of the reindeer's winter grazing areas. This is an important indicator of when animal pelts are of the best quality. From this point on, snow can be expected to cover the ground until spring. Squirrels are about to start their migration, and therefore many people start hunting around the villages. The reindeer herders and hunters of the Zhumaneev-Aruneev family move to their fur-hunting territories in the Nercha River basin, far from their summer herding territories. They take along only a few reindeer to carry the tents and groceries. Only a few reindeer herders stay in camp, as the village hunters also leave for their log cabins.

Fur hunting lasts until New Year's Day, when most hunters return to the village to spend a few weeks celebrating. Vladimir Torgonov says that hunters have to do a lot of walking before the New Year, since sable run up to twenty-five kilometres per day in search of food.

Because there is usually little snow (Oro. *imanda*) before New Year's Day, hunters call this period 'the time of big walking'. During this 'big walking time' they hunt mostly sable, typically with the help of a dog. It can be expected to snow much more after the New Year, and the hunters have to adapt to these changes. They say that the peak of the cold weather comes after New Year's Day. As there is more snow on the ground, it is a period of 'little walking'. One can hardly walk because of the fresh snow, and the sables continually retrace their own tracks (Oro. *oktol*). Hunters also break their own paths and use them regularly when trapping sables. It is considered almost inevitable that by the end of the 'little walking' period, hunters in remote areas run out of meat and have to stalk birds and small animals. The days are now sunnier, and the snow is covered with a crust of ice, which makes moving around difficult for large game. People must seize the opportunity to hunt during *giravun*, the time of the snow crust. This is the best time for tracking moose on skis. Soon the warmer weather will signal the sable mating period and their fur will diminish in quality. It is said that as soon as the snow feels wet, the fur-hunting season is over.

Reindeer herders were not interested in celebrations like the New Year. They rarely referred to calendars when talking about their experience of hunting and reindeer herding; instead, they cited certain spatial or seasonal activities. Hunters of the Zhumaneev-Aruneev family arranged meetings with each other with statements like 'I will arrive in the lowlands of the Bugarikhta River after the first call of the cuckoo'. Hunters talk about events that are important to them with reference to weather conditions or places. Aleksei Aruneev told me: 'I shot my first bear near the rutting-season camp of Biromiia, when the small rivers were frozen but water could still be found beneath the ice [Oro. *birakan*]'.

This case study demonstrates that Orochen temporality can be described not as a fixed and abstract calendar, but as a flow of intertwined signs and changes, situated in places, to which people have to adjust their activities in order to succeed in their subsistence. In this context luck is achieved through the successful prediction of, and influence upon, the weather to ensure that hunters and herders make the best use of certain hunting areas and certain animals.

Notes

1. On various types of Evenki calendars, see Orlov (1858b: 21), Shirokogoroff (1935: 57), Tugolukov (1969: 93), Mazin (1992: 62–67).

CHAPTER SEVEN

Herding, Hunting and Ambiguity

Humans' involvement with hunting and herding is considered a way of life that sustains life, health, the environment and luck. Living with animals every day is held to generate value by itself. In this chapter I describe the social nature of humans' interactions with domestic reindeer and dogs, as well as with predators like wolves and bears. In pre-Soviet times the Orochen perceived their relations with bears and wolves as a cooperation based on respect, autonomy and sharing between humans and animals. Today, hunters say that in an environment of shortage and state constraints, they have to dominate and even poach animals just to survive. In this chapter, I will continue my description of the Orochen's interaction with wild and domestic animals, arguing that it can be understood as a complex, dynamic process of competition that involves both cooperation and domination on certain occasions and structures people's spatial experiences.

In describing human-animal interactions in circumpolar societies, Ingold (2000: 72–73) proposed the two opposite modes of *trust* and *domination* as a framework for understanding hunters' and pastoralists' interactions and relations with animals. On the one hand, the relationship between hunter and game is based on trust, that is, the hope and expectation that the other partner will do likewise and respond in ways that are favourable to you (ibid.). Domination, on the other hand, is a form of human-reindeer relationship found among pastoralists that is based on the presumption that domestic animals lack the capacity to reciprocate and care about themselves and therefore control over them has been relinquished to humans (ibid.). While these modes of interaction may apply to some communities of pure reindeer herders or hunters, contemporary Orochen see the hunting of wild animals as a form of ever-shifting competition involving an ambiguous ensemble of practices and ideas of cooperation and exchange. By contrast, the Orochen perceive their interactions with domestic animals like reindeer and dogs as cooperation, based on people's competence and reciprocity as well as their respect for the animals' autonomy and agency. Among the Orochen, both reindeer herding and dog breeding are closely intertwined with hunting, so these separate economic modes must be understood as elements of an interdependent subsistence strategy that encompasses an integral system of skills, knowledge and notions of personhood. A person's interaction with animals is based on his or her intimate engagement with both living and dead animals and their living places. In this context there is no clear distinction between wild and domestic animals.

Reindeer Herding: Reciprocity and Autonomy

Before the Soviet policy of collectivization was implemented, Orochen reindeer herding activities were part of a hunting-based subsistence economy that was typical of many indigenous groups in the sub-boreal forest region of Southern Siberia. Orochen elders remember that before collectivization, their parents owned about thirty reindeer on average, with individual variations ranging from ten to a hundred and fifty head (see also Titov 1926a: 5). Some reindeer herders, having retired from the collective farm, maintained their way of life of hunting with small reindeer herds of thirty to fifty head until the early 1990s. Reindeer were slaughtered only rarely and were mainly used for riding and transporting camping or hunting gear. Some female reindeer were also milked. Domestic reindeer were tame and easily approached and harnessed and could be used as pack animals and ridden in the camp or the taiga. The herd usually grazed fairly close to the camp, and most female animals wore bells around their necks that protected the herd from predators. The sound of the bells also told the herders the location of the herd in the taiga. The elder Bultai recalled that reindeer could easily be called back to the camp by shouting in the direction of their assumed location or shaking a salt pouch with hooves attached like a rattle. Fiodor Zhumaneev's grandsons told me that their 'grandpa set up camps where he had everything at arm's length' (Rus. *vse tam bylo u nego pod rukoi*), including his reindeer. Although the reindeer were tame and well cared for, they still could be driven off by wolves, lured away by wild reindeer in the rutting season or stricken with disease, so the herders inspected their grazing herd constantly. If unharnessed, any reindeer used for riding or transportation on a hunting trip would leave camp right away and keep moving farther away every day. Therefore various devices, like the piece of log attached to reindeer to impede his movements called *moonmokan,* were used to impede the reindeer's movements and to be able to track it in the morning.

In 1970s, collectivized reindeer were raised mainly for the value of their meat, and herd sizes could reach two thousand head. Such large reindeer herds had to be monitored regularly. In periods like the calving or rutting season the herders had to spend all day and night watching the herd's movements and behaviour and scouting the vicinity for the tracks of predators. In addition, collective farm specialists built large corrals and fenced areas for different seasons that were intended to minimize the loss of reindeer and increase the animals' biomass. Wild reindeer offspring were usually killed, as they might become leaders of a group of reindeer and become uncontrollable. As one retired veterinary specialist explained, 'the wild and tame subspecies had a different grazing biology, a different phenotype and behaviour and therefore must not interbreed'. Wild reindeer were skinnier and taller, and their grazing areas were larger and mostly confined to the uplands. Maintaining such large herds in the mountainous taiga would have been impossible without the service of indigenous hunters called in Russian *volchatniki* (wolf hunters), employed by the collective farms to hunt such predators as wolves. The reindeer herders also left bait poisoned with a chemical *barium* on the wolves' tracks. Nevertheless, the reorganization of collective and state farms and the shifts in grazing areas, along with many irrational decisions by officials with little knowledge of reindeer, caused a tremendous loss of reindeer stock. Even today, upon seeing wild reindeer, hunters and herders still recognize the colours and shapes of domestic reindeer that belonged to the state farm in the Olekma District of the Zabaikal Province.

Today, only fifteen to thirty tame and trained reindeer usable for transportation are left from the Zhumaneev-Aruneev family's large herd of five hundred head. Recently this number has decreased even further. In 2004 only one reindeer that could be used for riding was left, and even the elder Olga rarely used it. Herders from Tungokochen District do not use sleds or snowmobiles, which would be useless in their mountainous, rocky territory. Every adult reindeer of the herd is known by age, sex, colour, name and character, and sometimes even by parentage and life history. Herders use an elaborate terminology to describe the use, role, colour and other characteristics of reindeer.

Well-tamed reindeer are called in Orochen *mongnan*. At the time of my stay in 2004–2005, the Zhumaneev-Aruneev family did not own many of these. The herd consisted of adult female reindeer called *niami* and adult male reindeer that have not been castrated called *siru*. The castrated adult reindeer are called *aktavna*, while a partially castrated reindeer that still has a passion for fights is called *naran*. Male yearlings are called *multakan* if already castrated; noncastrated yearlings were *sirukan*. Reindeer are carefully selected for certain roles. The largest and healthiest male reindeer are chosen for breeding and therefore are not castrated, but other tame male reindeer who are chosen for transportation are castrated.

Newborn reindeer are called *ongnokan* (male) or *songnachan* (female) and female yearlings *niamikan*. At two years reindeer are fully grown. Females of this age are called *satiari* and males *evkan*. Not every female reindeer calves at this age. A barren cow is called a *ialova*. Luck in reindeer herding would be impossible to achieve without the herders' successful interaction with the leading reindeer (usually an elder female animal) called the *nioraki*, *diuloptun* or *ioraptyn*. Reindeer are chosen to perform different kinds of work. A trained, castrated reindeer called a *gilga* is used for transportation, whereas adult female reindeer – *umiri* – are used for milking. An *iktan* is a reliable three-year-old reindeer that is used for transportation, while *niuorkana* means a reindeer that is ill. An *uvuchak* – a reindeer used for riding – is considered the kind most closely related to the hunter. In the village of Bagdarino in Buryatia, such an animal was killed in its owner's funeral ceremony in order to carry the soul of deceased to the world of the dead. Many Orochen stories tell of how an *uvuchak* or a hunter's dog can be killed as a substitute by spirits seeking revenge for the hunter. Loss of an *uvuchak* is seen as huge misfortune, and sometimes even as an indication of the loss of hunting luck.

Zabaikal'ia has few reindeer herders with whom the Zhumaneev-Aruneev family can exchange reindeer to enhance their herds' bloodlines, so interbreeding of their animals with wild reindeer is not uncommon.[1] Hybrids of wild and domestic reindeer are called in Orochen *boiutkan* or *mongnotutkan*. The offspring of wild and domestic reindeer are very hard to control. However, the second generation of crossbred reindeer is easier to manage, herders note. Crossbred reindeer are also thought to be much healthier and stronger than domestic ones. Some herders have even tried to domesticate young wild reindeer. Interbreeding has never been a matter of open discussion among reindeer herders. Successful interbreeding of domestic and wild reindeer depends on constant selection, as the herders have to choose and slaughter the 'wildest offspring'. Hybrids often become leaders of the herd and lead all the other animals far away from the camps. Therefore the attitude to interbreeding is ambivalent, since it blurs the distinction between domestic animals, with which humans cooperate, and wild animals that are slaughtered for consumption.The second or third generation of hybridized reindeer are said to have all the character traits of domestic animals and be also very healthy.

The Orochen villagers who were previously involved in reindeer herding call the Zhumaneev-Aruneev family's reindeer 'wild' (Rus. *dikie*). Other villagers do not even hesitate to hunt such reindeer because, according to them, they 'wander everywhere' (Rus. *vezde shorahaetsa*). About meeting such an animal, people ask rhetorically, 'What should I do, should I just look at it?' (Rus. *tolko smotret' na ego chtoli?*). In this context, daily interactions between humans and reindeer are all the more critical to maintaining a relatively large herd in a hilly territory covered with sub-boreal taiga.

The Orochen describe reindeer herding luck as being achieved when a person who owns as many reindeer as are needed for hunting and transportation maintains that herd without significant losses through the years. They also say that a person is extremely lucky to maintain a herd that is healthy and looks pretty. A pretty herd is well-fed and includes many female reindeer and strong bulls with large antlers. Its individual animals are of various colours, preferably light, white or a mixture including white or light colours. Successful herders can recognize each reindeer by its 'face' and can tell when one is missing or has not been seen for a while as soon as they look at the herd. They are also familiar with the herd's 'social life', including such details as which animals gets along with each other. Most adult reindeer are called by name. They are known by their physical features and character, and are rarely counted. Skilful and lucky herders do not state the exact number of their reindeer, as one must not boast about one's reindeer. Similarly, Oskal (2000) noted that among the Sami, 'determining the exact number of animals in a herd can spoil reindeer luck and lead to reindeer misfortune (*guorzuvullot*)'. Hence, Evenki reindeer luck depends on the herders' actions and is premised on their interaction with reindeer, master-spirits and the landscape. Moreover, reindeer-herding luck is also seen as something of a personal character trait.

Orochen elders tell many stories about how reindeer became angry at humans who put inadequate effort into cooperating with them and caring for them. The elder Agafia Dandeeva from Rossoshino illustrated the interdependence of reindeer and humans in the following story (as retold by Anna Naikanchina):

> Orochen life is worthless without reindeer. Therefore, the Orochen love reindeer like a brother. Many years ago, when reindeer could understand and speak in the Orochen language, one reindeer lived with a hunter's family. He was very clever and all the people loved him. However, he became old and the head of the family decided to kill him. The reindeer heard about the decision, but he did not want to leave the humans. He was not afraid of death, but he was thinking about his devotion to people and he started to cry about being separated from his family. When the Orochen saw him crying, they decided to let him live. Since then, the heads of families have decided to go hunting together. Since then, reindeer and humans stay together, and they stay together even after death.

Reindeer herding luck is based above all on people's enactment of cooperative relations with reindeer by feeding them with salt, providing smudges, protecting them from predators and creating and maintaining proper resting and grazing areas. The elder Gena Kirilov told me the following story about the cooperation with reindeer:

> The reindeer is a special animal that was sent down to earth from the sky by Seveki. Reindeer landed everywhere, but many people did not take care of the animals and therefore the animals ran away to the taiga. However, in places where Orochen lived reindeer were welcomed with a soft lair and a smudge fire providing smoke that protects them from mosquitoes. This way the reindeer landed safely and stayed with the Orochen people. But, in some places of the world reindeer fell, got hurt and ran away.

Nikolai warns that 'when a reindeer is not made welcome in camp, it gets wild and starts living on its own'. Hospitality for reindeer includes the herders' creation of culturally modified places like burnt fields and their maintenance of smudge areas where the animals can get respite from the mosquitoes in summer. It also includes the building of corrals (Oro. *kure*) in autumn. At any time of the year but especially in winter, salt plays a crucial role, as it is used to lure reindeer to a camp and attract the herd's lead animals in the taiga. To maintain the cooperation between humans and reindeer, the herders must adapt their movements to the herd and shift the location of their camps according to the reindeer's preferences. In doing so they have to be attentive to the herd's movement in a certain direction and establish their camp fairly close to the herd at the right time. It is said that reindeer who feel the presence of humans are more interested in maintaining contact with them. However, reindeer that are kept in the same place for a long time may become diseased. Herders have to acknowledge the reindeer's autonomy and respect their choice of grazing areas (see Table 7.1).[2] At the same time, it is important 'to have reindeer close at hand' so that they can be used to carry gear during the rutting season or on hunting trips.

Table 7.1. | *The main grazing areas and diet of the Zhumaneev-Aruneev family's reindeer herd, 2004–2005.*[3]

	Reindeer
Dec.	Lived on treeless mountain slopes (Oro. *yanil, goltsy*), feeding on lichen (Oro. *lalbuka*, Rus. *lishainiki*).
Jan.	Lived on treeless mountains (Oro. *toksokol*, Rus. *khrebty*), visiting lichen areas when the snow was not too deep. If the temperature fell, the reindeer moved farther up the mountains.
Feb.	Moved to narrow valleys (Oro. *ikon*) on the northern slopes (Oro. *bosoo*). In other areas, especially on the southern slopes, the snow crusted over when it became wet in the daytime.
March	Lived in the northern part of the lower mountain valleys.
April	Lived on hills (Oro. *ural*, Rus. *sopki*) and mountain ranges (Oro. *toksokol*) in places where the snow had melted in the sun and the soil, along with lichen and grass, was uncovered. They spent the night on the northern slopes and the day on the southern slopes.
May	Migrated to the lowlands to give birth and graze on *kever*. They preferred to live in sites called *diapko* (Rus. *zakraika*), between the forest and the fields (Oro. *kever*). They fed on young grass (Oro. *irgekta*) in the daytime and lichen (Oro. *enkel*, Rus. *yagel*) at night. By mid-May the reindeer had moved to shrub fields (Oro. *maril*) and into the birch forest to feed on the young leaves.
June	Fed on *kever*, grass, and blossoms.
July	Continued to movie between *kever* and *maril*, feeding on everything.
August	Lived in *diapko*, feeding on mushrooms and bushes. Later the reindeer migrated to wet, flat lowlands that are rich in mushrooms (Oro. *dainaktal*).
Sept.	Lived near springs between the mountains and the fields of the uplands. According to Nikolai Aruneev, 'the reindeer visited the flat uplands where they played rutting games', feeding on lichen and hydrophytes (Oro. *sivakil*) found in springs. They also moved to mineral water springs (Rus. *nakip'*, Oro. *bukte*) and freshwater sources (Oro. *silki*), where they fed on *sivak* and lichen (Oro. *lalbuka*, Rus. *lishainik*).
Oct.	Stayed near springs, in the foothills (Oro. *duval*) and mountains. Diet similar to that in September.
Nov.	Moved to their winter grazing areas on treeless mountain slopes, where they fed only on lichen.

When feeding on mushrooms in autumn, the herd splits into many small groups that roam independently of each other. During this period the herders must expend much effort controlling the herd, which always tries to move away from its grazing areas. The lead animal selects the routes and grazing areas for the group. Contact must be maintained with all groups of reindeer, especially those that have moved far from camp or beyond mountain ridges. Searching for the various groups of reindeer can be difficult and may take days or weeks. Hence, herding luck is also based on the skills and knowledge that characterize a competent reindeer herder. To maintain a reindeer herd, one must be able to walk twenty to thirty kilometres each day across river basins, following the tracks of various groups of reindeer. These searches usually start by circling the grazing area until the tracks of reindeer or of game are found. Spotting the scattered reindeer in the taiga would be impossible without skills in tracking and knowledge of the weather. Knowledge of individual reindeer's – and especially the leader animals' – character, as well as physical features like the shape of their hooves, is also indispensable for bringing the herd back to camp.

When a group of reindeer has been spotted, it must be approached carefully. The herder attracts the animals' attention by talking and offering salt. Sometimes it is impossible to bring the herd to the camp without subduing and leashing the lead animal by force. This can pose quite a challenge. In other cases, it is sufficient to turn the whole group in the direction of the camp. Herders tell many stories of how a herd stood silent and motionless in the bushes, trying to hide from the herder. Some herders are considered to have special skills in approaching a herd without spooking it. Reindeer are believed to be very smart and able to trick an inexperienced herder. The animals may hide in the bushes or bring mosquitoes to the herders' camp and then run away. Herders therefore need various strategies of persuasion and deception when approaching reindeer, returning them to camp or luring them into the corral. When a herd arrives in camp, the experienced herder can tell which reindeer are missing.

As soon as I heard the reindeer's barking and the herd approached the camp, I would run to put some green logs and wet moss on the fire to create as much smoke as possible. The reindeer usually run straight to the area of the smudge fires (Oro. *samningsal*) and gather in compact groups around the fires. A smudge fire in the shadow of trees sheltered from the wind provides the most comfort for resting reindeer. The dense smoke of smudge fires – *samning* (Rus. *dymokury*) – gives them a good protection against blood-sucking insects like mosquitoes (Rus. *komary*, Oro. *imikta*), black fly (Rus. *moshka*), bot-flies (Rus. *paut*, Oro. *irgekta*), ticks (Rus. *klesch'* or *karpisha*, Oro. *daikta*) and other kinds of flies that lay eggs in antlers, cause them to rot (Rus. *mukhi*, Oro. *dylkachan*). Harassment by insects exhausts the animals and can cause disease or even death in the summertime. Their constant visits to the camp accustom the reindeer to the smudge fires. They may visit the camp of their own volition to rest in the smoke in the daytime, when insects are most active. Herders even wait for certain insects to appear so that they can manage the herd with the help of smudge fires, rather than spending hours searching for the scattered animals every other day. The Orochen elder Ania Semirekonova from Mongoi village told me that reindeer stay with people only because people build smudges for them: as soon as dark falls and the mosquitoes disappear, the reindeer move away to graze in the taiga. Only certain types of wood are used for smudge fires. These may be moist deadwood (Oro. *irakta*), larch damaged by fungus when the wood is still white (Oro. *ilty*) or green larch. However, red-coloured larch (Oro. *kuchu*) must not be used because its smoke can be harmful to the reindeer's health. Adding wet moss to the fire increases the amount of white smoke. People also extensively use smoke to protect themselves and their horses and dogs from insects.

The reindeer's regular visits to the herders' camp offer the best opportunity for sustaining cooperation and intimate relations. Herders observe the animals' movements and condition in order to judge their health. Animals that appear to be sick are drawn away with an offering of salt or bread and then tied to a tree with a rope thrown around the neck. This makes it easy to approach a reindeer to tend to rotting antlers, for example, which are cleaned, sprayed with medicine or even cut off. Before the autumn of 2005, Zhumaneev-Aruneev family removed the antlers of almost all the male reindeer in their herd to keep them from exhausting the females and injuring each other in rutting fights. Salt is crucial to successful reindeer-human interaction. Salt is given to reindeer in their feed the year round, and the trees growing in the *samnisal* area are usually rubbed with salt for them to lick. The reindeer become so used to salt that individual animals fight for places close to the trees. The herders can use salt to attract any reindeer and leash it for further use. Reindeer also usually fight to lick the herder's hand and rush towards him when he urinates near the tree. It is said all across the taiga that reindeer are attracted by urine. They also visit scattered natural salt licks. Reindeer are so accustomed to receiving salt from humans that they react to any kind of behaviour linked to salt offering and urinating. Even wild reindeer encountered in the taiga overcome their fear of humans when they are offered salt or watch other reindeer approach humans for salt.

The herders also use controlled burning of wet lowlands, grass and bushy fields to create attractive places for reindeer to live in the area. Controlled burning of meadows (Oro. *diagdichiucha*, Rus. *opalka*) is a widespread practice among reindeer herders, hunters and villagers, as such burning helps to restore a foundation for domestic animal feed after a long winter. Every spring, herders and hunters burn last year's grass to allow fresh grass to grow more easily in hummock fields (Oro. *kever*). Usually the first grass stems (Oro. *irgekta*) grow on hummocks, whereas the grass blades called *nergakta* appear later. This grass is an important food source for reindeer from early spring through summer.

Parts of the *kever* that have not been burned for a couple of years are covered with young bushes and trees like ash, birch and willow. Nikolai Aruneev said that the reindeer eat the young shoots of these plants even in winter, and that both leaves and shoots are an important part of their diet in spring and summer. Herders and hunters also burn some areas covered with willow bushes (Oro. *maril*). According to Nikolai Aruneev, *maril* should be burned with special care: some *maril* need attention every two years, while others must be burned every five years. It is important to leave some bushes standing at a controlled burning because animals need places to hide. The burning must be done in the early spring, when the earth is still wet or frozen. The controlled burning practised in early spring and in autumn is a key element of the reindeer herding and land use strategy.

Orochen talk about the burning of patches in terms of reciprocal and balanced relations created with animals and landscape. Reindeer herders stress that if particular areas go too long without being grazed by domestic reindeer, they will be vulnerable to forest fires. Therefore, it is said that reindeer's presence means these areas will never be destroyed by fire. Furthermore, reindeer are seen as closely attached to certain places. Female reindeer are believed to always return to their own place of birth for calving. Several reindeer that Nikolai Aruneev had traded to Baunt Orochen from Buryatia returned to their place of birth, more than five hundred kilometres from their new location. Nikolai Aruneev contends that reindeer are the real master (Rus. *khoziain*) of the land and influence the well-being of other animals, humans and the land itself: 'If somebody took the reindeer from the land, it would definitely be completely destroyed.'

Many herders stressed that an Orochen has to live with reindeer to sustain health, *kutu* (luck) and joy of life (Rus. *zdorov'e, udachiu i zhizneradost'*). According to Nikolai, 'reindeer are a gift' (Rus. *olen' po-darok*), so a herder must not slaughter reindeer unless it is absolutely necessary. When herders need to slaughter a reindeer, they select an animal that is ill, wounded, old or rebellious. Nikolai slaughtered only animals that were hurt or in poor condition. Once he slaughtered a young, skinny reindeer that did not yet have a role in the herd, saying that 'this reindeer asked to be killed'. Reindeer may be slaughtered in rituals, as in the case of the death of a reindeer herder, shamanic healing rites or a visit by scientists, in which I participated as well (see Anderson 2012). Reindeer are slaughtered to carry a deceased person's soul to the world of the dead or as an offering to calm the master-spirits. In such cases the reindeer is specially skinned so that the hooves, eyes and penis remain attached to the skin, which is hung on a pole (ibid.). Nikolai says it is important to ask forgiveness from the reindeer before the killing and to constantly make offerings to the master-spirit by feeding the fire during the butchering. He typically sprinkled rice, sugar and vodka, apologizing to the reindeer, when his brother Yura slaughtered and butchered an animal. Elders say that before slaughtering a reindeer, one must explain to it that the herder has no other choice. A herder who kills a reindeer for money or drink may lose luck in reindeer herding and even health, and be abandoned by the herd. In some cases, however, reindeer may be sacrificed to sustain a human's well-being: Nadia Zhumaneeva told me about her brother, who suffered from epilepsy in his childhood. After a bad seizure, her father performed a special rite, killing a young reindeer, cutting out its beating heart and placing it on the boy's breast. Only this helped the boy to recover. The idea of exchanging strength with reindeer is widespread among the Orochen.

Communication with the spirits in charge of reindeer herding luck is maintained through specially selected reindeer called by Orochen *angun* (see also Vasilevich 1957: 170–183, on *iasil* and *ongun*, see Shirokogoroff 1929: 194). For this purpose an especially pretty and healthy reindeer is chosen, often white or bright in colour, with well-developed antlers. According to Yulia Semirekonova, the *angun* was spirit and animal at the same time and was connected to the master-spirit. Therefore it could ensure a herd's successful reproduction. The elder Pavel Naikanchin told me that the *angun* reindeer was chosen by the spirits and usually had a distinctive colour. According to Nikolai Aruneev, the *angun* was decorated with coloured stripes and had a special halter called a *mongalan* that was decorated with bullets and images of guns in order to protect the whole herd from predators and malevolent spirits. These reindeer were the first to be fed salt and bread when coming to camp. In Vladimir Torgonov's family, the *angun* were the only reindeer that were tethered when smudged, and 'women should not even look at it'. *Angun* were often smudged with smoke from the plant *senkire* (Lat. *Ledum palustre*, Rus. *bagulnik*, marsh labrador tea) as soon as the caravan arrived at a new campsite. Used to carry the idols locally called *seveki* or *barilak*, and bundles of amulets that provided hunting luck, these reindeer always walked at the head of the caravan. They never carry camp gear. Through interaction with this reindeer, a herder ensured the well-being of the herd. The Zhumaneev-Aruneev family considers white reindeer to be 'marked by the spirits'. They are never used as pack animals, their antlers are not cut and they are not castrated. In the Zhumaneev-Aruneev herd, one special reindeer called Mama (mother) was shown extraordinary respect and care. At more than twenty years of age she was very old, and she was the first to be fed salt and the only reindeer that received a piece of bread. Olga Zhumaneeva believed that Mama protected the herd and brought well-being to the other reindeer, so this reindeer was always well cared for. The herders thought and talked about it almost daily. It was a lead animal and carried a special bell that, according to Olga, 'was used by Mama to invite all reindeer to be safe around Mama'.

According to Vasilevich (1957: 170–183) such a reindeer was considered the protector of the herd and could also ensure the well-being of the herders. Many Evenki groups select such a reindeer for elaborate shamanic rituals conducted to heal sick clan members, or in the case of the unexpected death of a child. The shaman would obtain *musun* (power), *omi* (soul) or *kutu* (luck) for such reindeer while curing the sick person, thus protecting the clan from future misfortune (ibid.). During these rituals, certain bags were manufactured as placings for human's luck or soul, called *kuturuk*, or of reindeer luck, called *oror kuturuktyn*. In other cases, a shaman stole reindeer souls from the upper world, brought them back in a special bag and then chose the special reindeer, *sevek*. The loss of such a bag was seen as damaging to both humans' and animals' life energy or soul (ibid.).

Raising Dogs

A hunter may not have a reindeer or horse, but always owns at least one dog (Oro. *ninakin*). Orochen like to describe their dogs' hunting activities in great detail, telling of how humans and dogs are attuned to each other's behaviour (on the Kurumkan Evenki, see Safonova and Santha 2012). The dog is held to be an exceptional animal that can help people catch hunting luck (Oro. *kutu*) or cause misfortune to a whole group of hunters.[4] Hunters say that a dog owner (man or woman) must have a 'good hand' to raise a dog properly, and that a person's luck can be shared with a dog and vice versa. Dogs are often given animal names or the name of a former lucky dog, which is believed to make them luckier in hunting. Aleksei had owned a long line of dogs named either Belchik (Squirrel) or Sobol' (Sable). Some people are said have no luck in raising dogs. Their puppies get sick or a successful dog's offspring fail to show the same skills as the parent. Puppies from 'lucky hunters' are considered most likely to perform well in hunting. Vladimir Torgovov's father said that 'a hunter may lend his wife to other hunters, but he must never lend his dog', lest hunting luck slip away.

According to Nikolai Aruneev, there is a special relationship between dog and human. Dogs can feel the hunters' wishes and moods and even share their pain. Hence dogs often howl when their human master is ill. There are also many stories about dogs letting people know that their master is either ill or dead. Dogs cooperate and communicate with their human master on the hunt. In Aleksei's terms, 'the dog is expected to understand what the hunter wants, and the hunter must know what the dog is telling him' (Fig. 7.1). As already mentioned, hunters watch dogs closely in camp, on the road or in the village. A dog's behaviour may signal to a hunter that reindeer are coming or passing close to the camp, that a wild animal is approaching or that a guest is coming. Gena Dushinov could even communicate with his dogs in his dreams when they told him where game could be found. Among the Tungus-speaking Ulchi, a person's soul is believed to be closely tied to his dog, so the dog of deceased person is specially treated and fed after the funeral and then given away to a distant village (Smoliak 1978). At a curing ritual, a dog could serve as an intermediary between the spirits and the sick person (ibid.).

The way hunters teach hunting skills to puppies resembles the way they share their knowledge with young men. According to Aleksei, one must follow the tracks of a wounded animal together with a dog to teach the dog to be persistent in hunting. Hunters let their dogs bite a dead animal and even play with it for a while, believing that the dog will develop a passion for hunting this way. Aleksei always splashed the nose of a young dog with blood after the first squirrel or sable was killed in its presence, expecting the dog to develop a passion for hunting this kind of animal in the future.

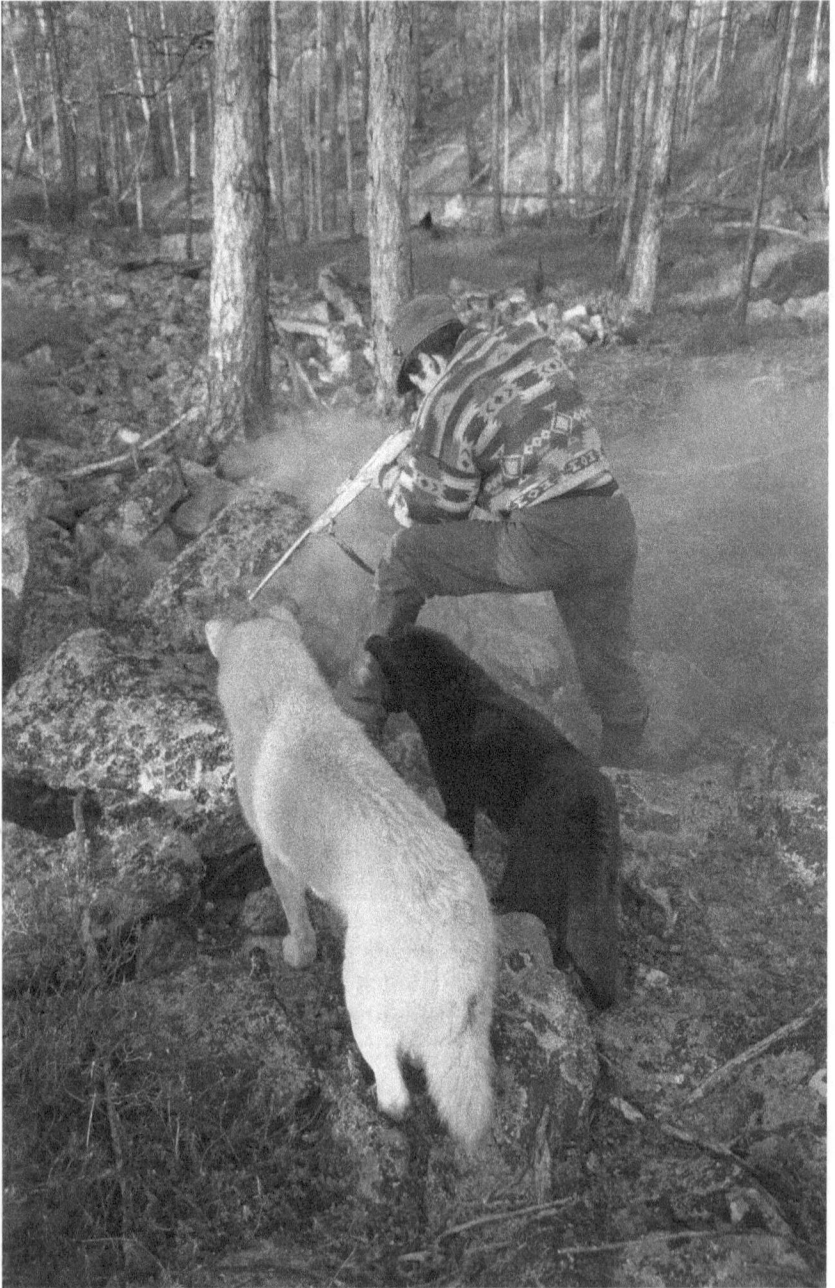

Figure 7.1. | *Aleksei Aruneev hunting sable in cooperation with dogs.*

Usually every hunter takes daily care of his or her dogs in camp or on a hunting trip in order to maintain a close relationship with them. Dogs live outside the tent in the Aruneev-Zhumaneev camp, but other herders and hunters build special shelters for their dogs. They cut grass from grass roots formed hummocks (Oro. *chiapchiako*) to make a sleeping area for them in the snow. Every successful hunt means a big feast for the dogs, who get as much food as they can eat. Food for dogs is cooked daily on a special fire. Their usual fare is dried food boiled in water, leftover intestines and salt (Oro. *dalavun*). Dogs are usually fed once per day, but working dogs that are being used for hunting are fed twice. Olga Zhumaneev feeds her dogs before going on a hunting trip, believing that the dogs will reciprocate with a good hunting performance. Skilful dogs are respected. They are never killed in old age but rather treated as if they were hurt and buried after they die. Hunters usually cover a dog's body with stones. Someone who shows disrespect towards a dog and kills it without reason will have no more luck raising good dogs. If a lucky dog dies, a puppy is often given its name with the expectation that luck will be passed on in this way.

A skilful dog knows how to bark in different ways to tell the hunter about different animals and waits until its master arrives when a hunted animal is surrounded. Such a dog will never refuse to hunt an animal, be it a moose, bear, sable, wild boar or squirrel. A skilful dog is like a hunter in that both must know how to live independently in the taiga. Aleksei never took food for his dogs along when he was hunting in summer and autumn. His dogs often caught rabbits, feeding on them as we rode along while hunting moose. Dogs are never cuddled like pets, and it is said that one should never praise a dog because doing so can 'damage' its abilities (Rus. *chtob nesglazil*). Many taboos are connected to dogs. The Orochen do not feed the heart of a lynx to the dogs, believing that dogs that eat it will become weak runners like the lynx. Hunters hang forbidden parts of animals (like the large intestine, called *moman*) in trees while butchering the carcass so that the dogs are unable to reach them and harm themselves.

Hunters, it is said, must not show aggression by beating any animal, including a dog. They must rely only on their relationship of reciprocity. Only once did I see Nikolai beat his dogs, after they started fighting among themselves. Indeed, it is widely believed that a dog fight before hunting brings bad luck (see Vasilevich 1969: 164). Nikolai explains that '*buga* looks after the dogs and if humans do not treat dogs well they are punished by *buga*'. Nevertheless, today every hunter punishes his dogs for their bad behaviour and failures. Punishment includes heavy beatings, which are intended to improve the dog's hunting performance. Some say that it has been impossible to breed skilful dogs ever since state administrators imported dogs that were unsuited for life in the taiga. All dogs move freely about the village, and many of the offspring lack any passion for hunting. Elders say there are no more good dogs today, since 'dogs are spoiled and become ever more spoiled' (Rus. *pakostnoi*). Nowadays dogs steal food and destroy food reserves, causing many difficulties for people. I was told that many hunters had killed their dogs in anger, attributing several misfortunes to them. Although everyone acknowledges that killing a dog is a sin, it is a common practice. Some hunters told me they had lost their luck in both raising dogs and hunting after killing one of their dogs.

Combating Wolves

In pre-Soviet times, the Orochen avoided areas where a pack of wolves lived, 'respecting the master-animal'. Elders say that wolves were rarely killed. Burnarkomzem (1934–1936) also states that only the Buryat, 'who hated wolves', killed them in early Soviet times and that the Evenki did not kill wolves. Wolves are among the few animals that can challenge humans for the use of territory and threaten their hunting and herding activities. In today's environment of shortage, Orochen interactions with wolves (Oro. *changa*) evoke much more ambiguity for hunters and herders than they used to. Orochen have to act aggressively against wolves in the competition for space. Herders say there is no more space for wolves to live separately from humans, and therefore more and more wolves are coming to people's living places. Wolves never touch reindeer when an abundant, wide variety of game is available to them. In such cases, wolves can even share their *bikit* with a reindeer herd, raising their pups without killing reindeer. Wild animals or reindeer killed by wolves are considered their property. Local elders treated wolves as neighbouring hunters. Sometimes parts of animals killed by hunters were even left for wolves or bears as the 'masters' of a place. Anna Taskerova told this story:

> Once we were moving to another camp with thirty reindeer. When we stayed on a flat mountain pass for the night, my father let his reindeer graze and after some time we heard a wolf howling. Father shot into the air but he was not very concerned since the reindeer were grazing quite close to our camp. However, we could not find a certain reindeer in the

morning. We found it killed by wolves, but my father did not let us take the meat although it had not even been touched by the wolves. He said that it is not ours, since the wolf killed it. The wolf was master of this killed reindeer. Formerly, Orochen would move away as soon as a wolf killed their reindeer.

The wolf is much respected and is also called 'the lucky one' and 'the strong one'. Wolves are seen as highly social beings and skilful hunters. A wolf family consists of a male, a female and their pups that live with the adults until they reach one year of age. The female gives birth in April or May in a den and then raises her pups together with the male. Nikolai says that these animals always protect their pups and take them out of their cave when they sense danger. Wolves are able to teach their pups all kinds of hunting tricks as well as to communicate and to coordinate their hunting. Once young wolves are two years old and can start their own family, they usually are banished from the pack. Then the young wolves start searching for new territory and may come to live near humans when there is a shortage of game.

According to Nikolai, cooperation between predators and humans was possible when the taiga was inhabited only by the Orochen, who would take a few animals for themselves and share the rest. Since the spread of 'poaching' by ATV, he says, only a few animals are left for anyone today. Wolves come constantly to the reindeer herding areas to compete over reindeer. Nikolai maintains that in this situation, is almost impossible to herd reindeer without waging war on the wolves. Nowadays life in the taiga necessarily involves a perpetual, risk-generating contest of aggression between humans and wolves. Wolves can cause heavy losses to reindeer herds by killing all the calves. One spring Nikolai had to move his herd to a remote area far from his regular grazing territory to keep it safe from large packs of wolves that came from the Kalar River.

Hunting wolves is risky. As Nikolai Aruneev says, 'the wolf can feel danger in advance and foretell the future'. It conceals its movements at all times, which makes it extremely difficult to kill. Wolves can signal danger to each other and share information about harm caused to them by humans. They can also predict the movements of hunters and game. It is well known that wolves have good hunting luck and even perform some rituals for luck. For example, a wolf always carries away the leg of its prey 'as an amulet for good luck'. For this reason hunters always find that animals killed by wolves are missing one leg. If you kill one wolf, you must be ready to kill the whole pack to keep the remaining wolves from forcing you out of your hunting territory.

It is also said that if a hunter touches a wolf's den, the wolf will kill his or her reindeer as punishment. Some say a wolf will seek revenge for at least a year. As Nikolai instructs, 'If you don't have the strength [Rus. *sily*] to kill wolves, do not touch this animal at all'. Struggles with wolves, he remarks, are also 'not for life but for death, since the weaker always dies'. The warlike struggle that has become part of the daily interaction between humans and wolves entails great danger for reindeer herders. Wolves always take revenge on humans who have killed one of their family. If wolves appear in one's hunting territory, they must be fought and eliminated.

One late spring, Nikolai Aruneev and I found the carcasses of three large reindeer killed by a wolf (Fig. 7.2). The wolf ate the meat of the rump, leaving the rest of the carcasses completely frozen. Nikolai stated that the reindeer had been killed by a male wolf that had lost his 'wife and children' in a fight with herders. Because wolves are extremely difficult to hunt in the taiga, they are mostly poisoned with barium. Expecting the wolf to return to its prey, Nikolai lit a fire about thirty metres from the carcasses to lace a piece of liver with poison and stuff inside a carcass. Nikolai walked backwards to sweep away our footprints. He believed that wolves had taken over this part of the grazing area, but he still acquired poison to continue fighting them.

Figure 7.2. | *Nikolai Aruneev and his reindeer killed by wolves.*

Table 7.2. | *Table of lost reindeer and predators killed by the Zhumaneev-Aruneev family.*

	Predators living close to the herd	Loss of reindeer (of a herd of 500)	Predator kills
Sept.	3 bears, 1 wolf	3 reindeer killed by predators	1 bear
Oct.	1 bear, 1 wolf		1 bear wounded
Nov.	1 wolf	7 reindeer killed by predators	
Dec.	1 wolf		Attempts to poison
Jan.	1 wolf		
Feb.	5 wolves, 1 wolverine		Attempts to poison
March	5 wolves	6 reindeer killed by predators	
April	5 wolves	100 newborn reindeer (out of 150) killed by predators	Attempts to poison
May	5 bears, 2 eagles		1 wolf, 1 eagle, 1 bear wounded

Bears: Hunting 'the Master of the Taiga'

The bear is another animal that can make people's life in the taiga difficult. Nikolai Aruneev says bears constantly hang around herders' camps because they too suffer from the shortage of game and space. Indeed, up to eight bears were living near our Poperechnaia reindeer herding camp in the spring of 2005. Each reindeer herder suffered several bear attacks that spring. Bears are considered dangerous, strong animals that may easily attack any hunter. Successfully killing a bear, by contrast, entails a risk because the soul of animal is capable of doing harm to people as well. The ethnographic literature contains numerous references to the iconic image of the bear as 'the master of the taiga' in indigenous Siberian societies (Gemuev, Alekseev and Oktiabrskaia 2000). The complex interaction between humans and bears has also been described for circumpolar societies (Hallowell 1926; Ingold 1986: 243–276). Shirokogoroff (2001: 92–93) suggests that the notion of 'bears' mastery' dates back to a time when the Tungus-speaking nomads were competing with bears over the use of the river valleys.[5] He notes that this struggle was resolved when the animals or the humans abandoned a place, or else upon the formation of a 'taiga commonwealth' (Rus. *taezhnoe obschestvo*) based on mutual dependence and regulated by norms and traditions (ibid.).

Hunters say a bear's soul is similar to a human's soul: it 'leaves the body after the bear's death and like any other soul it may harm a man if he does wrong' (ibid.: 80). Hunters also point out that a skinned bear's carcass looks exactly like a human's body, saying, 'look, this is a person lying on the ground, it is so frightening to look at'. Perhaps this is why the bear is considered an ancestor (Oro. *nanaptyl*) that was formerly human (Rus. *kak chelovek*).[6] People refer to bears in Orochen as *diedo* or *ama* (grandfather), *amikan* or *animikan* (my little father).[7] It is said that bears could once walk on two legs and even speak. Hunters stress that bears still have many habits and behaviours that are similar to humans', including getting drunk.[8] A hunter named Andrei Dogonchin told me his grandfather's story. Once, bears lived in the upper world; they liked to visit humans and had many children with them. However, *seveki* banished the bear from the sky after finding out about the bear's passion for humans. A well-known story in Tungokochen tells of a bear that had sexual relations with an Orochen woman (for a similar story among the Evenki, see Vasilevich 1936: 38–40). Therefore, elders say that bears and Orochen are relatives.

It is even known that in the old times a bear would share its den with a hunter, helping him survive when he lost his way in the harsh winter. The bear allowed the hunter to spend the entire winter in its den and offered the hunter its paw to suck on, thus feeding him through many cold days and nights. According to Voskoboinikov (1965: 745–746), the Baunt Evenki thought it was a bear that had given the reindeer to the Orochen. The following story, told to Vladimir Torgonov by Agafiia Dandeeva, a 105-year-old female hunter, illustrates the close relationship between bears and human well-being:

> Three girls were picking berries. They went to search for berries and then came back home. There was no food left in their *chum*, only hunger. Next time, when they came back home, they found some food and a small child in a cradle. The girls were happy that they got a child and decided to see where the food came from. The child got up and started to grow and turned into a bear. Then the bear defecated a fish, saying '*oldo beldy, oldo beldy*'. The girls decided to kill it by pouring a kettle of boiling water on its head. Before its death, the child-bear started to shout: 'make a bowl from my head, make arrowheads from my bones, make beads from my eyes, make skin-tanning tools from my ribs, make sewing tools from my nails, make a chum and clothing from my skin, make flintstones from my teeth and fire from my eyes.' The dying bear gave everything that people needed for their lives.

Killing many bears is considered dangerous, as the bear's soul is capable of doing harm to the hunter. Nadezhda Zhumaneeva told me that after her brother killed about forty bears, he died in an accident, whereupon bears devoured part of his body in revenge. Given such events, it is said that a bear must not be killed just for its meat or for fun. I have observed a few times how hunters avoided killing a bear that spent the winter near their hunting camp. A hunter called Andera from Mongoi village told me, 'You give him time to sleep through the winter and he leaves you in peace and moves to another place. If I encounter him I say "get the fuck out of here [Rus. *idi nakhui otsiuda*]" and he goes away'. Due to the shortage of herding and hunting space and widespread 'poaching', however, people nowadays often clash with bears over territory and game. According to Nikolai, 'bears and people have to fight with each other for food and space, since bears are pushed closer to reindeer herders by poachers'. Therefore, herders are forced to kill bears and risk their own well-being.

This situation causes much ambivalence and increases the risk for humans and bears alike, as many bears show up close to the reindeer herds in the springtime. They try to kill reindeer calves and also pose a threat to the people in camp. Nikolai stated simply that 'if we do not hunt *taptygin*, *taptygin* destroys us'. People may even deny that they hunt bears even though they have recently killed one. Nikolai always deliberately misled me when our camp's hunters killed a bear. He once told me that it had been a group of geologists in an ATV that killed a bear and left it. Although I explicitly indicated to Nikolai that I did not believe that story, he never related any details about hunting that bear. I found out who killed the bear only when I saw who carried the bear's skin from the taiga to the village. Even the word bear is rarely used in conversation; instead a bear was referred to as *babai* (terrific) or *taptygin* (the one who walks clumsily). Hunters strive to deflect a bear's revenge by performing rituals of cooperation that show respect for the bear by hiding the fact of the killing, either through denial (e.g. by refusing to talk about it) or by disposing of the remains. As many stories show, a bear is not 'killed' but is 'invited as a guest' to Orochen households to be 'treated', 'entertained', 'adored' and then 'escorted'.[9]

Nevertheless, bear body parts have become commodities widely used in the villages for medicine, food, camp gear and trading. Throughout Siberia, bear gall bladder (Oro. *dzho*) is used to treat liver diseases, including cirrhosis. Bear fat is a remedy for common taiga illnesses such as cough, lung disease and even tuberculosis, and is also applied externally to treat burns and skin diseases. Hunters often say that if you feel physically exhausted, you need only eat bear fat and your strength will be restored. Today, bear meat is considered the perfect food for winter hunting, since a small piece lasts the hunter a whole day and 'the meat can warm you' as well. Bearskins are used to make winter mattresses called *dyrkovun* and sleeping bags. A bear's dried paw (Oro. *mana*) is considered powerful medicine. After it is heated over a fire, it is brushed over a reindeer or a cow udder to cure mastitis.

The bear is also seen as an intermediary between people and master-spirits. The Orochen believe bears are sent to punish humans for their sins (see also Voskoboinikov 1965: 251). Bears are said to punish people for robbing a shaman's grave, living in old camps without establishing proper relations with the spirits, or plundering storage platforms.[10] According to Nikolai Aruneev, the master-spirits always 'send the bear as a powerful animal to deal with a sinful person' (Rus. *posylaiut taptygina na razborki s greshnikom*). Many elaborate stories describe how a bear pursued a 'sinful person' year-round, constantly stalking and attacking the perceived sinner (Rus. *karaulit i delaet zasady*) wherever he or she went. Indeed, one hunter told me how bears chased him all over the taiga several times and also appeared in his dreams, roaring and driving him crazy. He felt the bear's presence everywhere and therefore fell into a long period of drinking and even attempted to commit suicide. He visited several medical institutions and various shamans, and finally gave up hunting for good. Other hunters interpreted this as the outcome of sinful behaviour towards the spirits.

Anisimov (1959: 13) noted that *amaka* (bear in Evenki) is called 'the threatener of humans' lives'. Orochen hunters and herders believe that bears never approach a camp without a reason or out of curiosity alone. Bears, they say, bring messages or come with the intention of taking a person's strength (Oro. *chinen*). Therefore, a bear's visit is believed to foretell the illness or death of a certain person. As hunters say, 'a bear comes to the camp looking for *buni* (a dead person)'.[11] Members of the Zhumaneev-Aruneev family tell detailed stories about how several relatives died after strange encounters with bears. A bear visited Nikolai's paternal grandfather in his tent before his death. His paternal grandmother killed a bear in her camp before passing away. Moreover, many uncles and nephews have been wounded by bears.[12]

Hunters say it is very unusual to come across a bear's den. Bultai, a hunter from Bugunda village, told me he finds bear's dens by chance, usually when hunting sables or squirrels. His friend, an old hunter named Chulan, told me no one ever finds a bear's den by looking for it. A dog can be so afraid of bears it does not tell hunters about a bear's presence. Hence, it is held that the person who does find a den is 'worthy of a bear's visit'. When a bear's den is found in the winter, hunters never state publicly that they are going to hunt bear. Gilton Aruniev would drop a hint: 'Tomorrow we will go to visit a weasel's den'. They say you should not clean your gun or prepare a kettle for cooking before leaving for bear hunting, or you will signal that the hunt is planned and thus interfere with your luck. When planning to hunt a bear, Bultai's father always waved his hands, imitating a bird and shouting *kukav kukav*, before drinking tea. Only then would he tell the other hunters 'let's go pay them a visit' (Rus. *poidemte v gosti*).

The Orochen's hunting of bears and treatment of their carcasses are more complex than the same procedures for other animals. A person's own well-being has to be protected, since the bear's soul, or the bear itself in revived form, may seek retribution for the killing. The hunters typically leave camp in late morning when the sun is high, without any overt hurry. Usually more than one person participates in bear hunting: one person blocks the den with two crossed logs (Oro. *kamka*), while the second guards the exit with a gun, ready to shoot in case of a sudden attack. Often a dog is leashed in front of the den so that when the bear bursts out it will attack the dog and not the hunter. Hunters from the village of Zelenoe Ozero make a fire a few hundred metres from the den, boil tea and offer tobacco by saying, 'grandpa, be quiet for your children' (Oro. *amai gudiandekol*). The elders say it is a sin to kill a sleeping animal, so before being shot, the bear has to be roused by poked it with a pole. During this act, Nikolai Aruneev would say, 'grandpa, get up, guests have arrived' (Oro. *amikan maatal, iramachal ichaulkal*). When the bear shows its face, the hunters shoot it, all the while shouting *kukav kukav*. Hunters notice a special vapour (Oro. *tamnaldal*) coming from the den when the bear is dead. Then its head is hooked or tied, and the carcass is dragged out of the den. Once the bear has been dragged out, there is time for a break. A fire is made and tea is boiled. At this time offerings are made by 'feeding the fire' and sprinkling tea. The bear's mouth is usually propped open with a stick.

Gilton Aruniev waited for almost an hour to give the bear's soul time to leave the body; only then did he start to skin the animal. This procedure includes 'undressing the bear' and 'the bear's travel' to camp to meet his 'guests'. All these activities are accompanied by references to or imitations of the sounds of other animals or birds in order to disorient the bear and divert bear's anger from the humans who killed it. When burying a bear, the hunters may imitate the calls of crow (Oro. *kere*) or raven (Oro. *turan*) and mention fox (Oro. *sulaki*) or insects like the ant (Oro. *irikta*) or even other people, for example Russians.

The first step in skinning a bear is to cut out its eyes to keep the bear from seeing its killers.[13] The bear is skinned on a specially prepared carpet of branches called *syktel*. The carcass is skinned, the fat cut out, the intestines removed, the gallbladder cut out, the inner fat collected, the paws cut off and the meat parcelled. Finally, the head is cut off. The animal is then packed for transportation. Gena Kirilov remembers leaving a wooden figure of an animal near the bear's den and pointing to it as responsible for the bear's death so as to direct the bear's anger away from himself towards the wooden figure and escape the bear's revenge. The elder Yulia Semirekonova says that all children in the camp were roused and expected to greet the bear when the hunters brought the carcass to camp. Everyone in the camp had to welcome the 'divine guest' and often had to make loud noises or imitate birds in order to disorient the bear. In camp, people entertain the bear. Its head may be put in the special 'master's' place (Oro. *malu*) in the tent to show respect.[14] The head is offered smoke and drink, and the participants in these ritual actions also eat the cooked bear meat. The bear's head is cooked for a whole day, and a special dish called *asimin* is prepared from its brain, lungs, heart and intestinal fat (all cut into small pieces). Some families do not let women eat *asimin*, while others believe that only pregnant women must not eat it.

The bear's bones were not broken but were collected in a pile after the meat was consumed. Then all intestines, bones and other remains were collected and taken to a place a few hundred metres away and separated from the camp by a river, where they were left on specially made platforms. Today's hunters perform many variations of the bear mortuary ritual. Some wrap up all the bones and some intestines and hang them on a pole in the bushes. Others just hang the head in a tree. A hunter named Pavel Naikanchin used to build a platform on which to arrange the skull, paws and intestines in the shape of a bear.[15] Aleksei used to hang the bear's head in a tree after skinning the carcass and now also leaves some of the bones near that tree's roots. The bear's head might point in certain directions – perhaps eastward, as in the positioning of a human corpse on a mortuary platform; or towards a river, with the expectation that the 'bear's spirit is carried away by the river'. Nikolai says it is important to escort (Rus. *provodiny*) the bear and leave its parts on a mortuary platform; otherwise the bear's soul will stay in the taiga and wander around, causing harm to humans. Elders remember how they uttered a cry when a 'bear's soul' was escorted. No humans or animals must disturb the mortuary platform, they said; therefore the trees around it are marked to warn others about the site. People leave the site walking backwards, as they do when leaving a human's mortuary scaffold. A bear is always shown as much respect as possible in order to calm his spirit and prevent his revenge.

Butchering and the Disposal of Animals

A hunter's close interaction with animals is also manifest in the butchering and disposal of animal remains (see also Shirokogoroff 1935: 89–92). Butchering skills are key to acquiring animal parts for trade, food and medicine. Butchering practices, the display of bones and the concealment of the butchering place are also tied to ideas of generating luck. Today butchering has increased in importance, since any part of an animal has a certain value. Large ungulates are butchered with a thirty-centimetre knife (Oro. *koto*) by cutting at the joints; sometimes the ribs are cut open with an axe (see also Vorob'ev 2013). No bones should be broken in the process, especially not large ones, as it is believed that the animal will be reborn and need all its bones intact. The hunters carefully remove the fat and separate the guts to be stored and used for making soup. It is considered very lucky if the animal has much fat. In Soviet times hunters left the animal's head at the butchering site, but today people say that the head contains fat and should be cooked first before eating the other parts of the animal. Nikolai Dimitrov from Bugunda village claims that eating the head is also related to the belief that the animal's soul (Oro. *omi*) dwells in its head.[16] Thus the hunter who leaves the head risks losing his hunting luck (see also Zelenin 1929: 55). At the same time, eating the head or any other special part of an animal that is believed to contain its soul may also bring more strength and luck to the eater (ibid.: 52). In general, ideas of living in the taiga and eating wild meat are often linked to notions of a moral and healthy life. Large game is believed to provide all vital vitamins, fats and other elements, and animal parts are important for handicrafts, magic and trade (see more in Brandis-auskas 2011).

The special treatment of an animal's bones is a way of showing respect to animals and is tied to the idea of their cyclical rebirth. Elders believe that such behaviour increases the number of available animals, since 'the animals' souls need their bones for rebirth'. Although hunters believe that any lucky incident helps to sustain one's flow of luck, killing more animals than can be consumed or carried away may cause luck to be lost. The simple rule is that 'all animals hunted must be consumed'. Breaking this rule is considered a 'sin'

Table 7.3. | *Reindeer herders' and hunters' uses of wild animal parts for food and medicine.*

	Domestic/wild reindeer	Roe deer	Musk deer	Elk	Moose	Boar	Bear
Head (Oro. *dyl*)	Consumed as food	Consumed as food or given to dogs	Consumed as food or given to dogs	Consumed as food or given to dogs	Consumed as food	Consumed as food or given to dogs	Can be cooked as food, left on open platform or hung on tree
Brains (Oro. *taraki*)	Consumed as food	Consumed as food or given to dogs	Consumed as food or given to dogs	Consumed as food	Consumed as food	Given to dogs	Can be eaten
Intestines (Oro. *syluptal*)	Consumed as food or given to dogs	Given to dogs	Given to dogs	Parts (Oro. *moman*) consumed; others given to dogs	Parts (Oro. *moman*) consumed; others given to dogs	Given to dogs or thrown away	No uses, one part of intestines is cooked by Orochen of Bugunda village
Bone marrow (Oro. *uman*)	Consumed as food	Not used	Not used	Consumed as food	Consumed as food	Not used	Not used
Visceral fat (Oro. *uluivcha*)	Consumed as food	Not used	Not used	Consumed as food	Consumed as food	Rarely consumed as food	Consumed as medicine
Liver and kidneys (Oro. *bososkto and olion*)	Consumed as food, often raw	Consumed as food (raw)	Consumed as food, often raw, reserved for males	Consumed as food, often raw, mostly from male elk in autumn, when they are fat	Consumed as food or used to tan hides	Given to dogs	Not used

Subcutaneous fat (Oro. *umukso*)	N/A	N/A	N/A	N/A	No meat fat	Consumed as food	Consumed as food
Special uses	The penis and velveted antlers (*panty*,[17] cut in April–May) can be sold to *komersanty* or used to treat different diseases. Orochen use the penis and pieces of hoof to cure men's diseases.	Musk glands (Rus. *struia*) are sold to *komersanty* and used in healing. The glands are also traded to China for fragrance production.	The penis and *panty* (velveted male elk antlers) can be sold to *komersanty*. *Panty* are made into an infusion to treat different diseases such as imbalanced blood pressure and generally strengthen the organism: 500 g of vodka is poured over 150 g of a chunk of dry *panty* and left in a dark place for ten days. The daily dose is one teaspoon.		The upper lip is sold to *komersanty* as a delicacy.		Skins are sold as trophies. Paws are sold for export to China to be used as medicine. Bear spleen is also widely used by Orochen and Buryat and exported to China. It is popular for treating disease. Visceral fat (Oro. *uluivcha*, Rus. *zhyr*) is used to treat lung diseases, coughs and exhaustion.

that may attract misfortune. Once Aleksei did not kill a bear he found sleeping in its den because he would not have been able to transport the carcass on his horse. Even though the bear could become a threat in spring, the thought of wasting meat seemed more dangerous to him. Given today's shortage of ways to transport game, most hunters have to run the risk of failing to reach their village before the meat starts to spoil. When an ATV or truck is used for night hunting, some wounded animals are likely to escape. These animals eventually die of their wounds, creating places that are believed to be spoiled since attract predators to the place. Hunters avoid these places for a few weeks in the belief that one will 'have no luck' (Rus. *ne budet farta*) there. Spoiled meat also attracts bears, which may frequent the area while living on the wasted meat.

As was outlined in previous chapters, hunting and herding can be understood as a dynamic form of competition that pits hunters and herders against individual animals and involves forms of reciprocity and respect for autonomy. However, in an environment of shortage and state constraints, hunters say they must dominate and even poach animals in order to survive. In pre-Soviet times the Orochen perceived their relations with bears and wolves as cooperation based on respect, autonomy and sharing between humans and animals, but today they believe they cannot successfully herd reindeer without 'warfare' with predators. To ensure food supplies or succeed in reindeer herding, hunters and herders thus have to engage in ambivalent interaction with other animals and rely on practices that remain hidden and may call for spirits' revenge.

Notes

1. At the time of my fieldwork in 2005 only few large herds remained in Zabai-kal'ia. The Chernoev family in Severobaikalsk (Buryatia) owned about two hundred reindeer, and there were a few reindeer herders with up to three hundred head in the Kalar District (Zabaikal Province).
2. The idea of following the herd is also found in Burch's (1991: 439–445) study of hunting practices among the Canadian Chipewyan, which he describes as following a caribou herd the year round.
3. This table, compiled by the author, does not represent all the dynamics among the scattered groups of animals, which sometimes roam quite far from each other. The migration of reindeer depends on the weather conditions in any season, so it may start two weeks earlier or later than indicated.
4. According to Voskoboinikov (1965: 259), Orochen tales always depict dogs in a positive way.

5. Shirokogoroff (1929: 143–147) believed that the Evenki lived in southern China between the rivers Huanhe and Yandze before migrating north to Siberia.

6. According to Badmaev (2000: 68), the Buryat believe that bears have power similar to that of shamans.

7. See Titov (1923: 92–94) for a linguistic analysis of Orochen names and nicknames for the bear.

8. It is said that bears 'get drunk' when consuming formic acid from eating ants.

9. See the descriptions of Orochen bear hunting in Dobromyslov (1902: 82) and Titov (1923: 94–97).

10. The Evenki ethnographer Titov (see in Vasilevich 1936: 278), who collected tales among the Nercha Orochen, also mentions that the bear punishes and takes revenge on all taiga animals.

11. Although animals can respond to people's actions and are strong enough to escape from a hunter, they are not seen as a source of direct danger unless they are controlled by spirits or acting on behalf of shamans or master-spirits (see also Shirokogoroff 1935: 83–84). In the Orochen perspective, some animals, like the eagle, owl, wolf and bear, can act as messengers and mediators for various powerful beings (humans and spirits).

12. Kwon (1998) describes the same beliefs among the Sakhalin Oroks (referred to as Orochons), going even further by saying that any killing of animals is considered dangerous to humans, since a human may turn into his prey and become the hunted.

13. The elder Kirilov usually left the eyes in special incisions made in a tree trunk near the mortuary scaffold.

14. *Malu* is an area at the back of tent that is reserved for the master of tent and certain hunting idols (Shirokogoroff 1929: 225, Sirina 2002: 224, Anderson 2007: 51).

15. For similar observation among the Barguzin Evenki, see Dobromyslov (1902: 82–83).

16. I was also told that *omi* can be located in any part of an animal's body (see also Vasilevich 1969: 225). If one respects and uses animal parts in the appropriate way, they will bring well-being (Rus. *dobro*) (ibid.).

17. Reindeer velvet antlers (Rus. *panty*) have been used for *rontarin* production in pharmaceutical factories in Irkutsk and Kirov, and at a scientific institute in Moscow. *Rontarin*, a medicine similar to *pantakrin*, is extracted from elk *panty* and widely used to 'strengthen the metabolism'. Prior to Soviet times there were even a couple of elk farms in Zabaikal'ia for *pantakrin* production.

CHAPTER EIGHT

Rock Art, Shamans
and Healing

As I have shown in previous chapters, luck – *kutu* – is inseparable
from moral conduct of life in collaboration with animals, spirits and
humans. In this chapter I will explore how the anxiety over luck is
linked to vernacular notions of health and illness and to interactions
with various ritual specialists and places. I will also demonstrate how
tangible monumental ritual sites in the landscape have become important sources of knowledge, health and well-being. Particularly, I will describe how the rock art sites scattered across the northern Zabaikal'ia
have served as a monumental manifestation of Orochen cosmology
throughout the past century.

Most people from the northern villages express a lack of trust in
the collapsing healthcare system. They have themselves experienced
failure in treating diseases and have also witnessed the retreat of state
healthcare institutions from the villages to the district centres and the
poor quality of the medicines that flood remote villages along with
numerous other low-quality goods. Notions of curing diseases and escaping misfortune have become closely linked to everyday knowledge
and engagement with the landscape. People believe that the master-spirits that have been neglected for decades exert an influence
– either positive or negative – on a clan and on the lives of those who
continue to use certain places in the taiga (see Mazin 1984; Alekhin
1999).

Monumental sites, as rock art, are the landscape's most transcen-
dent manifestations of human interaction with nonhumans over centuries (see Brandisauskas 2012). In search of supernatural help, Orochen
elders and educated people (Rus. *inteligentsia*) have visited distant
Buryat and Evenki shamans for consultation and begun visiting the

old ritual sites, mortuary scaffolds, old reindeer herders' camps and storage platforms scattered across the taiga that belonged to their kin. In this context, the elders' memories have become an important source for solving problems caused by disease or clan curses (Rus. *rodovoe prokliatie*) as well as for finding appropriate remedies or taiga medicines. Knowledge of simple rituals like smudging, curing or predicting misfortune is in many cases manifested in actions that shape the Orochen's daily activities. Inherited amulets, certain placings and ritual sites in the taiga have also gained value and are used by individuals and the community alike as important intermediaries in the quest for luck, healing power, spiritual support and divination. Reindeer herders and hunters have revived extinct rituals, creating new public celebrations and marking the landscape of both taiga and villages with their own identities. Decorated idols or trees by the main roads and paths have become important sites of ritual respect for all people travelling between villages. Such re-created sacred landscapes, marked by humans' reciprocal appeal to the spirits and infused with anxiety over luck, have became an important source of individuals' well-being. They also reinforce Orochen identities in the post-Soviet rural community, now that ritual specialists like shamans are no longer the main cosmological intermediaries.

Figure 8.1. | *Nikolai Kirilov pouring vodka offerings at his ancestor's grave.*

In the scientific community, research on rock art sites was a key topic in the Soviet archaeology of Siberia. Scientists debated the dating and classification of rock art styles and also offered some explanations of rock art images. Almost none of these researchers, however, were interested in how the rock art sites are related to the beliefs and practices of contemporary indigenous people. The perception and use of rock art sites can be much more productively understood with reference to the people who use them than to those who created them. The meanings associated with the images found at the rock art sites continue to play an important role in Siberian hunters' and herders' everyday lives.

Healers, Hospitals and Taiga Medicines

Early ethnographies (Fisher 1774; Lindenau 1983 [1742]) described Siberian indigenous people's perceptions of illness and ways of healing, and several generations of Siberian ethnographers (e.g. Zelenin 1935, 1936; Shirokogoroff 1935; Mikhailov 1987) have examined healing as part of the shaman's specialized role in indigenous societies. Shirokogoroff (1935) refered to shamanism as a baseline for determining the complex actions of individuals, groups and societies. Although he focuses on the 'shaman's art of controlling spirits,' his rich ethnography also provides information on the Tungus' perception of various spirits and on the manifestation and causes of various diseases and symptoms, including descriptions of how these diseases can be treated. The ethnographer Zelenin (1935) even argued that the shaman's main role was that of a medical specialist, rather than securing luck in hunting or performing divinations for his group. These ethnographies aimed to describe the evolution and main features of Siberian religions by elaborating on the activities, worldviews and psychology of shamans.[1]

Countless statements in early Soviet ethnographic publications repeat the opinion that there was no proper medical treatment among the Orochen of Zabaikal'ia before Soviet rule (see Paladimov 1929; Samokhin 1929; Neupokoev 1928). These reports, which were written for the Soviet authorities, stated that the nomadic way of life was very 'unhealthy and caused many diseases among the Orochen' (Samokhin 1929).[2] The nomads' conical tent *chum* was considered unsanitary because 'it was rarely cleaned' (Neupokoev 1928; Samokhin 1929; Paladimov 1929). Paladimov (ibid.) stressed the Orochen's overall unsanitary habits, maintaining that they washed only their faces. These accounts also referred to the widespread notion of their extreme spirit-drinking habits. Such descriptions reinforced belief in the imminent extinction of indigenous Siberians and served to justify the state's paternalistic attitude toward them and the nonindigenous Siberian population (Titov 1926a; Neupokoev 1928; Rouillard 2013). The Soviet authorities aimed to transform the Orochen's material culture, beliefs and identity via a civilizing project that included sedentarization, professional healthcare and hygiene (see also Leete 2004). As Paladimov (1929: 84) stated: 'There is no alternative to sedentarizing the Orochen, since their hunting way of life and constant movements, life in the *chum* and even the cold lead to their dying out [Rus. *vymiraniiu*]' (see also Zolotarev 1938).

In the early Soviet years, professional physicians often competed with shamans and other indigenous specialists for patients. The prominent Evenki ethnographer Vasilevich (1971: 58) stated that shamans had a monopoly on healing because they 'created [their] own explanations of the cause of disease, thus influencing people's belief that one's spirit can leave the body'. Ethnographers often proclaimed shamans to be mentally ill (see Zelenin 1935). They came to be called 'enemies of the people' (Rus. *vragi naroda*) and, accused of 'cheating' and 'exploiting' people, were severely persecuted all across the region in the 1930s (see Suslov 1936).[3] Yet indigenous people continued to resist the forced introduction of professional medicine and the removal of shamans from their communities, and many conflicts ensued between the two different healing traditions (Koledneva 2009; Paladimov 1929).

Shamans were not the only knowledgeable individuals who continued to practice traditional ways of healing in the taiga camps and remote villages. Various other medical specialists knew how to use medicinal plants for healing, set broken bones, administer head massages, stop bleeding or perform divinations (see Koledneva 2009). Shirokogoroff (1935: 133) also mentioned specialist 'painters' who were able to neutralize disease-bringing spirits with the creation of 'placings'. The Tungus (i.e. horse-herding Evenki) acknowledged that although shamans were unable to cure many diseases, there were some experienced humans who could pray and offer a sacrifice for the idol in order to cure disease (Shirokogoroff 1935: 134–135). Among the Orochen of Manchuria the ethnographer Pu (1983: 109) also mentioned respected medical specialists like the *wutuoginil*, who cured smallpox or measles, and the *agagin*, who used divination in healing. Finally, a variety of folk healers (Rus. *sheptuny*) and people knowledgeable about repelling curses, setting bones or using medicinal plants are also part of the old Russian settlers' and Buryat traditions in Zabaikal'ia. Today as in the past, the villagers consult any available healer, including so-called lamas, shamans or *sheptun* (see Paladimov 1929; Basharov 2003). The state authorities often showed no interest in these 'non-shaman' specialists, who nonetheless continued to provide healing in many rural areas throughout the Soviet period.

As elsewhere in Siberia, the popularity and influence of the various healers, locally known as shamans (Rus. *shamany*), lamas (Rus. *lamy*) or *znakhari* (also called *sheptuny*), has increased in the northern part of Zabaikal'ia over the last decade (see Znamenski 2003). Orochen, Buryat, Russians, people of Cossack descent and horse herders of Tungus origin travel hundreds of kilometres across Zabaikal'ia from their remote northern villages in search of healers who can treat their diseases or addictions. Today, ritual specialists are especially asked for help in fighting alcoholism, the 'evil eye,' bad dreams, misfortune and myriad other complaints such as constant pain in the joints. This coincides with the official plan to close the Tungokochen hospital in the near future. The only other way people in many remote villages can obtain clinical medical care is to travel long distances to hospitals in Verchnii Usugli the centre of Tungokochen District or even to the city of Chita. Local people regard medical doctors as representatives of a formal bureaucracy that has no willingness to help. The decline of trust in medical institutions is also caused by a general belief that anything made in Russia or China is *potdelka* (fake). As one hunter stated, 'there is no benefit from hospitals' (Rus. *bol'nitsa paria stala bezpoleznaia*).

During my fieldwork in May 2010 I tried to help a prosperous hunter get a simple blood test done so I could help him to obtain special Western-made medicines for his arthritis. Due to the indifference or absence of doctors and the lack of even the simplest equipment, we had no success, even though we travelled hundreds of kilometres to visited a hospital three times, made agreements with relatives working in hospitals and negotiated for the test. After this experience, I was told that it is best to visit a hospital when you are almost dead. Other people added that you must be able to walk to a hospital since nobody will take you there. The mistrust in professional healthcare and the popularity of healers among the Orochen are reminiscent of their view of the first medical doctors to arrive in the newly established Tungokochen village in the late 1930s (Koledneva 2009) and of Paladimov's (1929) description of Buryatian Orochen's experiences with public healthcare.

As in the early Soviet period, Orochen go to hospitals today, but they also rely on a variety of healers, attend ritual sites and use their own taiga medicines to treat disease. As I have already described, medicinal knowledge has become increasingly important, given the growing dependence on taiga resources and economic self-reliance. People living in the taiga commonly suffer injuries caused by falls, freezing, burns, cuts or animal attacks (Shirokogoroff 1929: 291). Knowledge of taiga medicines and individual curing practices are crucial to Orochen autonomy and self-reliance. Items such as animal parts, oil, fat, stones and plants are used in treating various diseases. The most valued medicines, which are referred to as 'the most powerful', are the so-called stone oil, items made from velveted antlers (Rus. *pantakrin*), and a bear's gall bladder and intestinal fat. These medicines are well known to foster health and fight a wide range of diseases. 'Stone oil' sites are often kept a secret to be shared only with close relatives and friends. The rocks exude oil only in winter, but it is harvested all year round – a dangerous endeavour that involves climbing steep rocks or using ladders. It is said that one should always leave offerings in exchange for the stone oil, and using a knife or rifle to scrape it from the cracks is not recommended. Orochen hunters believe that stone oil can hide from humans if they do not show it proper respect or speak too loudly about harvesting it. Small quantities of this medicine can be shared only between very good friends and close relatives; it must not be sold. Stone oil is used for strengthening one's health, and more specifically as a remedy for stomach aches and diarrhoea.

Bear gall bladder (Oro. *dzho*) is used to treat liver problems, including cirrhosis. It is also popular among the Southern Buryat and Chinese. A bear's intestinal fat can be used in various ways. It is said to increase strength; hunters often say that eating fat helps prevent physical exhaustion. It is also used to fight coughs – a common complaint among hunters, who tend to be heavy smokers of strong, unfiltered cigarettes – and as an ointment for treating burns. Other bear products, such as paws or hides, can also be used in medicine but are more often sold to *komersanty* for export to China (see Fig. 1.1).

Velveted antlers, called *panty*, are processed to produce *pantakrin* in pharmaceutical factories in Irkutsk, Kirov, the Moscow Okhotovodsk Scientific Institute, and China.[4] Hence, the *panty* of wild reindeer, moose and elk are always cut off and cooked, then dried to preserve them for export.[5] *Pantakrin* is widely used in Russia; it is popular as a strong medicine that helps 'strengthen the metabolism', as noted earlier, and as a medical supplement among athletes. In the taiga and villages, medicines are made from the *panty* of wild animals and vodka. Reindeer herders never cut off the *panty* of domestic reindeer because 'it makes the reindeer sick'. Elk penises and tails are also exported to

China or used for making a similar medicine to strengthen metabolism and balance blood pressure. Prostate problems are treated with a soup made from the hooves of large animals (Oro. *chimchen*).

A variety of medicines are used on a daily basis to prevent serious diseases and treat simple ones. A birch fungus (Lat. *inonotus obliquus*) called *chaga* is consumed to prevent cancer, while a tea made from Siberian dwarf pine (Lat. *pinus pumila*) is drunk regularly as a blood enhancer. I walked for twenty to thirty kilometres per day with the hunters and often developed sores on my feet, which were treated with larch gum. Puffballs are used to treat saddle sores on reindeer and horses. A common cold was treated with the blood of the white ptarmigan (Oro. *elaki*), and a soup made from partridge (Oro. *oribko*) was consumed to induce coughing, clean the lungs and even prevent tuberculosis. When I had a toothache, I was given a sable's gallbladder to put on the aching teeth, to reduce the pain. Aleksei Aruneev used various plants and shrubs in compresses to help his aching joints. He had recently learned from the elders how the clay of certain hills had been used in healing in the old days and was planning to try it too.

People who continue to follow a subsistence lifestyle or have recently adopted it have also become interested in ways to avoid misfortune and maintain good health while spending long periods in taiga. Good health is seen as bound up with maintaining relationships through respect and obligations of reciprocity with the human and nonhuman beings inhabiting a landscape. Failing to observe certain moral obligations when interacting with master-spirits can threaten a hunter's life. Healers always try to find out whether their patient has *porcha*. *Porcha* and *zglaz* are understood as 'bad energy' that can reside in items like salt, kettles or coins and may be directed (Rus. *navesti porchu*) at a person to cause illness. This may be accomplished by throwing 'cursed' salt or coins into the targeted person's path or spitting into his or her backyard or house. One woman taught me how to do *porcha* to another person, wishing him disease. The simplest way is to write a negative wish on a piece of paper and cover it with salt, leaving it for a few days so 'negative energy' will infiltrate the salt. When the salt is thrown in the path or close to the house of the targeted person, the person will certainly be harmed. Indeed, people say that one can spoil a hunting ground by leaving different items carrying 'bad energy' on one's route in that area. These notions (*porcha* and *zglaz*) are not unique to Zabaikal'ia and exist among many old settler communities in Siberia and North-Eastern Europe (for old settlers of Chukotka see Khakarainen 2007; for Komi see Il'ina 2008).

'Bad energy' can also be transmitted by speaking ill of a person or wishing someone bad luck. Hunters do not trust other people and prefer to keep their plans secret from other villagers rather than arouse conflict or risk having their luck spoiled by magic. They avoid malevolent people and *porcha* (spoil) when entering and leaving the village, and they try to mislead malevolent spirits before leaving on a hunting trip. Indeed, when I left the village together with Orochen people, we never talked about our route. Occasionally we even waited for darkness before leaving. Once, when we were packing our gear on a riverbank, other people observed us from far away with great interest. This kind of curiosity (Rus. *liubopytsvo*) caused great concern among the hunters because it was perceived as harmful; I was told to make certain signs (Rus. *kukish*) with all five fingers. Aleksei also recommended using swear words to 'send the people away' (Rus. *poshli ikh podalshe*). We did not manage to kill any game that week, and I was told this was due to the curiosity shown by the people we encountered on the riverbank. Smudging (cleansing one's body) with the smoke of *senkire* (Rus. *chiushachii bagulnik*, Lat. *ledum palustre*, Marsh Labrador tea) is one way to protect oneself against various negative influences or reduce the harm caused by them. Herders and hunters often did this before and after leaving the village, before visiting mortuary scaffolds and during various rituals. Reindeer herders also believed that predator attacks on the herd were caused by the doings and malice of malevolent people.

The following story illustrates the creative ways in which the Orochen handle medical care in the context of socioeconomic transformation and shortage (see also Anderson 2011). I met an Orochen man named Vova who was considered a very successful hunter. He had good dogs and often returned to his village from the taiga with bags full of meat. He owned a good hunting territory where he harvested much fur during the winter hunting season. His household owned many cattle and horses. Moreover, he was in good health and had no problems with alcohol. However, one spring he fell seriously ill and became unable to walk because of severe pain in his joints. He visited several healers, who all told him he was suffering from *porcha* because many people were jealous of his success and prosperous life. When he first started to feel the pain, Vova visited a female shaman in her sixties known as Khamnigan (the name of another Tungus Manchu-speaking group), who was very popular among the people of Tungokochen. She lived about eight hundred kilometres away from Tungokochen in Zagulai (former Aga Buryat Autonomous District) and could only be reached by travelling over bad roads. The healer used a bottle of vodka without a label as a 'clean source' for divining diseases and future events. In performing healing rituals over individuals, she used a variety of methods common to the healers of Zabaikal'ia. She fed candies, cookies, milk and butter to the spirits close to her house in order to lift the *porcha* from her patient. She gave patients suffering from certain illnesses a black tea (Rus. *nasheptanyi chai*) charged with a specific energy that was delivered through words mouthed silently while holding a knife above the tea.

Vova did not feel better after his visit. For the next two months he could barely walk or even hold a spoon. He decided to visit the local hospital in Tungokochen, where he was prescribed pills and given various injections. He did not trust the local medical doctor, however, whom he called a poacher. He then travelled to Usugli, the capital of Tungokochen District, where he spent several weeks in the hospital getting the same treatment he had received in the local clinic. Vova then heard that a famous female shaman of Orochen origin from the Baunt District was visiting the Orochen community of Usugli at that time, so he took the opportunity to visit her. He did not feel better after her healing rituals but said that the lack of success was probably due to his having seen her very late at night and being not well prepared, bringing only one bottle of vodka that was used for treating two patients. Later Vova travelled to the city of Chita, the urban centre of Zabaikal Province, to see a Buryat healer who tried to heal him by beating his joints with a hammer. This procedure did not help either – it only resulted in more pain. Vova also visited a hospital in Chita, where he was examined and given many papers. However, his health still did not improve; therefore he visited Usugli again a few weeks later. People advised him to see a local Russian healer whose custom was to perform his healings only at night, but this too failed to help and left Vova feeling sceptical.

He soon returned to Tungokochen, where he spent several weeks in the hospital taking pills and receiving more injections. After several more months, other villagers advised him to visit a Buryat lama who managed to reduce the pain with massages. Vova was also told to use different charms bought in a Buddhist *datsan* as a protection against malevolent spirits, and to perform certain rituals that involved the sprinkling of vodka. This healer, like the others, tried to diminish the power of the *porcha*. He instructed Vova not to travel in the eastern part of the taiga since five illnesses were located there, and he also told him he might encounter an malevolent spirit in the north-eastern part of the taiga. Vova was prohibited from attending large gatherings of people, lest he be cursed. After visiting the lama several times he started to feel much better and drew the conclusion that 'the hospitals are useless' (Rus. *bol'nitsa bezpoleznaia*). To strengthen his body, he took different taiga medicines that he learned about from relatives and neighbours. He also became interested in the healing capacities of massage, minerals and medicinal plants. The elders interpreted his long-lasting illness as a possible call to become a ritual specialist.

Most shamans are based in large villages or even cities and have no knowledge of life in the taiga. For this reason, hunters or herders visit them only when they have very serious health problems that they are unable to solve on their own (Humphrey 2002). During my fieldwork in the Aga Buryat Autonomous District in the summer of 2005, I noticed that almost every Buryat family knew about many generations of their ancestors. Buryat shamans say the Orochen's social problems, like alcoholism, fatal accidents, violence and internal strife, are explained by their neglect of their ancestors and failure to treat them properly. These shamans always recommend rituals to contact the spirits of ancestors dwelling in the landscape. They also advise the Orochen to visit their ancestors' ritual sites or clan territories (Rus. *rodovye zemli*) in the taiga and leave offerings near the mortuary scaffolds of former shamans.

Although the Orochen do not believe in disturbing mortuary scaffolds and leave offerings only when passing in the immediate vicinity, the post-Soviet years of misfortune have pushed them to appeal to all kinds of spirits and former ritual sites. Thus they started to search for neglected mortuary scaffolds scattered across the taiga and attend to them by leaving offerings. The Orochen have traditionally used scaffold burials, and the practice was continued until recently in several villages of Buryatia. Elders complain that it has been difficult to find old mortuary scaffolds because many taiga areas have been burned in the past decades. Many scaffolds of former shamans are also perceived as alien because people have not tended them for a long time and often are unaware of their location, 'walking on scattered bones'. One of the reindeer herders' tasks was to perform rituals to re-establish relations with various spirits in order to calm them. Elder Nadia Zhumaneeva complained to me that having a shaman for a relative meant much trouble, since shamans' souls exerted a negative influence on their descendants. Her deceased grandfather, a shaman (see Fig. 1.3) famed throughout Zabaikal'ia named Shuman, is thought to be angry with all the male Zhumaneev kin and has kept 'taking their lives' every decade since Nadia's father fought with him.[6]

Various inherited ritual items also became sources of inspiration for rituals (see Fig. 8.2). When I visited the village of Bagdarin, I met a young Orochen hunter named Andrei Dogonchin, who had inherited a *seveki* – a bundle of dolls, animal-shaped amulets and an iron mask – from his grandparents. Andrei and his brother had never observed their grandparents' use of the *seveki*, but they believed that it brought strength and well-being to their kin and that an attached wooden icon had healing power. The item was also used for protection. Andrei often took the *seveki* from his house to the backyard and sprinkled it with vodka. He told me that anyone in the village who wished him bad luck would hide their faces after seeing him shaking the *seveki*. He said people will be less curious later (Rus. *ne liubopytnye*) and therefore 'causing less trouble and showing more respect' to him. Andrei wished to become a shaman and believed that the *seveki* was calling him to perform rituals.

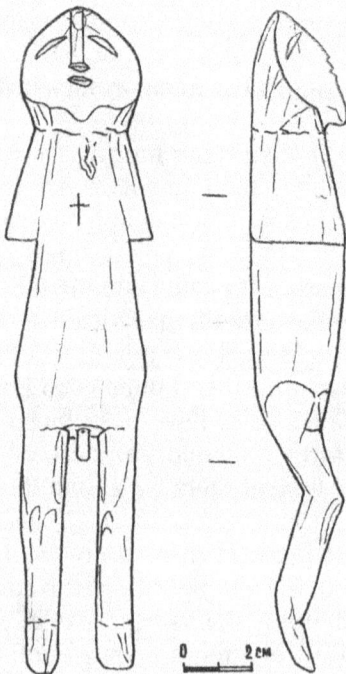

Figure 8.2. | *Sketch drawing and photo of Orochen* seveki *by Aleksei Arbatskii in Kalar County, Zabaikal Province. In the photo, the* seveki *is adorned with pieces of wild reindeer jaw and dried fat, given as offerings (see Arbatskii 1982).*

Rock Art and Rituals

In the days of intensive collectivization and industrialization, many ritual sites were eliminated from Zabaikal'ia's landscape. In Tungoko-chen, mortuary sites were removed when roads to the reindeer herd-ers' *baza* were built across the taiga; others were consumed by the extensive forest fires of the 1980s and 1990s. The monumental rock art on the surfaces of cliffs and boulders, however, were impossible to remove. In cracks at the Dukuvuchi rock art site, well-preserved rouble coins with Lenin's head, cartridges and musket balls bear wit-ness to the ritual use of the site by generations of hunters. These offerings continue to inspire local hunters, and nowadays rituals are performed at the site. Today people strive to establish relationships of respect and mutual obligation with the master-spirits of such sites, intending to ask for a successful hunt, good health and a good life. Such relationships entail obligations in terms of reciprocity and mo-rality. Rock art images are polysemic and easily lend themselves to reinterpretations connected to a person's biography, state of health, changing luck or experiences in subsistence activities. The archae-ologists Norder and Carr (2009) note that rock art sites should be understood in the context of their user/caretaker rather than their maker, since the act of creation of the site and the original meanings associated with the images do not hold an essential place within a group's memory. People believe that images found at rock art sites can shift, hide, show, inform and forecast and also stand as powerful agents that shape people's ideas of reproduction and their sense of well-being, health and luck.

The performance of rituals of respect and reciprocity at river cross-ings, rocks, lakes and rock art sites has been documented across Za-baikal'ia since the early colonial encounters. According to Vasilevich (1930: 62) these ritual practices can be attributed to a wider belief system that encompasses myriad master-spirits inhabiting the land-scape, with whom humans create a relationship of reciprocity by leav-ing offerings, bringing their domestic reindeer and asking for hunting luck. Archaeological findings show that in Soviet times many Evenki groups continued to perform rituals at rock art sites all over eastern Siberia (see Vasilevich 1957: 62; Okladnikov and Mazin 1976: 112; Tugolukov 1977: 41–44; Kochmar 2002: 52–55). At some rock art sites archaeologists have excavated artefacts from several different time periods, including recent offerings. These included stone tools, iron arrowheads, musket balls, cartridges and wooden idols that were found leaned against the rock (Okladnikov and Zaporozhskaia 1970).

In the Soviet academy, rock art archaeology was a privileged discipline that explored so-called archaeological monuments (Rus. *archeologicheskie pamiatniki*) all across Central and Northern Asia up to the Far East. Okladnikov declared rock art to be a 'window to an unknown world' (Rus. *okno v nevedomy mir*), attracting the attention of laypeople and mass media (Derevianko and Medvedev 2008).[7] The Soviet state supported many expeditions to search for rock art sites in areas where industrial development projects like hydroelectric plants or dams were planned. The bulk of this research was undertaken by Aleksei P. Okladnikov – an emblematic luminary of Soviet archaeology, member of the Soviet Academy of Sciences and head of the Institute of History, Philology and Philosophy at the academy's Novosibirsk branch – and his students. Most of Okladnikov's scientific career was dedicated to the discovery, registration, excavation and dating of rock art in Altai, Mongolia, the Amur Province, Zabaikal Province, Pribaikal'ia and Angara, as well as Tajikistan, Turkmenistan and Uzbekistan.

Rock art was considered the most characteristic feature of the Neolithic era. Attempts were made to study the style and, to a lesser degree, the semantics of rock art images (see Okladnikov and Mazin 1979; Kochmar 2002). The sites were seen as important locations of past ritual activity, where artefacts from numerous offerings could be found (Okladnikov and Mazin 1979: 99). In the general scientific literature, rock art was said to show the primitive hunters' world view, former subsistence practices and artistic expressions, and to demonstrate how primitive cultures developed into more complex ones. Okladnikov (1975) claims that Neolithic rock art expressed a feeling of peace, in contrast to the later Bronze Age rock art that presented more dramatic expressions and was created by societies that were already divided into classes. In his book on the Shishkino rock art site, Okladnikov and Zaporozhskaia (1959: 54) infer the meanings of rock art images from the indigenous peoples' belief in animism. They suggest that the Evenki called the site Bugady in the past, and that such sites were presumably the places sacred to clans (Rus. *sviatilishcha*) that were linked to zoomorphic ancestors. Okladnikov and Mazin (1976: 105) also surmise that rock art sites were important places for various social activities, feasts, rituals and clan cults. In his analysis of rock art images, Okladnikov's student Mazin (1984: 12) goes even further by suggesting that many heroes of Evenki folk tales and even some mythic events and personages are represented in rock art images. He even identifies certain personages, such as *Mangi*, 'the moose hunter who stole the sun', at a rock art site near the Maia river; *Agdy*, 'the thunder, a human-like being that had eagle wings and a bear's head', in the Zeia River basin; the malevolent beings known as Kadykakh in Shishkino rock art and *Khargi* in the Onon River basin; and *Seli* (mammoth) and *Kulin* (snake) in rock art drawings of the Arbi River basin (East Siberia). Mazin (1984: 194) also believes that the rituals of *sinkelevun* and *ikenipke* are depicted in rock art.

Although most discoveries of rock art sites relied on the knowledge of indigenous hunters and guides on archaeologists' and ethnographers' expeditions, the scientists showed little interest in contemporary indigenous peoples' interaction with rock art sites. Both Mazin and Okladnikov interpreted rock art on the basis of Evenki folktales and cosmology, taken from Anisimov's early ethnography (1958, 1959). They regarded ritual performances at such sites as events of the past that no longer existed, as was expected from the vantage point of Soviet ideology. A good example found in a book by Mazin (1986: 129) book describes how his Evenki guide Trofim Pavlov told him a story about a rock art site that was powerful in the past, but 'does not work' (Rus. *ne deistvuet*) in the present. This trope is commonly found in Soviet ethnographies (see also Tugolukov 1963).

Seven rock art sites in the basins of the rivers Vitim and Nercha have been continuously tended by the hunters and herders of Tungokochen District (and Baunt District in the Republic of Buryatia), at least throughout the last century. Most of these sites are, in archaeological terms, 'undiscovered rock art sites' included on the list of archaeological monuments protected by the state. According to archaeological information, the rock art sites of Zabaikal'ia are painted with red ochre mixed with glue and blood. The drawings are painted on the flat rock surface, mostly in spectacular places. These sites are special features of the landscape of Tungokochen District. The drawings are visible from the east or south-east, and the rocks are of unusual shapes, such as an arch or tunnel, or are located in the vicinity of river junctions or caves. The characteristics of the places are usually conveyed by their names: Dukuvuchi (Drawing One) (there are at least four sites of that name) or Kadavun (Rocky).

The best known rock art site in Tungokochen District is a complex of three sites located short distances from each other in the Muishin River basin. The most prominent of them is called Dukuvuchi and is located at the junction of the Dukuvuchi and Muishin Rivers (Fig. 8.3). Another site called Dukuvuchi is on the other side of the Vitim River in Buryatia. The Muishin river Dukuvuchi is well known not only to local hunters and herders, but also to most inhabitants of the villages of Krasnyi Yar, Yumurchen, Tungokochen, Ust' Karenga and even the Tungokochen District centre, Usugli. Local peoples have recently come to know it as the 'most powerful place' in northern Zabaikal'ia. More and more people want to visit the site and come to Tungokochen village in search of a guide. The Orochen have known about the Dukuvuchi site since the early twentieth century, when the ethnographer Aleksei Makarenko visited the camps of the Vitim River Orochen to collect shamanic artefacts for the St. Petersburg Ethnographic Museum. Nikolai's and Aleksei's great grandfather a shaman called Shuman took Makarenko to the rock art site, where he documented the paintings in his fragmentary diaries. He also documented Shuman's shamanic tools and photographed a shaman's tent that had been erected for a ritual performance.

In the 1960s the site was explored by Aleksandr Arbatskii, a student of archaeology and ethnography at Irkutsk State University who spent several summers with Fiodor Zhumaneev. The latter was married to Shuman's daughter and was the grandfather of Aleksei and Nikolai Aruneev. In the 1960s and 1970s Fiodor was a member of a work brigade at the *kolkhoz* reindeer farm and the most prominent hunter in the region. The reindeer farm, a very successful enterprise at that time, owned up to two thousand head of reindeer. Herders kept the herd in the Muishin River basin area, which offered large fields and treeless hills for grazing, excellent campsites and many natural salt licks (Rus. *solontsy*, Oro. *tala*), which were important for hunting. After the herd was moved to a new grazing area in the course of the consolidation of collective farms, Fiodor retired and spent his time migrating with his wife and reindeer herd in the rock art area of the Muishin and Ima river basins until his death in 1994.

Arbatskii (1978) questioned elders and recorded some stories of hunting luck from hunters who had visited Dukuvuchi and performed rituals of respect and reciprocity at the site in the past. All the stories of left offerings and observed pictures told to Arbatskii end with the successful killing of game that was send to the hunter by spirits as reward (see also Tugolukov 1963). His short article and field report contain descriptions of similar perceptions and practices which are continued until the present. Visiting hunters usually first build a fire some distance from the site and make tea, which is sprinkled in the direction of the drawings. Only then will they approach the site, keeping some distance and carefully examining the drawings, trying to see what the rock is showing them (Rus. *chto ona pokazhet*). Then they leave some offerings, usually bullets, and ask for good luck. All the reindeer herders of the *kolkhoz* farm and their family members visited the Dukuvuchi rock art site to perform rituals over the next thirty years. Every hunter tells his or her own stories about strange events that are attributed to the spirits of Dukuvuchi. These are not always success stories. Events like a plane crash in the Muishin basin and an ATV's sudden bursting into flames in 1970 were interpreted as punishment sent by spirits of Dukuvuchi.

In the 1990s, after many elders had passed away, the Muishin River basin was used by Orochen hunters in their twenties who knew nothing about the powers of Dukuvuchi. Today these hunters tell many stories of how Dukuvuchi's spirits punished them for various sins like making too much noise at the site, fighting (Rus. *borolsia*) with their domestic reindeer, hunting animals that were hiding among the rocks or defecating there. These stories usually ended in misfortune: one hunter fell off his reindeer on his way home and severely injured his leg; gangrene set in, and he remains disabled today. Another experienced hunter named Sopka once went fishing near the site without showing it the appropriate respect. He lost a large bag of fish, and his friend even lost his gun. Other hunters tell of how, when the master-spirits refused to accept them, they were attacked by a hawk, shot at or pelted with stones. They say that animals also get crazy there; dogs bark a lot and chase after invisible things. The unusual behaviour of animals is generally taken as an indicator of the presence of spirits. Gena Dushinov told me of his concerns upon approaching the site: he never knew how he would be received. He worried about whether he would manage to hide his 'sins' (Oro. *ngelome* singular, *ngelomel* plural) or whether his offerings would be accepted.[8] Hunters say that they are often afraid to go there, as they may see signs that predict trouble, misfortune or even death. Olga Zhumaneeva told me that once, as she was approaching Dukuvuchi, she even saw a burning cross (a sure sign of death). Georgi (1779: 38) wrote that the Evenki used to resolve conflicts at rock art sites. A hunter or herder who was accused of stealing was brought to the rock art site and made to take an oath along with his kin to prove his innocence (ibid.). It is said that even if you are afraid, you must continue to approach the site. You may be lured away from the site by fresh tracks that suddenly appear on the way and induce you to go hunting. Thus do the master-spirits test the visitor's intentions.

Children are advised not to go there because 'it can drive them crazy', so only adults visit these places. Orochen hunters stress that the drawings were not made by humans, but most likely by spirits or maybe shamans. They also say that the master-spirit keeps changing the images, and that one may receive specific information when approaching with offerings. The elder Nadia Mordonova from Rossoshino village told me about seeing an image at Dukuvuchi that has been meaningful to her ever since. As a teenager, she said, she went to the site to see the pictures and saw many children standing in a row. Having later became the mother of nine children, she believes the rock art site empowered her to bear so many offspring. Indeed, the notion of empowerment is reiterated in a story told by Shuman's daughter. She told about a Buryat lama or shaman who spent a week fasting at the site and left many cloth offerings. He managed to survive there without any food or kettle. According to Nadia Taskerova from Ust' Karenga, some local soldiers survived World War II because they had performed rituals at the Kadavun rock art site before joining the army. When visiting the smaller rock art site of Dukuvuchi, one must first undergo purification by passing through the rock arch.[9]

I visited Dukuvuchi with Aleksei in 2004 before the autumn hunting season. We walked about eighteen kilometres from our camp to the site, taking just offerings and a kettle and leaving our horses and dogs in camp. Aleksei did not want to take his animals, saying that 'animals often get crazy when they meet spirits'. He added that spirits can even kill domestic animals or take them away in exchange for certain demands. After four hours of difficult walking, we built a fire about two hundred metres from the site and made tea. We silently sprinkled the tea in the direction of the rock (Oro. *kadar*) and had a snack. Only then did we walk closer to the site to leave our offerings of bullets and coins in a crack or on top of the rock. Aleksei stepped back to look at the drawings, giving me a short time to photograph all the paintings. Observing my work with some suspicion, he soon stopped me, in saying, 'Let's go back, the drawings never show on photographs anyway'. This was a reference to Arbatskii's (1978) visit to the site with Aleksei's grandfather some decades earlier, 'when he did not manage to take a single picture'. It is widely known in Tungokochen village that Arbatskii's attempts to excavate the site caused many troubles for him. It is also said that it is extremely dangerous to take anything from the site. Recently, I was told that the rock had started to flake because Arbatskii's attempts at excavation had shifted large rocks that had previously been moved only by giants.

Soon after we left the site, and as predicted by our view of the drawings, we encountered a moose and killed it, afterwards giving thanks to the master-spirit of Dukuvuchi by putting pieces of meat into the fire. As Tamara Naikanchina says, 'if you pray [Rus. *molitsa*] well, then the rocks always show or give something to you'. Another elder said that the master-spirit is as good to you as your parents and always giving. Sites that are inhabited by a master-spirit can be felt with one's whole body on approaching the place. Many hunters describe

Figure 8.3. | *A hunter visiting the Dukuvuchi rock art site in the Muishin River basin (Zabaikal Province).*

the feeling they often get when visiting rock art sites as a strong 'inflow of energy' (Rus. *pritok energii*). However, the master-spirit may also meet hunters with a strong gust of wind, and sometimes people hear voices when approaching the site. It is advisable to refrain from speaking in a loud voice or otherwise polluting a ritual site. It is also dangerous to cut trees down; shoot; quarrel with dogs, horses or reindeer; or hunt before performing the ritual.

When I conducted my long-term fieldwork in 2004, it was mostly hunters and reindeer herders from the villages of Tungokochen, Krasnyi Yar, Yumurchen and Bugunda who visited the Dukuvuchi site. Today the site is well known as place where people can find remedies for economic failure, misfortunes, clan curses (Rus. *rodovoe prokliatie*) and disease. During my fieldwork in the autumn of 2011, two groups of people came from the city of Chita to ask the successful, reliable Orochen hunter Aleksei Aruneev for help in visiting the Dukuvuchi site. A husband and wife brought their son Vova, a young man in his twenties who had experienced several serious misfortunes, including a car crash and a suicide attempt. They also brought along a grandmother who was born in Tungokochen village and had Khamnigan-Evenki ancestors. The shaman from former Aga Buryat Autonomous District had recommended performing a ritual in an ancestral ritual place, and they had chosen the rock art site of Dukuvuchi. On another day, we were surprised to see a surgeon from the Chita state hospital taking a trip to Dukuvuchi. In both cases Aleksei helped the people perform the ritual of feeding the spirits at a special place called a *burkhan* that had been established by an Evenki female shaman from the Baunt District near Tungokochen village. I was able to participate only in the first ritual, since the medical doctor was uncomfortable with a foreigner's presence. He had even kept his visit a secret from his aunts who lived in Tungokochen village.

Rock art sites are located in regions used extensively by hunters and reindeer herders in the past The remnants of their activities – old campsites, mortuary scaffolds, old fireplaces, offerings left in various places – create a meaningful landscape for a new generation of people who use the area. Hunters who acquire new hunting territories that they have never visited before leave offerings at any rock art site they spot in their new environment. Several hunters told me long stories of how they found a rock art site in a remote part of their hunting territory and started using it to generate luck in their subsistence activities.

The sites have been kept alive in the stories of generations of hunters and reindeer herders. Today people's experiences at rock art sites legitimate their use of the environment for subsistence. Hence, rock art is a good example of how people strive for information, experience and empowerment in a changing sociopolitical environment. Through their interaction with master-spirits, the hunters become masters themselves, creating and maintaining their own living places (*bikit*). Rock art sites are by no means the window to the past imagined by Okladnikov. In a way they are a window to the past, present and future alike. Today Orochen reindeer herders and hunters believe in showing respect to and reciprocating with nonhuman beings by leaving offerings in return for taking something from the taiga. Ignoring this ethical imperative may lead to lost hunting luck, disease or even a encounter with a spirit, which is considered extremely dangerous. To sustain luck and well-being, it is imperative to interact and reciprocate properly with the master-spirits.

Many more ritual sites linked to ideas of exchange, luck and divination dot the region. One of them is a cave called Dolgan, located about eighteen kilometres south-east of the village of Bagdarin. It is said that the site predicts (Rus. *podskazyvaet*) luck and well-being. Anna Semirekonova used to visit that place before the hunting season, making tea and camping there for three days. She always strove to prepare tea with reindeer milk and leave items like bannock as offerings, tying a strip of cloth to a nearby birch. After placing the offerings and drinking tea, the hunters would approach the cave and lie down on their stomachs to view the images of animals. Anna told me that 'Dolgan master-spirit is so good, like a parent, that it always shows, always foretells something. If you see a moose moving in the darkness of the cave, you will kill that moose. Then the image disappears and you see only the colour of blue. Then you go and kill as many different animals as you can see'. She said it was common to see deer, sables, squirrels and even bears in Dolgan. Other hunters came to learn about their reproductive prospects: 'the more children you see, the bigger the family you will have'. Various caves in Tungokochen District are also considered to be meeting places of ancestors and humans. One may invite various deceased relatives there in order to ask them for help. It is believed that human souls fly into caves after death and meet their ancestors, who may turn the soul back if it still has to stay in the 'middle world'.

In Soviet times, ritual practices that were connected to everyday routine, like feeding the fire, never attracted censure and therefore continue to be practised; however, the Soviet state strictly prohibited public rituals performed by the community or kin group. In Tungokochen District, members of geological expeditions, forest workers and scientists destroyed mortuary scaffolds and shamans' platforms, which they saw as dross – relics of the past. Meanwhile, many cultural features of the landscape like rock art sites or caves that were known as ritual sites were excavated and registered as 'monuments of archaeology or nature' (Rus. *pamiatnik prirody*), whereupon Orochen ceased to attend them because hunters and herders believed such sites had lost their power.

The reindeer herders of Tungokochen have reclaimed several monumental ritual sites, re-enacted rituals of reindeer sacrifice and created new ritual sites in the taiga and near their villages (Anderson 2012). The Orochen believe that the rituals performed at public celebrations like Aboriginal Day (Rus. *Den' Aborigena*) today are very important for communicating with local spirits. Former leader of the Evenki Indigenous Association Mariia Grigoreva aptly conveyed the importance of such revived rituals: 'There are many unexplained tragic deaths, suicides, and diseases – even young people die. We need rituals very much.' The Orochen intelligentsia from villages and cities have joined the hunters and herders in performing and reconstructing rituals aimed at ensuring the well-being of their clan. In the early 1990s, two well-known and respected indigenous communist party leaders – Vladimir Torgonov from Bagdarin village (Buryatia) and Gilton Aruniev from Tungokochen (Zabaikal Province) – started to play an intermediary role in interactions between Orochen communities and spirits as well as formal powers. Both men were sons of shamans repressed in the latter part of the 1930s. They were raised in boarding school, educated at St. Petersburg University and sent back to serve as ideological leaders of indigenous communities for decades as mouthpieces of the State and communist ideology. After the collapse of Soviet state, both of them became active supporters of Orochen ritual practices, leading some public rituals as well as performing occasional healing practices.

Furthermore, Orochen have revitalized ritual forms that were practised many years ago. For example, upon a herder's death in the past, reindeer were slaughtered and the deceased's main belongings – clothing, personal dishes and bowls, hunting equipment, personal idols and even reindeer skins – were hung on poles at the gravesite. Today, reindeer may again be slaughtered as a gift to the master-spirits and a reindeer skin mounted on a pole next to structures for meat offerings (Oro. *kundulo*). Such ritual sites are established in remote taiga places as well as near villages. Carved wooden idols placed at the roadside on mountain passes have become focal points for offerings and respect shown to the spirits. Today these carved idols have become very popular among villagers and even urban people. All vehicle drivers stop at such sites, and their passengers usually offer cigarettes, vodka, food, coins, bullets and pieces of cloth or toys 'in order to avoid misfortune on the journey'. Herders and hunters have carved several new idols and established ritual sites by using cloth to decorate trees on mountain passes along the paths leading to their main reindeer herding and hunting camps. Every hunter stops at such sites for a smoke, a snack or a short break from riding. Because they highlight a person's responsibility to pay respects to the spirits, these structures are also a reminder to behave in a moral way.

The regularly celebrated Aboriginal Day (Rus. *Den' Aborigena*) involves the Orochen intelligentsia, villagers, hunters and reindeer herders, politicians and various visiting officials. People remember that local party activists used to organize Aboriginal Day celebrations to honour the reindeer herders. These occasions usually involved public speeches, various shows with reindeer and the cooking of food. The Orochen observed the holiday by presenting their identity, performing rituals and communicating with state officials. Nikolai Aruneev always acted as the leader in such public rituals. He provided reindeer meat for the feast and for feeding the fire, and communicated publicly with the master-spirits in the Orochen language, making it explicit that the taiga is inhabited by Orochen spirits. At the Aboriginal Day celebration in the autumn of 2005, he placed near the village a carved idol resembling those placed at the roadside on mountain passes in the taiga. Everyone who participated in the celebrations fed the master-spirits of the taiga by leaving an offering at either the idol or the fire. In doing so they created a ritual site to be used in the future. Thus, Nikolai and the community left their own landmark, in the form of the idol, in the territory of village.

It is not only cash and various goods that are in short supply in the post-Soviet environment: even ritual sites and spirits have become objects of contestation among different communities. The Orochen community of the Baunt District of the Republic of Buryatia has also started to revive ritual practices in one of the most prominent sites of the district, the White Mountain (Rus. *Belaiai Gora*) near Bagdarin village, led by the young female Evenki shaman Svetlana Voronina. The rituals are performed near some impressively shaped rocks said to symbolize the Orochen clans of Kindigir and Chilchagir.[10] Buryat shamans and Buddhist lamas also visit the White Hill to conduct rituals and consider it a sacred site. The Orochen believe that some spirits that formerly belonged to them have been taken over by the Buryat, who have been much more active in performing rituals. Recently, some Orochen have even made a ritual site in the hills and left the clothing of deceased reindeer herder there, thus infusing their own identity into an area that is contested among Buryat, Tungus and Orochen villagers. I once witnessed Svetlana Voronina perform the ritual of feeding the spirits, asking for their support for her daughter, who had to take a school exam. During the ritual the shaman struggled to bring the spirits back under her control after Buryat shamans had used them for their own needs. This ritual was seen as something like a contest over 'the mastery of spirits' (Rus. *kto khoziain dukhov*) between shamans of different groups.

At the end of my fieldwork in late autumn of 2005, a new ritual site was established near Tungokochen village. Svetlana Voronina visited Tungokochen village for the first time and invited everyone to participate in a public ritual. The Orochen of Tungokochen claim there are no Orochen shamans and therefore travel more than six hundred kilometres to visit shamans in the Aga Buryat Autonomous District. Svetlana had spent all her life in Bagdarin village in Buryatia and learned to shamanize from Aga shamans after the collapse of the Soviet Union. However, the Aga shamans soon noticed that Svetlana spoke Evenki during her rituals and liked to jump over the fire, which was considered an Evenki way of shamanizing. Hence, as she said, the spirits of Aga no longer wanted her to stay in the region and she began to grow (Rus. *rosti*) into an Evenki shaman. She began to expand her knowledge of the Evenki language and visited the old shaman Savelii in Neriugri in Southern Yakutia. From the Buryat shamans she learned the importance of her genealogy, the shamans of her clan and their mortuary scaffolds.

Eventually Svetlana decided to visit the Orochen of Tungokochen to get in touch with her ancestors and the local Orochen spirits. A site for the shaman's ritual was selected at the edge of Tungokochen village near a path leading into the taiga. The shaman gave all kind of instructions to specially selected helpers – mostly female elders and successful hunters – who prepared a variety of foods for the spirits and built a large fire. Everyone had to bring a bottle of vodka, candies, cookies, butter and milk. The shaman, who was dressed in her shaman's costume, fed the fire with many dishes and offered vodka to all the spirits of the taiga. Beating her drum, she cleansed people for well-being (Rus. *blagopoluchiia*) and luck (Rus. *udacha*). She also performed healing rituals for people who approached her, using either a whip or her hand to heal different parts of their bodies. People asked for the shaman's help in healing alcoholism, treating different diseases, lifting *porcha* or *zglaz* and making luck return to them. Some

Orochen brought their children who suffered from epilepsy or speech impediments. Even those who were sceptical about the existence of spirits used this opportunity to participate in rituals or attend visiting shamans 'just in case'. Hunters requested information about when there would be an 'open way' (Rus. *otkrytaia doroga*) to luck in fur hunting.

At the end of the ceremony, the shaman asked that pieces of cloth be left as offerings on a nearby birch tree. She closed the ritual by inviting everyone to join in a traditional dance called *adiora* (Fig. 8.4). This dance is taught to local children in school, yet it was strange to see adult male hunters dancing in the circle. Elders said that only in childhood had they previously witnessed their clan performing such dances. When the shaman proclaimed that 'the spirits ask for a dance to entertain them', everyone had to dance and sing. Many elements of the ritual performed by Svetlana are also part of the ritual practices of Buryat shamans in Zabaikal'ia. With the singing and performing of the old dance, however, this ritual became something very Orochen. In fact, the shaman said, it was important to sing in the Orochen language because the spirits that were present could only understand that language. The site was called by the Buryat term *burkan* – god by the shaman (on *burkan*, see Shirokogoroff 1935: 123 and Tsintsius

Figure 8.4. | *Svetlana Voronina, a shaman (right), leading a dance near Tungokochen village.*

1975: 113) and later became the main ritual site for Tungokochen villagers. Nevertheless, Svetlana Voronina never visited Tungokochen again. Visiting shamans regarded the village as harbouring bad energy from an excess of 'black activities' (Rus. *chernota*). In this context, the rock art site of Dukuvuchi has served continuously as an icon of superhuman power where various problems can be solved.

In Baunt District there is a place called Ikendek (Oro. *ike* to play) that is known as a former site of Orochen competitions, singing and dancing. The leading reindeer herder Vitalii Morodnov says that 'formerly the Orochen celebrated and competed in this site by lifting up these rocks'. Elders believe that today, as in the past, humans can acquire luck by performing rituals or celebrating near the Ikendek rocks. The ethnographer Mazin (1976: 43) describes how the Orochen sang and danced and competed in archery at special places like rock art sites. Lavrillier (2007) also describes how playing, singing, competitions and ritual practices are interlinked both semantically and practically among Tungus peoples. All such practices bolster people's claims of influence on the world, since an act of imagination or imitation is the first step towards accomplishing any task.

Various rituals are performed publicly in the villages to reaffirm the indigenous identity and well-being of an Orochen community gathered in one place from all across the region (see also Vaté 2005). Reindeer herders' and hunters' ritual performances at various taiga sites signal respect for the master-spirits and establish a claim to the mastery of land in competition with other groups striving to claim the use of taiga territories. Reindeer herders and hunters revive extinct rituals also to calm forgotten and malevolent spirits and ensure well-being for various taiga territories. Thus these rituals demonstrate how Orochen strive to achieve healing and luck at the same time, emplacing their own identity and 'energies' on the land. This is how, in a context in which specialists like shamans have become rare visitors or ceased altogether to be the main cosmological intermediaries, both monumental ritual sites like those with rock art and rituals have become important sources of knowledge and empowerment for all people based in taiga and villages.

Notes

1. In Siberian ethnographies, the shaman was described as a spiritual leader, which was supposed to be a characteristic of 'primitive societies' (Hutton 2001).

2. Such a statement was characteristic of explorers' and ethnographers' reports over a long period of time. The ethnographer Titov (1926: 8) may be cited as an exception, since he courageously criticized state policies and voiced the opposite opinion, namely, that settled life had many negative consequences for the Orochen, including poor health.
3. The people of Zabaikal'ia suffered particularly harsh Soviet repressions. Many more shamans survived in other Orochen communities in the Amur Province, Southern Buryatia and Evenkia (Turaev 2008; Zabianko, Mazin and Kobyzov 2002; Troshev 2002).
4. A few elk farms were established in Zabaikal'ia in the Imperial era for harvesting *panty*.
5. *Panty* is a Russian term for the buds of a growing antler that has spread across Siberia.
6. In battles between Evenki shamans, see Yampolskaia (1993: 114–115).
7. Today the exploration of rock art sites continues to be of special interest to archaeologists working in Zabaikal'ia (see Tsibiktarov 2011). Their activities mainly concern efforts to classify rock art sites and excavate artefacts that could serve as evidence of the region's archaeological cultures. Any discovery of a new rock art site is celebrated as a sensation in today's mass media and the popular scientific literature in South-East Siberia.
8. The Orochen of Karaftit village in Buryatia interact with a large monster-like creature with an animal's head and a fish tail that inhabits thirty-three interconnected lakes and is believed to be the ruler of a large area. The Orochen say that when this monster-fish shows up, 'sinful people' (Rus. *greshniki*) lose their ability to talk; they may even die after meeting the monster.
9. See the description of the Evenki ritual *chipikan* in Kagarov (1929).
10. It is said that Orochen clans used to come to the hills not just to seek well-being and good luck, but also to celebrate weddings and hold competitions, games and dances.

CHAPTER NINE

Conclusions

Ambivalence, Reciprocity and Luck

Domination and Reciprocity

The Orochen always experience notions of cooperation and domination as interactions that are based on reciprocity. The reindeer herders and hunters are aware that the master-spirits might demand a human life in return for human aggression or coercion.[1] By giving hunting luck, the master-spirit follows an ethic based on reciprocity, while hunters must be able to 'catch' the luck and prove themselves worthy of it. An Orochen hunter who establishes cooperation with a master-spirit as part of 'awareness of such moral responsibilities' (see Anderson 2000b: 234) may kill a type of animal for a certain period without risking her or his well-being. That hunter's hunting luck is acquired (Rus. *dobyta*) because of the generosity of a master-spirit, as well as through the hunter's ability to 'take an opportunity' by successfully employing knowledge and skills in a contest with an individual animal.[2]

In hunters' and herders' experience, however, cooperation with master-spirits in the chaotic and unstable post-Soviet environment also imposes some 'limits' (Rus. *ogranichenie*) on their hunting results. They believe that the master-spirits have to maintain a balance among animals dwelling in different taiga places. Therefore they occasionally give away just enough for the hunter's daily needs (Rus. *tol'ko dlia prozhivania*), but not enough to make him wealthy (Rus. *ne na bogatsvo*) or even make a better living. Thus, one must wait for a master-spirit's 'goodwill' (Rus. *chto khoziain dast*) or hope that other hunters will share their hunt with him or turn to domination and 'poaching', in this way risking the master-spirit's revenge.

In his book on the Siberian Yukaghir, Willerslev (2007: 43) suggests that hunters interact with master-spirits in the belief that they are 'obliged to share their abundance of game with them in much the same way as fellow humans who possess resources beyond their immediate needs are obliged to give them up'. He thus (ibid.: 38–47) expands on Peterson's (1993) idea of 'demand sharing', proposing it as a frame that shapes interactions among humans and between humans and nonhumans. He also draws on Peterson's (1993: 870–871) criticism of the idea of 'generous giving' to propose that resource transactions can be construed as 'coercive' and even as 'an aggressive act' when humans are not eager to share yet at the same time feel entitled to make demands on anyone who has any kind of wealth.[3] In contrast to Peterson (1993: 869), who describes the morality of 'demand sharing' in positive terms, as generosity, Willerslev (2007: 45) argues that Yukaghir sharing is based on an ambiguity that also includes forms of domination. Hence, Yukaghir hunters, expecting sharing to be unconditional, can accuse master-spirits of being stingy if their demands are rejected, while at the same time the master-spirits can equally demand human lives in return (ibid.). Criticizing Sahlins' (1972: 193–194) notion of 'generalized reciprocity' and drawing on Gell (1992: 150–151), Willerslev (2007: 39) argues that such sharing among the Yukaghir is not a form of reciprocity because of the absence of 'mutual indebtedness'. He suggests that hunters are never sure whether the master-spirits will fulfil their moral obligation to act as 'parents' or whether they are about to trick them into the position of 'donors' (ibid.).[4] Hunters deal with these ambiguities by inducing 'lustful play' (ibid.) in master-spirits. By imitating a prey animal, a hunter can take on its identity while at the same time striving to seduce the animal into sacrificing its life against its own will (ibid.).[5] However, Willerslev's (2007: 44–45) example of a Yukaghir hunter's one-way transaction could also be interpreted as a two-way interaction at a later stage, and therefore also as a reciprocal relation. For example, Willerslev (ibid.) mentions the widespread Siberian trope of a lucky hunter who harvests an enormous amount of fur and meat but whose son eventually falls ill as a result of the spirits' response.

Furthermore, Orochen hunters and herders see sharing as part of an established relationship of trust. One always shares with the expectation of reinforcing one's luck (Rus. *na fart*, Oro. *kutu*) in the relationship between hunters known as 'friendship' (Rus. *druzhba*) (see Chapter 3). In this case, sharing constitutes an act that is 'moral for its own sake' (Widlock 2004: 61). It always evokes emotions and strengthens 'friendship' among hunters in the taiga. Sharing may also be framed as allowing access to resources, knowledge and skills. When sharing is enforced, however, the relationship lacks trust. The Orochen frame such interaction as coercion, since it has potential to bring misfortune to both actors. A relationship is challenged when one actor 'takes' what is not given willingly by other beings, fails to share himself or excludes others from their share.

Such coercion or aggression is intrinsic to a way of hunting that hunters and herders call 'poaching' (Rus. *brakonerstvo*) or 'sin' (Oro. *ngelome*). Poaching is seen as the opposite of the ethic of 'equal contestation' with animals, since poaching denies the animal the use of its volition. The aggressive nature of poaching also excludes other persons from the 'equal contest', thus interfering with their right to acquire luck or enter the contest. Poaching includes the use of elaborate hunting equipment or hunting strategies that are likely to waste meat, lack of respect toward nonhuman beings, and leaving hunting places in a 'messed-up' state. Such acts may 'spoil' the luck of various human actors. Poaching can also endanger the hunter, who risks being the target of the spirits' revenge. The recycling of animals' souls by means of domination is thus seen as a potential threat to the hunter's life, once domination becomes a part of a reciprocal relationship.[6]

Although cooperation is the preferred and commonly practised strategy of interaction with the environment, in the post-Soviet context of shortage people also have to rely on aggression, imposing their will on other humans and nonhumans or 'spoiling the luck' of others (Rus. *napakostit' fart*). In this way people increase their own chances for success in their subsistence activities. A hunter who acts aggressively and sinfully will most likely succeed in harvesting animals; however, the animals' master-spirit may attack him in return. Hence, hunters and herders hide their future plans and past and present subsistence activities from other beings. Various strategies of misleading spirits, animals and humans have become extremely important to Orochen who hope to escape their revenge. The complex mixture of aggression and cooperation creates ambiguity, risk and tension among people and nonhuman beings.

The long history of state domination and the post-Soviet competition for resources have led to different modalities of indigenous subsistence strategies and interaction with various beings. In the context of a 'wild' market economy and shortages of resources, practices of domination appear almost unavoidable in the taiga and villages.[7] Many ethnographic accounts of hunter-gatherers describe a 'giving environment' and suggest that hunting success is based on the idea that animals offer themselves to the hunters as long as they are treated with respect, but present-day Siberia presents a very different image.

Comparative studies of hunter-gatherer societies by Ingold (2000) and Bird-David (1990) describe the interaction between humans and nonhumans as based on dependency and noncoercive relations such as trust and a 'cosmic economy of sharing' among different actors. Much ethnography of Athapaskan and Algonquian societies in sub-arctic North America reiterates the idea of giving and sharing. There, animals give themselves to the hunter willingly out of love or pity. Hunters are deemed trustworthy when they observe the many responsibilities entailed by such relations, like showing respect for the animal in the process of killing, butchering and disposing of its remains. Hunting based on obligations and responsibilities towards animals is thus described as a practice that does not threaten the relationship between humans and animals.

Brightman (2002: 189) proposes an 'adversary' – as opposed to a 'benefactor' – mode of relationship between the Cree people and animals. In the benefactor mode, animals are seen as offering themselves to be killed, an act that requires the hunter to offer a gift or reward. Here, the killing of an animal is understood as part of a reciprocal relationship. Human-animal interactions in the benefactor model are seen as 'an endless cycle of reciprocities' where the relationship must satisfy both animals and humans (ibid.). In the adversarial model, by contrast, the animal is seen as the opponent of the hunter. In order to succeed, the hunter must overcome the animal. Therefore, according to Brightman (ibid.), such relations are more likely to be characterized as domination.

Tanner (1979: 136) also describes how Cree hunters pay respect to their game and acknowledge the animals' superior position. They may build a friendship, or at least a relationship of exchange, with a particular animal. Tanner (ibid.) proposed three models of interaction between hunters and animals based on three types of social relationships that he identifies as the 'symbolism of hunting rites'. These models are: (1) male-female, (2) domination-subordination, and (3) equivalence. The first model emphasizes the loving relationship between hunter and prey, which can be seen as either sexual attraction or parent-child love. In domination and subordination model, Tanner (ibid.) describes the use of magical practices to compel an animal to approach the hunter or allow itself to be caught in some other way. Although 'powerful' hunters may use their ability to attract game this way, the emphasis in this mode still rests on the generosity of animals or their 'masters', rather than on the hunters' skills of coercion. Tanner (1979: 148) states that the 'magical power' that a hunter establishes through coercion, which causes the animal to approach him against its will, can be found only in oral traditions about past hunting. The third mode emphasizes 'friendship' between animals and humans, specifically hunters who have killed a large number of animals of a particular species. According to Tanner (1979: 138–139), such a person would be seen as a 'friend' and 'partner' of these animals. Tanner (ibid.: 150) also wrote that the model of domination differs from other models in that the transaction is conducted by means of coercion rather than cooperation or exchange.

Both Tanner and Brightman construct a rough opposition between hunter-animal relations based on domination and those based on reciprocity. They claim that the concrete behavioural mode that causes an animal's 'good will to offer itself' should be understood as grounded more in ideology than in practice. However, they do not present a contextual account of how such oppositional models can be integrated in practice, but refer only to functional or psychological explanations. Tanner (1979: 148) notes that although some coercive rituals take place before the hunt, only after the hunt is the animal discursively transformed from victim to benefactor and finally friend. Brightman (2002: 211) sees the idea of exchange, when applied to the animal after it has been killed, as softening the violent act and providing a more reliable ideology for securing material benefit.

A certain ambivalence may inhere in this relationship, but the 'benefactor' mode nevertheless dominates in subarctic ethnography. At the same time, some historical examples demonstrate that in periods of extreme misfortune, disease or animal extinction, people adopted strategies of domination in their interaction with other beings (see Krech 1981). The prevailing belief was that the spirits of offended animals could also inflict sickness (see Martin 1978). Nevertheless, there are also hints that 'medicine power' could be connected to domination in the Canadian subarctic. References are made to 'bad medicine' among the Ojibwa (Black 1977: 150), to aggression in the 'shaking tent ceremony' among the Cree (Feit 1994: 304–305) or to uses of medicine power called *inkoze* for dominating animals among the Chipewyan (Smith 1982: 51–52). Furthermore, as Krech (1981: 88–89) remarks, among the Chipewyan, Dogrib or Slavey *inkoze* 'can be used to make people sick, to kill people, to kill dogs, to help starving people, and to send bad luck to hunters when hunting'. Power *inkoze* can be used for malevolent ends, including sickness (ibid.). Krech (1981: 89–90) cited the Jesuit Jetté's (1911: 102) reporting on the Koyukon, who described shamans as controlling good or malevolent spirits and capable of either causing people harm like disease, misfortune or ill luck, or benefiting them by curing disease, bringing prosperity and good luck. Spirits who were protecting animals or humans as punishment for mistreatment could also cause harm. Among the Koyukon, lack of hunting luck was also blamed on sorcerers or shamans from other groups of Athapaskans, Cree, Inuit or Euro-Canadians (ibid.: 86–97).

Recent studies (see Fausto 2007; Brightman, Grotti and Ulturgasheva 2012) of Amazonian hunters have shown how the dominance mode can be seen as a distinct way of producing people and their sociality with animals. Hunting is described as warfare that exposes humans to danger, since animals also engage in predatory acts against them. Notions of respectful consumption of animals can also be found in the anthropological literature on Amazonia. Meanwhile, the result of disrespect toward animals is held to be more dangerous than the extinction of animals or the loss of luck, as it always causes counter-predation (Fausto ibid.). Hunting is always disguised as something other than warfare for human and animal persons; therefore, the animal is de-subjectivized through ritual acts that are always performed before consumption of animals (ibid.). In a recent comparative study of Yukaghir and Altaians, Broz and Willerslev (2012) suggest that hunting luck can be understood in terms of the ambiguous manifestation of two ontologically antithetical phenomena, with either positive or negative consequences. Hunting luck may at any point be exposed as misfortune since the spirits can trick the hunter and turn him into prey (ibid.).

The Orochen view even warfare as a game based on reciprocity, mutual agreement and strict rules (see Anisimov 1936; Vasilevich 1968; Maksimova 1992). The oral traditions of several Evenki groups, including the Orochen, tell how rival groups agreed on a certain place for fighting and set it apart with a fence or other markers. Maksimova (1992: 96) states that all warlike activities were based on notions of honour and respect. Many a war party ended with a peaceful settlement and the exchange of gifts. Members of rival groups who visited the camp were usually received as guests; only after some time were they asked the reason for their visit (ibid.). Sometimes visiting rivals were compensated with women, and then the parties made peace. If no agreement could be reached, the sides came to mutual agreement on when and where to meet for a fight, and each group selected a representative to be the so-called *soning* (war chief).

When the fighting groups met, they held first a dance and then a wrestling duel between the two chiefs (ibid.), followed by races. Only then was there a fight with weapons. Sometimes the opposing groups exchanged arrows to make the fight more equal. They also agreed on the distance between the groups of archers. It was considered unethical to kill a person who was lying wounded on the ground or someone with his eyes open. Women, elders and children were never killed either. The victors marked trees on their way back to give their opponents a chance to follow them, should they wish to resume the fight. When a *soning* killed someone he had to die at the hand of his enemies in return (ibid.). Therefore a *soning* would give his own arrows to the enemies, asking to be killed and recommending that they eat his heart, thus to share in his strength (see Vasilevich 1968). This kind of warfare centred on the demonstration of skills, competition and negotiation rather than the actual killing of enemies. It served to diffuse tension between rival groups and restore peace and balance. The use of cunning and stealth was excluded unless the enemy did not 'play fair'.

Enacted and Emplaced Luck

This book has approached the Orochen luck – *kutu* – as a vernacular theory of causality based on Orochen hunters' and reindeer herders' dynamic interaction with various beings and entities, including other humans, animals, spirits, material objects and places. I have illustrated this point with interrelated ethnographic vignettes that show how *kutu* can be caught, sustained, contained, shared or lost in daily subsistence practices. I have also shown how *kutu* can be emplaced into various material objects (amulets, tools, camping structures) and places (such as *bikit*), and sustained through networks of reciprocity with humans and nonhuman beings. Practices of attracting, catching and sustaining *kutu* are also inseparable from active discursive and behavioural patterns. Thus *kutu* is neither a superstitious relic of old religious practices nor an abstract theoretical concept, but something perceived and experienced as an indigenous reality that is inseparable from everyday subsistence practices, embodied knowledge and quotidian interactions. In certain contexts, *kutu* can also be seen as an intrinsic component of personhood that can be shared with other people, thus sustaining kin or wider social relations that embrace humans and nonhuman beings.

In particular, this study has aimed to show how Orochen communities of reindeer herders and hunters based in taiga camps and villages have struggled to revive their life with domestic animals in remote taiga places since the collapse of Soviet state. This includes not only economic activities like reindeer herding and hunting, but also rituals that were suppressed but are now being rediscovered and reinvigorated through adaptions and transformations that are consonant with contemporary realities. Hence, I demonstrated how the desire for luck, accumulation of it and occasional forms of domination became an important ways for people to try to control and adapt to shifting natural, social and economic environments.

In pre-Soviet times master-spirits were seen as rulers of the landscape, animals and humans destinies, while shamans and other knowledgeable people were masters of spirits that controlled the clans' and individuals' well-being and, derivatively, hunting luck. However, the Soviet state's dominance was so harsh that not only were ritual leaders like shamans supressed, but any objects linked to spiritual practices, such as sites of ritual importance, mortuary scaffolds and shamanic material sacraments, were also destroyed. In this context the omnipresent Soviet state replaced shamans and master-spirits in many spheres of human life, providing the jobs, goods and necessities needed to work and live in the taiga and villages. Orochen elders once sang for me an old indigenous song that had the refrain 'Lenin is a master of hills and valleys and Lenin is everywhere' which illustrates how the shamanic and master-spirits' agency was partly transferred into communist force and new masters of humans' life and destinies.

Despite the Soviet suppression of traditional religious practices and institutions, hunters and herders living in the taiga continued to perform embodied ritual practices, particularly those that were deemed crucial to gaining luck in hunting and reindeer herding. At the same time, various features of landscapes (e.g. boulders, caves and rock art sites) and of intra-house environments (e.g. the fireplace) continuously served as secret spaces for these rituals. These silent rituals of reciprocity and respect were probably hardly visible and therefore little censured by the Soviet powers.

The unexpected collapse of the socialist state, concurrent with the rise of the market economy, placed economic burdens on people living in remote northern villages. At the same time many families started to feel that they were literally flooded with health problems and poverty, and had suddenly lost control of many spheres of their life. Indeed, the great number of tragic events, deaths, problems with drunkenness and disabilities that occurred in Orochen communities over the decades significantly marked the local landscape and social relations. Most villagers had no option but to subsist on taiga goods and domestic animals. Having inherited domestic reindeer and taiga territories from the state, Orochen now had to deal with their autonomous life and subsistence in taiga.

Today, hunters and herders believe that various tragic places scattered throughout the taiga, as well as old and empty reindeer herders' camps, unattended mortuary sites, old log-houses, hills, rocks and lakes, have became sites where malevolent spirits and monsters can become manifest. Infused with misfortune, these places have started to shape the Orochen experience of place, land use and well-being. Furthermore, in the post-Soviet environment of transition, malevolent spirits displaced from the taiga have become localized in villages or neglected industrial sites, or can be met wandering around routes in the taiga and villages. Indeed, such Orochen place-making practices can be seen as extensions from a geographic locale to the wider spatial and temporal field of relations, linking a place with histories of colonial contact, global forces and markets, governments and various forms of industrialization (Gupta and Ferguson 1997; for Cree in Canada see Feit 2004: 94,).

Today, one can witness the state institutions' step-by-step retreat from the formerly prosperous northern villages as various state institutions and officials lose the trust of the people. In villages, the evil eye and black magic activities have become central themes in daily accusations regarding the diminished luck and health of individuals and families. These conflicts between various groups have released previously suppressed and unknown spirits, which have begun to bother people in taiga and villages, reaching even cities. Thus claims of sorcery and possible harm to others affect most social relations between neighbours and different groups of hunters and herders. The risk and danger are further increased by outbursts of contemporary immoral activities in the taiga and harsh competition between herders, hunters, officials, entrepreneurs, villagers and state power representatives.

Many spirits, forgotten for almost half a century, are held to have caused multiple misfortunes, illnesses and even deaths of relatives, hitting all spheres of Orochen life. Some have begun to interpret these outcomes as resulting directly from the accumulation of debts to spirits. Thus understood, spirits have become important actors shaping contemporary Orochen perceptions of sociality, morality and ritual life and are now widely feared, avoided and discussed. In this way, nonhuman beings that have existed in Orochen cosmology for centuries are continuously experienced and employed in contemporary storytelling by hunters and herders.

Even as people turn their attention towards master-spirits, old and reinvented rituals and rock art sites have again become powerful agents in luck-generating practices and healing.[8] The Orochen communities and individuals have revived interaction with these beings through rituals based on reciprocity as well as creation of ritual sites in the taiga and next to villages. These interactions with master-spirits in various places have become one of just a few important options for dealing with present-day calamities and uncertainties. In an environment where people cannot rely on state supplies and facilities or high-quality goods, it comes as no surprise that hunters and herders are creatively re-enacting many old rituals, skills and strategies for generating luck and escaping misfortune.

In a context of shortage of resources and absence of hunting luck, people can devolve into domination of other humans and animals, cause harm to each other and engage in 'poaching' activities, showing unwillingness to share with each other. They may also take up risky illegal mining for gold or nephrite, exposing themselves to the possibility of magical or physical revenge by other humans. Exploitative, dangerous and greedy people who act disrespectfully towards humans, animals and spirits are easily associated with various malevolent spirits and mythological monsters. Contemporary Orochen narratives depict people's immorality and self-will, linking these to the emergence and revenge of malevolent spirits.

Despite the increase in people's anxiety over their control of spirits and their own destinies, there were few knowledgeable people in the villages. The infrequent interactions with newly evolved shamans in Aga or Buryatia helped to fill some gaps in the explanations and memories of forgotten or unknown spirits and provide details about the proper performance of rituals to tame various spirits. In this context rock art sites, elders' stories, shamanic ancestry and one's own experiences become the main sources of knowledge about engaging with and knowing the spirits. Today, rituals led by skilful hunters or former indigenous Communist Party leaders might even be reconstructed by relying on the works of ethnographers, memories of elders or images in museum photos. In the same way that animal tracks left on the landscape reveal information about the animals and point to ways of dealing with them while hunting and herding, changes observed in rock art pictures, ashes, fire, springs or caves, as well as interpretations of dreams and stories, lead to answers to many existential questions. Dreams, birds, sounds, sparks, rock art and one's embodied awareness are all important sources of knowledge that guides one's strategy of catching luck (Oro. *kutu*) and escaping misfortune, and also helps people tame spirits and control their own destinies. This knowledge-generating process, combined with attunement to the flow of a changing social or natural environment, can be seen in terms of the persistence of intuitions that shape how people use various opportunities build a secure living environment and landscape (also Anderson 2006a, 2012). Hence, hunters' and herders' ontology of luck stands as an important epistemology dealing with socioeconomic and spiritual changes and the uncertainties of the transition.

Aiming to understand how hunters and herders managed their luck, I have analysed a wide variety of hunters' and herders' tactile and bodily techniques, along with the skills, knowledge, empathy and awareness that are activated when they move through the landscape and compete with animals, spirits and other humans. I have also demonstrated how walking, forecasting weather and selecting and organizing campsites in accordance with shifting environmental conditions allow people to avail themselves of various subsistence opportunities. Catching luck means being in the right place at the right time, which is inseparable from success in competing with animals, reading the landscape and predicting the weather. In this book I have therefore extensively described how hunters and herders enact Orochen knowledge, skills and perceptions in everyday practices of subsistence and movements in the taiga and villages. These strategies permeate embodied and discursive activities, the use of landscape for habituation and subsistence, and attentiveness toward places of memory or ritual importance when a person creates her or his own living place (Oro. *bikit*) linked to her or his own identity. Success in subsistence also revolves around 'traditional knowledge' and skills developed to make the best use of animal parts and various taiga goods in tool, clothing and equipment production.

Domestic animals like reindeer, horses and dogs have become crucial to subsistence and are also considered a source of physical strength and spiritual inspiration. Like a person's relationship with other humans, relations with reindeer can be described as cooperation based on sharing and exchanges of favours within the framework of human-animal sociality, which Beach and Stammler (2006) aptly called 'symbiotic domestication'. The continuation of inherited subsistence practices like reindeer herding is perceived as bringing balance to the set of relationships between spirits, animals and landscape. Interactions with reindeer depend on both the herders' skills in competition and the maintenance of reciprocal relations and respect for the animals' autonomy and agency. Living with reindeer in the taiga and creating living places (*bikit*) for humans and reindeer sustains not just an indigenous identity but also knowledge of spiritual landscape. Any hunting or reindeer herding activity involves a contest between humans and individual animals. These separate modes of subsistence – hunting and herding – can be seen as elements of one integral strategy that relies on similar sets of skills and knowledge and similar notions of personhood.

It would be impossible to gain knowledge and communicate in the taiga without extensive movements, knowledge about how to leave and read tracks and signs, and the ability to forecast the weather and seasonal change. Hunters and herders consider walking a source of health and a vital skill in the context of generating luck. Movement itself is framed by a symbolic discourse of expertise, knowledge and morality and is semantically linked to ideas like 'life energy', 'soul', 'strength' and 'luck'. Old tracks left on the ground and old campsites are important indicators of a person's mastery of a place, be it a live human or a soul. Movements across the taiga, prints and tracks left on the landscape and enacted rituals of luck carried out by individuals serve to maintain an identity based on people's ties to life and places in the taiga. Movement on foot through the landscape and walking with animals while harvesting game or herding reindeer are crucial to becoming a full-fledged hunter and creating living places (*bikit*). One cannot sustain the *bikit* of humans or animals without adapting the rhythm of one's daily activities and movements to the agency of various beings. Such a *bikit* evolves from the successful coexistence of humans, wild and domestic animals, and spirits to become an area emplaced with one's 'life energy' (Oro. *musun*) and luck (Oro. *kutu*).

I have also described how luck is caught not only because of the master-spirits' goodwill, but also because of the hunter's ability to overcome individual animals by using his skills and knowledge. The contestation among humans, animals and spirits striving to overcome each other recalls Lavrillier's (2007) observations on the Amur Evenkis' notion of 'play' (Oro. *evi*). She aptly describes the latter as the ability to perform rituals, compete, produce crafts, play instruments and games, perform shamanic practices, move around skilfully and perform stories. In this context, Orochen do not wait for a gift from the environment, but actively strive to achieve their desired hunting results via skilful negotiation with various kinds of beings.

The master-spirit in control of the balance among animals can set limits to a human's *kutu*, and successes that any individual has achieved through domination may turn into misfortune or danger. Regardless, hunters and herders occasionally resort to strategies of domination over other beings or accumulate resources by ignoring the ethics of reciprocity and sharing. Both forms of sinful behaviour cause much tension among humans and nonhuman beings. Hence, both luck and success that is achieved through domination depend increasingly on covert practices meant to sustain well-being or escape misfortune, vengeful spirits or the evil eye. Hiding and maintaining silence have became important ways of trying to maintain the beneficial environment in which luck can be realized, as has sharing information about animals, spirits and subsistence activities. Participating in storytelling empowers Orochen to inject some predictability into their lives and subsistence, and promote awareness of potential dangers while also teaching appropriate moral behaviour and judgements. Storytelling can also serve strategic needs, such as protecting one's storage platforms, taiga resources, domestic animals, hunting and herding territories, and possessions. Reproductions of old narratives linked to malevolent spirits' revenge and to morality play an important role in explaining the past and present difficulties and building a potentially secure future.

The description of relationships between various kinds of beings has challenged the standard view of hierarchical relations among supreme beings, animal masters, shamans/humans and wild or domestic animals in hunter-gatherer societies (see Ingold 1986: 264–273) with an alternative picture of temporally and situationally shifting patterns of interaction between individualized beings. Humans interact and struggle daily with individual animals, other humans and, occasionally, individual spirits. Any such interaction may involve ambiguous relations and covert strategies. Anxiousness about hunting luck or success based on domination is the driving force making these relationships dynamic, situational and essentially a-hierarchical. Thus, the complex relationship of cooperation and domination constitutes a Bakhtinian *dialogic* between actors, where meanings are continuously re-created (Bakhtin 1981).

To the Orochen, *kutu* and success are a game played against various human and nonhuman beings. The Russian ethnographer Alekhin (2001: 162) vividly describes the sense of tension expressed by Evenki hunters and herders of Surinda village (Krasnoiarsk Province):

> Life is a game where one must follow the rules (described by the Evenki as norms called *ngolomo* – 'sin' or *nengo* –'sign, prediction') in order to escape an untimely death. Where breach of these rules inevitably leads to death, following them does not automatically make you a winner.

Although the Orochen experience their interactions with other beings as dramatic and dangerous in the post-Soviet environment, their life can nevertheless appear much less predestined than that of the Yukaghir. Aiming to predict and control their life, people overplay the role of animals and malevolent spirits, and therefore reciprocity remains intrinsic to all social relations as the most predictable element of social life. People also do have hope that any misfortune or illness can be traced back to a specific sin committed in the past that, once known, may be remedied. In this context, Orochen values like making offerings (Oro. *kundulo*), sharing (Oro. *nimat*), avoiding sins (Oro. *ngelomel*) and observing the system of prohibitions (Oro. *odel*) continuously serve as moral guidelines bringing balance to the displaced field of relations between humans, nonhumans and landscape (see Vasilevich 1969: 201; Alekhin 1998; Varlamova 2004: 51–59).

Any kind of misfortune and unexpected death or revenge that may lie ahead can be predicted and known through awareness and observation of various predictive signs (Oro. *nengo*), and avoided by means of rituals. While any form of cooperation or domination is also seen in terms of a reciprocal relationship, humans can switch from one mode to the other, thus aiming to retain some control of their life and believing that they are able to turn a negative outcome into a positive relationship. When it comes to catching luck, tricking spirits and animals, and escaping revenge when harvesting game by means of domination, the importance accorded to skill highlights the role of the individual player in the game of his own destiny. The Orochen reindeer herders' and hunters' ambiguous relations with their environment, which I have described in term of domination and cooperation, can be understood as fluid, enmeshed and co-implicated forms of interaction among human and nonhuman beings.

My ethnography is intended to stress the Orochen's flexibility in terms of the strategies, knowledge and skills they use to adapt to their changing natural, seasonal, economic and political circumstances. In his description of the Orochen of Buryatia, Neupokoev (1928) noted almost a century ago:

> This nation is capable of escaping death and accepting everything that can support their living culture. ... There is a dramatic decrease of game and they use predatory ways of hunting. There is an increase in newly arriving hunters as well, reindeer herding is declining and they are treated unfairly in the fur trade – all of this threatens the Tungus of North Buryatia with a catastrophic future. At the same time, the history of the Tungus nation has borne witness of their ability to survive [Rus. *zhiznesposobnosti*] and their persistence [Rus. *stoikosti*].

As the past century has shown, the core of the Orochen's ontology of luck and success is their capacity to adjust their daily lives to change and to create and maintain subsistence strategies that give them the best possible chances for survival in both the taiga and the post-Soviet socioeconomic environment. Orochen life does not consists of simply moving *with* the flow of the environment: life is mastered both *over* the environment and *together with* it, whether by catching luck or achieving success through domination in their subsistence activities.

Notes

1. Reciprocity, which has been described in classical studies as the practice of gifting and counter-gifting, is generally seen as involving 'obligations' to repay as well as receive gifts (Mauss 1967: 10–11).
2. Anderson (2000a: 126–127) also advances the idea of 'taking opportunities', opposing it to the somewhat romantic image of the 'giving environment' that can be found in several circumpolar ethnographies.
3. See more examples on demand sharing in Myers (1988: 52–74) and Woodburn (1998: 48–63).
4. The so-called sexual seduction of animals includes the hunter's actual and perceptual engagement with his prey (Willerslev 2007). My findings concur with numerous descriptions linking certain sexual prohibitions to hunting luck, but I have never come across an Orochen female hunter who described her dreams of animals or hunting luck in sexual terms. Though the question of female hunters' perception of animals needs to be explored further, I would suggest that in the Orochen world there are no gender divisions at all with respect to hunting.
5. Willerslev (2007), though he also elaborates on the Yukaghir hunters' negotiations of the space between becoming the animal through mimicry and remaining human, does not address humans' spatial experiences and the agency of places that are an important part of animist cosmologies across Siberia.
6. For the risk of soul recycling among the Orochon of Sakhalin, see Kwon (1998: 119); for Siberia, see Hamayon (1990: 365–72).
7. Through the years 2008–2014, the situation became even more infused with conflict due to the impact of climate change: the landscape of Northern Zabaikal'ia became unusually dry and was devastated by forest fires. This made the taiga easily accessible to vehicles driven by city- and village-based hunters who had started to harvest game, reaching and overhunting remote areas.
8. Even small animals and birds are believed to be stronger than humans (see also Varlamova 1996: 51). However, the Orochen believe that any human or nonhuman being has its own agency to cause misfortune as well as foretell luck.

Glossary of Orochen and Russian Terms

arenkil (sing. *arenki*) (Oro.)   souls of hunters or herders who did not reach the world of the dead due to sudden or accidental death, or because they were not escorted by the proper rituals. These souls had to remain in this world and became malevolent.

baza (Rus.)   base camp.

bikit (Oro.)   a living place (of humans and/or animals) where humans, animals and nonhuman beings as well as landscape can fit together to harbour one's subsistence life and well-being for a sustained period.

bosoo (Oro.)   northern mountain slope.

botolo (Oro.)   reindeer's bell.

brakonerstvo (Rus.)   poaching

changa (Oro.)   wolf.

chernota (Rus.)   black magic.

chinen (Oro.)   strength.

chum (Rus.)   conical tent made from canvas, tanned skins and bark of larch or birch.

dalavun (Oro.)   boiled dog food.

datsan (Bur.)   Tibetan Buddhism monastery.

delken (Oro.)   elevated open storing platform.

dido (Oro.)   stone.

dovan (Oro.)   A mountain passage connecting different river basins.

dukh-khoziain (Rus.)   'master-spirit' a spirit in charge of different geographical locations and having influence on rebirth and procreation of wild and domestic animals and the life of humans.

dzho (Oro.)   gall bladder.

emchure (Oro.)   winter footwear made from moose buckskin.

Evenki   the ethnonym chosen by the Soviet state as an administrative category in the 1920s after the end of the civil wars. It was used as a unified reference to many scattered groups in Siberia and the Far East that spoke dialects of the Tungus-Manchu language group.

fart (Rus. fortuna)   luck

fufaika (Rus.)   winter coat filled with cotton-wool.

irakta (Oro.)   larch.

ikenipke (Oro.) ('imitation of life', 'playing for life', Oro. *ike* 'play')   an elaborate ritual performed in the spring. It lasted eight days and featured singing, competitions and divinations as well as hunters' performance of chasing moose to obtain luck and well-being.

irgekta (Oro.)   fresh grass growing in spring on hummocks.

kabarga (Rus.)   musk deer, an smallest deer in Siberia hunted for valuable musk glad.

kever (Oro.)   open marshy fields of hummocks (Rus. *kochki*).

kiltera (Oro.)   bread.

kolkhoz (Rus.)   collective farm.

kolokochan (Rus.)   kettle.

komersanty (Rus.)   entrepreneurs such as fur traders and owners of all-terrain vehicles and grocery shops.

koto (Oro.)   knife.

kundulo (Oro.)   offering, offering site.

kure (Oro.)   reindeer corral.

kutu (Oro.)   Orochen word denoting luck (also Rus. *fart*).

kuturuk (Oro.)   placing of luck, see *placing*.

labaz (Rus.)   elevated storing cache built on stomps of trees.

lokovun (Oro.)   rack- tripod or horizontal pole.

mahin (Oro.)   luck among Orochen of Buryatiia.

malu (Oro.)   master's place located in the back of the tent.

maril (Oro.)   shrub bush fields.

moonmokan (Oro.)   special wooden log attached to the neck that prevents from fast animal's movement.

murchen (Oro.)   'horse people' (Bur. *murin* 'horse'), i.e. Evenki who raised cattle and horses.

murin (Oro.) see *murchen*.

musun power, 'life energy', power of movement, an ability to have influence on other beings. *Musun* can be intrinsic to different places, material objects, phenomena and nonhuman beings as well as spoken words.

nengo (Oro.) a sign (such as the weird behaviour of a bird) by which a hunter may foretell a (mostly negative) incident, a particular future event or possible outcome.

ngelome (Oro.) (plural *ngelomel*) sinful behaviour linked to violations of taiga ethics such as not sharing, or showing disrespect to domestic and hunted animals, spirits or mortuary and ritual sites.

nimat (Oro.) cultural rule or ethical norm obliging hunters to share after a successful hunt.

ode (Oro.) (pl. *odel*) certain ethical guidelines and principles to be followed in daily practices of subsistence and life.

odzhen (Oro.) see *dukh-khoziain*.

oktol (Oro.) taiga paths.

omi (Oro.) a soul of human or animal or soul associated with place.

omiruk (Oro.) a soul placing (see placing) *Orochen* (Oro.) 'reindeer people', a self-designation used by reindeer herding and hunting groups of Evenki inhabiting the Vitim, Olekma and Aldan river basins.

oron (Oro.) reindeer.

pakostnoi (Rus.) harmful, *pakost'* (Rus.) harm. *porcha* (Rus.) a conscious magical attack meant to cause illness to another person.

paktyravun (Oro.) rifle.

peshkov'e (Rus.) a walking trip.

placing (Rus. *vmestilishcha*) a Tungus (Evenki) notion, which means a material object (idol, crafted item, place) or alive being (tree, human or animal) inhabited by the spirit or humans' soul.

porcha (Rus.) literally 'spoil'- a negative magic damage.

senkira (Oro.) (Lat. *Ledum palustre*, Rus. *bagulnik*, marsh labrador tea) a plant used for smudging and protecting/cleansing from evil influence.

seveki (Oro.) the main master of spirits, ancient creator of world or a wooden idol, also referred to as master of taiga.

sinkelevun (Oro.) a special ritual that can be semantically translated as 'searching for hunting luck' or mean 'imitating luck' or 'obtaining hunting luck'.

siru (Oro.)   dried pieces of meat.

solontsy (Rus.)   sites consisting salt in the soil.

stram, stramnoi (Rus.)   bad, unacceptable.

taiga (Rus.)   sub-boreal forest consisting of predominantly larch as well as birch and pine trees.

tauseruk (Oro.)   ammunition bag.

toksokol (Oro.)   mountain ranges.

tungus   an old colonial name for the scattered Tungus-Manchu-speaking groups of hunting and reindeer-herding people. Today, the Orochen also use the term Tungus to refer to horse and cattle raising groups known as Barguzin Tungus (Buryatia) and Shilka Tungus (Zabaikal Province).

turan (Oro.)   raven.

tyevun (Oro.)   a tool consisting of two attached sticks that can be used as walking stick or as twopod for rifle.

ural (Oro.)   hills.

yagel (Oro.)   lichen.

yanil (Oro.)   treeless hills.

zglaz (Rus.)   a negative influence on human activities that is passed unconsciously from one person to another.

Bibliography

Alekhin, K. A. 1998. 'Kommunikativanaia kul'tura evekov v otechestvenykh issledovaniiakh: narabotki i perspektivy', in I. N. Gemuev (ed.), *Sibir' v panorama
tysiacheletii: Materialy mezhdunarodnogo simpoziuma*. Novosibirsk: Izdatel'stvo Instituta archeologii i etnografii SO RAN, pp. 12–16.
Alekhin, K. A. 1999. 'K voprosu o traditsionnoi meditsine taezhnykh evenkov', in
Gumanitarnye nauki v Sibiri. Arkheologiia I etnografiia 3: 93–95.
Alekhin, K. A. 2001. 'Etnokul'turnaia kharajteristika lokal'nogo soobschestva (po
materialie Surindy). Problemy kommunikativnoi kul'tury', unpublished PhD
dissertation. Novosibirsk: Novosibirsk University.
Alekseev, N. A. 1975. *Traditsionnye religioznye verovaniia iakutov v XIX – nachale
XX v.* Novosibirsk: Nauka.
Anderson, D. G. 2000a. *Identity and Ecology in Arctic Siberia: The Number One
Reindeer Brigade.* Oxford: Oxford University Press.
Anderson, D. G. 2000b. 'Tracking the "Wild Tungus" in Taimyr: Identity, Ecol-
ogy, and Mobile Economies in Arctic Siberia', in Peter P. Schweitzer, Biesele,
M. and R. K. Hitchcock (eds), *Hunters and Gatherers in the Modern World:
Conflict, Resistance, and Self-Determination.* New York and Oxford: Berghahn
Books, pp. 223–243.
Anderson, D. G. 2000c. 'Surrogate Currencies and the Wild Market in Central
Siberia', in P. Seabright (ed.), *The Vanishing Rouble: Barter Networks and
Non-monetary Transactions in Post-Soviet Societies.* Cambridge: Cambridge
University Press, pp. 318–344.
Anderson, D. G. 2006a. 'Dwellings, Storage and Summer Site Structure among
Siberian Orochen-Evenkis: Hunter-Gatherer Vernacular Architecture under
Post-Socialist Conditions', *Norwegian Archeological Review* 39(1): 1–26.
Anderson, D. G. 2006b. 'The Turukhansk Polar Census Expedition of 1926–1927:
At the Crossroads of Two Traditions', *Sibirica* 5(1): 24–61.
Anderson, D. G. 2007. 'Mobile Architecture and Social Life: The Case of the Coni-
cal Skin Lodge in the Putoran Plateau Region', in S. Beyries and V. Vaté (eds),
*Les civilisations du renne d'hier et d'aujourd'hui. Approches ethnohistoriques,
archéologiques et anthropologiques, actes des XVIIe rencontres internationales
d'archéologie et d'histoire d'Antibes.* Antibes: Éditions APDCA, pp. 43–63.
Anderson, D. G. 2011. *The Healing Landscapes of Central & Southeastern Siberia.*
Edmonton CCI Press.

Anderson, D. G. 2012. 'Neo-Shamanism in a Post-Socialist Landscape: Knowledge, Luck and Ritual Among Zabaikal' Orochen-Evenkis', in P. Jordan (ed.), *Landscape and Culture in the Siberian North*. London: UCL Press.

Anisimov, A. F. 1936. *Rodovoe obshchestvo evenkov (tungusov)*. Leningrad: Izdatstelstvo Institutanarodov CIK SSSR im. P.G. Smidovicha.

Anisimov, A. F. 1949. 'Predstavleniia evenkov o shingenakh i problema proiskhozhdeniia pervobytnoi religii'. *Sbornik Muzeia Antropologii i Etnografii* 12: 160–194.

Anisimov, A. F. 1958. *Religiia evenkov v istoricheskom izuchenii problemy proiskhozhdeniia pervobytnikh verovanii*. Moscow and Leningrad: Nauka.

Anisimov, A. F. 1959. *Kosmologicheskie prestavleniia narodov severa*. Leningrad: Akademi Nauk.

Anisimov, A. F. 1963. 'The shaman's tent of the Evenki and the origins of shamanistic rite', in H. N. Michael (ed.), *Studies in Siberian Shamanism*. Toronto: University of Toronto Press, pp. 84–123.

Arbatskii, A. I. 1978. 'Nekotorye dannye o religioznyh perezhitkakh Vitimskikh evenkov', in *Drevniaia istoria narodov iuga vostochnoi Sibiri*. Irkutsk: Irkustk State University, pp. 177–180.

Arbatskii, A. I. 1981. 'Otchet o polevyvkh issledovaniiakh Vitimskogo etnograficheskogo otriada v 1980 godu', unpublished fieldwork report, Laboratory of Archaeology and Ethnography, Irkutsk State University.

Arbatskii, A. I. 1982. 'Evenkiiskoe antropomorfnoe izobrazhenie iz poselka Srednii Kalar', in *Drevniaia istoria narodov iuga vostochnoi Sibiri*. Irkutsk: Irkutsk State University, pp. 140–148.

Archakova, O. B. and L. L. Trifonova. 2006. *Mifologicheskie predstavleniia evekov: po materialam narodnykh skazok*. Blagoveschensk: Amur State University.

Aruneev, N. I. 1994. 'Zemlia predkov-sokhranim ee dlia sebia', *Vesti Severa*, 12 November, pp. 2–3.

Badmaev, A. A. 2000. 'Relikty kul'ta medvedia v kulture Buriat', in I. N. Gemuev (ed.), *Narody Sibiri: istoriia i kul'tura. Medved' v drevnikh i sovremenykh kul'turakh Sibiri*. Novosibirsk: SON RAN, pp. 68–71.

Bakhtin, M. 1981. *The Dialogical Imagination: Four Essays*. Austin: University of Texas Press.

Basharov, I. P. 2003. 'Predstavlenie o dukhakh-khoziaevakh mestnosti u russkogo promyslovogo naseleniia Vostochnogo Pribaikal'ia', in A. G. Generalov (ed.), *Narody i kultury Sibiri. vzaimodeistvie kak factor formirovaniia i modernizatsii*. Irkutsk: Mezhregional'nyi Institut Obschestvennykh Nauk, pp. 4–14.

Basso, K. 1996. 'Wisdom Sits in Places: Notes on a Western Apache Landscape', in S. Feld and K. Basso (eds), *Senses of Place*. Santa Fe, NM: School of American Research Press, pp. 53–90.

Batashev, M. S. 2007. 'Materialy Krasnoiarskogo muzeia po kul'tovym sooruzheniiam Evenkov', *Eniseiskaia provintsiia* 2: 77–106.

Beach H., and F. Stammler. 2006. 'Human-Animal relations in pastoralism' in F. Stammler, and H. Beach (eds) *People and Reindeer on the Move*. Special Issue of the journal *Nomadic Peoples* 10,2. Oxford: Berghahn, pp. 5–29.

Belikov, V. V. 1994. *Evenki Buriatii: istoriia i sovremenost'*. Ulan Ude: BNC SO RAN.

Bender, B. 1993. 'Introduction: Landscape-Meaning and Action', in B. Bender (ed.), *Landscape: Politics and Perspectives*. Oxford: Berg, pp. 1–17.

Bender, B. and M. Wiget. 2001. *Contested Landscapes: Movement, Exile and Place*. Oxford and New York: Berg.

Berkes, F. 1999. *Sacred Ecology: Traditional Ecological Knowledge and Management Systems*. Philadelphia and London: Taylor & Francis.

Bird-David, Nurit. 1990. 'The Giving Environment: Another Perspective on the Economic System of Gatherer-Hunters'. *Current Anthropology* 31(2): 189–196.

Bird-David, N. 1999. 'Animism Revisited: Personhood, Environment and Relational Epistemology', in *Culture: A Second Chance?* Special issue of *Current Anthropology* 40(S1, February): 67–91.

Black, M. 1977. 'Ojibwa Power Belief System', in R. D. Fogelson and R. N. Adams (eds), *The Anthropology of Power: Ethnographic Studies from Asia, Oceania, and the New World*. New York: Academic Press, pp. 141–151.

Bloch, A. 2004. *Red Ties and Residential Schools: Indigenous Siberians in a Post-Soviet State*. Philadelphia: University of Pennsylvania Press.

Bloch, A., 2005. Longing for the kollektiv: Gender, power, and residential schools in central Siberia. *Cultual anthropology*, 20(4), pp. 534–569.

Bodenhorn, B. 1990. 'I'm Not the Great Hunter, My Wife Is: Iñupiat and Anthropological Models of Gender', *Etudes/Inuit/Studies* 14(1–2): 55–74.

Bogoraz, V. 1919. 'Narodnaia literatura paleoaziiatov', in *Literatura Vostoka*. Petrograd: Izdatelstvo vsemirnoi literatury, pp. 50–68.

Brandisauskas, D. 2007. 'Symbolism and Ecological Uses of Fire among Orochen-Evenki', *Sibirica* 6(1): 95–109.

Brandisauskas, D. 2011. 'Contested Health in the Post-Soviet Taiga: Use of Landscape, Spirits and Strength among Orochen-Evenki of Zabaikal'e (East Siberia)', in D. G. Anderson (ed.) *Health and Healing in the Circumpolar North: Southeastern Siberia*. Alberta: CCI Press.

Brandišauskas, D. 2011. 'Hide tanning and its use in taiga: the case of Orochen-Evenki reindeer herders and hunters of Zabaikal'e (East Siberia) '. *Journal of Ethnology and Folkloristics* 4 (2): 97–114.

Brandišauskas D. 2012. 'Making a Home in the Taiga: Movements, Paths and Signs among Orochen-Evenki Hunters and Herders of Zabaikal Krai (South East Siberia) '. *Journal of Ethnology and Folkloristics* 6(1): 9–25.

Brennan, C. A. 1999. 'The Buriats and the Far Eastern Republic: An Aspect of Revolutionary Russia 1920–22', unpublished PhD thesis, Department of Anthropology. Aberdeen: The University of Aberdeen.

Brightman, R. A. 1993. *Grateful Prey: Rock Cree Human-Animal Relationships*. Berkeley, Los Angeles, Oxford. University of California Press.

Brightman, R. A. 2002 [1993]. *Grateful Prey: Rock Cree Animal-Human Relationships*. Regina: Canadian Plains Research Centre.

Brightman, M., Grotti V. E and O. Ulturgasheva (eds) 2012. *Animism in Rainforest and Tundra Personhood, Animals, Plants and Things in Contemporary Amazonia and Siberia*. N.Y, Oxford: Berghahn Books.

Brody, H. 1982. *Maps and Dreams*. New York: Pantheon Books.

Broz, L. and R. Willerslev. 2012. 'When Good Luck Is Bad Fortune: Between Too Little and Too Much Hunting Success in Siberia', *Social Analysis – The International Journal of Social and Cultural Practice* 56, pp. 73–89.

Burch, E. 1988. 'Modes of Exchange in North-West Alaska', in Tim Ingold, D. Riches and J. Woodburn (eds), *Hunters and Gatherers: Property, Power and Ideology*. Oxford: Berg, pp. 95–109.

Burch, E. 1991. 'Herd Following Reconsidered', *Current Anthropology* 32: 439–445.

Burnarkomzem. 1934–1936. 'Ekonomicheskii-Geograficheskii ocherk ekspeditsii Burnarkomzema Bauntovskogo Tuzemnogo Raiona', unpublished fieldwork report. Ulan-Ude, Archive of the Museum of Native People of the Village Bagdarin.

Buyandelgeriyn, M. 2007. 'Dealing with Uncertainty: Shamans, Marginal Capitalism, and the Remaking of History in Postsocialist Mongolia', *American Ethnologist* 34(1): 127–147.

Casey, E. S. 1996. 'How to Get from Space to Place in a Fairly Short Stretch of Time: Phenomenological Prolegomena', in S. Feld and K. Basso (eds), *Senses of Place*. Santa Fe, NM: School of American Research Press, pp. 13–52.

Cruikshank, J. 1998. *The Social Life of Stories: Narrative and Knowledge in the Yukon Territory*. Lincoln: University of Nebraska Press.

Da Col, G. 2012. 'Introduction: Natural Philosophies of Fortune-Luck, Vitality, and Uncontrolled Relatedness', *Social Analysis* 56(1): 1–23.

Damasio, A. 1999. *The Feeling of What Happens: Body and Emotion in the Making of Consciousness*. New York: Harcourt.

Derevianko, A. P. and V. E. Medvedev (eds). 2008. *Okno v nevedomyi mir: sbornik statei k 100- letiiu so dnia rozhdeniia akademika Alekseia Pavlovicha Okladnokova*. Novosibirsk: Izdatel'svo Intituta arkheologii i etnografii SO RAN.

Dobromyslov, N. M. 1902. 'Zametki po etnografii barguzinskikh Orochen', *Trudy Troitskogo Kiakhtinskogo Otdela Priamuria Rossiskogo Geograficheskogo Obschestva* 5(1): 78–87.

Dolgikh, B. O. 1960. *Rodovoi i plemennoi sostav narodov Sibiri v XVII veke*. Moscow: Izd. AN SSSR.

Empson, R. 2011. *Harnessing Fortune: Personhood, Memory and Place in Mongolia*. Oxford: Oxford University Press.

Empson, R. 2012. 'The Dangers of Excess: Accumulating and Dispersing Fortune in Mongolia', in G. da Col and C. Humphrey (eds), *Cosmologies of Fortune: Luck, Vitality and Uncontrolled Relatedness*, special issue, *Social Analysis* 56(1): 117–132.

Ermolova, N. V. 2010. 'Predstavleniia o dushe, smerti i zagrobnoi zhizni v traditsionom mirovozrenii evenkov', in Y. E. Berezkin and L. R. Pavlinaskaia (eds), *Ot bytiia k inobytiiu: Fol'klor i pogrebalnyi ritual v traditsionnykh kul'turakh Sibiri i Ameriki*. St Petersburg: MAE RAN, pp. 93–158.

Fausto, C. 2007. 'Feasting on People: Eating Animals and Humans in Amazonia'. *Current Anthropology* 48 (4): 497–530.

Feit, H. A. 1973. 'The Ethnoecology of the Waswanipi Cree, or How Hunters Can Manage Their Resources', in B. Cox (ed.), *Cultural Ecology: Readings on the Canadian Indians and Eskimos*. Toronto: Carleton Library, pp. 115–125.

Feit, H. A. 1994. 'Dreaming of Animals: The Waswanipi Cree Shaking Tent Ceremony in Relation to Environment, Hunting and Missionization', in I. Takashi and T. Yamada (eds), *Circumpolar Religion and Ecology: An Anthropology of the North*. Tokyo: University of Tokyo Press, pp. 289–316.

Feit, H. A. 2004. 'James Bay Crees' Life Projects and Politics: History of Place, Animal Partners and Enduring Relations', in M. Blaser, H. A. Feit and G. Mc Rae (eds), *In the Way of Development*. London and New York: Zed Books, pp. 92–110.

Ferrara, N. and G. Lanoue. 2004. 'The Self in Northern Canadian Hunting Societies: "Cannibals" and Other "Monsters" as Agents of Healing', *Anthropologica* 46: 69–83.

Fisher, I. E. 1774. *Sibirskaia istoriia*. St Petersburg: Imperial Academy of Sciences.

Fondahl, G. 1989. 'Native Economy and Northern Development: Reindeer Husbandry in Transbaikalia', unpublished PhD thesis, Department of Geography. Berkeley: University of California Press.

Fondahl, G. 1998. *Gaining Ground? Evenkis, Land, and Reform in Southeastern Siberia*. Boston, London, Toronto: Altyn and Bacon.

Forsyth, J. 1992. *A History of the Peoples of Siberia: Russia's North Asian Colony 1581–1990*. Cambridge: Cambridge University Press.

Foucault, M. 1980. *Power and Knowledge: Selected Interviews and Other Writings, 1972–1977*. New York: Pantheon Books.

Gabysheva, T. P. 2012. 'Predaniia evenkov basseina reki Olekma', PhD dissertation. Elista, Russia: Rosiiskaia akademiia nauk Sibirskoe otdelenie Intituta Gumanitarnykh issledovaii I problem malochislenykh narodov Severa.

Gell, A. 1992. 'Inter-tribal Commodity Barter and Reproductive Gift-Exchange in Old Melanesia', in C. Humphrey and S. Hugh-Jones (eds), *Barter, Exchange and Value: An Anthropological Approach*. Cambridge: Cambridge University Press, pp. 142–168.

Gemuev, I. N., Alekseev, N. A. and I. V. Oktiabrskaia (eds). 2000. *Narody Sibiri: istoriia i kul'tura. Medved' v drevnikh i sovremenykh kul'turakh Sibiri*. Novosibirsk: SON RAN.

Geniatulin, R. F. (ed.). 2000. *Entsiklopediia Zabaikal'ia*, vol. 1. Novosibirsk: Nauka.

Georgi, I. G. 1779. *Opisanie vsekh v Rossiiskom gosudarsve obitaiuchikh narodov, takzhe zhitelei obriadov, ver obyknovenii, zhilishch, odezhd i prochikh dostopamiatnostei. Chast' tret'ia: O narodakh Samoedskikh, Mandzhurskikh i Vostochno-Sibirskikh kak i shamanskom zakone*. St Petersburg: Imperatorskoi Akademii Nauk.

Gordillo, G. R. 2004. *Landscapes of Devils. Tensions of Place and Memory in the Argentinean Chaco*. Durham, NC, and London: Duke University Press.

Goulet, J. G. 1998. *Ways of Knowing: Experience, Knowledge, and Power among the Dene Tha*. Lincoln: University of Nebraska Press.

Gupta, A. and J. Ferguson. 1997. *Culture, Power and Place: Explorations in Critical Anthropology*. Durham, NC: Duke University Press.

Gurvich, I. S. 1977. *Kul'tura severnykh iakutov-olenevodov*. Moscow: Nauka.

Halemba, A. E. 2007. *The Telengits of Southern Siberia*. London and New York: Routledge Press.

Hallowell, A. I. 1926. 'Bear Ceremonialism in the Northern Hemisphere', *American Anthropologist* 28(1): 1–175.

Hallowell, A. I. 1960. 'Ojibwa Ontology, Behaviour, and World View', in S. Diamond (ed.), *Culture in History: Essays in Honour of Paul Radin*. New York: Columbia University Press, pp. 19–52.

Hallowell, A. I. 1966. 'The Role of Dreams in Ojibwa Culture', in G. E. Grunebaum and R. R. Caillois (eds), *The Dream and Human Societies*. Berkeley: University of California Press, pp. 267–292.

Hamayon, R. N. 1990. *La chasse à l'âme*. Nanterre: Société d'ethnologie.

Hamayon, R. N. 1996. 'Game and Games, Fortune, and Dualism in Siberian Shamanism', in J. Pentikainen (ed.), *Shamanism and Northern Ecology*. Berlin and New York: Mouton de Gruyter, pp. 134–137.

Hamayon, R. N. 2012. 'The Three Duties of Good Fortune "Luck" as a Relational Process among Hunting Peoples of the Siberian Forest in Pre-Soviet Times', *Social Analysis* 56(1): 99–116.

Harris, M. 1998. 'The Rhythm of Life on the Amazon Floodplain: Seasonality and Sociality in a Riverine Village', *Journal of the Royal Anthropological Institute* 4(1): 65–82.

Harvey, D. 1989. *The Condition of Postmodernity: An Enquiry into the Origins of Cultural Change*. Cambridge, MA: Basil Blackwell.

Helm, J. 1994. *Prophecy and Power among the Dogrib Indians*. Lincoln: University of Nebraska Press.

Hirsch, E. and M. O'Hanlon. 1995. *The Anthropology of Landscape: Perspectives on Place and Space*. Oxford: Clarendon Press.

Huber, T. and P. Pedersen. 1997. 'Meteorological Knowledge an Environmental Ideas in Traditional and Modern Societies: The Case of Tibet', *Journal of the Royal Anthropological Institute* 3: 577–597.

Humphrey, C. 1996. *Shamans and Elders: Experience, Knowledge, and Power among the Daur Mongols*. Oxford: Oxford University Press.

Humphrey, C. 2002 *Unmaking of Soviet Life: Everyday Economies after Socialism*. Ithaca. NY: Cornell University Press.

Hutton, R. 2001. *Shamans: Siberian Spirituality and the Western Imagination*. London: Hambledon.

Il'ina, I.V. 2008. *Traditsionaia meditsinskaia kul'tura narodov evropeiskogo severo-vostoka (konets XIX–XX vv.)*. Sykhtyvkar: Komi Nauchnyi Tsentr.

Ingold, T. 1983. 'The Significance of Storage in Hunting Societies', *Man* 18(3): 553–571.

Ingold, T. 1986. *The Appropriation of Nature: Essays on Human Ecology and Social Relations*. Manchester: Manchester University Press.

Ingold, T. 1996. 'The Optimal Forager and Economic Man', in P. Descola and G. Pálsson (eds), *Nature and Society*. London: Routledge, pp. 25–44.

Ingold, T. 2000. *The Perception of the Environment: Essays in Livelihood, Dwelling and Skill*. London: Routledge.

Ingold, T. 2004. 'Culture on the Ground: The World Perceived through Feet', *Journal of Material Culture* 9(3): 315–340.

Ingold T. 2005. 'On the Social Relations of Hunter-Gatherer Bands', in R. B. Lee and R. Daly (eds), *The Cambridge Encyclopaedia of Hunters and Gatherers*. Cambridge: Cambridge University Press, pp. 399–411.

Ingold T. 2011. *Being Alive: Essays on Movement, Knowledge and Description*. Taylor & Francis e-library.

Ingold, T. and T. Kurttila. 2000. 'Perceiving the Environment in Finnish Lapland', *Body and Society* 6(3–4): 183–196.

Ingold, T. and J. Vergunst. 2008. 'Introduction', in T. Ingold and J. Vergunst (eds), *Ways of Walking: Ethnography and Practice on Foot*. Aldershot: Ashgate, pp. 1–19.

Janes, R. R. 1983. *Archaeological Ethnography among Mackenzie basin Dene, Canada*. Calgary: Arctic Institute of N.A.

Jetté, J. 1911. On the superstitions of the Ten'a Indians. *Anthropos* 6: 95–108, 241–259, 602–615, 699–723.

Jordan, P. 2003. *Material Culture and Sacred Landscape: The Anthropology of the Siberian Khanty*. London: Rowman & Littlefield.

Kagarov, E. G. 1929. 'Shamanskii obriad prokhozhdeniia skvoz' otverstie', *Doklady Akademii Nauk SSSR*: 189–192.

Kahn, M. 1990. 'Stone-Faced Ancestors: The Spatial Anchoring of Myth in Wamira, Papua New Guinea', *Ethnology* 29(1): 51–66.

Khakarainen, M. V. 2007. 'Lokal'nye predstavleniia o bol'nykh i lechenii (Poselok Markovo, Chukotka)', PhD dissertation. St Petersburg: European University.

Khoroshikh, P. P. 1950. 'Putevye znaki evenkov-okhotnikov', in *Kratkoe soobshchenie Instituta Etnongrafii* 10. Moscow: Akademiia Nauk, pp. 57–59.

King, A. 1999. 'Soul Suckers: Vampiric Shamans in Northern Kamchatka, Russia', *Anthropology of Consciousness* 10(4): 57–68.

Klitsenko, Y. 2009. 'Evenkiiskaia detskaia igra "Umuken Khalganchuluk"', *Ilken*, October 15.

Kochmar, N. N. 2002. 'Isledovanie zhertvenikov pisanits srednei Leny', in *Narody i kul'tury Sibiri: Vzaimodeistviia i modernizatsii*. Irkutsk: Ottisk.

Koester, D. 2003. 'Drink, Drank, Drunk: A Social-Political Grammar of Russian Drinking in a Colonial Context', *Anthropology of East Europe Review* 21(2): 41–47.

Koledneva, N. V. 2009. *Planeta Evenkiia: Nauchno-populiarnaia literatura*. Chita: Ekspress- izdatel'stvo.

Kornai, J. 1980. *Economics of Shortage*. Amsterdam: North-Holland.

Kozulin, V. N. 2004. 'Etnicheskie i khoziaistvennye sviazi evenkov Barguzinskogo, Bauntovskogo i Nerchinskogo ostrogov', in E. F. Kurenaia (ed.), *Bauntovskie Evenki. Sled na zemle*. Bagdarin and Chita: Zabtrans, pp. 105–106.

Krech, S. 1981 (ed.). *Indians, Animals and the Fur Trade: A Critique of 'Keepers of the Game'*. Athens: Univ. of Georgia Press. 207 p.

Krech III S. 1999. *The Ecological Indian: Myth and History*. New York: W. W. Norton & Co.

Kureiskaia, E. A. 2000. *Kak zovut tebia bee? Slovar' evenkiiskikh imen*. Krasnoiarsk: LAA.

Kwon, H. 1993. 'Maps and Actions: Nomadic and Sedentary Space in a Siberian Reindeer Farm', unpublished PhD thesis, Department of Anthropology. Cambridge: University of Cambridge.

Kwon, H. 1998. 'The Saddle and the Sledge: Hunting as Comparative Narrative in Siberia and Beyond', *Journal of the Royal Anthropological Institute* 4: 112–147.

Lavrillier, A. 2003. 'De l'oubli à la reconstructin d'un rituel collectif: L'Ikènipkè des Évenks', *Slovo* 28/29: 169–191.

Lavrillier, A. 2007. 'Evenkiiskaia 'igra' evi-/ike: mezhdu igroi I ritual'nym deistviem', *Religiovedenie* 1: 3–8.

Lavrillier, A. 2009. 'Creation and Persistence of Cultural Landscape among the Siberian Evenki: two conceptions of "sacred" space', in P. Jordan (ed.), *Landscape and Culture in Northern Eurasia*. Walnut Creek, California, Left Coast Press Inc. Pp. 215–231.

Leacock, E. 1982. 'Relations of Production in Band Society', in E. Leacock and R. Lee (eds), *Politics and History in Band Societies*. Cambridge: Cambridge University Press, pp. 159–170.

Lee, J. and T. Ingold. 2006. 'Fieldwork on Foot: Perceiving, Routing, Socialising', in P. Collins and S. Coleman (eds), *Locating the Field: Space, Place and Context in Anthropology*. Oxford: Berg, pp. 67–86.

Lee, R. B. and I. De Vore. 1968. *Man the Hunter*. Chicago: Aldine.

Leete, A. 2004. 'Invasion of Materialism into the Soviet North: Sedentarisation, Development of Professional Medicine and Hygiene in the 1920–40s', in E. Kõresaar and A. Leete (eds), *Studies in Folk Culture*. Tartu: Tartu University Press, pp. 69–86.

Legat, A. 2007. 'Walking the Land, Feeding the Fire', unpublished PhD thesis. Aberdeen: Aberdeen University.

Lindenau I. I. 1983 [1742]. *Opisanie tungusov, kotorye zhivut u Udskogo ostroga 1744–1745. Opisanie narodov Sibiri (pervaia polovina XVIII veka). Istoriko- etnograficheskie materially o narodakh Sibiri i Severo-Vostoka*. Magadan: Kniga.

L'vova, E. L., I. V. Oktiabrskaia, A. M. Sagalaev and M. S. Usmanova. 1988. *Traditsionoe mirovozrenie tiurkov Iuzhnoi Sibiri: Prostranstvo i vremia*. Novosibirsk: Nauka.

L'vova, E. L., I. V. Oktiabrskaia, A. M. Sagalaev and M. S. Usmanova. 1989. *Traditsionoe mirovozrenie tiurkov Iuzhnoi Sibiri: Chelovek i obschestvo*. Novosibirsk: Nauka.

Lyarskaya, E. 2010. 'Women and the Tundra: Is There a Gender Shift in Yamal?' *Anthropology of East Europe Review* 28(2): 51–84.

MacArthur R. H. and E. R. Pianka. 1966. On Optimal Use of a Patchy Environment. *The American Naturalist* 100 (916): 603–9.

Mainov, I. I. 1898. *Nekotorye dannye o tungusakh Iakutskogo kraia*. Trudy VSORGO 2. Irkutsk: Typography of P.I. Makushin.

Maksimova, I. E. 1992. 'Voenoe delo u symskikh evenkov', in *Voprosy etnokul'turnoi istorini narodov Zapadnoi Sibiri*, pp. 92–103.

Maksimova, I. E. 1994. 'Tungus Oikos: Po materialam symsko-ketskoi grupy evenkov', unpublished PhD thesis, Department of History. Tomsk: Tomsk State University.

Martin, C. 1978. *Keepers of the Game: Indian-Animal Relationships and the Fur Trade*. Berkeley: University of California Press.

Mauss, M. 1967. *The Gift: Forms and Functions of Exchange in Archaic Society*, trans. W. D. Halls. New York: W.W. Norton.

Mazin, A. I. 1976. 'Naskal'nye risunki IV-III tys. Do nashei ery taezhnoi zony verkhnego Priamur'ia', in *Pervobytnoe iskutstvo*. Novosibirsk: Nauka, pp. 97–110.

Mazin, A. I. 1984. *Traditsionnye verovaniia i obriady evenkov-orochonov (Kon. XIX–nach. XX vv.)*. Novosibirsk: Nauka.

Mazin, A. I. 1992. *Byt i khoziaistvo evenkov-orochonov (Kon. XIX–nach. XX vv.)*. Novosibirsk: Nauka.

Mermann-Jozwiak, E. 1997. 'His Grandfather Ate His Own Wife': Louise Erdrich's Love Medicine as a Contemporary Windigo Narrative', *North Dakota Quarterly* 64(4): 44–54.

Mikhailov, T. M. 1987. *Buriatskii shamanism: istoriia, struktura i sotsialnye funktsii.* Novosibirsk: Nauka.

Mikheev, V. S. 1995. *Traditsionoe prirodopolzovanie evenkov: obosnovanie territorii v Chitinskoi oblasti.* Novosibirsk: Nauka.

Morphy, H. 1995. 'Landscape and the Reproduction of the Ancestral Past', in E. Hirsch and M. O'Hanlon (eds), *The Anthropology of Landscape: Perspectives on Place and Space.* Oxford: Clarendon Press, pp. 184–209.

Myers, F. R. 1986. *Pintupi Country, Pintupi Self, Sentiment, Place, and Politics among Western Australian Society.* Washington, DC: Smithsonian Institution Press.

Myers, F. R. 1988. 'Burning the Truck and Holding the Country: Property, Time, and the Negotiation of Identity among Pintupi Aborigines', in T. Ingold, D. Riches and J. Woodburn (eds), *Hunters and Gatherers: Property, Power and Ideology.* Oxford: Berg, pp. 52–73.

Nadasdy, P. 2003. *Hunters and Bureaucrats: Power, Knowledge and Aboriginal-State Relations in the Southwest Yukon.* Vancouver: UBC Press.

Nadasdy, P. 2007. 'The Gift in the Animal: The Ontology of Hunting and Human-Animal Sociality', *American Ethnologist* 31(1): 25–43.

Nelson, R. K. 1973. *Hunters of the Northern Forest: Designs for Survival among the Alaskan Kutchin.* Chicago: University of Chicago Press.

Nelson, R. K. 1983. *Make Prayers to the Raven: A Koyukon View of the Northern Forest.* Chicago: University of Chicago Press.

Neupokoev, V. 1928. *Tungusy Buriatii.* Verkhneudinsk: Izdatelstvo zhurnala 'Zhizn' Buriatii'.

Nirguneev, D. 1928. 'Religioznye predstavlenii evenkov', *Taiga i Tundra* 1: 44–47.

Norder, J. W. and D. Carr. 2009. 'From Maker/Meaning to User/Caretaker: Shifting Paradigms in Understanding the Rock Art of the Canadian Shield', *74th Annual Meeting of the Society for Americam Archeology*, Atlanta, GA, 22–25 April 2009.

Novik, E. S. 1984. *Obriad i folklor v sibirskom shamanisme: opyt sopostvaleniia struktur.* Moscow: Nauka.

Novik, E. S. 1989. 'The Archaic Epic and Its Relationship to Ritual', *Soviet Anthropology and Archeology* 28(2): 20–100.

Novikova, N. I. 2014. *Okhotniki i neftianiki. Issledovanie po iuridicheskoi antropologii.* Moscow: Nauka.

Nuttall, M. 1992. *Arctic Homeland: Kinship, Community and Development in Northwest Greenland.* Toronto: University of Toronto Press.

Okladnikov, A. P. 1975. 'Izuchenie istorii v Sibirskoi otdelenii AN SSSR', *Voprosy Istorii* 6: 37–61.

Okladnikov, A. P. and A. I. Mazin. 1976. *Pisanitsy reki Olekmy i Verkhnego Priamur'ia.* Novosibirsk: Nauka.

Okladnikov, A. P. and A. I. Mazin. 1979. *Pisanitsy basseina reki Aldan.* Novosibirsk: Nauka.

Okladnikov, A. P., & Zaporozhskaia, V. D. 1959. *Lenskie pisanitsy: Naskal'nye risunki u derevni Shishkino.* Moskva: Izd-vo Akademii nauk SSSR.

Okladnikov, A. P. and V. D. Zaporozhskaia. 1970. *Petroglify Zabaikal'ia.* Leningrad: Nauka. T. II.

Orlov, V. 1858a. 'Amurskie Orocheny'. *Vestnik Imperatskogo Russkogo Geografich-eskogo Obschestva* 21(6): 193–199.

Orlov, V. 1858b. Bauntovskie i angraskie brodiachie tungusy. *Vestnik Imperatsk-ogo Russkogo Geograficheskogo Obschestva* 21(2) 181–192.

Oskal, N. 2000. On nature and reindeer luck. *Rangifer* 2–3: 175–180.

Paladimov, P. 1929. 'Barguzinskaia Taiga', *Zhizn' Buriatii* 5: 82–89.

Pallas, P. S. 1788. *Puteshestvie po raznym provintsiiam Rossiiskogo gosudarstva.* St. Petersburg.

Pálsson, G. 1994. 'Enskilment at Sea', *Man* 29: 1–27.

Pedersen, M. 2002. 'Prominence, Humour and Dharhars in Northern Mongolia', unpublished PhD thesis, Department of Anthropology. Cambridge: University of Cambridge.

Pestrev, V. 1994. 'Tungusskoe vosstanie', *Severnye Prostory* 2: 48–50.

Peterson, N. 1993. 'Demand Sharing: Reciprocity and the Pressure for Generosity among Foragers', *American Anthropologist* 95: 860–874.

Petri, B. E. 1930. *Okhota i olenevostvo u tuturskikh Tungusov v sviazi s organizatsiei okhotkhoziaistva.* Irkutsk.

Petrov, A. A. 2000. 'Tabu i evfemizmy tungusov', *Kul'turnoe nasledie narodov Sibiri i Severa* 4: 328–331.

Pika, A. 1999. *Neotraditionalism in the Russian North: Indigenous Peoples and the Legacy of Perestroika.* Seattle: University of Washington Press.

Podruchny, C. 2004. 'Werewolves and Windigos: Narratives of Cannibal Monsters in French-Canadian Voyageur Oral Tradition', *Ethnohistory* 51(4): 677–700.

Potanin, G. N. 1883. *Ocherki Severo-Zapadnoi Mongolii,* vol. 4. St Petersburg.

Potapov, L. P. 2001. *Okhotnichii promysel altaitsev.* St Petersburg: MAE RAN.

Povoroznyuk, O., O. Habeck and V. Vaté. 2010. 'Introduction: On the Definition, Theory, and Practice of Gender Shift in the North of Russia', *Anthropology of East Europe Review* 29(2): 1–37.

Pu, Q. 1983. *The Oroqens:China's Nomadic Hunters.* Beijing: Foreign Languages Press.

Rastsvetaev, M. K. 1933. *Tungusy Miamialskogo roda.* Leningrad: Izdatelstvo Akademii Nauk SSSR.

Ridington, R. 1976. 'Wechuge and Windigo: A Comparison of Cannibal Belief among Boreal Forest Athapaskans and Algonkians', *Anthropologica* 18(2): 107–129.

Ridington, R. 1988. 'Knowledge, Power and the Individual in Subarctic Hunting Societies', *American Anthropologist* 90(1): 98–110.

Ridington, R. 1990. *Little Bit Know Something: Stories in a Language of Anthropology.* Vancouver and Toronto: Douglas and McIntyre.

Rogers, C. 1975. 'Empathic: An Unappreciated Way of Being', *The Counselling Psychologist* 2: 2–10.

Rouillard, R. 2013. 'Nomads in a Petro-Empire: Nenets Reindeer Herders and Russian Oil Workers in an Era of Flexible Capitalism', unpublished PhD dissertation. Montreal: McGill University.

Rushforth, S. 1992. 'The Legitimation of Beliefs in a Hunter-Gatherer Society: Bear-lake Athapaskan Knowledge and Authority', *American Ethnologist* 19: 483–500.

Rychkov, K. M. 1917. 'Eniseiskie Tungusy', *Zemlevedenie* 1–2: 1–149.

Ryden, K. C. 1993. *Mapping the Invisible Landscape: Folklore, Writing, and the Sense of Place.* Iowa City: University of Iowa Press.

Safonova T. and I. Sántha. 2012. Stories about Evenki People and their Dogs: Communication through Sharing of Contexts // M. Brightman, V. E. Grotti and O. Ulturgasheva (eds) *Animism in Rainforest and Tundra Personhood, Animals, Plants and Things in Contemporary Amazonia and Siberia.* N.Y, Oxford: Berghahn Books, pp. 82–95.

Sahlins, M. 1972. *Stone Age Economics.* New York: Aldine de Gruyter.

Sakharov, N. T.-Z. 2000 [1869]. 'Ob inorodtsev, obitaiuschikh v Barguzinskomo-kruge Zabaikal'skoi oblasti', *Ogni Kurumkana,* 29 June, p. 2.

Samokhin, A. T. 1929. 'Tungusy Bodaibinskogo raiona', *Sibirskaia zhivaia starina* 8–9: 5–66.

Scott, C. 2006. 'Spirit and Practical Knowledge in the Person of the Bear among Weminji Cree Hunters', *Ethnos* 71(1): 51–66.

Sem, T. 2002. *Vklad Makarenko i ego korrespondentov v komplektorivanie shamanskikh evenkiiskikh kolektsii REM/Muzei. Traditsii. Etnichnost' XX–XXI v.* Kishinev: SPB.

Sharp, A. S. 1986. 'Shared Experience and Magic and Death: Chipewyan Explanation of a Prophet's Decline', *Ethnology* 25: 257–270.

Sharp, A. S. 1994. 'The Power of Weakness', in E. S. Burch and L. J. Ellanna Key (eds), *Issues in Hunter-Gatherer Research.* Oxford: Berg, pp. 35–60.

Sharp, H. S. 2001. *Loon: Memory, Meaning, and Reality in a Northern Dene Community.* Lincoln: University of Nebraska Press.

Shirokogoroff, S. M. 1919. 'Opyt izucheniia osnov shamanstva u tungusov', in *Uchenye zapiski istoriko-filologicheskogo fakulteta,* vol. 1. Vladivostok.

Shirokogoroff, S. M. 1929. *Social Organization of the Northern Tungus.* Shanghai: Commercial Press.

Shirokogoroff, S. M. 1935. *Psychomental Complex of the Tungus.* London: Kegan Paul, Trench, Trubner and Co.

Shirokogoroff, S. M. 2001 [1936]. *Etnograficheskoe isledovanie: Izbranoe.* Vladivostok: Dalnevostochnogo Universiteta Izdatel'stvo.

Shirokogorov, S. M. and E. N. Shirokogorova. 1914. 'Otchet o poezdkakh k tungusam i orochenam Zabaikal'skoi oblasti v 1912 i 1913 gg. S.M. i E.N. Shirokogorovykh', *Izvestiia Russkogo komiteta dlia izucheniya Srednei i Vostochnoi Azii* 2(3): 129–146.

Shubin, A. S. 1969. 'O religioznykh perezhitkakh u evenkov Severnoj Buriatii', *Etnograficheskii sbornik Ulan Ude* 5: 170–174.

Shubin, A. S. 2001. *Evenki Pribaikal'e.* Ulan Ude: Belig.

Shubin, A. S. 2007. *Evenki.* Ulan Ude: Respublinkanskaia Tipografiia.

Simonov, M. D. 1983. 'Materialy po shamanstvu symskikh evenkov', *Izvestiia Sibirskogo otdeleniia Akademii Nauk SSSR* 11(3): 102–112.

Simonova, V. V. 2013. 'Living Taiga Memories: How Landscape Creates Remembering among Evenkis in the North Baikal, Siberia', unpublished PhD thesis. Aberdeen: Aberdeen University.

Sirina, A. A. 2002. *Katangskie evenki v 20 veke. Rasselenie, organizatsiia sredy zhiznedeiatel'nosti.* Moscow and Irkutsk: Ottisk.

Sirina, A. A. 2006. *Katanga Evenkis in the 20th Century and the Ordering of their Life-World.* Edmonton: CCI Press.

Sirina, A. A. 2008. 'Chiustvuiushchie zemliu: ekologocheskaia etika evenkov i evenov', *Etnograficheskoe obozrenie* 2: 121–138.

Sirina A. A. 2012. *Evenki I eveny v sovremennom mire: samosoznanie, prirodopol'zovanie, mirovozzrenie.* Moscow: Vostoch'naia literature.

Slezkine, Y. 1994. *Arctic Mirrors: Russia and the Small Peoples of the North.* Ithaca: Cornell University Press.

Smith, D. M. 1973. *Inkonze: Magico-Religious Beliefs of Contact Traditional Chipevyan Trading at Fort Resolution, NWT.* Ottawa: National Museum of Man.

Smith, D. M. 1982. 'Moose Deer Island House People'. National Museum of Man Mercury Series, Canadian Ethnology Service Paper 81. Ottawa: National Museums of Canada.

Smith, D. M. 1998. 'An Athapaskan Way of Knowing: Chipewyan Ontology', *American Ethnologist* 25(3): 412–432.

Smith, E. A. and B. Winterhalder. 1992. *Evolutionary Ecology and Human Behaviour.* New York : Aldine de Gruyter.

Smoliak, A. V. 1980. Rol' sobaki v zhizni religioznykh verovaniiakh ul'chei. *Polevye issledovaniia* 1978: 227–234.

Smoliak, A. V. 1989. Traditsionnye kalendari korennykh zhitelei Nizhnego Amura. *Novoe v etnografii: polevye issledovaniia* 1: 45–53.

Smoliak A. V. 1991. *Shaman: lichnost', funktsii, mirovozzrenie.* Moscow: Nauka.

Speck, F. G. 1935. *Naskapi: The Savage Hunters of the Labrador Peninsula.* Norman: University of Oklahoma Press.

Ssorin-Chaikov, N. 2003. *The Social Life of the State in Subarctic Siberia.* Stanford: Stanford University Press.

Stépanoff, C. 2009. 'Devouring Perspectives: On Cannibal Shamans in Siberia', *Inner Asia* 11(2): 283–307.

Suslov, I. M. 1936. 'Shamanstvo i bor'ba s nim', *Sovetskii Sever* 3–5: 89–152.

Swancutt, K. 2012. *Fortune and the Cursed: The Sliding Scale of Time in Mongolian Divination.* Oxford: Berghahn.

Takakura, H. 2012. 'The Shift from Herding to Hunting among the Siberian Evenki: Indigenous Knowledge and Subsistence Change in Northwestern Yakutia', *Asian Ethnology* 71(1): 31–47.

Tanner, A. 1979. *Bringing Home Animals: Religious Ideology and Mode of Production of the Mistassini Cree Hunters.* Social and Economic Studies 23. St John's, Canada: Institute of Social and Economic Research.

Teicher, M. I. 1960. 'Windigo Psychosis: A Study of a Relationship between Belief and Behavior among the Indians of Northeastern Canada', in Verne F. Ray (ed) *Proceedings of the 1960 Annual Spring Meeting of the American Ethnological Society.* Seattle: University of Washington Press.

Titov, E. I. 1923. Nekotorye dannye po kultu medvedia u nizhne-angarskikh tungusov Kindigirskogo roda. *Sibirskaia zhivaia starina: Etnograficheskii sbornik. 1:* pp. 90–105.

Titov, E. I. 1926a. *Otchet o rabote po izucheniiu olennykh tungusov.* Archive of Chita Museum of Kuznetsov, Nr. 15319.

Titov, E. I. 1926b. *Tunguskii-Russkii slovar'*. Irkutsk: Vlast' Truda.

Troshev, Z. P. 2002. Shamany i shamanstvo. *Evenkiiskaia zhizn'*, 29 August, 41 (8354): 176–186.

Tsibiktarov, V. 2011. *Petroglify Zabaikal'ia: formirovanie istochnikovoi bazym istoriografiia i voprosy kul'turno istoricheskoi interpretatsii*. Ulan Ude: Izdanie Buriatskogo gosudarsvennogo universiteta.

Tsintsius, V. I. 1975. *Sravnitel'nii slovar Tunguso-Man'chzhurskikh iazykov*, 2 vols. Leningrad: Nauka.

Tugolukov, V. A. 1962. 'The Vitim-Olekma Evenki', *Sibirskii ethnograficheskii sbornik* 4: 15–40.

Tugolukov V. A. 1963. 'Dzheltulakskie pisanitsy', *Kratkie soobschenie instituta etnografii* 35: 82–89.

Tugolukov, V. A. 1969. *Sledopyty verkhom na oleniakh*. Moscow: Nauka.

Tugolukov, V. A. 1977. 'Polevye isledovanie v Severnoi Priamur'e', in *Polevye isledovanie instituta etnografii 1975*. Moscow: IE RAN.

Tugolukov, V. A. 2004. 'O polozhenii evenkiiskogo naseleniia v Tungokochenskom, Kalarskom i Tungiro-Olekminskom raionakh Chitinskoi oblasti', in Z. P. Sokolova and E. A. Pivneva (eds), *Etnologichekiaia ekspertiza: narody severa Rossii 1959–1958*. Moscow: Institut etnologii i antropologii RAN, pp. 342–368.

Tugolukov, V. A. and A. S. Shubin. 1969. 'Kolkhoznoe stroitelstvo u evenkov Severnoi Buriatii i ego vliianie na ikh byt i kul'turu', *Etnograficheskii sbornik Ulan Ude* 5: 42–65.

Turaev, V. A. 2008. *Dal'nevostochnye Evenki: Etnokul'turnye i etnosotsianlye protsesy v XX veke*. Vladivostok: Dal'nenauka.

Turov, M. G. 1974. 'Nekotorye svedeniia ob evenkakh Chunskogo raiona', *Drevniaia istoriia narodov iuga Vostochnoi Sibiri* 4: 237–248. Turov, M. G. 1975. 'K proiskhozhdeniia i evoliutsii evenkiiskogo labaza "noku"', *Drevniaia istoriia narodov iuga Vostochnoi Sibiri* 3:193–209.

Turov, M. G. 1990. *Khoziastvo evenkov taezhnoi zony srednei Sibiri*. Irkutsk: Irkutsk State University.

Turov, M. G. 2000. 'Kul't medvedia v folklore i obriadovoi praktike evenkov', in I. N. Gemuev, N. A. Alekseev and I. V. Oktiabrskaia (eds), *Narody Sibiri: istoriia i kul'tura. Medved' v drevnikh i sovremenyh kul'turakh Sibiri*. Novosibirsk: SON RAN, pp. 48–59.

Ulturgasheva, O. 2012. *Narrating the Future in Siberia: Childhood, Adolescence and Autobiography among Young Eveny*. Oxford, New York: Berghahn Books.

Varlamov, A. N. 2011. Igra v evenkiiskom folklore. PhD dissertation. Yakutsk: Rosiiskaia akademiia nauk, Sibirskoe otdelenie Intituta Gumanitarnykh issledovanii I problem malochislenykh narodov Severa.

Varlamova, G. I. 1996. *Epicheskie traditsii v evenkiiskom fol'klore*. Yakutsk: Severoved Press.

Varlamova, G. I. 2002. *Epicheskie i obriadovye zhanry evenkiiskogo folklora*. Novosibirsk: Nauka.

Varlamova, G. I. 2004. *Mirovozrenie evenkov: otrazhenie v folklore*. Novosibirsk: Nauka.

Vasilevich, G. M. 1930. 'Nekotorye dannye po ohotnich'im obriadam i predstavleniiam u Tungusov', *Etnografiia* 3: 57–67.

Vasilevich, G. M. 1936. *Sbornik materialov po evenkiiskomu folklore. Trudy po folklore*, vol. 1. St Petersburg: Trudy narodov severa.

Vasilevich, G. M. 1949. *Fol'klornye materialy i plemennoi sostav evenkov (tungusov). Trudy II Vsesoiuznogo geograficheskogo s'ezda*, vol. 3. Moscow: Geografiz , pp. 355–364.

Vasilevich, G. M. 1957. *Drevnie ohotnich'i i olenevodcheskie obriady evenkov.* Sbornik MAE 17. Leningrad: Nauka, pp. 152–187.

Vasilevich, G. M. 1961. *Ugdan- zhilishche evenkov Iablonogo i Stanovogo khrebtov.* Sbornik MAE 20. Leningrad: Nauka, pp. 30–39.

Vasilevich, G. M. 1968. 'Narody Sibiri pered prisoedineniem k Russkomu gosudarstvu: Tungusy', in *Drevniaia Sibir'* T. 1. Leningrad: Nauka, pp. 395–402.

Vasilevich, G. M. 1969. *Evenki: Istoriko-etnograficheskie ocherki (XVIII–nachalo XX v.).* Leningrad: Nauka.

Vasilevich, G. M. 1971. *O kul'te medvedia u Evenkov.* Sbornik MAE 27. Leningrad: Nauka, pp. 150–169.

Vasilevich, G. M. and M. G. Levin. 1951. 'Tipy olenevodstva i ikh proiskhozhdenie', *Sovetskaia Etnografiia* 1: 63–87.

Vaté, V. 2005. 'Kilvêi: The Chukchi Spring Festival in Urban and Rural Contexts', in E. Kasten (ed.), *Rebuilding Identities: Pathways to Reform in Post-Soviet Siberia.* Berlin: Dietrich Reimer Verlag, pp. 39–62.

Whaley, L. J.; Grenoble, Lenore A. and Li, F. X. 1999. Revisiting Tungusic Classification From the Bottom up: a Comparison of Evenki and Oroqen. *Language* 75, (2). 286–321.

Vitebsky, P. 1995. 'From Cosmology to Environmentism: Shamanism as Local Knowledge in a Global Setting', in K. Pardon (ed.), *Counterworks: Managing the Diversity of Knowledge.* London: Routledge, pp. 182–203.

Vitebsky, P. 2002. 'Withdrawing from the Land: Social and Spiritual Crisis in the Indigenous Russian Arctic', in C. Hann (ed.), *Postsocialism: Ideals, Ideologies and Practices in Eurasia.* New York and London: Routledge, pp. 180–195.

Vitebsky, P. 2005. *Reindeer People: Living with Animals and Spirits in Siberia.* London: Harper Collins.

Vitebsky, P. and S. Wolfe. 2001. 'The Separation of the Sexes among Siberian Reindeer Herders', in A. Low and S. Treamyne (eds), *Sacred Custodians of the Earth? Women Spirituality and the Environment.* Oxford: Berghahn Books, pp. 81–94.

Vorob'ev, D. 2013. 'Sovremennye verovaniia okhotnikov na dikogo severnogo olenia (na primere evenkov Chirindy)', *Etnograficheskoe Obozreniia* 2: 37–52.

Voskoboinikov, M. G. 1965. 'Prozaicheskie zhanry evenkiiskogo fol'klora', unpublished PhD thesis. St. Petersburg: Institute of A. I. Gertzen.

Vreeke, G. and I. Van der Mark. 2003. 'Empathy, an Integrative Model', *New Ideas in Psychology* 21: 177–207.

Weiner, J. F. 1991. *The Empty Place, Poetry, Space and Being among the Foi of Papua New Guinea.* Bloomington: Indiana University Press.

Widlock, T. 2004. 'Sharing by Default?' *Anthropological Theory* 4(1): 53–70.

Willerslev, R. 2007. *Soul Hunters: Hunting, Animism, and Personhood among the Siberian Yukaghirs.* Berkeley, Los Angeles and London: University of California Press.

Winterhalder, Bruce. 1981. Optimal Foraging strategies and Hunter-Gatherer Research in Anthropology: Theory and Models. In Bruce Winterhalder and Smith Eric (eds). *Hunter-Gatherer Foraging Strategies: Ethnographic and Archeological Analyses.* Chicago: University of Chicago Press. pp. 13-35.

Wispe, L. 1986. 'The Distinction between Sympathy and Empathy: To Call Forth a Concept, A Word Is Needed', *Journal of Personality and Social Psychology* 50(2): 314–321.

Woodburn, J. 1982. 'Egalitarian Societies', *Man* 17(3): 431–451.

Woodburn, J. 1998. 'Sharing Is Not a Form of Exchange: An Analysis of Property Sharing in Immediate-Return Hunter-Gatherer Societies', in C. Hann (ed.), *Property Relations: Renewing the Anthropological Tradition.* Cambridge: Cambridge University Press, pp. 48–63.

Yampolskaia, I. A. 1993. 'Shamanskii chum evenkov: istoriia otkrytiia, rezul'taty issledovanii, gipotezy', in *Etnosy i etnicheskie processy.* Moscow: RAN.

Zabianko, A. P., A. I. Mazin and O. A. Kobyzov. 2002. 'Shamanizm evenkov Priamur'ia I Yuzhnoi Yakutii (sovremenoe sostoianie)', in *Traditsionaia kul'tura Vostkoka Azii.* Blagoveschensk: Amur State University. Pp. 294–304.

Zelenin, D. K. 1929. *Tabu slov u narodov Vostochnoi Evropy i Severnoi Azii.* Sbornik Muzeia antropologii i etnografii 8. Leningrad: SMAE.

Zelenin, D. K. 1935. *Ideologiia sibirskogo shamanstva.* Izvestiia AN SSSR 8. Moscow and Leningrad: AN SSSR.

Zelenin, D. K. 1936. *Kul't ongonov v Sibiri. Perezhitki totemizma v i ideologii sibirskikh narodov.* Trudy instituta antropologii, arkheeologii i etnografii 14. Etnograficheskaia eriia 3). Moscow and Leningrad: AN SSSR.

Zelenin D. K. 2004. *Izbrannye Trudy: Stat'i po Dukhovnoi Kul'ture 1934–1954.* Moscow: Indrik Press.

Zhukov, A. V., A. G. Iankov, A. O. Barinov and A. V. Drobotushenko. 2003. *Sovremennaia religioznaia situatsiia v vostochnom Zabaikal'e.* Chita: Museum of Local History.

Ziker, J. P. 2002. 'Raw and Cooked in Arctic Siberia: Seasonality, Gender and Diet among the Dolgan and Nganasan', *Nutritional Anthropology: Hunter Gatherers* 25(2): 20–33.

Znamenski, A. A. 2003. *Shamanism in Siberia: Russian Records of Indigenous Spirituality.* Dordrecht, Boston, and London: Kluwer Academic Publishers.

Znamenski, A. A. 2007. *The Beauty of the Primitive: Shamanism and the Western Imagination.* Oxford: Oxford University Press.

Zolotarev A. M. 1938. 'Novye dannye o tungusakh i lamutakh XVIII veka', *Istorik Marksist* 2(66): 63–88.

Index

dolls. *See also* idols
  avoiding misfortune using, 86
  omiruk, 81
domestic animals, 32, 254
domestic reindeer, 190. *See also* reindeer
domestic world, 146
domination, 94–98, 189, 244–50, 256
dom kultury (Rus. large villages), 72
dovan, 173
drag (Rus. *taskat'*), 68
dreams, 89, 90
drinking water, 161
drug (Rus. friend), 112
druzhba (Rus. friendship), 112, 113, 165, 245
dukh (Rus. spirit), 3
dukh-khoziain (Rus. master-spirit), 3, 4, 5, 7, 11, 69
  butchering animals, 170
  revenge, 244
  sensing presence of, 99
Dukuvuchi, 235, 236
  rock art site, 229. *See also* rock art
  stories about spirits, 233
Dushinov, Gena, 118, 233
  bikit (Oro. living place), 147
  raising dogs, 201
dwelling intuition, 71

E
economies, 12
  game as means of income, 31
  hunting animals for cash, 58
educated people (Rus. *inteligentsia*), 218
elections, 37
elk (Lat. *cervus elaphus*), 32
embodied experience, place as, 99
emchure (Oro. footwear), 65, 67, 74, 95, 131, 186
empathy, 88
emplaced luck, 250–258
enacted luck, 250–258
enemies, killing, 250
entrepreneurs (*komersanty*), 27, 31, 33, 36, 38, 58, xiv
environment, difficulty of, 24
epic (Oro. *nimngakan*), 83, 184
Epov, Yura, 68
ermine (Lat. *mustela erminea*), 32
Esserovtsy, 42
European calendar, 184. *See also* calendars

European Christian calendar, 185. *See also* calendars
Evenki, 20, 130
  Association of Tungokochen District, 63
  calendars, 184
  of Chirinda, 2, 3
  clans, 22
  flexibility of land ownership, 40, 41
  indigenous population of, 25
  languages, 20
  Nerchinsk, 63
  oral traditions, 249
  rock art sites, 229. *See also* rock art
Eveny, Lavrillier, 20
  theme of luck of, 12
evil eye *(zglaz)*, 8

F
fairy tales, 86
Far East Republic, 42
fartovyi okhotnik (Rus. lucky hunter), 29
fat, bear, 223
fear and moral awareness, 106
fighting wolves, 204–07
fires
  for human needs, 169
  smudge, 196, 197
  zones around, 163
firewood, 161, 165
First Chilchagir, 39
folk healers, 221. *See also* shamans
food, game as food source, 31
footprints
  gathering information from, 135
  leaving, 157
footwear (Oro. *emchure*), 65, 67, 74, 95, 131, 186
foragers, 145
forecasting weather, 179. *See also* weather
forgiveness for slaughtering reindeer, 199
friend (Rus. *drug*), 112
friendship (Rus. *druzhba*), 112, 113, 165, 245
fur-bearing animals, cash income from, 32
fur-hunting camps, 163, 164
fur trading, 33

G
gainakta (moose tooth amulet), 91
gaino (Oro. nest), 159
game. *See also* animals

www.ingramcontent.com/pod-product-compliance
Lightning Source LLC
Chambersburg PA
CBHW070911030426
42336CB00014BA/2372